P9-ARY-473

Gateway to Judaism:
Encyclopedia Home Reference

Gateway to Judaism:
Encyclopedia Home Reference

VOLUME II

by

Albert M. Shulman

Thomas Yoseloff
South Brunswick · New York · London

© 1971 by A. S. BARNES and Co., Inc.
Library of Congress Catalogue Card Number : 69-15777

Thomas Yoseloff, Publisher
Cranbury, New Jersey 08512

Thomas Yoseloff Ltd
108 New Bond Street
London W1Y OQX, England

Second Printing, 1972

SBN 498 06896 X

Printed in the United States of America

Contents

6

The Institution of the Synagogue

The story of the synagogue is the history of Israel and the Jew's constant search for God. Throughout its history it has been the heart that sustained the life stream of the Jewish people. Although it was known primarily as the building used for public assembly and prayer, within the synagogue the Jew also found an outlet for his social, economic, and communal interest. It served as a school for the education of children and adults; it was the original "town-hall" for assemblages on special occasions; it was the law court where grievances were heard and judged; it was the scene of weddings, Bar Mitzvahs, and funerals; and in the hours of Israel's tragedies, it was often the last refuge. Within its precincts were to be found quarters for the Shammus, a hostel for wayfarers, and the Mikveh, the ritual purification bath.

Historical Development

HIGH PLACES— במות —BAMOTH

A high place was usually an elevation of land or a mound on which an altar or shrine was erected for worship and for sacrificial purposes. All religions established such shrines or temples. The Greeks had their Mt. Olympus; the Babylonians created artificial hills called Zigguroth. The Temple in Jerusalem was on an elevated site. The people "went up" to the shrine where they prayed, tithed, consulted priestly oracles, and sacrificed to God.

Early high places were cultic centers, usually associated with lewd pagan rites and immoralities. With the centralization of religion at Jerusalem, reforms were instituted and these centers, with their false priests and adulterous rites, were extirpated. Common to many such High Places were the special chambers maintained for sacred prostitution by men and women known as Kedeshim and Kedeshoth.

575

THE TEMPLE— בית המקדש —BETH HA-MIKDOSH

The Tabernacle that Moses constructed in the wilderness was the blueprint for the Temple erected by Solomon in Jerusalem. Its purpose was to be a shrine for the Ark of the Covenant, and a place for sacrifice and the housing of sacred vessels. It had three main divisions —a Hall or Temple Court (Azarah), a Shrine (Hechal), and an inner Sanctum (Devir).

In 586 BCE the Temple was destroyed by the Babylonians. The date marks the end of the First Commonwealth and the beginning of the post-Exilic period. In the year 516 BCE it was reconstructed by Zerubbabel after the return from Exile. This Second Temple existed until the time of Herod the Great, who in the year 8 BCE decided to rebuild and enlarge it. The Temple remained as the center of Jewish life and worship until the year 70 CE, when the Romans conquered the land and leveled the city of Jerusalem to dust. This date marks the end of the Second Commonwealth.

The Temple consisted of a complex of buildings in which the royal and priestly families were housed, as well as the large personnel required to administer the affairs of the priesthood and the monarchy. The Temple proper was situated on a hill (Mt. Moriah), the highest elevation in the complex. At the present time the Mosque of Omar occupies the Temple site, and only a remnant of the western wall of the ancient sanctuary remains. It is about 160 feet long and 60 feet wide and as "the Wailing Wall," it is a center for worship and for religious pilgrimages.

THE SYNAGOGUE— בית התפילה —HOUSE OF PRAYER

No record is available concerning the date, the structure, or the organization of the first synagogue. When Jacob dedicated the place where he dreamed of angels, as BETH-EL— בית אל —HOUSE OF GOD, it was in the wilderness and it was but a bare rock. When the prophet Ezekiel brought messages of comfort to his exiled people in Babylonia after the destruction of the Temple (586 BCE), it was to small scattered groups, probably meeting in open places or in sections within larger buildings. In the absence of the Temple with its sacrificial cult, oral petitions or prayers became the pattern of worship.

The conclusion reached by most scholars is that the synagogue did develop in the Exile and when the people returned to Jerusalem they brought with them practices that became the basis of the present synagogue.

Upon examination of the conditions existing in pre-Exilic times, as recorded in the Bible, one finds ample references to prayer distinct from, but complementary to, Temple worship and sacrifices. Isaiah (1 : 15) reproaches those whose offerings to the Temple he considered meaningless by saying, "Yea, when ye make many prayers, I will not hearken." In the famous quotation, "And I will bring them to my holy mountain and make them joyful in my house, their burnt offerings and their sacrifices shall be accepted upon my altar, for mine house shall be called a house of prayer for all people," (Isaiah 56 : 7) the prophet indicates that the joint practice of prayer and sacrifice was familiar to the people. When King Solomon dedicated the Temple, he made no reference to the sacrifices that pilgrims could bring, but only to their prayers, using the words TEFILLAH and HITPALLEL—PRAYER and PRAYING.

Historically, religious assemblies were known to take place outside the precincts of the sanctuary. Samuel convened them at Mizpah, where he offered prayers on behalf of the people and exhorted them to fasting and repenting of their sins. During the days of the prophets, meetings of this type are described in the Bible.

It is known that in the post-Exilic period, synagogues were coexistent with the Second Temple and worship included verbal prayers and animal sacrifice. There was a room in the Temple known as the "Chamber of Hewn Stone," which was used for worship services involving the reading of the Ten Commandments, the Shema, special benedictions, and the priestly blessing.

From the Mishnah (Sotah 40b) we learn that there was a synagogue situated on the Temple Mount, in which the Torah was read on Yom Kippur, with the officials of the Temple, including the High Priest, participating. In time it became general practice for a prayer service to complete the worship and sacrificial rites on the holy days. The participation of the public was marked by simple responses at appointed times.

Some of the terms used to describe assemblies and the places where they occurred furnish clues to the various needs served by the synagogue. In Jeremiah 38 : 8 there is a description of the burning of the BETH HA-AM— בית העם —the HOUSE OF THE PEOPLE. Rashi and Kimchi, Bible commentators, conclude that this place was a synagogue. In Psalm 74, concerning the destruction of the Temple, is found the reference to the burning of the MO'ADAY EL— מועדי אל —MEETING PLACES OF GOD. These must have been recognizable buildings apart from the Temple, and have been translated as "synagogues." There is a Talmudic reference that mentions that there were 480 synagogues in the city of Jerusalem during the days of the Bar Cochba revolt. (J. Meg. 3 : 1) Before the fall of the Second Temple (70 CE), well known synagogues existed in such cities as Alexandria, Rome, Babylonia, Damascus, and Antioch.

The gathering of people is known by the Hebrew word KNESSETH— כנסת —which means ASSEMBLY or MEETING, and the place was called BETH HA-KNESSETH— בית הכנסת —THE HOUSE OF ASSEMBLY or THE HOUSE OF MEETING or THE MEETING PLACE. The Greek word for Knesseth is SYNAGOGUE. While originally the word denoted any kind of meeting place, in the course of its usage it fell into the same category as words like cathedral, church, and mosque, and came to designate the Jewish house of worship. Another name for the synagogue is BETH TEFILLAH— בית התפילה —HOUSE OF PRAYER. The popular Yiddish name is SHUL or SHOOL, which is taken from the German SCHULE and literally means "school." The Latin name for school is SCHOLA.

TALMUDIC—HOUSE OF LEARNING

After the destruction of the Jewish Kingdom by the Romans, the synagogue began to function not only as a "House of Worship" but also as a BETH HA-MIDRASH— בית המדרש —HOUSE OF LEARNING or STUDY. Babylonia became the center of Jewish learning and communities like Sura and Pumbeditha rose to fame because of their academies. The Talmud is a product of these scholastic institutions.

The tradition of Jewish study through the synagogue is evident today in the study groups, the adult education classes, and the emphasis on the religious education of the children. The Cheder, "class room," for the elementary instruction of children, had its origin within the precincts of the synagogue. Today many of them are disassociated and function as Talmud Torahs. The waiting period between the late afternoon (Minchah) service and the evening (Ma-ariv) service was traditionally devoted to learned discourses by the daily worshipers. Saturday afternoon was given to Torah study and interpretation.

MEDIEVAL—HOUSE OF ASSEMBLY

It was in the middle ages that the synagogue developed to its highest degree as a place of meeting. Many factors contributed to this.

The synagogue was the community house that provided hostel accommodations to strangers and visitors, especially prior to the Sabbath and holidays.

The synagogue and the Yeshivah were usually in one building. Students lived within its walls until they finished their course of study.

The institution of the Ghetto closed all avenues of social life for the Jew in the outside world. Hence the synagogue became the center of social life and activity.

During the Crusades and other periods of Jewish persecution, the synagogue served as a haven of refuge against the attacks of bigoted mobs.

The cultural life of the Jew was bound up in his religion. In the synagogue the religion of Israel found expression through the joyous observance of its festivals and ceremonial rites.

In the modern world the synagogue became identified with townsmen grouped by countries of origin, or the type of observance. Thus, in the Diaspora the synagogue would often bear such names as the "Synagogue of Greek-speaking Jews," the "Synagogue of Roman Jews," the "Hungarian Synagogue," the "Russian Synagogue," the "Chassidic Synagogue," and so forth. Sometimes synagogues were known by the trade of the worshipers, such as the "Synagogue of the Copper Workers in Jerusalem." Artisans frequently congregated together to form their own synagogue.

MODERN—THE COMMUNITY HOUSE OR CENTER

Up to recent times the task of teaching the young was delegated to Cheders and Talmud Torahs. The social aspects of synagogue life, except for occasional entertainment in connection with religious celebrations, were not well developed. With the advent of Reform Jewry, the ancient three-fold purpose of the synagogue, namely worship, study, and assembly, became implemented. The newer buildings provided more classrooms for religious education, meeting rooms for lectures and assemblies, recreation facilities for dancing, socials, and entertainment, and in some instances gymnasiums and swimming pools. In many communities there are Jewish centers that sponsor cultural-religious-social programs, and often conduct summer day camps.

Conservative synagogues are tending to follow this pattern, but Orthodox congregations generally still adhere to the tradition of providing only for worship.

Architecture of the Synagogue

It is strange that, since the synagogue served as the model for buildings used for prayer-worship by other religions, there is no inherited tradition in synagogue architecture or originality in design. Builders became imitative, especially in exterior design, although the interiors also reflected the influence of contemporary trends. The modifications were always based on the needs of the worship service, which underwent some change in the various parts of the world.

CONFORMITY WITH TEMPLE PLAN

The earliest synagogues attempted to copy the courts, the chambers of the Tabernacle, and the Sanctuary of the original Temple. The Bible makes specific mention of the outer court, the inner court, and the inner chamber called the "Holy of Holies." Symbolically, the interior of the synagogue is still patterned after the Temple. The sanctuary or place of divine worship represents the CHATZER— חצר —the OUTER COURT of the Temple, the place where the people gathered. The INNER COURT— קדוש —KADOSH, housed the altars of sacrifice. Inside the synagogue, it is symbolized by a raised platform in the center or in the front. The HOLY CHAMBER—קדש הקדשים—KODESH HA-KADASHIM (Holy of Holies) is the Ark or the receptacle of the Torah and is situated on the east wall behind the altar.

INFLUENCE OF THE CHURCH

Some synagogues copied the pattern of Christian church structures as they became established. At one period, the church followed the Roman basilica pattern, which consisted of three sections : a portico or porch entrance, a Narthex or vestibule, and a Nave, which was the main body or sanctuary where the congregation assembled. This seemed to fit the general plan, so most synagogues throughout the ages contain these three areas, with the addition of a gallery or women's section.

SEPARATION OF SEXES

The Biblical law against mixture (Shaatnez) was extended to women in the synagogue, where the sexes were forbidden to sit together or to be in mixed company. During the existence of the Temple there was a special section for women called AZARETH NASHIM—עזרת נשים— the COURT OF WOMEN. This was later replaced by an elevated section or gallery on the three sides of the courtyard to enable the women to view the service from above the court without permitting them to mingle with the men.

The partition separating the sexes is called MECHITZAH—מחיצה—
and in many orthodox synagogues it took the form of a gallery or
balcony that surrounded the sanctuary. If the balcony were low, it
could be curtained or latticed to prevent the women from being seen.
Some synagogues had side chambers for the women, who were then
not able to see or participate in the services. This room was sometimes
an annex and, in many European congregations, women precentors
were engaged to direct their worship. Where the synagogue structure
does not permit separate places for women worshipers, arrangements
may be made to seat the women on one side of the room or in the rear.

EXTERIOR

There are no historic regulations as to the exterior construction of
synagogues, but many were and are columned structures, perhaps as
a reminder of the pillars that were basic to the Temple. Exteriors
usually varied according to the prevailing mode of the country or the
century. The history of architecture is reflected in the following general
types of construction that are in evidence in synagogues throughout
the Jewish world.

Egyptian and Babylonian—These were featured by massive limestone
and granite blocks. The Temples and synagogues of Bible times
followed this mode.

Graeco-Roman—These were rectangular basilicas, some with ornamented, columned porticos, gabled roofs or round arches.

Byzantine, Moorish—This architecture gave the synagogue a bulbous
design with domes and minarets.

Gothic—This style was more florid Baroque and was characterized
by pointed arches, towers, and spires.

Renaissance—The early synagogues of America followed this pattern
with simple fronts and horizontal lines, rather than the vertical
ones of the massive and basically Romanesque buildings.

Modern—This uses all the idioms current in church architecture in
the various geographic areas. Often the differences are apparent
only in the Hebrew letters and artistic embellishments.

SITE AND LOCATION

Synagogues, according to the Talmud, were to be built on the heights
of a city because, like the Temple of old, it had to be on an eminent
elevation and be visible from all directions. When the Christian and
Moslem churches came into power they decreed that no edifice should

be taller than the church or mosque. Later, restrictions forbade the erection of a synagogue within the vicinity of a church. Considerations of personal safety also made it sometimes necessary to situate synagogues on the outskirts of a city.

Various reasons involving purification rites have been advanced for the construction of a synagogue near a body of water. Also, in the interpretation of the verse "Out of the depths have I cried unto thee, O Lord," (Psalm 130 : 1) the reason why some synagogues were built in basements or below ground level may be found.

Where no restrictive covenants are in force, synagogues may be found anywhere—in residential sections, on main thoroughfares, or in the heart of business districts. In cities with large Jewish populations, services are ofttimes conducted in rented halls or auditoriums, particularly on the High Holy Days.

In memory of the destruction of the Temple and as an act of national mourning, Orthodox synagogues are so placed that the worshipers face the direction of Jerusalem while praying.

The Interior and its Decorations

Through the centuries, the one constant characteristic in interior synagogue construction seems to be the desire to invest it with beauty and dignity. As the styles of the exteriors changed, so did the interiors. Traceable to the Gothic influence, some were built in the form of a double nave, with central pillars supporting a vaulted roof, which, in turn, formed several bays, each with crossvaults. These conveyed an impression of loftiness. At another time, the sanctuary was a simple room with a vaulted ceiling and buttressed walls, which resembled the monastic refectory. This form gave a feeling of spaciousness and did not hinder vision of the Ark and the Bemah, since there were no pillars. The Moorish structures had parallel arcades of pillars that supported a series of circular arches. These were intricately ornamented with gilt designs. There has seemed to be a retention of pillars in most synagogue construction, because of a traditional association with their use for separating the areas used for study and worship. The synagogues of antiquity were not equipped with seats or pews, since the people stood throughout the service.

ART IN THE SYNAGOGUE

Rigid adherence to the commandment "Thou shalt not make any graven image," has resulted in creating a house of worship bare of pictures or statues of the Patriarchs, Moses, the Prophets, or any other figures. Until recent times, secular Jewish art was almost completely ignored everywhere in the synagogue structure. At certain times there were attempts at artistry in interior design, such as mosaic floors and religious motifs, borrowed from non-Jewish houses of worship. When stained glass windows became the vogue, some synagogues used them, incorporating the names and symbols of the tribes of Israel, ritual emblems, and verses from Scripture into the designs.

The modern structures are not bound by any tradition in style or physical layout. They follow current trends in art and architecture, reflecting the wishes of the congregation.

APPURTENANCES OF THE SYNAGOGUE

AHRON HA-KODESH— **ארון הקדש** —THE HOLY ARK

This is the oldest and usually the most ornate object used in Jewish worship. It is also called TEBA—**תבה**—BOX or CHEST, with reference to the outer casing of the Torah. Another name for it is TIK— **תיק**. In Sephardic congregations the Ark is called HECHAL— **היכל**—SANCTUARY, because of its holy character. In the early history of the Jewish people it was associated with the movable Ark of the Covenant mentioned in the Book of Numbers. (10 : 33) During the wanderings in the wilderness, the Ark was kept in the DEVIR—**דביר**—the HOLY OF HOLIES chamber, and was taken out in times of national crisis. When the Temple was completed by King Solomon, the Ark was permanently placed in the sacred chamber and only the high priest was permitted to enter this room on the Day of Atonement.

The cover of the Ark had two golden Cherubim (winged angels) facing each other, symbolizing the divine presence of God. It is not known what happened to the Ark after the Temple was destroyed in 586 BCE.

The Ark in the synagogue today has a two-fold meaning : (1) to remind the people of the original "Ark of the Covenant" and, (2) to keep alive the idea of the inner sanctuary, the "Holy of Holies," of the Temple. It is a receptacle for the Torahs, or Scrolls of the Law. As a reminder that the Holy of Holies chamber was separated from the other parts of the Tabernacle by a veil, in most synagogues the Ark has a curtain (Parocheth) before it. In Jewish tradition the Ark also contained a pot of manna and Aaron's rod.

In the Western world, the Ark usually takes the form of a recess in the east wall facing the congregation, because that is the direction of the city of Jerusalem. In other parts of the world the location of the Ark is determined by its relative position to Jerusalem.

The idea of "ascending unto the mountain of the Lord" (Psalm 24) has led to the erection of steps just before the Ark. A reading desk at the foot of the altar, or a platform in the center of the sanctuary was designed to carry out the precept "to descend before the Ark." (Pesachim 113b) A custom of long duration is to bow toward the Ark when entering the synagogue.

There is no restriction as to style or materials used for the inside walls or the exterior of the Ark. Often, across the front or above the curtain of the Ark there may be verses from the Bible or the Talmud such as

Ain zeh ki eem beth elohim   אין זה כי אם בית אלהים
   This is none other but the house of God.   (Genesis 28 : 17)
Da lifnai me atoh omade   דע לפני מי אתה עומד
   Know before whom thou standest.   (Berachoth 28b)
Shevisi adonoy l'negdi tamid   שויתי יי לנגדי תמיד
   I will set the Lord always before me.   (Psalms 16 : 8)

ALTAR— מזבח —MIZBAYACH

An altar is a place for sacrifice and worship; an elevation; a table, mount, or platform. In the Temple service, altars were made of stone, clay, metal, or wood. Unhewed stone is described in Exodus 20 : 21 because the use of iron was not permitted in the construction of sacred objects.

In early religious history "High Places" and "Groves" were common sites for worship. Hence, the erection of the Temple on Mt. Zion. Tables made of brass were used as altars for sacrifices and burnt offerings.

The first altar on record is one built by Noah. (Genesis 8 : 20) Individuals, like the Patriarchs, erected altars unto God for sacrificial purposes. In the Temple there were a number of altars used for different purposes.

   The Brazen Altar, used for sacrifices and burnt offerings. This was located in the outer court near the gate. The corners of this altar terminated in horns. In Jewish tradition, seizing the horns offered asylum to an accused.

   Altar of Incense (The Golden Altar). This was placed before the "Devir" (Holy of Holies), where the Ark of the Covenant was kept.

   Altar of Showbread. This was a table on which the symbolic loaves of bread were kept in the Hechal (Holy Place). These were replaced by fresh loaves each Sabbath. (Exodus 25 : 30)

After the fall of the Temple the altar was retained in the synagogue as a platform, on which were placed the Ark and a reading desk for the use of the leader of the services.

The Two Tablets of the Law

The Decalogue, according to the Biblical account, was received by Moses at Sinai, engraved upon two tablets of stone. These are known by the Hebrew name SH'NEI LUCHOTH HA'BRITH— שני לחות הברית (Exodus 32 : 15) They may be of marble, wood, metal, or ceramic, and fixed above the Ark, sometimes supported by the figure of a lion on each side.

In the Book of Genesis, one of Jacob's sons, Judah, is compared to a lion. (49 : 9) In the course of Israel's history, Judah's name was used to designate the entire country of Palestine. The lion decoration has long been popular in Orthodox synagogues, with this motif appearing on the Ark curtain and on Torah Mantles. A quotation from "Ethics of the Fathers," (5 : 23) "be bold as a leopard, light as an eagle, swift as a deer, and strong as a lion to do the will of your Father who is in heaven," has prompted some synagogues to use the deer, also, to decorate the Ark.

The Parocheth— פרכת —Curtain or Veil

In Temple days, separating the innermost chamber of the Tabernacle, the Holy of Holies, from the Holy Chamber or Court, was a curtain or veil called "Parocheth." This curtain is retained symbolically in the synagogue to this day. It may be made of fabric, wood, glass or plastic, but it always covers the front of the Ark. White curtains are used for the Holy Days and during the rest of the year they are customarily red, blue, or purple. Like the mantles of the Torahs, they are embroidered with designs, symbols, or Bible verses.

The Menorah— מנורה —Seven Branched Candlestick

Instructions for making the Menorah are found in the Book of Exodus, chapters 25 and 37. The Menorah, which was used in the portable Tabernacle (Mishkan— משכן) and later in the Temple, was made of hammered gold with three branches or arms extending from a central shaft on each side. It was placed in the Holy Sanctuary together with the Golden Altar of Incense and the Table of Show-bread.

The Menorah, like many of the Temple holy vessels, disappeared after the destruction of the Second Temple. An idea of its form and construction comes to us from the Arch of Titus, a Roman memorial depicting the spoils taken from the captured city of Jerusalem. This shows the candelabrum with its seven lamps in a straight line. In Temple times all the lamps were kindled from evening to morning, (Exodus 27 : 21) but the center lamp was kept burning throughout the day.

After the fall of the Temple, the Menorah became a fixed symbol of the Jewish faith. It found its place in the synagogue on the altar, near the Ark, or on the reading desk in the center of the sanctuary. In many synagogues two Menorahs are used, one on each side of the altar. Often the lighting fixtures on the walls incorporate the Menorah design.

In the home, a pair of candlesticks or a candelabrum varying in the number of branches is used as the chief feature of the Sabbath Eve ritual. During the Chanukah holiday a special eight-branched Menorah is used, with an additional light on the center shaft or fixture to act as pilot.

The symbolism of the Menorah is not definitely known. The seven lights have been associated with the seven days of creation, with the center light representing the Sabbath day, the seven planets, the seven continents, and the tree of life.

The Ner Tamid— נר תמיד *—Perpetual Light*

The light that burns constantly before the Ark is called the Ner Tamid or Perpetual Light. It may be traced to the oil light that burned continually outside the veil of testimony in the Mishkan, (Exodus 27 : 20) and to the perpetual fire that was kept burning on the altar. (Leviticus 6 : 6) It has been suggested that the ever-burning light in the central shaft of the golden Menorah of the Temple, which was used to kindle the other lamps each day, is the source for the Ner Tamid.

As a symbolic fixture of the synagogue it represents the truth contained in God's Torah; it is also associated with the idea of immortality and the "Shechinah," the invisible presence of God. It also identifies the Jewish people as "a light of the nations." (Isaiah 42 : 6) Another explanation is that God's House of Worship should never be in total darkness.

There is no law concerning the use of the perpetual light nor any regulation of its form. Its use is of comparatively recent date. The original oil-wick light gave way, in turn, to candlelight, to gaslight, and now to electric light.

The Almemar— אלמימר *—or Bemah—* בימה *—Reading Desk*

This raised platform in the center of Orthodox synagogues is called an Almemar, from the Arabic "Almimbar," meaning "elevated stand." It is also called "Bemah," from the Greek Bema (Tribune), from which speakers addressed the public. It is secondary in importance only to the Ark. It is usually surrounded by a railing and serves as the reading desk or pulpit from which the lessons of the Torah and the prophets are read, prayers are recited, and sermons or discourses delivered. Here also, the Chazan and choir usually perform on Sabbaths and holidays.

One explanation of the "Bemah" is associated with the return from Exile when Ezra stood on a "pulpit of wood" to read the Book of the Law to the people. (Nehemiah 8 : 2) When seats and benches came into vogue, they were arranged around the "Bemah" so that the worshipers could observe the participants in the service. In the Conservative and Orthodox synagogues the Bemah may be combined with the Altar, directly in front of the Ark, and in some synagogues it may be found to one side on the Altar.

Lectern—Amud—Pulpit Stand

Individual pulpits or lecterns are frequently used by worshipers to this day in many Orthodox synagogues. Sometimes these are folding pulpits attached to the walls or the back of benches or pews. An individual such as the rabbi, Cantor, or any other leader usually has his own "Amud" or reading stand.

Mogen David— מגן דוד —Shield of David

The "Shield" or "Star of David," which is a distinctive decorative motif in the synagogue, is a six-pointed star or two triangles superimposed upon each other. One has been found in a Capernaum synagogue of the third century and another on a tombstone in Italy from about the same period.

The name "Shield of David" is of unknown origin. There is no mention of it either in the Bible or in any rabbinic literature. Some claim that it may have been the emblem of a war shield used in Bible times, or it may have served as a symbol for astral worship. The first Jewish reference to it is in a Karaite work "Eshkol Ha-Kofer" about the middle of the 12th century, which describes it as an amulet or charm with protective powers.

The first Zionist Congress in 1897 adopted it as the symbol of Zionism. It came to serve as the Jewish emblem and, later, of Israel, in the same way that the Cross represents the Christian religion and the Crescent, the Mohammedan religion. It is a common motif in synagogue architecture today.

Mizrach—מזרח—Eastward

The word "Mizrach" means East and designates the direction of the rising sun. It applies to the seats of honor closest to the Ark, which

are usually reserved for the officials of the congregation or other ex-
tremely pious individuals. The word "Mizrach" also refers to decorative
designs that may be elaborately embroidered on velvet "Bemah" covers
or painted on cards or plates that could be hung on the altar wall of
the synagogue or in the home. The Bible source for this is in the 93rd
Psalm : "From the rising of the sun unto the setting thereof, the name
of the Lord is praised."

Tzedakah Boxes—קפה—Charity or Money Box—Kupah

To encourage the people to practice the virtue of charity, and to
support worthwhile Jewish causes, small containers, usually made of
tin, were placed in the antechambers and meeting rooms of the synagogue. These Tzedakah boxes are still in evidence today and some
organizations place them in Jewish homes.

In Yiddish this box is called a PUSHKI.

Memorial Tablets

To commemorate the passing of the dead, the custom arose in
recent times of inscribing the name and anniversary of the deceased
on some form of tablet or plaque. These tablets, made of marble, metal,
or wood, are hung on the walls of the synagogue or in the halls. Modern
tablets are equipped with individual lights next to the nameplate so
that they can be illumined on the occasion of the Yahrzeit or memorial services.

The Organization of the Synagogue

THE AUTONOMY OF THE SYNAGOGUE

Every synagogue is an independent unit, formed traditionally by
ten Jewish men on their own authority and volition. They elect their
respective officers, secure officiants to fill their spiritual and educational
needs, and account to no jurisdiction. There is no Jewish ecclesiastical
hierarchy, although some communities may elect a chief rabbi and
some countries may have a religious head who is appointed by the
government. In early Christian communities, some congregations were
governed by an ARCHISYNAGOGUS, an honorary title meaning "Ruler of
the Synagogue."

MEMBERSHIP OF THE SYNAGOGUE

Synagogue membership is voluntary and is based on family units,
with the head of the family determining the affiliation. No formal

initiation or consecration takes place when a family joins a congregation, unless conversion from another faith is involved. An application for membership is sometimes submitted to the officers and directors of a synagogue who seldom, if ever, exercise their power to accept or disapprove.

Though synagogues are maintained by members and function for their benefit, nonmembers may attend and participate in the worship and some activities of the congregation. On the High Holy Days, however, seats are usually reserved for members and their families.

HOW THE SYNAGOGUE IS SUPPORTED

Synagogues are financed by membership fees pledged annually and by donations. Membership pledges vary according to the circumstances and desires of the individual. Donations may be made on various occasions, such as in honor of participating in the Torah service, in memory of a loved one, or for some happy family event. Synagogue income is also derived through the sale of seats for Holy Day services and from special appeals and fund-raising affairs held throughout the year.

Offerings

There is no offering or weekly collection in synagogues, as a rule, although some Reform congregations have been known to take up collections on occasion.

THE OFFICIANTS OF THE SYNAGOGUE

When the synagogue became established as an institution in Jewish life it was necessary to create offices and officiants for the promotion of its various activities. Prior to the Babylonian Exile (586 BCE), all religious affairs were supervised by the Priesthood and all community functions were under government jurisdiction.

After the destruction of the Commonwealth (70 CE), Jewish communities were led by unpaid officials who were responsible for administering the affairs of the people. The important leaders were the Parnas (President), Gabbai (Treasurer), and trustees or council members. Among the religious functionaries who received remuneration for their services were the Shochet, the Mohel, the Sofer, and the Meshullach.

Every community, known as a Kehillah, supported one or more synagogues and employed professional officiants to conduct services and fulfill religious functions. The more important of these were the

Rabbi, the Chazan, and the Shammash. Others with special skills were selected to conduct various parts of the worship services.

Religious Functionaries

The Rabbi

The name RABBI—רִבִּי—literally means MY TEACHER. The term came into popular use after the fall of the Second Temple when the spiritual leadership passed from the priesthood to scholars and heads of academies who were teachers of Torah. In the Talmudic age many of these scholars were designated as RABBAN—רִבָּן—OUR MASTER or RAV—רַב—MASTER.

The title of "Rabbi," was bestowed upon a person in recognition of his learning, his standing in the community, and his qualifications as a judge in Jewish law. As an authority on Halachah—Jewish Law, he was called upon to adjudicate religious problems that required legal decisions. In practice he also served as marriage counselor, expounder of Halachah, recounter of Haggadah, and the final authority in disputes among his members.

During Talmudic times and for centuries following, rabbis were laymen, engaged in their respective livelihoods. After their day's work they served as rabbis without compensation. It was not until the 15th century that they became salaried officiants.

Rabbis receive their preparation and training in various Jewish theological seminaries. Orthodox rabbis are educated in Yeshiboth, the traditional schools for the study of Bible and Talmud. Since these schools are concerned with Jewish law and procedure, less emphasis is placed on the other functions of the rabbinate. Conservative and Reform rabbis are trained in modern schools or seminaries corresponding to colleges and universities. The curriculum of these schools takes into consideration more modern personal needs and changing ways, as well as the problems of the Jewish community.

Upon completion of the training course the graduate receives s'MICHAH—סְמִיכָה—ORDINATION, or a diploma that entitles him to assume the duties and responsibilities of the rabbinate. On the principle that "one who is ordained may ordain," S'michah could be conferred by any rabbi. The act of ordination involves the "laying of hands" upon the individual. The Biblical phrase v'SAMACHTOH ES YADICHAH—וְסָמַכְתָּ אֶת יָדְךָ—LAY THY HAND (upon him), (Numbers 27 : 18) which gives us the word "S'michah," is the source of transferring authority to another in the presence of the congregation. This has led to the practice of conferring S'michah on a qualified candidate by three or more rabbis.

Though S'michah is a requisite for the rabbinate, congregations are free to select anyone they desire, regardless of qualifications. In small traditional congregations a MELAMED—מלמד—TUTOR or TEACHER, or the SHOCHET—שוחט—SLAUGHTERER often assumes the role of spiritual head of the congregation.

The Rabbi today serves many other functions in the administering of his duties. He receives special training in the following fields:

PUBLIC SPEAKING

Since sermons form an important part of the worship service, he is trained in the field of homiletics, which is the art of preparing and delivering sermons.

EDUCATION

To organize and direct the religious instruction for the youth and adults of the congregation.

PASTORAL

To counsel and comfort the members of his congregation whenever the occasion demands. This duty frequently brings him into the field of psychology, psychiatry, marriage counseling, and social work when dealing with problems of individuals.

ADMINISTRATION

To be familiar with the organization, financing, and administrative work of the synagogue.

SPIRITUAL LEADER

To espouse the cause of Judaism and to make its history, heritage, and teachings available to his people.

PUBLIC RELATIONS

The rabbi is often called upon to represent his people on civic and welfare boards, to appear before religious and secular groups on various occasions, and to champion the civil rights of people whenever necessary.

The Chazan— חזן —Reader—Cantor

The office of Chazan goes back to Temple times. Originally, he was the administrative overseer of the community, and was subordinate to the "Parnas," the head of the community. Later, he served as a "Shammash," the superintendent or sexton of the Temple. In Gaonic times he assumed the office of "Reader" in public worship services. In this role he was expected to chant the liturgy.

The Chazan today is usually called the Cantor. He may chant the service, accompanied by a choir, but he also may be the professional soloist and choirmaster. He may use the centuries-old cantillation modes, or sing modern musical versions of prayers, or create original liturgical compositions. The Chazan was not a permanent synagogue official. Any qualified layman could be invited to conduct the service. In time, a pleasant musical voice came to be a prerequisite for the office of Chazan, because of the emotional appeal he could impart to the service.

Many congregations employ Cantors only for the Holy Days. In some instances prominent Jewish singers in the field of entertainment are invited to sing the Holy Day liturgy as Cantors.

Shammash—שמש—Sexton

A multitude of duties have fallen to this person in the course of the history of the synagogue. In olden times he was a "Shulkiopper," knocking on doors to call people to services. He had to provide the proper ceremonials for the holidays, prepare boys for Bar Mitzvah, superintend funeral arrangements, and assist in marriage ceremonies. Today, the Shammash is the warden or caretaker of the synagogue. In very small congregations he acts as rabbi, teacher, Chazan, and reader of services.

The Sheliach Tzibur—שליח צבור—Messenger of the Congregation

Historically, the title of "Sheliach Tzibur" applied to an appointed or voluntary leader of public prayer. He was the public spokesman for worship at a time when there were no prayer books and the congregants relied solely on an expert leader during public devotions. As a "messenger," his primary task was to direct the attention of the congregation to the prescribed prayers and to the selected readings from the Torah and the Haftorah, and to lead them in their responses.

The ROSH KNESSETH—ראש כנסת—HEAD OF THE CONGREGATION was selected on the basis of scholarship, diction, enunciation, accuracy, pleasing voice, piety, and unblemished reputation.

In the Gaonic period, the Chazan acted in the capacity of a public reader. Later, this privilege was extended to worthy and qualified individuals of the congregation.

The Baal Tefillah—בעל תפילה—Master of Prayer

Another name for the office of "Sheliach Tzibur" is BAAL TEFILLAH—MASTER (READER) OF PRAYER. This title is now in common use today. In many congregations he is a full-time officiant.

It is the custom in many synagogues to invite someone who is worthy and suitable to lead the worshipers in prayer and intone the liturgy. Often this service is performed by one observing a Yahrzeit. He intones the "Eighteen Benedictions" called the "Amidah" and other parts of the liturgy. More than one individual may be so honored in the course of a service. Well-trained and gifted Bar Mitzvah boys are sometimes accorded this privilege.

The Baal Koray—בעל קורא—Master (Reader) of the Torah

This function of reading and intoning the weekly lesson from the Torah and Haftorah was originally associated with the office of the Chazan and the Sheliach Tzibur. A knowledge of cantillation is necessary and since the words of the Torah are unvocalized, only a trained person can qualify. On special occasions, such as Rosh HaShanah, he may be called upon to be a BAAL TOKEAH— בעל תוקע —A SHOFAR BLOWER, although this function can be assumed by any one who is qualified and experienced in the sounding of the Shofar.

Lay Community Officials

The Jewish community and the synagogue were inseparable. The leaders of the Kehillah were also the leaders and important officiants in the synagogue. The growth and diversification of the Jewish community brought about functions separate and distinct from the synagogue, yet religious in essence. The rabbi was usually identified with the synagogue but he was also a community leader. He was part of a BETH DIN—בית דין—COURT OF JUDGMENT that included lay leaders and was involved with every aspect of community life. The leaders of the Jewish community were primarily concerned with law and ritual pertaining to the health, welfare, protection, and continuity of Jewish life. The respective roles played by them date back to Bible and Talmudic times.

The Parnas—פרנס—Administrator

The Hebrew word "Parnas" means "to support," "to provide." In Bible times the Parnas was known as the ROSH HA-KAHAL—ראש קהל—THE RELIGIOUS HEAD OR ADMINISTRATOR OF THE COMMUNITY. He presided over a group of council members or trustees, varying in number, called TOBAY HA-IR— טובי העיר —THE GOOD MEN OF THE CITY. The Talmud speaks of them as YECHIDIM—יחידים—SELECT ONES or the ELITE of the community.

The Parnas was an unpaid, elected, or appointed lay leader of high repute. He was selected for the office because of his scholarly attainment and his qualifications to supervise religious services. As religious head of the community he was called MANHIG— מנהיג —LEADER OF THE CONGREGATION. Until the 16th century he was the chief synagogue functionary. As president he was responsible to the community for the support, maintenance, and religious conduct of the synagogue.

The Gabbai—גבאי—Collector

The Hebrew term "Gabbai" means "Collector." This title is traced back to the first century when the Roman government designated the

Gabbai to be the Jewish tax collector. Before the office became associated with the synagogue he was known as GABBAI TZEDAKAH— גבאי
צדקה —CHARITY COLLECTOR. The Talmud speaks of the Gabbai as
a "tax officer." In this capacity and as a collector of charity he was
the official treasurer of the community.

In medieval times he was the fiscal head of the synagogue and also
served on a committee of trustees appointed by the Parnas to supervise
Jewish institutions. With the dissolution of the Kehillah and the emancipation of the Jew in the 19th century, the Gabbai became a lay
treasurer official of the synagogue. One of his duties was the distribution or sale of ALIYOTH (the privilege of being called to the reading
of the Torah on Sabbath and holidays).

Darshanim and Maggidim—דרשנים-מגידים—Preachers and Teachers

The earliest preachers and teachers of the Jewish religion were the
prophets. They were the "anointed of God" and their purpose was two-
fold; (1) to admonish, denounce, and castigate the people for their
moral laxity, and (2) to explain the true nature of God and plead for
a return to the just, forgiving, and compassionate "Father."

The successor to the prophet was the teacher-rabbi. Among his
duties was to translate the Torah into the vernacular. As such he became known as a Methurgeman (translator) and his chief task was to
follow the reader, verse by verse, in translating the Torah into the
Aramaic language. As a teacher-rabbi he would deliver discourses at
Sabbath morning services in the form of homilies. Later, the Sabbath
afternoon discourse became a popular feature of the synagogue.

The afternoon sermon was called DERASHAH— דרשה —which means
TO SEEK. The person preaching the sermon was called DARSHAN—דרשן.
These preachers developed the homiletical art of interpreting the
Torah, using stories and illustrations from the Talmud and Midrash.
Another group of expounders of the Bible text was known as BAALEI
AGGADAH—בעלי אגדה—MASTERS OF NARRATION.

In the 16th century, the preacher, known as MAGID— מגיד —RELATER,
replaced the Darshan. The Hebrew form HAGGAD— הגד —means TO
TELL. The Magid was an itinerant preacher, relying primarily on
moralistic themes in reaching his listeners. He was also known as a
MOCHIACH— מוכיח —REPROVER. In addition to a fee in the form of a
collection, he received food and lodging.

The Shochet—שוחט—Slaughterer

The ritual slaughterer of the community is called a SHOCHET—שוחט.
The Dietary laws and Kashruth regulations prescribe special proce-

dures for the slaughtering of meat and fowl. For this task a Shochet, trained and licensed with a certificate of KABALAH—קבלה, is retained by the orthodox community. In some communities, in addition to his service fees, he is supported by the synagogue. He may also operate as an independent butcher. In slaughter houses he has the authority to determine whether or not animals are fit for consumption.

The Mohel—מוהל—Professional Circumciser

Training, experience, and certification (Kabalah) qualify this person to initiate male children into the covenant of Abraham by the rite of circumcision. For this task the Shochet and the Mohel may often be the same person.

The Sofer—סופר—Scribe, Copyist

In Bible times the "Scribe of the King" was an important official and acted in the capacity of Secretary of State. The name is derived from the word SEFER—ספר—which means "Book." Certain sages of the Talmudic period were known as SOFRIM. They were learned men and trained in the art of writing. In addition to making copies of the Torah for use in synagogues, they made the insertions for the Phylacteries and Mezuzoth. They also drew up marriage contracts and bills of divorce.

The Mashgiach— משגיח —Supervisor of Dietary Laws

This individual is appointed to supervise the laws of Kashruth and the strict observance of the Dietary regulations in public institutions. Any Jewish layman or rabbi who is qualified in this aspect of Jewish law can perform this function.

The Meshuloch—משולח—Emissary, Collector

These people, also known as SHADARIM—שדרים—THOSE SENT FORTH, were traveling emissaries for charitable causes. They were sent abroad by Jewish organizations in Israel and Europe to collect funds for needy people and for the support of Jewish education. Many well-known Yeshiboth and orphanages were represented by these Meshulachim.

The Chevrah Kedisha—חברה קדישא—Holy Fellowship

Every Jewish community had a society of men or fellowship made up from the membership of the synagogue. The chief duty of this group was to take full charge of funeral arrangements and properly prepare the body for burial. Membership in this fellowship was voluntary and no charge was made for services performed. In many communities the society manages the cemetery and is responsible for its care.

The Shtadlan—שתדלן—Mediator or Interceder

This Jewish functionary of medieval times represented the community as a special agent in dealing with non-Jewish officials and dignitaries. The name is derived from the Aramaic and literally means "Persuader." Because of his eloquence, ability, and influence, he was selected to intercede for his people against discriminatory and abusive measures.

Contemporary Synagogue Officials

The President

All the offices of a synagogue are honorary. The president is selected by the members of the congregation to be the administrative head. With him are also elected one or more vice-Presidents, Secretary, Treasurer, and other officers.

Board of Directors

These people are chosen by the membership to assist the officers in formulating and executing the policies of the synagogue. The chief function of the board is to select a rabbi, approve candidates for membership, arrange budgeting and financing, authorize synagogue maintenance, supervise religious education, and coordinate all synagogue activities. The members of the board are elected for a limited time and serve without remuneration.

SYNAGOGUE ACTIVITIES

Men's Club—An organization of the men of the congregation for the purpose of fostering social, cultural, and religious activities.

Sisterhood—The women's organization of the congregation. Their primary purpose is to promote social-religious activities and to sponsor fund-raising projects.

Religious School—To provide Hebrew and religious education for the children of the congregation; usually directed by the rabbi or Religious Educator.

Youth Groups—The young people who comprise the junior congregation of the synagogue. Many such groups are sponsored by national Jewish organizations.

Bible Classes—Study Groups—Forums—These cultural activities are for the benefit of the adults of the congregation. They are usually open to the nonmembers of the community.

The Worship of the Synagogue

THE NATURE AND FORM OF PRAYER

Jewish prayers are based upon the idea of a personal covenant between God and man. In general they express faith in Him, submission to His will, commitment to the furthering of His kingdom, and exaltation of His name. His power and His majesty are supreme, regardless of the destiny which might befall Israel or the individual Jew.

The sacrificial cult of Bible times was devoted to bringing the presence of God to man's consciousness. "Hear, O heavens, and give ear, O earth, for the Lord hath spoken," says Isaiah in 1 : 2. Zechariah (2 : 17) declaims, "Be silent, all flesh, before the Lord; for He is aroused out of his holy habitation." Some prayers of this period were primitive, addressed to a God who would be benevolently disposed toward men whose conduct was deemed worthy, and one who would guard them against the evil forces and harmful spirits that surrounded them. Other prayers, which were in the spirit of thanksgiving or in petition, have their counterparts in the prayers of today. Later, others came into use : penitential prayers, expressions of distressed minds, and enunciation of moral ideals.

Prayer was purely voluntary during the time of the first Temple. Then the Davidic hymns were sung by the Levites and vows of repentance accompanied the sin offerings. But later, according to Maimonides, (Yad Tefillah 1 : 3) there was one obligatory daily prayer, the Shema. Subsequently the prayer of the "Eighteen Benedictions" was added to the daily devotions. Regular daily prayers must have originated sometime after the destruction of the First Temple (586 BCE), in Babylonia, because the first related reference is found in Daniel (6 :11), which states that he prayed three times a day, indicating that this was the custom of the time.

After the return from Exile and during the days of the Second Temple, prayer in synagogues and sacrifices in the Temple were co-existent. Following the destruction of this Temple (70 CE), prayer became the binding and unifying force that helped the Jewish people retain their identity. As time went on, special preparations and set times for certain prayers received more attention. Consideration was also given to posture, to time and place, to solemnity and decorum. The day came when the prayer routine of each day, from rising until retiring, was prescribed. Penitential prayers, as expressed in the Selichoth prayers, asking for forgiveness, developed as Judaism concen-

trated upon expanding the moral consciousness of the people. Supplication prayers tended to become universal, especially in the form
Judaism has taken in the Western world. They encompass the welfare
of all mankind and include pleas for peace for all the world.

PUBLIC AND PRIVATE WORSHIP

As the religion of the Jewish people developed, it encouraged and
provided for private worship in the home and public worship in the
synagogue. No matter how scattered and how different the Jews of the
world, nor how dissimilar their prayer books, when they pray they are
united by a common prayer language, Hebrew, and by a belief in
the Oneness of God. They adhere to the same basic code of Jewish
law and give utterance to many of the same traditional hopes and
aspirations.

While public worship identifies the Jew with his people, Judaism
stresses individual responsibility and man's personal connection with
God as exemplified in private prayer. Each Jew stands before God
in his own right. No one can utter his prayers for him except when he
is under severe disability. A Rabbi can only lead and direct him. Much
of public prayer is concerned with the collective welfare of Israel and
all mankind. Only in private devotion does the Jew commune with
God on matters of personal concern, as is the practice in many
religions.

REVERENCE AND DECORUM

From earliest times, the deference demanded for the Temple in
Leviticus 19 : 30, "Ye shall reverence my sanctuary," was claimed for
the synagogue. However, the situation is anomalous because standards
of decorum have been difficult to maintain, especially in traditional
Judaism where many believe in doing as the Psalmist says, ". . . I will
pray and cry aloud, and He shall hear my voice." (55 : 18) Those who
justify the lack of decorum claim that the worshipers feel "at home"
and therefore do not need to be concerned with disciplined conduct.
They do not consider praying aloud and spontaneously as disrespectful.

However, there are those who disagree and point out that historically
much attention was given to the physical and spiritual preparation of
the worshiper so that he would enter the house of worship in a reverent
mood. "The Lord is in His holy temple; let all the earth keep silence
before Him." (Habakkuk 2 : 20) In this spirit it is customary for many
to bow in silence toward the Ark when entering the synagogue, and to

recite in undertone special Scriptural verses based on the ideas of reverence and self-dedication.

Indecorum follows naturally from worship that requires oral prayers. These are sometimes of great volume when an individual is oblivious of others and is emotionally keyed to a full-throated response uttered at his own pace and his own tempo. To avoid this, the Liberal service formalizes participation by having the leader guide the congregation in prayer and having him call for the various responses that are rendered in unison.

Conversation

An age-old breach of etiquette remains the apparently disrespectful practice of holding personal, social, or business conversations before and during the worship service. Efforts have been made from earliest times to correct this abuse of reverence but to date no measure has successfully coped with it. As a result, authorities delineated certain portions of the liturgy where various degrees of silence were demanded. Attempts were made to forbid conversation during the reading of the portions of the Torah, but there was no objection during the interval when individuals were called for Aliyoth.

Some prayers are rendered silently, and it is expected that at this time no voice be heard. Other practices included the displaying of notices asking for silence, the employing of a beadle who was designated to preserve silence, or the reproaching of the congregation by the Rabbi or congregational official.

Interruptions in Prayer

Respect for the synagogue was also to be manifested in behavior in parts of the building other than the sanctuary. The freedom of the synagogue permits one to enter or leave as he pleases, thereby encouraging lack of consideration for the officiants. Bad manners, restlessness, changing pews, unnecessary entering and leaving, and idling within the vicinity of the building have always been considered to be in poor taste.

Physical Preparation for Prayer

Since the day of the Holy of Holies in the original Tabernacle, the sanctuary has been associated with purity. Therefore personal cleanliness became a prerequisite for prayer. Preparation for worship, whether on the Sabbath or holiday, included cleansing of both body and personal effects. Maimonides listed the wearing of the best available clothes as desirable. Upon arising, before his first prayer, and for daily prayers, each worshiper was expected to wash his hands. In the Temple, as well as in the synagogues that followed, a laver was provided for this purpose. Dirty shoes had to be wiped or scraped of mud before entering the building.

THE SPIRIT OF KAVANAH

Much has been said about the relationship between the mood of one who is about to pray and resulting emotional experience. In Judaism, much attention is given to the matter of self-attunement or KAVANAH—כוונה—which comes from the Hebrew word meaning INTENTION or TO DIRECT. There are no fixed rules for the achievement of "Kavanah," but primarily it is an awareness that all worldly affairs should be excluded from the mind, and one should be in a calm, contemplative mood and regard himself as standing before the "Shechinah," the Divine Presence. (Maimonides, Hilchoth Tefillah 4 : 16) Essentially, "Kavanah" is an attempt to direct the heart and the emotions so that prayer, during which man confronts and communes with God, shall have the most beneficient result.

Without this preparation, prayer is apt to be mechanical and perfunctory, with the reading of the printed word just an empty gesture. Both the mind and the heart must be involved. Isaiah said, "This people draws near unto me with their mouth and with their lips to honour me, but have removed their heart from me and their fear of me is a command of men learned by rote." (29 : 13) The wearing of "Tefillin" during morning devotions, with one phylactery on the head and the other near the heart, is intended to create a better disposition to sincere prayer. "Rather a little prayer with intention than much without it," say the sages. Prayer is not supposed to be speeded up nor the words slurred, but this is very difficult for those who are so familiar with the liturgy that they hurriedly mumble the words by rote without thinking about the subject matter of the prayer.

POSTURE

Since prayer is an emotional expression, there developed, in time, gestures and postures which accompanied it. Purely individualistic in origin, they included bowing or inclining the head; kissing certain appurtenances of worship, such as the Torah and the Mezuzah; standing or sitting as the liturgy indicated; prostration before the Ark; covering the head and the eyes; swaying and bending, and the like. All these are meant to reveal the deeper feelings of the worshipers, whether of reverence, humility, adoration, or solemnity. They are outward manifestations that are supposed to aid the power of concentration or devotion.

Standing—Originally, all worshipers stood throughout the service. There were no seats or pews in the Temple and when public and private prayer developed after the destruction of the First Temple, standing was the common posture. "Standing before the Lord" is an expression that occurs frequently in the Bible and also in many prayers. This posture still adds solemnity to the recital of certain prayers, such as the Shema, personal petitions, public confessions, declarations of praise (Hallel), the K'dushah, a prayer of holiness, and the raising of the Torah when taken from and to the Ark.

The Hebrew word for "stand" is AMAD— עמד, and from it comes the name AMIDAH— עמידה, which describes one's posture during the thrice-daily recited collection of benedictions and personal petitions known as the SHEMONEH ESREH— שמונה עשרה —THE EIGHTEEN (Benedictions). There are specific directions to be observed when standing for the "Amidah." (Berachoth 10b) One must stand firmly, placing both feet closely together, and must not lean on anything nearby, so that one's stance is not slovenly. When the prayer is concluded, the worshiper should step backward three paces as an act of reverence. As man humbles himself before an earthly king and withdraws backwards from his presence, so is he supposed to reflect the attitude of respect in which he holds his religion and his God, the King of Kings.

Sitting—Sitting is allowed during most prayers. The Hebrew YASHAV — ישב —means TO SIT or TO DWELL. Sitting in the synagogue is regarded as dwelling in God's house. This is to predispose one to commune with God and to contemplate His ways. These two aspects are noted in Lamentations, "He sits alone and is silent." (3 : 8) Since contemplation is related to study, the congregation is seated during the reading of the Torah and other portions of the Prayer Book derived from the Bible, the Mishnah, and the Talmud, which are meditative.

Kneeling and Prostration—Bowing, kneeling, prostration, and genuflection as acts of adoration have undergone many changes and modifications since ancient times. In the Scriptures there are many references to kneeling. Solomon knelt in prayer (I Kings 8 : 54); it was a posture of petition for Daniel (6 : 10); to "bow the knee" infers worship and prayer for the people. (I Kings 19 : 18)

The Hebrew root for KNEEL— ברך —BARACH is the same as for the Hebrew word BLESSING, which suggests that a blessing was received in a kneeling position. This would seem to indicate that the recital of prayers of adoration was accompanied by some act of genuflection. Whatever its form, Biblical and rabbinic sources tell us that prostration was practiced as an expression of complete humility and submission.

When the Christian church required genuflection as a general practice among its adherents, kneeling all but disappeared in Judaism because of its association. What remained of the practice was in modified form, as bending the knee, bowing and "falling upon the face." The latter, known in Hebrew as NEFILLATH APPAYIM— נפילת אפים, involved the bending of the body until the head touched the ground. This, too, was modified to a sitting position with the worshiper's head resting upon his arm. There are religious mystics who observe prostration by extending their whole bodies prone on the ground. This is called HISHTACHAVAYAH— השתחויה —THE COMPLETE HUMBLING OF THE BODY. In traditional synagogues today, remnants of this practice of prostration appears in the "Duchanin" service on the High Holy Days when the Priestly Blessing is pronounced.

Spreading and Raising the Hands—The spreading of the hands was used in some of the standing and kneeling positions. Moses "spread his hands to the Lord" while pleading the cause of the Israelites. (Exodus 9 : 33) Solomon "stood before the altar and spread his hands heavenwards." (I Kings 8 : 22) Repeated references may be found in the Bible, most of which tend to show that hand gestures added expressiveness, especially to prayers of intercession.

The "raising of hands" heavenward, similar to spreading the hands, indicated an expression of affirmation or assertion. In Ezra 9 : 5, the people who were assembled "answered, Amen with the uplifting of their hands." In post-Temple times, this gesture was no longer used by the worshipers but was retained by the priests, usually in the priestly benediction.

Associated with the raising of the hands is the "spreading of the fingers." This is called NESIATH KAPPAYIM— נשיאת כפים, and was a daily practice of the priests. In the Priestly Blessing the fingers of each hand are separated to form two open spaces. When the two hands are joined there is a space between the thumbs, thus making a pattern of five spaces. The allegorical explanation of this gesture is based on a verse in the Song of Solomon (2 : 9) that is interpreted to mean "five windows." The formation of the fingers has also been said to have a sexual connotation.

Other postures of the hands were clasping, folding, or interlacing the fingers, covering the eyes during the recitation of the first sentence of the Shema prayer, beating of the breast with clenched fist when offering penitential prayers, and palm against palm. Because the latter is so closely associated with Christian worship, it has been discontinued in Judaism.

Swaying or Swiveling—A posture common to Orthodox and especially Chassidic Jews is the swaying or swiveling of the body. It is supposed to add fervor to the prayers. Involvement of the whole body has been suggested at various times. The sentence "All my bones shall say, Lord, who is like unto thee" (Psalm 35 : 10) has been interpreted to mean the sense organs of the body, such as the head, eyes, mouth, tongue, throat, lips, heart, hands, and feet.

The founder of Chassidism, Baal Shem Tov, explained the need for impassioned swaying by comparing the worshiper to a man who is drowning in a storm-tossed sea, and can save himself only by waving his whole body. The backward, forward, and sideward movements serve to heighten the fervor of prayer. The swaying of the head is a gesture to accentuate the different cantillation modes during the reading of the Torah. The movement of the body, in any form, serves not only to expel all extraneous thoughts, but also to emphasize the meaning of the Shema prayer, "to love the Lord thy God with all thy heart, with all thy soul, and with all thy might."

Traditions of the Synagogue

HEAD COVERING— כסוי ראש —KESUEY ROSH

The head covering, common to most Jewish people, is called a YARMULKEH— יארמולקה, a word of Slavic derivation. Another name for the head covering is KIPPAH— כפה —CAP or SKULL CAP. The name KAPPAL is also used sometimes. It is derived from the Italian word CAPPELO, which means hat.

The Yarmulkeh is a small peakless cap, similar to the "Sarum" worn by Catholic priests. It is made of various materials and in differing shapes. Some authorities claim that it may be traced to the MITRE, a cone-shaped headgear worn by the High Priest in the Temple.

There is no Biblical or Talmudic law concerning the covering of the head, although the practice seems to have originated in Babylonia in the Talmudic period. It was not until medieval times that this custom (Minhag) became binding through the acceptance of the Shulchan Aruch by traditional Jews.

Prior to official codification there was widespread divergence in the observance of the custom. The Talmud (Nedarim 30b) says : "Men sometimes have their heads covered, and sometimes go bareheaded. Women always cover their heads; children always go bareheaded." This would imply freedom of choice and involved many opinions and interpretations by the rabbis. Maimonides (12th century), commenting on the practice, said that scholars and teachers should not study or teach while bare-headed and suggested that worshipers "ought" to keep their heads covered.

The *Shulchan Aruch*— שׁלחן ערוך —*The Prepared Table*, written by Joseph Karo (16th century), is the authoritative compendium of all Orthodox Jewish practice. It refers to the covering of the head as follows :

> One may not read from the Torah with uncovered head.
> (Orach Chayim 282 : 3)
> One may enter the synagogue with one's staff, knapsack and purse;
> but some prohibit entering with a long knife or uncovered head.
> (Orach Chayim 151 : 6)
> One may not walk four cubits (about six feet) with uncovered head.
> (Orach Chayim 2 : 6)

The first of these injunctions would apply only to the reading of the Torah at public worship and not outside the synagogue or in the home. It might also imply that men did worship with uncovered heads as late as the 16th century. The second injunction deals with decorum in the synagogue, inferring that bareheadedness is compared to nakedness and is repugnant in contact with God. The last citation is in keeping with standard Orthodox practice; that covering one's head at all times is a sign of reverence for God.

There were some opponents to the Minhag of wearing head coverings at all times. Rabbi Meir of Rothenburg (1215–1293) maintained that bareheadedness was not forbidden except for women. Moses Isserles (1513–1572), author of "Mappah," a popular code of Jewish practice, stated that the custom stemmed only from good manners. Elijah Vilna Gaon (1729–1797), a noted Talmudic authority, denied that praying or entering a synagogue with uncovered head was rooted in Jewish law. In France it was the custom of rabbis to pray with uncovered heads.

Minhag has the effect of law and the custom of wearing a head covering became a universal practice among Jews. Today, Orthodox Jews adhere strictly to the tradition of keeping the head covered during the prayer services at the synagogue, at private devotions in the home, at meals, at all religious functions and during the instruction of the young in Hebrew classes. Ultra-pious Jews wear the head covering constantly. There is no rule about the kind of Yarmulkeh used. Sometimes street hats or caps are worn or skull caps are provided, depending upon the circumstances.

Liberal Judaism does not require the wearing of hats during the religious services or at any other time, but since there is no uniformity, some congregations may insist that all worshipers be uncovered while in others it is left to the option of the worshiper.

Some Explanations for the Covering of Heads

Covering the head was a sign of humility among ancient peoples. Among oriental peoples, Hindus, Arabs, and Persians, it is a symbol of respect and reverence.

To go uncovered exposed the individual to the dangers of the desert sun and wind.

Tribal beliefs of early Israelites held the notion that human hair invited demons to inflict harm; hence the concealment of hair. This applied especially to women.

Bareheadedness was regarded as a form of nakedness and an imitation of the ways of the heathen.

The head covering is a symbol of separation and enables one to differentiate between the sacred and the profane. Because the Shechinah was above man, it was construed to be an act of irreverence to uncover the head in the presence of God.

The imposition of wearing the "Jew Hat" as a badge of humiliation. demanded of most Jews in the Diaspora, became an emblem of self-identification and a crown of distinction.

Moses, upon seeing the manifestation of God in the burning bush, (Exodus 3 : 6) hid or covered his face because of fear and awe.

In the orient, covering the head in the presence of an elder or scholar was considered to be a gesture of respect.

The act of covering the head not only prevents sin, but reminds the wearer of his obligation to perform good deeds.

MUSIC IN THE SYNAGOGUE

Music, singing, and dancing have always been an integral part of the culture of the Jewish people. All through the history of the Jewish religion we find references to music, starting with Jubal (Genesis 4) as the inventor of the first musical instrument. Moses sang praises unto God, and Miriam and her maidens danced with timbrels following the crossing of the Red Sea. (Exodus 15 : 20f.) Victorious soldiers were welcomed home with music and dancing, (Judges 11 : 34) Jeremiah (7 : 34) speaks of marriage processions accompanied with music and song. King David was a master of the harp and also introduced the great Levitical choirs in the Temple. A description of Temple offerings accompanied by music is given in II Chronicles 29. Temple music marked the religious festivals, and the sound of the Shofar was heard on numerous occasions.

Hallel or Praise Psalms were marked by joyous chantings. Psalm 150 calls attention to some instruments used in the Temple.

Praise Him with the blast of the horn; praise Him with the psaltery and harp. Praise Him with the timbrel and dance; praise Him with stringed instruments and the pipe. Praise Him with loud-sounding cymbals; praise Him with the clanging cymbals. Let everything that hath breath praise the Lord. Hallelujah.

Instruments of Bible Times

WIND INSTRUMENTS

Oohgab	עוגב	Similar to a bagpipe
Chalil	חליל	Flute or reed instrument
Chatzotzarah	חצוצרה	Trumpet
Shofar	שופר	Ram's horn (this was also made of metal, corresponding to the trombone)

STRINGED INSTRUMENTS

Kinnor	כנור	Harp
Nebel	נבל	Lyre or Guitar

PERCUSSION INSTRUMENTS

Toff	תף	Tamborine or hand-drum
M'tzalteem	מצלתים	A round metal gong
Shaleeshim	שלישים	A triangular steel gong
Tzaltzilim	צלצלים	Bells or castanets

Instrumental Music in the Synagogue

With the destruction of the Temple a period of national mourning set in and instrumental music was not permitted in the worship service. Since that time it has not returned to the orthodox synagogue. Another explanation of this ban was that playing an instrument on the Sabbath or Holy Day was construed as work.

Reform Jewry and some Conservative congregations use the organ as a regular part of their religious services, and on special occasions various other instruments are used.

Cantors and Choirs

Vocal renditions have always been part of the liturgy of the synagogue. In the Orthodox liturgy especially, choral singing has been developed to great heights of artistry through the Chazzan and his all-Jewish male choir. Although some Reform synagogues employ a Cantor today, most of them resort to mixed choirs and permit non-Jewish singers to participate.

The Prayers of Israel

THE LANGUAGE OF PRAYER

The language of the Prayer Book is Hebrew. It belongs to the Semitic family of languages and its alphabet, consonantal in form, was similar to that used by the Phoenicians and Arameans. Originally it was written in script form and did not appear in its present square style until the time of Ezra, about 400 years before the common era.

In every place where the Jew has lived throughout his history, he has used the Hebrew language in talking to his God. Hebrew was the language heard at Sinai at the time of the Revelation. It is the language in which the Bible and most of the great literature of the Jew is written. Hebrew is the Holy tongue of Israel and is called LASHON HA-KODESH— לשון הקדש —the HOLY SPEECH. (Sotah 7 : 2)

PRAYER IN THE VERNACULAR

Although Hebrew has been the medium of public prayer, it has not been the spoken language of the Jews at all times. At various periods in Jewish history, Israel prayed in the language of his time and country. In Bible times, when Aramaic was the popular spoken language of Palestine, an Aramaic translation of the Bible was printed alongside the Hebrew text. Many Aramaic prayers became part of the Jewish liturgy. The Kaddish prayer, which persists to this day in its original Aramaic version, is a typical example.

Despite the fact that the rabbis of old agreed that it was permissible to pray to God in any language that "the heart understands," tradition had kept the prayers of Israel in their original Hebrew form for collective worship. Individual prayers have been written in the vernacular, but those that proved acceptable were invariably translated into Hebrew before being incorporated into the Prayer Book.

Reform Judaism has broken with tradition by permitting its adherents to pray in the language that suits their desire and understanding. The essential Hebrew prayers, however, that form the framework of Israel's belief and ideology have been retained in the Hebrew, although in abbreviated form.

THE DAILY DEVOTIONS

Evening, morning and at noon will I pray and cry aloud; and he shall hear my voice. (Psalm 55 : 18)

And he (Daniel) kneeled upon his knees three times a day, and prayed, and gave thanks before his God, as he did aforetime. (Daniel 6 : 11)

The pious Jew offers prayers unto God three times every day. Tradition has set a fixed hour for these prayers, which are supposed to correspond to the daily sacrifices of the Temple. Actually, there were only two services of sacrifices in the Temple—morning and afternoon. The late evening prayer was added after the destruction of the Second Temple. At first it was considered optional, but later it became obligatory. The times for these daily devotions are :

SHACHARIT —שחרית— MORNING (near dawn)

MINCHAH   — מנחה— LATE AFTERNOON (before twilight)

MA'ARIV ——מעריב— EVENING (when first stars are visible)

THE PRAYER BOOK

In the ninth century, the Gaon Amram (870 CE) prepared a Prayer Book that he called SEDER— סדר —ORDER (of service). Although the text of the Prayer Book, known today by its Hebrew name SIDDUR— סדור, varies among Jewish sects, it ranks next to the Bible as a source book of Jewish faith and creed. It is a compilation of centuries of religious thinking and devotion, dating back to the Gaonic period. Within its pages are contained the essential elements of all prayer, of praise through adoration and exaltation, of intercession through petition and supplication, of appreciation and gratitude through thanksgiving, and of guilt release through confession and forgiveness. Behind these essentials of prayer is the desire of man to know and understand God.

The Prayer Book interprets the Jewish religion through poetry, psalm, and song. It quotes from the Bible, Talmud, and kindred Jewish literature. It gives expression to the creeds and dogma of Judaism and it serves as a guide for individual and collective conduct. It can well be said that the Prayer Book is Israel's book of poetry in which the worshiper uses the language of the gods in describing the wonders of God, man, and the universe.

The Prayer Book is the product of many contributors over a long span of time. Because each generation tries to seek God in terms of its own knowledge and understanding, there has never been one uniform Jewish Prayer Book, although most editions have the same traditional arrangement. In our present age, the three dominant groups in American Judaism—Orthodox, Conservative, and Reform—have each their own version of the Prayer Book. Among Orthodox groups, differences are marked in the Ashkenazic, Sephardic, and Chassidic liturgy.

Whatever the differences, however, whether in the inclusion or exclusion of certain prayers, in the lengthening or shortening of the services, in the use of Hebrew or the vernacular, the framework of the Prayer Book has always remained the same. It still continues to serve as the common denominator for Jewry.

THE FRAMEWORK OF THE PRAYER BOOK

The Jewish Prayer Book is built around two themes that can be traced back to Bible times. These are the SHEMA— שמע —HEAR, taken from Deuteronomy 6 : 4–9, and the SHEMONEH ESREH— שמונה עשרה —the EIGHTEEN Benedictions said to be composed by the Men of the Great Assembly during the Second Commonwealth. The Shema Prayer and the Ten Commandments were recited only in the Temple.

The Shema Prayer—The prayer known as the Shema is a confession of Jewish faith. The name comes from the opening word of the prayer, "Hear (Shema) O Israel, the Lord our God, the Lord is One." It is always followed by the response, "Praised be His name whose glorious Kingdom is forever and ever."

As the central theme of Israel's faith, the Shema declaration negates the concepts of polytheism, the belief in and worship of many gods; of paganism, the deification of people, objects, or forces; and of dualism, a belief in the rival forces of good and evil striving to control man. The pure monotheism of the Shema excludes Trinitarianism—the belief in three gods in one, and concepts of Virgin birth and intermediaries between God and man.

The Shema prayer is recited at all Jewish worship services. It is repeated by the congregation when the Torah is taken from the Ark. It is the first prayer taught to children and the last prayer recited at death. It is the prayer of Israel's martyrdom and the rallying cry to strengthen Jewish faith.

The required Shema declaration is accompanied by two other prayers, one taken from Deuteronomy 11 : 13 and the other from Numbers 15 : 37–41. The former sets forth the justice of God through reward and punishment; the latter contains the law concerning the wearing of fringes as a reminder of God's commandments. These were recited separately at one time, but are now a part of the morning and evening service.

The Three Sections of the Shema Prayer

Deuteronomy 6 : 4–9
Hear, O Israel : the Lord our God, the Lord is One. And thou shalt love the Lord thy God with all thy heart, and with all thy soul, and with all thy might. And these words, which I command thee this day, shall be upon thy heart; and thou shalt teach them diligently unto thy children, and shalt talk of them when thou sittest in thy house, and when thou walkest by the way, and when thou liest down, and when thou risest up. And thou shalt bind them for a sign upon thy hand,

and they shall be for frontlets between thine eyes. And thou shalt write them upon the door-posts of thy house and upon thy gates.
Deuteronomy 11 : 13–21

And it shall come to pass, if ye shall hearken diligently unto My commandments, which I command you this day, to love the lord your God, and to serve him with all your heart and with all your soul, that I will give the rain of your land in its season, the former rain and the latter rain, that you mayest gather in thy corn, and thy wine, and thine oil. And I will give grass in thy fields for thy cattle, and thou shalt eat and be satisfied. Take heed to yourselves, lest your heart be deceived and ye turn aside, and serve other gods, and worship them; and the anger of the Lord be kindled against you, and He shut up the heaven, so that there shall be no rain, and the ground shall not yield her fruit; and ye perish quickly from off the good land which the Lord giveth you. Therefore shall ye lay up these My words in your heart and in your soul; and ye shall bind them for a sign upon your hand, and they shall be for frontlets between your eyes. And ye shall teach them your children, talking of them when thou sittest in thy house, and when thou walkest by the way, and when thou liest down, and when thou riseth up. And thou shalt write them upon the doorposts of thy house, and upon thy gates; that your days may be multiplied, and the days of your children, upon the land which the Lord swore unto your fathers to give them, as the days of the heavens above the earth.
Numbers 15 : 37–41

And the Lord spoke unto Moses, saying : "Speak unto the children of Israel, and bid them that they make them throughout their generations fringes in the corners of their garments, and that they put with the fringe of each corner a thread of blue. And it shall be unto you for a fringe, that ye may look upon it, and remember all the commandments of the Lord, and do them; and that ye go not about after your own heart and your own eyes, after which ye use to go astray; that ye may remember and do all My commandments, and be holy unto your God. I am the Lord your God, who brought you out of the land of Egypt, to be your God : I am the Lord your God."

The Shemoneh Esreh—These "eighteen" prayers, known as TEFILLAH —תפילה—PRAYERS, are also designated by the term AMIDAH—עמידה (from "Amad" to stand) because they are recited while standing. Actually, there are nineteen prayers, since one directed against slanderers and apostates was added during the first century of the common era.

Numbers play a mystical and symbolic role in the Jewish religion, and the number eighteen is used many times. The Hebrew letters of 18 form the word CHAI—חי— which means LIFE. In the Shema prayer and Psalm 29 the name of God is mentioned eighteen times. The names of the Patriarchs, Abraham, Isaac, and Jacob, appear together eighteen times in Scripture. The Talmud (Berachoth 28b) mentions the fact that in man's spinal column there are eighteen essential vertebrae.

The "Amidah" is divided into three groups of prayers. The first three prayers are in praise of the Creator. The second group of thirteen is combined into one prayer for the Sabbath and holidays. The reason for this is that since these call attention to man's shortcoming, they would not fit the spirit of joy and gladness called for in Sabbath worship. They are prayers of supplication and petition for the needs of the individual and the community. The last group contains three prayers of thanksgiving.

Around these two themes, the Shema and the Shemoneh Esreh, have grown all the prayers of Israel, varying with the holidays and special occasions. The basic pattern of the daily service is as follows :

THE STRUCTURE OF THE TRADITIONAL PRAYER BOOK

Opening Hymns

Two poems about God and faith. The first is known as the "Yigdal" prayer and sets forth the thirteen principles of faith as formulated by Maimonides. The second, called "Adon Olom," is a statement on the nature of the Jewish God.

Morning Benedictions

Six blessings, which originally were recited before the formal prayers began, are included in this group. The first concerns the washing of hands and the last is the three-fold priestly benediction.

Excerpt from Jewish Literature

Taken from Mishnah Peah, Chapter I, this prayer touches upon charity, hospitality, consideration for the sick and dead, and the establishment of peace.

Benedictions

A prayer concerning the nature and purity of the soul, followed by sixteen short blessings thanking God for having made man as he is and acknowledging God's interest in Israel.

Supplication Prayers

Three prayers petitioning God to deliver man from evil. The last is a long, subdivided prayer on man's responsibility to God.

Jewish Literature

Four excerpts from the Bible and Mishnah pertaining to Temple sacrifices and rules for the study of Scripture.

Tallith and Tefillin Benedictions

The ritual ceremony of enwrapping oneself with fringes and donning the Phylacteries is accompanied by seven blessings and meditations. The last is a betrothal meditation taken from Hosea 2 : 21.

Passages of Song

The Hebrew name for this group of prayers is PESUKAY D'ZIMRA—פסוקי דזמרא—PASSAGES OF SONG. There are five sections containing twenty-five passages taken from Scripture. The third section is known as "Halleluyah Psalms."

Half Kaddish

This prayer, exalting God, marks the end of this part of the daily service.

Invocation Before the Shema Prayer

The Shema is the most important prayer in the Jewish liturgy. It is preceded by an invocation to prayer with the words, "Bless ye the Lord who is to be blessed."

Benedictions Before the Shema

The first five prayers are known as the YOTZER or CREATOR prayers and conclude with the prayer of sanctification, "Kadosh, Kadosh, Kadosh." The sixth benediction in this group is known as the AHAVAH or LOVE prayer. It expresses a desire for spiritual light and man's yearning for God.

The Shema Prayers

Three passages from Scripture constitute this group, which proclaims Israel's unity of God, reward and punishment, and the command to wear the fringes. Three additional prayers speak of the validity of the moral law, the eternity of God's word, and God as the redeemer of Israel.

The Shemoneh Esreh or Amidah Prayers

This group contains three sections of 19 benedictions. The first group of three is about the Patriarchs of Israel, the powers of God, and the sanctification of God's name. The second group of thirteen has petition benedictions for the individual's personal welfare such as understanding, health, good harvest, forgiveness, and so on. The ninth prayer in this group, "against slanderers, apostates and sectarians," was added at a later date. The last group of three prayers contains thanksgiving blessings for God's providence and petitions for universal peace.

Concluding Prayers After the Amidah

The first of two prayers concerns personal self-restraint and is recited in an undertone. The second is a short prayer for the rebuilding of the Temple.

Tachanun—Supplication Prayers

These penitential prayers are recited on weekdays at the conclusion of the Shemoneh Esreh section. On Mondays and Thursdays a longer version is recited.

Half Kaddish.

This notes the conclusion of another section of the prayer service.

Torah Readings for Monday and Thursday

These were market days, when people gathered in the towns. Readings from the weekly portion were read with accompanying benedictions before and after. Psalms were also read in praise of God's attributes and His holiness.

Kaddish Tithkabal

An extra paragraph is added to the regular Kaddish petitioning for the acceptance of Israel's prayers and supplications.

Concluding Prayers

Two prayers proclaiming the kingship of God conclude the regular daily liturgy service.

Mourner's Kaddish

The final Kaddish at the end of the service is said by mourners during their year of mourning or at Yahrzeit time.

THOUGHTS ON PRAYER

Whoever performs the will of the All-present and directs his heart to Him in prayer is heard.   (Exodus Rabbah 21 : 3)

Whoever has it in his power to pray on behalf of his neighbor and fails to do so, is called a sinner; as it is said, 'Moreover, as for me, far be it from me that I should sin against the Lord in ceasing to pray for you.' (Berachoth 12b.)

If it is impossible to pray in the synagogue pray in the field. If that is impossible, pray in thy house. If that is impossible, pray on thy bed. If that is impossible, pray in thy heart.

(Midrash Tehilim 4 : 5)

One should not pray in moments of melancholy, listlessness, frivolity, loquacity, levity, or idle talk. (Berachoth 31a)

He who makes his voice heard during prayer is of small faith.

(Berachoth 24b)

When you pray, regard not your prayer as a fixed task, but as an appeal for mercy and grace before God. (Aboth 2 : 18)

Anyone whose mind is not at rest should not pray.   (Erubin 65a)

If a man can concentrate, let him pray; not otherwise.

(Berachoth 30b)

When you pray, know before whom you stand.   (Berachoth 28b)

Do not let your prayer become perfunctory.   (Aboth 2 : 13)

7

Jewish Groups, Sects, and Languages

THE HOUSE OF ISRAEL

Judaism, as a religion, begins with the revealed word of God. To an unorganized slave people was given the Decalogue and the Oral Law, with Moses as the first leader. In spite of his talents as law-giver and leader, Moses was unable to cope with the many civil and religious problems that daily confronted him. Upon the advice of his father-in-law, Jethro, he divided the people into groups of given numbers and appointed judges or elders to rule over them.

Thus we have the first organization in the house of Israel—a body of judges vested with the power to guide the people and to make decisions. From this group arose the political judges or elders who held sway over the tribes of Israel until the establishment of the monarchy under Saul (1053 BCE).

Jewish history, however, is marked by strong conflicts and tensions that resulted in schisms, new movements, and sects. These had their origin in clashes of personalities, in national crises, and in periods of national stagnation.

Religious Groupings in Bible Times

Within the framework of Israel's religious and political development there functioned an ecclesiastical caste institution created by Moses. This was the priesthood, a religious organization with duties and obligations minutely described in the Bible.

KOHANIM— כוהנים —PRIESTS

Aaron, the brother of Moses, was appointed the first High Priest of Israel. The office of the priesthood was hereditary and functioned until the destruction of the Second Temple (70 CE), when Israel lost her independence and became dispersed among the nations of the world.

615

The word KOHEN literally means "one who officiates." His duties are clearly defined in the Bible. He was responsible for the Menorah lamps, the incense altar, the offering of the prescribed sacrifices, the show-bread, the blessing of the people, and the instruction of the law of God. The high priest made atonement for all the people and was the chief authority in all religious matters.

In the centuries that followed, the institution of the priesthood played a dominant role in the political life of the people. Its influence and power were great, but used, too often, to protect and secure its office.

The specific privileges of descendants of a priest were to receive the redemption money paid for the first-born males, to pronounce the priestly benedictions at specified services, to be called first to the reading of the Torah, and to lead in the recitation of the benediction prayers at the conclusion of meals. Biblical prohibitions do not permit a Kohen to come into contact with the dead or marry a divorced woman.

The purity of the line of descent of a Kohen today is highly question-able, but the custom of recognizing a person who claims to be a Kohen or a Levite is accepted without question in traditional Judaism.

LEVI'IM—   לוים   —LEVITES

The first-born of all the male children of Israel were to be conse-crated to God for the purpose of administering the service of the Temple. (Numbers 3 : 13–8 : 7) This law proved impractical and difficult to carry out and it was therefore decreed that only the mem-bers of the tribe of Levi should be designated as administers of Temple worship.   The ceremony of the "Redemption of the First-born," (Leviticus 27 : 26) known as "Pidyon HaBen" was instituted as a re-lease from Temple service.

In Bible times the Levites were a caste of people who separated themselves from family and community life and dedicated them-selves to a monastic career in the service of God.   In post-Exilic times the Levites constituted the lower order of the priesthood, under the Kohanim. As a select or consecrated group, the Levites did not share in the division of the land of Palestine, but received free and perpetual residence in designated cities of the various tribes.   They were also supported by special tithes and offerings.

The Levites of the Temple were assistants to the priests and worked under their supervision. Their duties embraced ecclesiastical, educa-tional, and legislative functions. As watchmen they were to guard the

Tabernacle and its holy vessels and to erect and dismantle it during Israel's wanderings. As porters they cleaned the Temple and its furniture and prepared all worship accessories, such as incense, showbread, oils, lamps, and sacrifices. They also provided the music, organizing choirs and training musicians. As administrators they collected Temple tithes and supervised the offerings. They gave instruction in the Law and guided the people in the way of proper observances. Like the Kohanim the Levites perpetuated their office by making it hereditary, and after the destruction of the Temple ceased to exist as a group. However, they still retain their synagogue honors in traditional Judaism.

YISRALIM—ישראלים—ISRAELITES

The Israelites were the masses of common Jewish people. They received their name from the Patriarch Jacob who was called ISRAEL—ישראל. (Genesis 32 : 24) They brought the sacrifices and offerings to the Temple and were subject to the law of the Priest and King.

These three Biblical groups exist and function to this day in symbolic form. In the Orthodox synagogue services a KOHEN (כהן) one who lays claim of being a descendant of the priesthood, is accorded the honor of being first to read the Torah. A Levite (לוי) is given the second honor and lastly, the Israelite. In the ceremony of the "Redemption of the First-born" a Kohen receives the redemption token or pledge. In Holy Day services special prayers are offered only by Kohanim and Levites.

NAZIRITE— נזיר —CONSECRATED ONE (To dedicate)

A Nazirite is a person who has taken a vow to abstain from intoxicants, from cutting or shaving the head, and from contact with ritual uncleanliness and the dead. Literally, the word Nazir means "to renounce," "to vow," "to abstain." As an early Bible sect, the Nazirites became consecrated people by dedicating themselves to the service of God.

The law of the Nazirite is found in Numbers 6 : 1–21. Many took such self-imposed vows for life; others, only for a specific time or purpose, the shortest allowable time being for thirty days. From a reference in Amos 2 : 11, Nazirites were looked upon as consecrated sons of God : "And I raised up your sons for prophets, and of your young men for Nazirites." The Mishnah devotes an entire tractate to the Nazirites, but in time the sect became less and less important and eventually the institution disappeared.

The word Nazarene, associated with the name of Jesus, refers to a native of a village situated in Galilee, in upper Palestine. It has no connection with the Nazirite person or oath.

NETHINIM— נתינים —TEMPLE SLAVES or SERVANTS

The origin of these people is uncertain, although they are mentioned in the books of Ezra, Nehemiah, and Chronicles as Temple servants. They were supposed to have been conquered Canaanites who were designated for service to the Temple under the supervision of the Levites. Another theory suggests that they were descendants of the Gibeonites. As Temple slaves their duties were of menial nature, and most often they lived on the Temple precincts. The name means "the given ones," implying that the person was given or appointed to sacred service.

KEDESHAH— קדישה —TEMPLE PRIESTESS

After the Israelites conquered Canaan and Solomon became King, they found and adopted some new religious practices, which included the worship of the goddess of fertility, Astarte (Ashtoreth). This practice contained rites in which sacred prostitutes, Kedeshoth, participated. Though Deuteronomy 23 : 18 specifically says that "There shall be no 'Kedeshah' of the daughters of Israel," this licentious pagan rite was not completely abolished until later times. The male prostitute who participated was called a "Kadesh."

PROPHETS— נביאים —NEBI'IM

Literally, the word means "one who brings" the word of God to man. The prophets of the Bible were looked upon as divinely inspired spokesmen to interpret the will of God. They rose usually from the ranks of the people, became teachers of religious truths, and preached on moral issues. As spiritual leaders pointing the way to God, they were characterized by the following attributes :

Emphasized the holiness of God.
Criticized the lax morals of their day.
Taught nobler way of living.
Dealt with judgment and retribution.
Opposed animal sacrifice and over-emphasis of Temple ritual.
Pleaded for righteousness, mercy, love, and justice.
Did not separate themselves from the daily life of the people.
Preached ultimate triumph of good and downfall of evil.
Yearned for ideal social order.
Foretold impending disaster when God was not obeyed.

RECHABITES

This early Bible sect goes back to the family of Jehonadab, who assisted Jehu in purging Israel of the cult of Baal. (II Kings 10 : 15) Rechabites are known also as KENITES. They were tent-dwellers and lived nomadic lives, abstaining from wine, and from cultivating vineyards or fields. What little knowledge we know of this ancient sect is contained in the writings and records of travelers. One such writer, Judah ben Bezaleel (1599), a Talmudist of Posen, claimed that the Rechabites had migrated to the Far East and had become Chinese Jews. Another traveler, Benjamin of Tudela, claimed that he had met a group of Rechabites while journeying through the land of Mesopotamia. Apparently they first lived in Samaria and went to Judah after the destruction of the Northern Kingdom (721 BCE) where they were known as the "sons of the water-drinkers."

Post-Biblical Groups and Sects

PHARISEES

In the Hasmonean period of the Second Temple there existed three major quasi-political groups among the Jewish people—the Pharisees, the Sadducees, and the Essenes. The first two were the main rivals for power to control the Temple.

The PHARISEES—P'RUSHIM—פרושים—meaning SEPARATISTS, were so called because they avoided contact with others for reasons of ritual purity. Their activities were directed to the masses. They were led by the rabbis and scholars and were known as the traditional expounders and interpreters of the Law. Originally they were called CHASSIDIM—חסידים — PIOUS ONES, because of their strict adherence to divine law and their strong opposition to the influence of Hellenism.

Under the rule of the Hasmoneans the Pharisees grew in strength and power. They followed the tradition of the scribes and teachers and sought to imbue the people with a spirit of holiness by propagating traditional values. They investigated and collected the growing storehouse of Jewish tradition and by their liberal interpretations laid the groundwork for the literature of the Mishnah and Talmud. They also incorporated into the framework of Judaism cult folk-customs not mentioned in the Bible.

They were not at all like the derogatory New Testament caricature. They were better known by the name of CHAVERIM—חברים —SCHOLARS or COMRADES. Because they represented the aristocracy of learning they frowned upon the ignorant and the violators of the ritual law. They coined a phrase for the unlearned Jews, AM HA-ARATZIM— עם הארצים —A PEOPLE OF THE EARTH, which is in current use to this day.

While the Pharisees represented the conservative and dogmatic element of Judaism, laying particular stress upon ritual observance and purity, they nevertheless remained the popular and more progressive party of their time. They attempted to adapt Judaism to the changing times without compromising their religion or beliefs. They sought to interpret the Law in accordance with the new conditions and circumstances of their day.

As a party they represented the poor, yet progressive, laity. They introduced popular education among the masses. They developed the liturgy of the synagogue and translated the Bible into the vernacular. They introduced the law of Prosbul, which indirectly abrogated the Biblical obligations of debt release during the Sabbatical year.

Though the Pharisees disappeared as a party after the Fall of the Temple, many of their leaders acquired great reputations as teachers and scholars.

THE SADDUCEES

The Sadducees were the opponents of the Pharisees and represented the ruling and priestly class. Their name is taken from TZADOK— צדק —A HIGH PRIEST and they were known as TZADAKIM—צדקים—JUST or RIGHTEOUS ones.

As an aristocratic political party they catered to the rich and controlled the priesthood. They furthered the inroads of Greek culture, called Hellenism, into Jewish life. Secularly, they were the assimilationists of their time, but their attitude toward Judaism was characterized by both fundamentalism and agnosticism. In their theology they denied the doctrine of Resurrection. While they rejected the Oral Law, they clung to the literal word of the Bible. They were more rigid in the observance of ritual and ceremony than were the Pharisees.

After the destruction of the Temple (70 CE) they too disappeared from the scene of Jewish history.

THE ESSENES

The Essenes shun pleasure as a vice. . . . They despise riches, and there is no one among them who owns more than another. . . . Like brothers they share equally what the community possesses. . . . They do not speak about worldly things before sunrise, but recite prayers that have been handed down to them from their forefathers. They work strenuously for four hours. They gather to one place, bathe in cold water, and meet in the dining room as solemnly as though it were a sacred shrine. . . . No noise ever desecrates the house; the silence that prevails is both mystifying and awe-inspiring.

Josephus : *History of the Jews*

The origin of the name Essene is not certain. The accepted meaning is PIOUS ONE from the Hebrew word CHASAYA— חסיה. At the time that the sect functioned, during the reign of the Hasmoneans, the members were stamped as ascetics—people who removed themselves from the materialism and worldliness of life. Information about them comes mainly from Philo and Josephus, who were contemporary writers. Recent discovery of Dead Sea Scrolls has shed more light on their organization and beliefs.

Originally the Essenes were members of the Pharisaic Party. Dissatisfied with secularism of their day they banded together and formed a collective based on joint and indivisible ownership of all property. They were essentially a celibate people, frowning upon all association with women, although some did marry. They did not believe in ownership of slaves. They earned their livelihood by farming and handcraft. In place of sacrifice of animals they substituted oil and flour. By principle they became strict vegetarians.

The Essenes were ultra-pious people. They believed in immortality of the soul, but not bodily resurrection. They literally followed the Mosaic laws of Sabbath observance and they were strict conformists to the laws of purity and holiness. They bathed daily and wore white clothes. As a brotherhood of "Pious Ones" they practiced self-denial and self-control. Only those who would subscribe to the vow of poverty could be admitted to the order.

The sect of the Essenes, which flourished in the reign of Herod the Great, was never large in number or popular. In the time of Philo, they numbered about 4,000 and lived in several different places. It is said that John the Baptist and Jesus were members of this sect and that they were greatly influenced by its way of life. Like other groups in Palestine, nothing was heard of them after the destruction of the Second Temple.

THE HEMEROBAPTISTS

These people were strict pietists. Like the Essenes, they believed in purification by bathing, except that immersion had to be at dawn each day. Hence the name Hemerobaptists, which means "Daily Dippers." Little is known about this sect or its organization.

THE HELLENISTS

Hellenism means Greek culture, which was diffused throughout the Mediterranean and Middle East countries after the end of the fourth century BCE, as a result of the victorious conquest of Alexander the Great.

In the life of the Jewish people during the close of the second commonwealth, Hellenism represented a struggle between conformity with Jewish law and assimilation into Greek civilization. The Hellenists of Palestine were Jews who followed the ways of the Greeks. They were a minority, but they exerted strong power and influence through the control of the priesthood and the Temple treasuries. These people openly imitated Greek ways of living; they dressed in Greek costumes, adopted Greek names, translated the Bible into the Greek language (Septuagint), developed a Judeo-Hellenistic literature, participated in Greek sports, and accepted the Greek Philosophy of Epicureanism—a philosophy that maintained that true happiness is derived solely through physical pleasures.

The influence of Hellenism reached its zenith in the day of Antiochus, ruler of Assyria, who sought to subject all Palestine to Greek paganism. The Temple was defiled and the Jewish religion proscribed. Revolt, led by the Maccabees, inevitably followed. Monotheism was restored to its rightful place under the rule of the Hasmoneans. Hellenism, however, continued to be a strong influence and was the cause of divisions and factions among the people during the Mishnaic period.

The opposition to this Greek influence came from a people who called themselves CHASSIDIM—חסידים—PIOUS ONES. They were so called because of their strong devotion to Judaism. From their ranks came the leadership of the Maccabean revolt. Their life was characterized by a piety or saintliness that was in sharp contradistinction to that of the Hellenistic Jews. The Chassidim were unable to stem the growth of Hellenism, but later a new group called the Pharisees emerged and met the challenge of Hellenism successfully.

BOETHUSIANS

The BOETHUSIANS—ביתוסים—BAYTHUSIM were a Jewish religious group active during the century preceding the destruction of the Second Temple. Closely associated with the high priesthood, they stemmed originally from the Sadducees. They acquired power and authority under Herod, who appointed Simon, a son of Boethus, High Priest of Israel. Their views were similar to that of the Sadducees, but not always identical. They denied the doctrine of immortality and resurrection. They controlled the priesthood and dominated the political life of Israel until the destruction of the Temple in the year 70 CE.

THE ZEALOTS

The Hebrew name for this group is K'NAIM— קנאים —and means ZEALOUS FOR GOD. The Zealots were the nationalistic branch of the Pharisees. They resisted Roman domination and labelled as traitors those Jews who accepted it. They were instrumental in raising the banner of revolt against powerful Rome. Their intense patriotism led them to denounce intermarriage and to oppose assimilation. Because many of their numbers carried daggers they received the name SICARII. Their assassination of idolators and pro-Romanists made them a dreaded terrorist group.

They developed their own theological and messianic outlook, proclaiming God as the sole ruler of the Jewish nation. Their leader, Judah the son of Hezekiah (6 CE), made popular the saying, "Neither death nor any dread should make them call any man Lord." They were in control of the Holy City of Jerusalem when it fell to the Romans. Most of the leaders were killed and the party disappeared after the fall of the Temple. Attempts have been made to relate this sect with the Dead Sea Scrolls.

AM HA-ARATZIM—עם הארצים—IGNORANT JEWS

The phrase AM HA-ARETZ means A PERSON OF THE EARTH. It came into use during the time of the Pharisees, who stressed learning and knowledge of Jewish law above everything else. People who neglected this privilege of learning and remained ignorant of the heritage received the appellation "People of the Earth."

YUDGHANITES

An eighth-century sect founded by Yudghan (Judah) of Hamadan, disciple of Abu Isa al-Isfahani, who believed himself to be a Messiah. The sect flourished in Persia and was strongly influenced by Christian and Mohammedan beliefs. Yudghan advocated a mystic interpretation of the Torah and declared all traditional religious symbols to be mere allegories. He kept the prohibition on wine and animal food. The sect did not long survive its founder.

THE KARAITES

Karaism stems from the Hebrew word KARAH—קרא—which means TO READ. The noun MIKRA—מקרא—refers to the Bible. The first followers of this movement called themselves ANANITES, after the name of the founder, Anan ben David. When the movement became well established the adherents called themselves BENE MIKRA—בני מקרא—SONS OF SCRIPTURE. Later they were known as KARAIM—קראים—BIBLE DEVOTEES or READERS OF SCRIPTURE. The English transliteration of the name gives us the term KARAITES.

Anan ben David lived in Babylon about 767 CE. He was a nephew of the Exilarch Solomon. He was next in line of succession, but because of his strong views against rabbinic authority, his younger brother received the appointment. Anan resented this slight and sought to oust his brother. He was arrested, imprisoned, and sentenced to death by the Caliph.

To escape his fate Anan proclaimed a new religion. He was released from prison and went to Palestine, where he was successful in gathering together dissident groups who still adhered to the old doctrines of the Sadducees and Essenes.

Anan explained his new movement "Back to Scriptures" in a book called SEFER HA-MITZVOTH— ספר המצות —THE BOOK OF COMMANDMENTS. (770 CE) He maintained that the guiding power of Judaism was the Oral Law of the Bible and not the rabbinical interpretation. He sought to re-establish the authority of the Bible as against the authority of the Mishnah and the Talmud. Typical of the principles and dogmas of Karaism are the following:

Rejection of all post-Biblical laws, such as Mishnah and Talmud.

The Bible was to be the sole authority of Judaism.

The laws of the Sabbath were to be strictly observed. "Ye shall kindle no light on the Sabbath" applied to non-Jews as well as Jews. "Abide ye every man in his place" meant staying at home all day on the Sabbath.

The laws of Levitical purity were to be strictly observed, according to the letter.

Eating of meat was forbidden. Dietary laws and laws of Kashruth were abolished.

There was to be no observance of the second day for festivals and holidays. The blowing of the Shofar and the wearing of Tallith and Tefillin were not to be observed. The Mezuzah was not used by them nor was the Chanukah holiday to be celebrated.

Karaism developed into a fast-growing movement that continued for several centuries and spread into European countries. But internal conflicts and dissension, plus vigorous denunciation by its opponents, the Rabbinites, finally weakened its influence. After the tenth century it began to decline as a distinct religious movement.

Though Karaism was a negative factor in Jewish life, it nevertheless made several positive contributions to Judaism. Because of its fanatical adherence to the Mosaic law, an intensified study of Scripture as literature developed. This in turn led to a study of the Hebrew language and was responsible for the standardization of the Bible text and introduction of vowel points known as Masorah.

The followers of Karaism today number about 12,000. About half of them reside in Crimea of Russia and speak a Tartar tongue, and about one-fourth of them live in Matzliah, in Israel. Though they do not consider themselves as Jews, they still adhere to ancient traditions and live an austere life.

Racial and National Groups

The term Jew is not a racial term or designation, yet the Jew belongs to the races of man. He is a Caucasian, a member of the white race, and he stems from its Semitic branch, which is characterized by its language and culture.

The Jew, however, has mixed with the people of every race and nationality. His sojournings throughout the world have made him an integral part of every culture and civilization. In this historical process of wandering about and mingling with peoples, the Jewish religion, at times, almost completely disappeared, leaving instead a people who either called themselves Jews, or as non-Jews managed to retain many of the traditions and customs of Judaism. Many are the instances in which Jews were forced into baptism yet inwardly remained Jews. And history records, also, non-Jewish groups that adopted the Jewish religion yet were not considered a part of the Jewish people. Following are some of the important segments of Jewry throughout history.

THE SAMARITAN JEWS

In the year 722 BCE the Kingdom of Israel lost its independence and most of its inhabitants were exiled to Assyria. The conqueror, Sargon I, sent natives of his land to replace the exiled Jews. These newcomers inter-married with the resident Jews and in time they became known as Samaritans after the capital city, Samaria. In literature

they are referred to as SHOMRONIM— שומרונים —KEEPERS OF THE LAW.
The Talmud calls them "Kutim." In the course of time they became
completely assimilated to Jewish life and proclaimed themselves to be
the true descendants of Abraham.

In the year 516 BCE they offered to help the exiles returning from
Babylon to rebuild the Temple. Because they were not considered to
be of pure Jewish descent, their help was refused. This attitude, and
the aggravating laws forbidding intermarriage with them, caused the
Samaritans to become antagonistic and hostile toward the Jews. In
retaliation they refused to acknowledge the authority of the priesthood and they gradually separated themselves from the Jewish
population. Subsequently they established a community of their own
and built a Temple on Mount Gerizim, which, they asserted, was the
site where God's word was originally revealed. This city was destroyed
by John Hyrcanus in 128 BCE.

The Samaritans remained distinct and different from the rest of
the Jews of Palestine. Their refusal to depart from the strict letter of
the Mosaic Law marked them as a narrow and obstinate people. Even
though they refused to identify themselves as Jews, they suffered the
fate of all Jews when Palestine was conquered by the Romans in the
year 70 CE. Some settled in Egypt and lasted there until the 18th
century. A Samaritan synagogue in Rome was destroyed about 500 CE.

Today, in the cities of Nablus and Jaffa, descendants of this oldest
dissenting group of Jews are still in existence. Though few in number
(about 246 in Nablus and 67 in Jaffa), this small remnant of strange
Jews lives by the old Mosaic law. They speak Arabic and worship in
the Hebrew tongue, although their original language was Aramaic.
Their religion is based on the Hexateuch (the five Books of Moses and
the Book of Joshua), and they are ruled by a high priest. They still
retain the sacrificial cult as of Bible times.

YEMENITE JEWS

Yemen is a little country on the southern tip of the Arabian Peninsula. Jews migrated there during Bible times, especially when Palestine
was under foreign rule and persecution there was severe. The early
history of Yemen records the fact that the ruling family, headed by
Abu Kariba Assad (390–420) and his followers, were converted to
Judaism.

When the Moslems took Yemen, many Jews migrated, leaving only
a remnant in the land. Jews were deprived of their property rights;
they were forbidden to ride animals or dress like Moslems; they were

insulted publicly and abused as unbelievers. In some places where Moslems ruled the Jews fared much better.

Not much information is extant about Yemenite Jewry, but it is known that the men received a Hebrew education, and their chief study was the Bible; the Cabala was popular among them; and they produced several liturgical poets, the most celebrated being Shalom Shabbazi. Though differing little in appearance from the Arabs, the Jews retained a distinct culture. They achieved renown as artisans, chiefly as silversmiths, a skill which served them well, when, because of the hostility of the Arab peoples, practically the entire Yemenite Jewish population, numbering about 47,000, was transferred to Israel in 1949–50, in "Operation Magic Carpet."

PERSIAN JEWS

Persia (Iran) has a special relationship to Jewish survival, because, about 50 years after Judah succumbed to Babylonian conquest (586 BCE), Persia conquered Babylonia. Under Persian rule, Jews were permitted to return to Palestine to rebuild the Temple. Many chose to remain in Persia. The Book of Esther tells of Jews living throughout the 127 provinces of the Persian Empire, and depicts them as numerous and influential in the capital city of Susa (Shushan). The fact that the Babylonian Talmud was put together during this period shows that there was a vigorous intellectual Jewish life.

Though conditions were favorable for centuries, a turn came with the rise of Zoroastrianism, which became the state religion of Persia. Yezdegerd II (438–57) sought to suppress Jewish observances. Persecution continued until the Arab conquest of 641, when a more tolerant policy was introduced. Under Moslem rule, the Jewish community flourished. They were controlled by Exilarchs and received their intellectual guidance under the leadership of the Gaonate. Persia was the cradle of many Jewish sectarian movements, i.e., the Issavites— formed by Abu Al Isfahani (c. 700); the Karaites—formed by Anan ben David (eighth century) and Messianic movements, one of which was headed by David Alroy. The lot of the Persian Jews was checkered for centuries. Many left Persia for other lands, because by the 19th century it was among the most depressed of the world's communities. With the rise of Arab nationalism, it became even worse.

Among groups tracing their origin to Persia are the following:

The Lost Ten Tribes

Bordering Persia are to be found a number of small Jewish communities which claim descent from the "Lost Ten Tribes of

Israel." The inhabitants of these communities were once natives of Persia, but fled the country during the periods of persecution. It is thought that remnants of the tribes of the kingdom of Israel might have been absorbed by the last Judean exiles, who, in 597–586 were deported to areas adjacent to Babylonia.

The Jews of Bokhara

This colourful community, formerly considered as a state in central Asia, is now in Russian territory. The Jews who live here are thought to have originated in Persia, coming to the region in the fourth or fifth century BCE. They, too, claim to be one of the lost ten tribes. For centuries they lived in complete isolation, unaware of the existence of other Jews, and up to recent times they rigidly preserved a form of their ancient faith modified by strong Moslem influences. When Islam spread, the Bokharan Jews veiled their women and covered the floors of their synagogues with rugs. The members of the congregation took off their shoes on entering, and they prayed in a squatting position.

They speak a Persian dialect and adhere to many of the Biblical laws. The men chew tobacco and the women smoke large water pipes or "nargilehs," known as "kilim." Their Jewish life was showing signs of decline by the 17th and 18th centuries, but new stimulation was supplied by Rabbi Joseph Maarivi, who arrived in 1793, and by new refugees from Persia, who came in 1839.

In the 19th century, the community was composed mainly of craftsmen, tradesmen, and merchants, especially in the silk trade. Very few were in agriculture. In the 1880's they started to migrate to Palestine, and most of what is known about them has come to light since then. From an estimated 50,000 at one time, today there are about four to five thousand Jews left there.

Kurdistan Jews

Today, Kurdistan is divided between Turkey, Iran, and Iraq and the Jews in that country are scattered among many communities. They have had a more continuous agricultural tradition than any other Jewish community in the world. They spoke an Aramaic dialect up to recent times, and claim descent from the Babylonian Jews, who migrated there at the time of the Exile. They practice child marriage and wife purchase, and live chiefly on the land, with a fair share of merchants, peddlers, and craftsmen. It is estimated that at the beginning of the 20th century, there were about 12,000 to 14,000 in this geographic area. After 1948 most of them emigrated to Israel, where their assimilation was made easier because of their agricultural background. When they prepared for their departure for Israel, they could not bear to leave behind them their beloved synagogue, Amadiyah, built in 1249 and named after the prophet Ezekiel. They took the building apart, stone by stone, and brought it to Israel.

Jews of the Caucasus

DAGHESTAN JEWS

In the region between the Black and Caspian Seas, dominated by the Caucasus Mountains, are to be found several ancient Jewish communities of Persian descent, who are now citizens of the Soviet Union. In the mountainous area known as Daghestan are about 25,000 Jews whose ancestors came there about 200 BCE. Their language is Perso-Judaic Tat, or Judeo-Tati, and they are a warlike group. At one time there were more Jews, but when this area was conquered by Islam, they were forcibly converted, and many of their descendants still live there as Moslems. As time passed, some Moslem superstitions even appeared in their rabbinic Judaism.

The Jewish household was composed of large collectivized family units. Often several such households would form a village. Property belonged to the family as a whole and all resources acquired by any member went into a common purse. This family structure guarded against assimilation and made it easier for Judaism to survive. Under Czarist Russia, this household structure disappeared and whole villages were destroyed. Jews dispersed to other areas in Daghestan. It has been surmised that the Jews intermarried with the Khazars, an Asiatic group, which converted to Judaism in the eighth century. This is thought to be the reason why they differ so little from their non-Jewish neighbors in physical appearance, being broad-browed and dark-eyed.

During the Bolshevik Revolution, White forces sacked the mountain villages, and their land was distributed among the Moslems. The Jews who were not killed were deported to the cities, where they met the familiar pattern of anti-Semitism so well known in Russian history, including the blood libel accusation.

Many famous Israeli pioneers come from this area. As good horsemen, they served in "Hashomer," who were forerunners of the "Haganah." Joseph Trumpeldor, who was one of very few Jews ever to become an officer in the Russian army, went to Palestine and joined Jabotinsky in forming the Jewish Legion, which fought on the side of the British during World War I.

GEORGIAN JEWS

Georgia lies along the southwest edge of the Caucasus Mountains. Jews have lived here continuously since the days of the Second Temple. They have become culturally integrated with their Georgian neighbors. They speak Georgian with no Hebraic admixtures, unlike the language spoken by the Jews of Daghestan. And yet, the Jews of Georgia have maintained their Jewish loyalties and traditions, and have kept up their knowledge of Hebrew. Before the Revolution, the Jewish population was urban, engaging mostly in commerce. Therefore they were particularly vulnerable to anti-bourgeois activity on the part of the government.

Georgian Jews settled in Palestine in the middle of the 19th century, establishing a community in Jerusalem, outside the Damascus gate. During the riots of 1929, this section was destroyed by the Arabs. Immigration continued until stopped by the Soviet accession to power and their ban on Zionist activity. There is a museum in the capital of Georgia, Tiflis, that is devoted to Georgian Jewry.

A recent Georgian delegation, which visited Jerusalem, brought some news of the present Jewish community there. The last census reported that about 100,000 had declared themselves as Jews. They are employed in industry, crafts, mining, and farming.

AZERBAIJAN

To the south of Georgia and Daghestan lies Azerbaijan, a region now divided between Russia and Iran. The majority of the people are Moslem, who stem, racially and linguistically, from the Turks. Generally, the history and culture of the mountain communities of Jews are similar to those of Daghestan. Centers of Jewish population were in Elizavetpol (Gandzha) and around Baku. In many areas only ruins of Jewish graves remain. In Talmudic times (second to seventh centuries) we find mention of distinguished Talmudists who lived in this area. A recent estimate of Jewish population puts their number at about 45,000, most of them of European origin. Only about 7,500 speak a Persian dialect. Since the civil war of 1918–1921, the majority of Jews live in the towns and cities.

OTHER GROUPS

Adjacent to this general area are to be found centers of historic Jewish settlement about which little is known. These areas are

Turkmenia, Uzbekistan, Kazakhistan, Tajikistan, and Kirghizistan. Physically, the Jews resemble their non-Jewish neighbors, which is slightly different in each case. Their speech is not uniform. Their dialects include Judeo-Persian, Tatti, and Turkish-Tataric. Many claim descent from the Ten Tribes.

JEWS OF INDIA

The Jews of India live in comparative freedom and security. Many have risen to high ranks in the armed forces and others have prospered in business and in the professions, but the majority are poor. There are many different types of observance of Judaism, ranging from the remnant of ancient tradition to the liberal practices of the more recent immigrants. Many Jews dress like the natives and have assimilated Indian social customs.

Some Jews of India claim that their ancestors settled there at the time of Solomon; some, after the destruction of the First Temple; and there is evidence, in the form of two large copper plates in the synagogue in Cochin, that a charter was granted to Jews giving them certain privileges in 379 CE.

There are three areas of Jewish settlement. The first one is around Bombay, on the northwestern coast of India, where the largest number live. They are known as BENE ISRAEL, and number about 21,000. According to tradition they arrived from Palestine about 586 BCE, and an ancient cemetery at Nowgow is shown as the place where bodies of those shipwrecked near the coast were buried by the 14 survivors. For centuries they managed to keep the laws and customs, but after a while almost everything was forgotten but a few rituals and practices. A world traveler, David Rahabi of Egypt, who visited India in the 12th century, recognized as Jewish the customs connected with the Sabbath, the rite of circumcision, and the dietary laws. He was responsible for a religious revival. He taught them the Sephardic rites and prayers that they have used since that time, translating the books into Maharati, their local tongue. They do not intermarry, and have produced scholars, authors, journalists, and newspaper publishers. About 5,000 have emigrated to Israel.

The second largest group is that of the Arabic-speaking Jews of Iraqi origin, who number about 7,000. They came in the early 19th century, chiefly from Baghdad. They live in Bombay and Calcutta and are engaged mainly in commerce. They are more educated than the BENE ISRAEL in religion and Hebrew, but there is otherwise little difference between them. It is said that they are descendants of the Jews who followed David Sassoon from Iraq in 1832, when he founded the house that has such a fine reputation for philanthropy. For a long time these Jews would not allow a BENE ISRAEL into their synagogue, but in late years such restrictions have disappeared. About 2,000 have migrated to Israel.

The third group consists of the Cochin Jews, who live on the Malabar Coast near the southern tip of India. No one really knows when they came, but they believe that their ancestors were members of the tribe of Manasseh, who arrived in the years following the destruction of the Second Temple. Most of the Jews are colored, but this area is stratified into three castes, a system common to India. The superior caste is white; the intermediary is brown; the lowest caste is black. The color line forbids them to worship together, so there are segregated synagogues in which they worship the same God with the same prayers. They are deeply religious and speak Malayalam, in their daily affairs, but use Hebrew in their religious lives. Benjamin of Tudela mentioned the black Jews of Cochin in his writings in the 12th century. They are farmers and artisans, and cultivate a love of Zion that has resulted in the migration of many to Israel. This group of immigrants is the only one that handed over their property to the Jewish Agency to help finance their settlement in the new state.

CHINESE JEWS

How early in time Jews arrived in China is not really known, but it is surmised that some might have settled there at the time of King Solomon, and they kept coming through the destruction of the two Temples, up through the beginning of the common era. It is claimed that the greatest influx came by way of Persia. By the eighth century, Jews were numerous enough to have the Emperor appoint a special officer to supervise them. Like Jews in other remote parts of the world, little was known about them until recently. Marco Polo, at the end of the 13th century, testified to the important role of the Jews of Cathay.

When the Jews fled from the Crusades, the Chinese emperors welcomed them with these words: "You have come to our China; revere and preserve your ancestral customs." There were many migrations of Jews into Honan during the centuries, and they must have been quite formidable to deserve the frequent official mention made of them in Imperial records. The Jewish newcomers resembled the Chinese in many ways, so they were readily accepted. They were gentle, scholarly, and devoted to their religion, and not the least, they revered tradition and their ancestors. This may be why Jews began to disappear as a group, since they were neither killed off nor forcibly converted. They were absorbed biologically and culturally. During the early years, the Jews avoided intermarriage, were faithful to Judaism, enjoyed complete equality and reached high office.

Their main community was in the city of K'ai-Fung-Foo, on the banks of the Yellow River, in the province of Honan, in the interior of China. This river is known as "China's Sorrow" for it was the cause of destructive floods. The Jews built a beautiful and elaborate Temple in 1163, which was destroyed in 1461 by a flood. It was rebuilt and destroyed several times in the years that followed. As time passed, the community deteriorated, with a rabbi last serving them in 1800. Eventually they were assimilated in language, manners, and dress into the Chinese community, and were different only in that they still practiced circumcision, removed the sinews from the rear quarters of their animals used for food, and abstained from pork. By the mid-19th century, the Temple was gone, and Jewish observance had virtually disappeared.

Meanwhile, Jews settled in other places in China, or what was China at one time. There were communities in Tientsin, Peiping, Harbin, Mukden, and Dairen, as well as a large Sephardic group in Hong Kong and Shanghai. These settled there in about 1840, when British Jews came from India and other areas. These communities absorbed large numbers of European Jewish refugees after the World Wars and the Communist Revolution. But, originally, settlement was expedited by the Sassoon and the Kadoorie families. Sir Matthew Nathan was governor of Hong Kong, and Silas Hardoon was a well-known philanthropist of the early period.

With the advent of the Communist Chinese regime, the economic situation of the Jews deteriorated. In 1948 there were about 26,000 Jews; today there are less than 400 in Chinese-controlled territory.

STRANGE JEWS OF NORTH AFRICA

Jews have lived in North Africa for at least 2,000 years. Although outwardly they resemble the natives, they have perpetuated variations of the Jewish tradition. In some of the countries they have lived as cave-dwellers and nomads; in others they were free to live in metropolitan cities or forced to reside in ghettoes, called "mellahs." In Ethiopia they are known as Falasha Jews; in Tripoli they are called "mountain Jews"; in Morocco, they go under the name of "Berber" or Daggutun Jews. Some are dark-skinned and some are light. All have been identified as Jews.

Falasha Jews

Falasha is an Abyssinian name meaning "exiled immigrant." These people cannot be distinguished in features, hair, or coloring from other Ethiopians. They call themselves BETA ISRAEL—"House of Israel," because they claim Abraham, Isaac, and Jacob as their ancestors.

Some scholars say that their physical characteristics resulted because the Jews who migrated from Palestine to Ethiopia at the time of the first exile (586 BCE) converted the African Negroes living there. Some trace their ancestry to a union between King Solomon and the Queen of Sheba. Other scholars think that the Yemenite Jews, who live just across a narrow body of water, came over and converted the local population.

Some scholars theorize that the Falashas are descendants of an ancient community of upper Egypt, founded before the Babylonian Captivity. The proof they cite is that these people have no knowledge of Tisha B'Ab, which commemorates the destruction of both Temples; they do not celebrate the festivals of Purim and Chanukah, both of which took place after the Babylonian exile. They know nothing of post-Biblical literature like the Mishnah, Gemara, the Talmud, or the Midrash. Their religion is Moses-centred.

Nothing was known of this people, who now number about 26,000 (1958) until the year 1790, when a publication by a Scotch traveler mentioned these black natives who called themselves Jews. It was not until 1904 that Jewish scholars made contact with them and learned their story.

The leaders of the community are divided into three groups
1. Nazirites—(Menokossie)
2. Priests   (Kahanes)
3. Learned Men—(Debteras)

Falasha Jews set themselves apart and until recent times did not permit non-Jews to enter their dwellings or synagogues, which they call MESGID. They are Sabbath observers, which is respected by the majority of the population, with Saturday's being referred to as the "little Sabbath," while Sunday is the "big Sabbath." Many Ethiopians observe the dietary laws. Sacrifices are offered upon occasion by the priests, some of whom live in monastic communities, maintaining strict purificatory rites.

Gheez, a combination of Hebrew and Arabic, is the language of religion among the Falashas. Only the priests read the language in which their religious literature was written between the fifth and seventeenth centuries. They speak the vernacular, Amharic, a Semitic language, although the northernmost tribes speak Tigrinya.

Cave-dwelling Jews

In the country of Tripoli, along the Jebul Nefuse mountain range in the Atlas Mountains, are to be found a number of primitive Jews closely related culturally and historically to the Jews of the Sahara. These people are known as "Cave-dwelling" Jews. In the 1940's their several communities numbered around 6,000. They received the name "Cave-dwelling" Jews because some live in caves in the high mountains, while most of them live in lower areas in a series of crater holes and stone labyrinths connected by underground passageways. Others built rooms of baked earth, reinforced with stone, above these volcanic stone dwellings. In each community there is a cemetery and an ancient synagogue headed by a CHACHAM, or rabbi. Instead of losing the feeling of attachment to Palestine, which might result logically from their dislocation from Jewish life, they have a consuming desire to return. Many of them have migrated to the new State of Israel.

Like the natives among whom they live, they are dark-skinned and speak the vernacular language. Little is known of their practices and background, but it is thought that they are probably descendants of Jews brought as captives by Titus after the Fall of the second Temple in 70 CE.

BERBER JEWS

Among the war-like tribes living in the Sahara desert country of Morocco are the Berber Jews. In 1942 there were 42,000 of them. They claim to be of Jewish origin and apparently practice Jewish rites. Upon completion of their fast on Tisha B'Ab (a date that commemorates the destruction of the two Temples), they march into the desert in search of caravan traces that they hope will lead them to the Messiah. They have an oral tradition, handed down from father to son, that relates them to Bible times. They dress, speak, and live as do the nomadic Berber natives, and are tall, healthy, and swarthy. Some speak a little Hebrew and "Cheder" training is their only education. Great poverty prevails, with livelihood gained from trade, handicrafts, and begging.

In the seventh century Berber tribes, professing Judaism, came into power when their priestess, Kahaniah, led all the Berber tribes to a temporary victory over the Moslems. But subsequently the Berbers were vanquished.

Another tribe living in the Sahara desert, the Daggatuns, observe certain Biblical customs and retain some Jewish traditions. It is thought that they might have been Jews originally, but at present there is no clear identification.

Converted or Proselytized Groups

Proselytism is the act of becoming a convert to another religion. It requires the performance of religious duties and the subsequent enjoyment of its privileges. In Jewish history there have been instances of non-Jews who accepted the Jewish faith, as in the case of the Khazars when their ruler made Judaism a state religion. There have been cases of individual Judaizers who sought to convert members of other religions to the Jewish faith, but never in large numbers or with any degree of success.

On the other hand, the conversion of Jews to Christianity or other religions occurred and still occurs over and over again. In some instances these conversions were voluntary or expedient. In most instances, however, it was a question of forced conversion or expulsion. In some countries the only alternative to conversion was death. In many other countries Jews were subjected to conversionist sermons, public disputations, and other forms of coercion and humiliation.

MARRANO JEWS

In Christian Spain and Portugal it was a frequent occurrence for Jews to be faced with the alternative of Baptism or death. Many of those who were baptized secretly professed their Judaism while outwardly they followed their new faith. Such Jews were called MARRANOS, neo-Christians, or crypto-(secret) Jews. The church labeled these Jews MARRANOS, which in Spanish means "Swine." The Hebrew word for such Jews is —אנוסים— "Anusim" meaning "coerced."

Those who were caught practicing their religion often suffered cruel torture and martyrdom through the office of the Inquisition. Church officials were constantly alerted to "back-sliding" Marranos. When caught in any form of Jewish observance they were branded as heretics and turned over to the Inquisition.

As late as 1920 in North Portugal there was still a large number of these neo-Christians, conscious of their Jewish descent and maintaining crypto-Jewish traditions that are hardly recognizable. An effort was made to bring them into contact with current Jewish practice and a synagogue was established for them at Oporto.

The Christian clergy decided that they could not adequately keep the neo-Christians in line unless all connections with their former relatives and friends were cut off. At their instigation the expulsion of the Jews took place in January, 1492. Many Marranos left their homes at this time and found refuge in the surrounding countries.

THE CHEUTAS

A number of Marranos who left Spain and Portugal found refuge in Majorca, a Spanish Island. The name applied to these Jews is CHEUTAS, which means "Pork-eaters," because they were forced to eat swine flesh in public to convince the authorities of the Inquisition that they were practicing Christians. These people were wholly excluded from normal community and social life and were subjected to all kinds of discrimination, which continues to this day. There is some question as to whether they have retained any of the Jewish tradition.

THE KHAZARS

The Khazars were a Tatar people living in a region in Southern Russia bordering the Caspian Sea. Because of its location it was a large commercial center. Its capital was Ityl, located at the mouth of the Volga river. Legend has it that in the eighth century, King Bulan embraced Judaism, to which he became converted after seeking a faith among those held by scholars of the major religions of the time. The story is told that he made his decision after listening to a disputation between an Arab Mullah, a Christian priest, and a rabbi.

News about this people came to Chasdai ibn Shaprut, a Spanish statesman who established communication with them. Their story is contained in the philosophic work of THE KUZARI, written by Judah HaLevi. In 1016, Khazaria was conquered and its people scattered throughout the Crimea. Practically all that is known about the Khazars comes from Arabic sources.

Members of the Karaite sect, who migrated into the Crimea, are sometimes associated with the Khazars, because they speak TSHAGATAISH, the Turkish dialect that was the language of the Khazars.

KRIMTCHAKI JEWS

This is the name given to a group of Jews of the Crimea. They claim descent from remnants of the Khazar population. Before World War I, they numbered some 7,500 and spoke the TSHAGATAISH language of the Khazars. Their dress and customs were Turkish. They were all but exterminated by the Germans in World War II.

DONMEH JEWS

This sect of Jews were followers of the false Messiah Sabbatai Zevi (1665), who turned Mohammedan when given the choice between conversion or death. So great was his hold on many of his followers that they, too, embraced Islam. They rationalized his conduct by saying that his ways, like God's ways, were inscrutable.

The Turkish name Donmeh or Doenmeh means "Renegade" and was applied to the Judeo-Moslem followers of Zevi. Their main center of community life was in the city of Salonica. About 15,000 of these people, who are divided into various sects, live in Turkey and speak the Turkish language. Donmeh settlements may be found in Constantinople and Izmir. They retain many Jewish rites despite the fact that they are considered to be Mohammedans. Their liturgy is in Judeo-Spanish and centres upon the Messiahship of Zevi. It was long kept in secrecy, but has recently been brought to light and partly published.

Cultural Groups

Cultural groups have their basis in movements or trends in Jewish history. The people who belong to these groups are identified by the traditions, ceremonies, and customs that have been developed in the course of their existence. Sometimes it is difficult to distinguish between the religion and the culture that dominated the life of the group. Very often both were closely identified with each other. As they came and went or remained on the scene of Jewish history, their life and thought and activity influenced their manner of living.

THE ASHKENAZIC JEWS

> And the sons of Gomer: Ashkenaz and Riphath
> and Togarmah.   (Genesis 10 : 3)

Ashkenaz, according to Scripture, was one of the grandsons of Noah. How the name came to be applied to a class of Jews is not certain. The first reference to the term is found in a letter written by Ibn Shaprut to the King of the Khazars, in which he refers to the Jews of Germany as being Ashkenazim.

In its present use the name Ashkenazim refers to the Jews and their descendants of Central and Eastern Europe. The countries having large numbers of Ashkenazic Jews were Germany, Poland, Russia, and the Balkan States. In the United States the term Ashkenazic is applied to any individual or group that follows the form and Hebrew pronunciation of the Ashkenazic prayers and rituals as contrasted with the Sephardic (Spanish), which is in use in Israel and many countries bordering on the Mediterranean.

The Ashkenazic Jews follow the custom known as the "Minhag Ashkenazim" or rite, which they trace back to Palestinian practice. There are marked differences between the Ashkenazic and Sephardic Torah service and ritual of the Prayer Book as well as in the dignity and decorum of the worshipers. Ashkenazic Jews comprise the majority of the Jewish population of the world and until the 20th century most of them spoke Yiddish.

THE SEPHARDIC JEWS

> And the captivity of this host of children of Israel...
> and the captivity of Jerusalem which in Sepharad,
> shall possess the cities of the south.   (Obadiah 1 : 20)

The Sepharad of the South, mentioned in the Bible by the prophet Obadiah, was associated in the middle ages with the Jews residing in the countries of Spain and Portugal. They and their descendants have been called Sephardic Jews in contradistinction to their co-religionists known as Ashkenazic Jews, who resided in Central and Eastern Europe. After the Expulsion from Spain and Portugal, these Sephardic Jews migrated to many parts of the world, establishing new communities and living in accordance with their particular custom or Minhag.

The "Minhag Sephardim" as practiced by Sephardic Jews is traced back to Babylonian times, and is marked by the use of Ladino, a Spanish-Hebrew language. Hebrew is written in Castilian-Spanish alphabet and the liturgical service lacks many of the poems and prayers used by the Ashkenazic Jews. Hebrew is pronounced differently from the Ashkenazic. It is in strict accordance with the grammar and rules used in Israel.

Sephardic groups existed as separate Jewish communities apart from their Ashkenazic kinsman. They believe that they are the direct descendants of the tribe of Judah. They have their own synagogues, prayer books, schools, and charitable institutions. In the past they felt greatly superior to the Ashkenazic Jews, whom they considered a lower class. They even went so far as to frown upon intermarriage with them. Differences were reflected in social patterns and literary fashions as well as in costume of worship, the wearing of which is conducive to greater formality.

Except for differences and variation in Jewish ritual and worship, most of the distinctions between Sephardic and Ashkenazic Jews have disappeared, partly because the Sephardic communities are dwindling. Only 15 per cent of the world's Jewish population is non-Ashkenazi.

CABALISTIC OR MYSTIC JEWS

Through the ages two opposite currents have run through Jewish thought. One was rationalism as represented by the Talmud, and the other mysticism as exemplified by the Cabala. To those who looked to reason, wisdom, and righteousness, as the best means of understanding God, the way of Cabala seemed childish and superstitious.

It is not difficult to understand why the supernatural should appeal to a persecuted, helpless people whose history was a constant repetition of being denied natural and normal rights. Their only means of coping with their human enemies and the evil spirits that beset them was by escaping into a mystical world. In this field they became experts in the use of magic formulas, amulets, and numerological and alphabetical exercises. At times charlatans claiming to be Messiahs took advantage of these simple, unhappy people and led them to disaster and disillusionment. Such men as Sabbatai Zevi, David Reubeni, Abraham Abulafia, Asher Laemmlein, and others attest to these unfortunate episodes in Jewish history.

The word "Cabala" means "doctrine received by tradition." It comes from the Hebrew word CABAL—קבּל—meaning TO RECEIVE. Like the Bible, Cabala is not one book, but a body of occult knowledge that originated in the second century. As a mystical doctrine it was not to be acquired by all men, but only by the elect of heaven, who could establish contact with God through the mystic illumination of the spirit. The movement was influenced by primitive occultism, which sought to subject mysterious powers to human control; by gnosticism, which sought a deeper knowledge of spiritual truth; by emanations, which held all creation as flowing from the Godhead; by dualism, which placed the universe under the power of two opposing forces; and by numerology, which gave occult significance to numbers.

Cabala has two aims. One involves the redemption of the suffering Jewish people, which they hoped to achieve by seeking and understanding God; the other is directed at spiritual purification, sometimes even to the mortification of the flesh, so as to hasten the coming of the Messiah. By the power of penance and prayer, Cabalists strove to break the fatal grip of Satan, which kept their spirits earthbound.

While numerous works collectively constitute Cabala, the two most important are the SEFER YETZIRA—ספר יצירה—BOOK OF CREATION and the ZOHAR— זהר —BOOK OF SPLENDOR. The former was supposedly written by Rabbi Simeon bar Yochai, during the second century in Palestine. Except for the Zohar, it is the most venerated Cabalistic work. It deals with the Creation story, which is explained by a symbolical system of numbers and letters, and it introduces the doctrine of SEPHIROTH—ספירות—HEAVENLY SPHERES, which is basic to Cabalism. The Zohar was compiled by the Spanish mystic, Moses de Leon (1230–1305). This is an encyclopedia of occult lore written in Aramaic, that is as well a mystical commentary on the Torah. It, too, deals with the creation of the world, but also contains treatises on astronomy, angels and demons, the physiognomy and the mystic science of numbers, the seven palaces of heaven, a journey through Paradise, the 613 Commandments of the Torah, and adds an analysis of the Shema prayer. Further, it gives numerical values to the Hebrew letters in various Scriptural words.

Other notable writings in this field were :

Hechaloth—הכלות—"Palaces," written by Rabbi Ishmael ben Elisha (about 120 CE). It describes God's throne and its heavenly administrators.

Bahir—בהיר —"Brilliance," helped popularize Cabala; written by Isaac the Blind (1190–1210) in France. He was the first of the medieval Cabalists.

Othiyoth or Alphabet of Rabbi Akiba—אותיות דרב עקיבא — A symbolic interpretation of the alphabet in relation to God and heaven.

Pirke de Rabbi Eliezer—פרקי דרב אליעזר—"Sayings of Rabbi Eliezer." Ninth century book of secrets of the heavenly bodies and the influence of the planets upon the world as revealed by the angel Raziel.

Sefer Bahir—ספר בהיר—"Book of Brilliance." Also called "Midrash of Nechunyah ben Hakanah." Treats of divine words serving as intermediaries between God and the world. These divine words were later called SEPHIROTH—Divine Emanations.

Sefer Ha-Chasidim—ספר חסידים—"Book of the Pious." Written by Judah He-Chasid (Judah the Pious) in Germany (died 1217), it achieved popularity among plain folk.

As time passed Cabalism spread from one country to another, in slightly varying forms and by a series of mystical personalities. Isaac the Blind popularized the movement in France and Spain. His disciple

Azriel ben Menachem of Catalonia was interested in poetic speculations about God, trying to reconcile the Biblical account of Creation
with Aristotle's concept of the eternity of the world.   There were
"scientific" Cabalists, like Isaac ibn Latif (1220–1290) of Spain, who
tried to bring their mystical ideas in line with the scientific spirit of
the age. Cabala went through a course of development in Germany
where it was entirely practical, devoid of any philosophic overtones.
It had a moral and emotional motivation that was lacking in more intellectual Spain and Provence.

Isaac Luria (1533–1571), better known as ARI, established Cabalism
in Safed, Palestine. His teachings were a blend of piety and superstition, oriented toward hastening the Redemption of Israel by bringing the Messiah as soon as possible. He wrote nothing himself, but his
teachings were recorded by his pupil, Chayim Vital Calabrese (d. 1620).
In this interpretation new ceremonies, customs, and prayer rites were
introduced.

The doctrine of Cabala covers the nature of God, the Divine
emanations or SEPHIROTH ("numbers" or "spheres"), the creation of
angels and man, their future destiny, and the character of the Revealed
Law. The theology is pantheistic. Everything emanates from God and
is called EN SOPH—"Without End," and all that we are and see is
the result of a process of Divine self-expression. God has ten SEPHIROTH,
expressed in triads, with the tenth one all-encompassing. Cabalism
introduced a diagram to illustrate how the SEPHIROTH are associated
with the various parts of man's body.

The Table of the Ten Sephiroth

The World of Thought	1. KETER—Crown 2. HOCHMA—Wisdom 3. BINAH—Intelligence
The World of Soul	4. CHESED—Love 5. GEVURAH—Justice 6. TIPHERET—Beauty
The World of Body	7. NETZAH—Eternity 8. HOD—Splendor 9. YESOD—Foundation

10. MALKHUT — The Kingdom
that encircles the other nine as
the SHECHINAH or Divine Halo.

When man attains the dominion of the Kingdom, he will achieve
D'VEKUT—Communion with God.

The ten SEPHIROTH form a strict unity, and cooperatively they produced, by their union, the universe, which consists of four different worlds, in order of decreasing spirituality.

The lowest—ASIYAH—The World of Action

Next higher—YETZIRAH—The World of Formation

Next highest—BERIAH—The World of Creation

The highest—ATZLIUT—The World of Emanations which proceeded from EN SOPH, the Transcendant God.

The Doctrine of the EN SOPH

According to this doctrine, God cannot be comprehended by the human intellect, nor described in words. Hence the expression EN SOPH, which means "infinite," "endless," or "boundless." Man's mind can only comprehend the SEPHIROTH, because they are affected by human action. Increase of sin forces the SHECHINAH into exile, and with it the people of Israel. Righteous endeavor, by good deeds, prayer, and the performance of Mitzvoth deliver the SHECHINAH from exile.

Reincarnation is implied in some of the teachings of Cabala, because souls bent on purification are supposed to be returned to earth several times until they succeed in returning to God, pure and unspotted. When all the souls shall have completed the mission, the Day of Redemption would dawn and the Messiah would descend from the World of Souls and a period of utter happiness would ensue, without sin or pain.

Symbolic Methods of Cabala

At least three basic symbolistic methods are used to probe the secrets of the letters and numbers in the Bible.

GEMATRIA—גמטריא—A cryptograph of interpreting words by their numerical value based on a predetermined value for each letter in the alphabet, to explain the hidden meaning of Scriptural words. It first appeared among the Tannaim in the latter part of the second century.

Example

Behold, I send an angel before thee, to keep thee by the way . . . Take heed of him and hearken unto his voice . . . For my name is in him. (Exodus 23 : 20ff.)

Because the name of God resides in this angel, his name must be METATRON, the high ranking angel of goodness. The numerical name of God SHADDAI is 314. The numerical equivalent of METATRON is 314. Hence, the name of God resides in the angel Metatron.

NOTARIKON— נוטריקון —An acrostic; a combination of words composed of initial letters of a word, making new words from the first or last letters of other words.

Example

The phrase YODEI CHEN— יודעי חן —means "Knowers of God's Grace," and refers to the great mystics of Judaism. Why are certain mystics possessed of God's grace? Because the first letter of Chen " ח " stands for CHOCHMA— חכמה —meaning "wisdom" and the last letter " ן " stands for NISTARAH— נסתרה —meaning "hidden" or "mysterious."

TEMURAH— תמורה —The permutation or a change of letters of the alphabet; the transposition of letters that alters the meaning of words or creates coded alphabets.

Example

Altered word: The words ONEG— ענג —"delight" and NEGAH — נגע —"pain" each have the numerical equivalent of 123. By transposing the letters, delight is changed to pain. The coded alphabet is to couple the first and last letters of the alphabet in their respective sequence.

CHASSIDIC JEWS

The word CHASSID— חסיד —(plural, CHASSIDIM— חסידים —) literally means PIOUS ONE or SAINT. In the post-Exilic period we hear of Chassidim who were followers of Judah Maccabeus in the revolt against the Syrians. From this group of Chassidim there later arose another movement known as the P'RUSHIM— פרושים —SEPARATISTS or PHARISEES. After the fall of the Temple (70 CE) the term Chassid was applied to anyone of saintly and pious character.

The name "Chassidism" appeared again at the beginning of the eighteenth century in Poland. It took the form of a new mystic cult that developed as a protest against the rigid formalism of Rabbinic Judaism. This was an outgrowth of Cabalism.

The first leader of this movement was ISRAEL ben ELIEZER MIEDZIBOZH (1700–1760). He was called BAAL SHEM TOB (BESHT), which means MASTER OF THE GOOD NAME. Besht was a man of humble origin who spent a great deal of his time wandering and meditating in the beauty and silence of the fields and mountains. Unsuccessful as an innkeeper, he spent days in a hut in the forest, praying and studying Cabala. Eventually he turned to teaching. He developed a deep religious fervor and at the age of 36 he suddenly gained renown as a healer and wonder-worker. In later stories and legends he became a miracle worker and a TZADIK, one who had mastered the secret and ineffable name of God. A Tzadik is usually defined as a most righteous person, but to his followers in the case of the Besht, the word Tzadik meant being an intermediary of God.

The Chassidim maintained that piety was more important than scholarship and that the Mithnagdim, as their rabbinic opponents were called, were more intent on fasting and mortification of the flesh than communing with God. They also contended that feasting, singing, and dancing in the name of God had more effect than the mechanical recitation of the prayers and the dryness of Talmudic legalistic lore taught by the Rabbinites. It must be remembered that at this time in history learning had deteriorated. The Dark Ages and the Ghetto had caused the great mass of Jews to turn to superstition and magic. Only the well-to-do could afford to study, and most Jews were poverty-stricken and ignorant.

As the Chassidic movement grew with the popularity of its leader, it incurred the criticism and protest of the rabbis, who, having been disillusioned by the mysticism of Cabala and misled by false Messiahs, held this new movement suspect. Rabbinic Judaism, which followed the traditional mode of prayer and worship for centuries, could not understand how a people could worship God in a cheerful spirit, with unrestrained singing and movement of body. They denounced the Chassidim as being irreverant, ignorant, and fanatical.

The principles of Chassidism centered around the nature of God and the purpose of prayer. God was good and beautiful, and so was man who was the center of God's creation. God is in everything and everything is in God. Man must serve God and love Him through every thought and act. Prayer, according to the Chassidim, was the means by which man could communicate with God, and it should be joyful, not mournful. Men must have faith in God and perform good deeds rather than utter meaningless prayers and go through punctilious observance of the 613 precepts of the Jewish religion.

Conflict and Tensions

The bitterness and hatred that developed between the Chassidim and the Mithnagdim seemed to threaten the unity of Jewry. When the Chassidim introduced the Cabalist prayerbook of Isaac Luria, the Besht and his followers were denounced and excommunicated by the Gaon of Vilna. Their leaders were proscribed and their books burned. But the movement could not be broken. It rolled on like a tidal wave over Galicia, Poland, the Ukraine, Hungary, and Slovakia, and about half of East European Jewry fell under its influence. The people wanted their rabbis to be Tzadikim, ultra-pious saints and intermediaries of God. They wanted to believe in men who proclaimed themselves healers and miracle-workers. They liked the emotional release of a happy religion.

Chassidism underwent many changes in the succeeding years. Dov Ber of Mezhirizh (d. 1773) succeeded the Besht as the leader of Chassidism. He was known as the Magid, the "Preacher." This title became a common appellation for many Chassids who became itinerant preachers. Dov Ber gave a firmer foundation to traditional Jewish learning and trained a large number of men who became important leaders in the movement, because he was convinced that good leadership was the only way to insure the future of Chassidism.

His successor, Shneour Zalman of Lyady (d. 1813), started a splinter group within Chassidism called HABAD, initial letters standing for Wisdom, Intelligence, and Knowledge. This off-shoot became a philosophical and rational movement and attracted scholars from White Russia and Lithuania.

After many years of bitter conflict and struggle, both groups started to change and compromise. Tradition and study, which were the pillars of rabbinic Judaism, were acknowledged and accepted by Chassidim, who even started Yeshivot. Some of the freedom and warmth of Chassidism was accepted by the Rabbinites. Though the two groups remained separate and distinct, they later joined hands to combat another new development in Jewish life, the Haskalah.

The decline of Chassidism was marked by the wave of emancipation of the 19th century which broke down the ghetto walls. During the Nazi period all the Chassidic centers in Poland and Russia were destroyed. Chassidic groups with a bizarre tinge are to be found in New York, and a very large center of Chassidic life is firmly established in Jerusalem. Chassidism will be remembered as a vitalizing force in the dark days of Judaism and for its contribution of a moral literature that still has validity in modern life.

TZADDIKIM

TZADDIK— צדיק —means a RIGHTEOUS MAN. The term goes back to Bible times (Habakkuk 2 : 4 and Proverbs 20 : 7) and has been used also to apply to the legend of the Thirty-Six "Lamed-vov-niks"— righteous men in each generation who keep the world in existence.

The title assumed importance in Jewish life with the development of Chassidism when the Tzaddik was regarded as the intermediary between God and man. Up to this time there was no personal agent representing God. At first the title was conferred by one Tzaddik on the most worthy of his followers, but later it became hereditary. His was the power to bring down divine blessings and his word was considered to be miraculous and prophetic. He held "court" where he dispensed his wisdom to those who came for help. His students and disciples lived on his premises and often followed him when he would tour the country. On Sabbaths and festivals his home was the gathering-place for his followers and visitors.

So anxious were the people for help in these troubled times that they were willing to accept the leadership of the Tzaddik without question. In many communities the rabbis were replaced by Tzaddikim who received greater favor and loyalty. The people came to assume that the Tzaddikim enjoyed God's special favor, not so much because of their learning, but because of their persons. Using this power, the Tzaddik was always in a position to choose his successor. Thus dynasties of Tzaddikim came into existence, some of which have lasted to this day. The most famous and affluent were those of Belz in Galicia, Sadagora in Bukovina, Ger in Poland, and Lubavitsch in Russia.

To some observers the Tzaddikim represented corruption and commercialism that sullied the purity of belief and practice of the Besht and his first followers.

RABBINITES

The scholars and students of traditional Judaism, who were centered around Babylonia and its Talmudic academies were called Rabbinites, to distinguish them from their opponents, the Karaites, who followed the strict literal interpretation of the Bible alone.

Rabbinites and Karaites continued as two rival movements until the tenth century when Saadiah Gaon (882–942), the most learned Jew of the time, was instrumental in stemming Karaism as a force in Jewish life. With the decline of the Karaites all Jewry subsequently became dominated by the legalism of Jewish law as interpreted by the Rabbinites.

Rabbinism, or Talmudic Judaism, was the instrument by which Judaism was able to adapt itself to the changing conditions of the time. A certain flexibility characterized these years, until the publication of the Shulchan Aruch— שֻׁלְחָן עָרוּךְ —"The Prepared Table" (1565), a codification of all Talmudic law, after which the Rabbinites permitted no changes. Jewish life became rigid and fixed, and so uncompromising were the leaders that inner revolt was inevitable. The new movements that arose in Israel because of domineering Rabbinism were Chassidism, Haskalah, and Reform.

MITHNAGDIM

The word MITHNAGDIM— מתנגדים —means OPPONENTS and was applied by the Chassidim to those people who stood in opposition to them. This name came into usage after the Vilna Gaon issued a ban against Chassidism in 1772. The Mithnagdim maintained that Judaism was being undermined by the pantheistic tendencies of the Chassidim, the use of Sephardic liturgy, the establishment of separate synagogues, and their belief in Tzaddikim. As the recognized Rabbinites of their time, the Mithnagdim had no alternative but to place the ban of excommunication upon the Chassidim. During the 19th century the conflict between the two groups became more conciliatory.

MASKILIM—(HASKALAH)

"Haskalah" means "Enlightenment" or "Understanding." It is derived from the Hebrew word SECHEL— שכל —meaning INTELLI-GENCE. Those who were associated with the "enlightenment" movement were called MASKILIM— משכלים —JEWISH INTELLECTUALS. The term was coined in 1832 by Judah Jeiteles. Haskalah started in Germany in the middle of the 18th century as a movement to spread modern European culture among Jews. The era of emancipation brought impetus to this movement and imbued the Jews with an egalitarian ardor.

About the same time, a similar movement began in other European countries. Moses Mendelssohn (1729–1786), is said to be the father of this movement of the intellectual, economic, and social emancipation of the German Jews. In Russia, Austria, and Galicia the ghetto walls started to crumble.

Haskalah found its expression through the cultivation of the Hebrew language and literature. Like its German counterpart, it sought to associate the Jew with the culture of Western Europe by modernizing Judaism and its customs. Out of this desire to open the windows of the Jewish mind to the light of the world and release the Jew from his ghetto psychology came many scholars who put new life and meaning into the Jewish spirit. Haskalah produced many famous Jewish poets and philosophers, novelists and dramatists, idealists and social reformers.

Haskalah grew into a protest movement against the dry and spirit-less Talmudism of the time. It paved the way for a group of traditional Jews who became imbued with Hebrew culture even while their thinking was permeated by the political and social ideals of the Western world. These men pioneered another movement that was to grip world Jewry—Zionism.

Haskalah and Jewish emancipation, however, did not touch the inner life of the masses of Israel's Jewry. The traditionalists forbade the reading of secular books, looked with suspicion upon reforms in the name of enlightenment, and viewed all Maskilim as assimilationists.

YIDDISHISTS

By the time Haskalah and Chassidism had become exhausted as movements in Jewish life, new voices were preparing to speak— Zionism and Socialism. The latter exerted a great influence upon early Yiddish writers because Yiddish was the medium of the masses, the "Mother Tongue," and Socialism was viewed as a solution to their problems. The Bund, as the Jewish Labor Alliance was called, gave the younger Yiddish writers a perspective that resulted in their seeing the Socialist way of life as the correlative of the prophetic conception of redeeming the world.

Consequently, the Bund exalted Yiddish, the language of the masses, and denied Hebrew, the language of the rabbis. Elementary and high school systems of education were established by the Socialists and also by the Labor Zionists, for whom Hebrew commanded a certain primacy. There were extensive adult cultural activities centering around the modern Yiddish literature and theatre. With the wave of newcomers from Europe came a noticeable burgeoning of the Yiddishist movement through newspapers, periodicals, books, theatres, lecture courses, and the like. So important did Yiddish culture become that in 1925 in Vilna, the YIVO was founded, the "Yiddish Scientific Institute." Since World War II, YIVO has had its main center in New York City. It fosters research in Yiddish literature, history, economics, statistics, psychology, and folklore.

Although the name YIDDISHIST is associated with the Socialist element in Jewish life, there were many gifted men of letters, like Sholem Asch, who used Yiddish because it was an integral part of the culture and romance that pervaded the lives of the people about whom he wrote. Piety, Jewish loyalty, and religious fervor were the favorite themes in Jewish literature. The Nazi tragedy and Russian suppression of the creative centers of Yiddish literature have caused them to shift elsewhere, but there are still healthy streams of Yiddish culture emanating from Tel Aviv and New York. With the number of Yiddish-speaking Jews declining, the future of Yiddish appears to be in doubt.

HEBRAISTS

"Hebraists" is a term applied to those who sought to establish Hebrew as a living language. The Jewish people, since the Diaspora, honored Hebrew as a holy language but confined its use to the Bible, Prayer Book, and kindred studies. They spoke the language of the country in which they resided, until they added variants like Yiddish and Ladino.

During the period of the Haskalah movement, efforts were made to make the Hebrew language the language of culture of the Jewish people. Maskilim, "Enlighteners," brought forth a Hebrew commentary on Mendelssohn's Bible—the BIUR. Dissertations on religious subjects and popular articles pertaining to Jewish life were printed in Hebrew periodicals, noteworthy among them being HA-ME'ASSEPH—"The Collector," founded in 1784 in Germany. The Hebraists of Germany, Austria, and Poland became known as ME'ASSEPHIM. Together with the Maskilim they used Hebrew in translation or imitation of foreign classics.

The movement to revive Hebrew gained impetus from the support of many new intellectuals and through the growth of Hebrew periodicals. Magazines like Ha-Karmel, Ha-Maggid, Ha-Meliz, Ha-Shachar, and Ha-Zefirah, though limited in circulation, opened the doors to Hebrew literature, poetry, philosophy, and fiction. The Hebrew language gradually assumed greater flexibility and was no longer considered the Biblical tongue.

From Germany and Austria the movement spread to Galicia, Russia, and Poland. In Lithuania, about the middle of the 19th century, the Hebrew novel made its appearance and from that time on modern Hebrew literature began to come into its own. Such names as Lebensohn, Mapu, Gordon, Smolenskin, and scores of others became household words revealing the inmost life of the Jewish people as recorded in their historic tongue.

By the end of the 19th century every phase of modern literature was found in Hebrew, which then started to develop into a language for common use. With the rise of cultural Zionism, Talmud Torahs (schools for the instruction of Hebrew) were established in the same way that Yiddishists organized their schools.

In spite of the efforts of Hebraists, the use of Hebrew failed to reach the masses. The intellectuals and writers lived in a little world of their own, supporting a few periodicals devoted to Hebrew literature. The masses stayed with Yiddish or with the vernacular.

The Zionist movement brought Hebrew to the fore through the

hope that Palestine would become their state and Hebrew would be the tongue of the land. Eliezer ben Yehudah (1857–1922) is the father of modern Hebrew in Israel. He published a Hebrew dictionary and under the British Mandate, the Hebrew language, along with English and Arabic, became one of the three official languages.

In the United States Hebraists concentrated their efforts upon the teaching of Hebrew in schools and colleges as a modern foreign language. *The Histadruth Ivrith—Hebrew Cultural Organization*—sought to spread the knowledge of Hebrew among Zionist groups. It published a Hebrew weekly, "Ha-Doar"—"The Post," and books of literary merit. The *B'rith Ivrith Olamith—World Federation of Hebrew Culture*—functions in the perpetuation and popularization of Hebrew as a language and in literature.

FOLKISTS

The immigrant workers who came to the New World from Yiddishist circles or "Shtetels" in Europe sought to continue the Yiddish-centred "folk" idea in this country and Canada. They had a strong feeling of Jewish peoplehood, but felt no need for formal identification with religion.

In origin, the Folkists might be said to be a part of the larger movement in which immigrants created organizations that were inspired by labor sympathies, nationalist ideologies, or Jewish philanthropic motives. They were possessed of a high sense of social justice, which was evidenced by their program of activities. They formed the ARBEITER RING, or "Workman's Circle," as a fraternal insurance society and had chapters throughout the country. They were oriented toward Socialism and were politically active. They formed unions in the needle and other trades, in which large numbers of Jewish immigrants found employment. They helped to form the Jewish Labor Committee, along with other groups interested in the Jewish labor movement.

In 1933 they sponsored a system of Yiddish-centered "folk" schools, particularly the *Sholem Aleichem School* and summer camps. Their publications all used the Yiddish language. The children who attended these schools were not taught Hebrew, and in large part, the families were not affiliated with or interested in institutions of traditional worship. They strongly supported Israel and assumed organizational responsibilities there. The folk organizations served as a resource for mutual help, either through loans or by personalized interest in the family problems of the members. These groups catered to the gregarious instincts of the immigrants.

Their best-known newspaper was the FORVERTS (Forward). It is the Yiddish organ of the Jewish Labor movement and Jewish Socialists, and has the largest circulation of any non-English newspaper in the country.

With time, the original needs of the Folkists have disappeared; most of them now are just social organizations seeking outlets for their accumulated funds.

THE LANDSMANNSCHAFTEN

The term "Landsmannschaften" has its English equivalent in the word "Countryman." Immigrants from the Old World found it easy to settle in places where previous countrymen had come, and with their help in finding employment, to adjust to their new environment and learn a new language. A Jew was never a stranger so long as other Jews were close by. When enough people from the same areas settled near each other they formed societies of fellow-countrymen. Hence, names like the "Federation of Hungarian Jews" or "Lithuanian Jews" or "United Rumanian Jews of America" are prevalent.

At first the function of the Landsmannschaften groups was to provide assistance for their needy members and to help families still remaining in the "old country." As they grew in membership they promoted cultural programs, aided in the establishment of synagogues, and incorporated as benevolent or relief societies, mutual insurance agencies, and burial societies.

New York City was the center for the Landsmannschaften movement. According to 1950 reports, from the time of the first Federation of United Galician Jews of America (1904), the groups have grown to some 2,000 in addition to women's auxiliaries. The Sephardic Jews have their own association called the "Union of Sephardic Congregations," organized in 1929.

With the closing of immigration in 1924, the Landsmannschaften movement began to decline. The destruction of European Jewish communities by Nazism closed their overseas relief program. The "coming of age" of American Jewry changed the pattern of Landsmannschaften to "peoplehood" instead of "fellow-countrymen." The new generation had little or no interest in old synagogues and societies, and instead, became identified with major national Jewish organizations such as the B'nai B'rith, Zionist Organization of America, labor groups, and the like. The only remaining feature of the Landsmannschaften is the *Family Circle,* for social gatherings.

LABORITES

The Jewish religion, through its Biblical legislation and its Talmudic interpretation, has always emphasized the mutual obligations that exist between the employer and the employee. The ideal of justice for both found expression in many famous passages.

The Emancipation era of the 19th century gave birth to a Jewish industrial proletariat. The social and spiritual importance of labor became one of the concerns of the Haskalah movement. It was the core of the philosophy of the "Prophet of Labor," Aharon David Gordon (1856–1922), who regarded physical labor as the basis of human existence. He believed that the solution to the Jewish problem and to exploitation of workers was a return to the soil, with no one person or group owning the means of production. In 1904 he settled in Palestine as an agricultural worker in a Kibbutz, Degania, where he lived out his life.

This labor philosophy, when transplanted to the United States by Jewish immigrants, did not adapt itself to an agricultural life. Most Jews went into the needle trades. Working conditions were intolerable when they arrived, and became worse because of the large supply of workers available to the manufacturers. Low wages, exploitation, and sweatshop conditions caused many Jews to react strongly, and to look for a political solution to the problem. Many went into left-wing radical and Socialist movements, as a result.

When a fellow immigrant, Samuel Gompers, in 1886 tried to organize them as a craft union, as part of the American Federation of Labor, he met with little success. Although they might gain in personal benefits, the evils would not be eradicated. So they formed their own union, the first "United Hebrew Trades" in 1888. In addition to the improvement of working conditions and wages, their goal included political activity that would do away with injustices and end the degradation of human dignity that plagued workers at that time.

In the pioneering efforts of Jewish labor, many organizations were formed and many leaders arose: Abraham Cahan, Morris Hillquit, Sidney Hillman, Sam Feigenbaum, Meyer London, Daniel de Leon, and hosts of others. Among the labor organizations we find the International Ladies Garment Workers Union (1900), United Garment Workers (1891), Amalgamated Clothing Workers (1914), and others.

Throughout the history of the American Labor movement, the Jewish labor segment has maintained its own identity. Labor Zionists and American Jewish labor groups have their counterparts in Israel and other nations. In the field of Jewish defense, the Jewish Labor Committee conducts its own extensive anti-discrimination campaign. It maintains its own philanthropies in the United States and abroad, wherever workers are affected. The foremost characteristic of Jewish laborites is their concern for their fellowmen.

ZIONISTS

The term ZIONISM was coined in 1893 by Nathan Birnbaum of Vienna. It is applied to those who are dedicated to Israel as the Jewish national home. In essence the term has been in use throughout Israel's dispersion following the fall of the Temple. Through the centuries the idea of a "return" to the homeland was kept alive in the hopes and prayers of the Jewish people. The dream gained impetus during the dark ages of Jewish history because of virulent anti-Semitism in cultured Germany and Austria, and the savage pogroms in Russia and Poland.

In 1862 in Germany, Moses Hess wrote "Rome and Jerusalem," in which he viewed the position of the Jews in a Christian world and explained the Zionist philosophy. He felt that emancipation was no solution to Jewish social and economic problems so long as they were subject to the will and power of a non-Jewish dominant majority. This was the Jewish experience of his day. Anti-Semitism knows no frontiers, and even in free countries Jews were subjected to discriminatory pressures. There was no hope in liberalism because with liberalism comes assimilation and in assimilation lay the seeds for the disappearance of the Jewish people. Hence the necessity for regathering the Jews in their ancient land as a political entity.

To Achad Ha'am (1856–1927), assimilation was a greater danger than anti-Semitism, nor did he see political Zionism as the answer. His solution was that the Jewish people should find a rebirth through culture that would stem from the Zionist ideology.

Varying Zionist ideologies are prevalent in Jewish life. In Russia in the 1880's, the CHOVEVEI TZION—LOVERS OF ZION—started training "Chalutzim," Pioneers, and encouraged their emigration to Palestine. Baron Edmond de Rothschild (1845–1934) of Paris provided resources for the establishment of several agricultural colonies. By the end of the century there was a slow but steady stream of pioneers on the soil, including a large number of Russian students calling themselves the BILU, an abbreviation for an Aliyah group. One of its founders was Menachem Mendel Ussishkin (1863–1941). He was also chairman of the Jewish National Fund from 1923 until his death. Leon Pinsker of

Odessa (1821–1891) wrote a pamphlet "Auto-Emancipation," in which he pleaded for a homeland as a solution to the Jewish problem.

The Dreyfus affair had the same kind of result in France as the pogroms and massacres had in Eastern Europe. It was this brazen form of anti-Semitism that kindled a fire in Theodore Herzl (1860–1904), founder of modern Zionism, and caused him to dedicate his short life to the settling of the Jewish people in a land they could call their own with complete autonomous rule. In 1896 he wrote "Der Judenstaat," "The Jewish State," in which he pleaded for the national rebirth of the Jewish people as a self-governing body. In 1897 he was instrumental in convening the first Zionist Congress at Basle for the purpose of establishing a Jewish national homeland.

Herzl interested many Jewish leaders. Among them were Dr. Max Nordau (1849–1923) who was one of his influential supporters; David Wolffsohn (1856–1914) who succeeded him as president; Hermann Schapira (1840–1898) who proposed the establishment of the Hebrew University and the Jewish National Fund; Nahum Sokolow (1860–1936) who was a key figure in negotiating the Balfour Declaration; Chaim Weizmann (1874–1952), first president of the State of Israel; Stephen S. Wise (1874–1949), one of the founders of the Zionist Organization of America; Louis Lipsky (1876–1963), co-founder of the World Zionist Congress; and David ben Gurion (1886–), first Prime Minister of Israel. Many auxiliary organizations came into being over the years. Among them were the Jewish National Fund, the Palestine Foundation Fund, and the Jewish Agency.

Fifty years later the State of Israel became a reality when the United Nations Organization partitioned Palestine between Jordan and Israel and granted political determination to the Jewish people.

The basic interest of Zionism took two general directions, cultural and political. Cultural Zionists hold that through emphasizing the arts the mission of the Jewish people would best be served in the Diaspora and that political power is not necessary to insure the flow of rich Palestine-centered culture. Political Zionists find fulfillment in the present state of Israel, which they feel is a national homeland for Jews everywhere.

On the other side of the coin are the non-Zionists and anti-Zionists. The former are noncommittal toward both cultural and political Zionism, but join in the spirit of peoplehood by giving financial and moral support to Israel. The latter feel that Israel is a threat to their security as nationals of the countries where they live, and they work actively at withholding support and denouncing its political ambitions.

Religious Divisions

ORTHODOX JUDAISM

The word ORTHODOX from "Orthos," "Right," and "Doxa," "Opinion," means "right," "true," or "correct." Applied to the Jewish religion, Orthodox Judaism means "Traditionalism." It was first applied to Jews by the French Sanhedrin, which was convened by Napoleon (1807) for the purpose of determining the attitude of Jewish leaders toward the Mosaic Law. The term, however, was not in common use until the advent of Reform Judaism in Germany about the middle of the 19th century. It referred to those Jews who refused to make any changes in their inherited religious practices regardless of changed conditions or environmental factors. They adhered strictly to Halachah, the authority of the Bible, to the Talmud, and to approved codes of Judaism. For centuries this tradition found expression through "Articles of Belief" formulated by Maimonides (1135–1204). He said,

> No one can be considered a true Jew who does not acknowledge these articles as true; he who denies a single one of them is a heretic, forfeits his membership in the community of Israel, and cuts himself off from all hope of future bliss.

The Orthodox "way of life," for both Ashkenazic and Sephardic Jews, is also expressed in a book called the SHULCHAN ARUCH— שֻׁלְחָן עָרוּךְ —THE PREPARED TABLE, or *Guide to Daily Jewish Life*. In it lies the authority of Rabbinic Judaism.

Basic to Orthodoxy is the belief in God's divine and immutable revelation at Sinai. The Torah is not the work of Moses, but the spoken word of God, and the Jew is obligated to live in strict conformity with the letter of the law without change or adaptation.

Orthodoxy is the essence of some three thousand years of Jewish history and dominates the lives of the majority of the world's Jews. In reality it embraces all Jews who call themselves Orthodox and who may accept the validity of the Mosaic law, but do not adhere to it strictly in daily life.

Orthodox Judaism in America is propagated by three primary institutions for Jewish education :

1. The Yeshivah schools, which prepare teachers and ordain rabbis. The most prominent schools are the Rabbi Isaac Elchanan Theological Seminary of New York (Yeshivah College) and the Hebrew Theological College in Chicago.

2. The Va'ad Hachinuch HaCharedi, supported by the Mizrachi Organization of America. It deals with Talmud Torahs and is Zionist oriented.

3. Torah Umesorah, organized for the promotion of day schools and Yeshivoth.

American-trained rabbis have introduced modern Hebrew schools to replace the old private Cheder classroom. Sunday schools offer religious courses in addition to Hebrew instruction. The late Friday evening service has become popular in some Orthodox congregations. Many synagogues have introduced auxiliary activities, such as Sisterhood organizations, Men's Clubs, Youth Clubs, Educational classes, and special cultural activities.

Zionism has been of primary interest to Orthodox Jewry. Through Mizrachi and religious labor parties it has helped shape the religious pattern of Jewry in Israel. Basic to Orthodox Jewish life, however, is the renascence of Torah, respecting and living in accordance with Halachah and its Talmudic interpretation.

Orthodox Judaism is represented by an international body called AGUDATH YISROEL— **אגודת ישראל** —ASSOCIATION OF ORTHODOX JEWS with authority to speak on Orthodox Jewish law. It was organized in 1912. The Sabbath Observance World Union was founded in 1923 for the purpose of promoting the observance of the Sabbath as a day of rest. In the United States Orthodox Judaism is represented by the AGUDATH HARABONIM— **אגודת הרבנים** —THE UNION OF ORTHODOX RABBIS. Most Orthodox congregations are affiliated with the Union of Orthodox Jewish Congregations. It is estimated that there are about 2,600 Orthodox congregations in the United States.

Some Fundamental Principles and Practices of Orthodoxy

Strict observance of the Sabbath day; prohibition of all work and business; obligation of prayer, meditation, rest, and mitzvoth.

The observance of two-day worship services for all Holy Days except Yom Kippur.

Prayers are to be recited three times daily, with not less than ten adult males (Minyan) constituting a quorum at synagogue services.

Use of ritual ceremonials, Tallith, Tefillin, and Mezuzah, is mandatory, as is the covering of heads.

The Biblical class distinctions between Priest, Levite, and Israelite are retained in public worship and religious ceremonies.

The exclusion of all instrumental music except the Shofar (Ram's Horn) in houses of worship. Music is intoned by a Cantor or reader, Palestrina style, either unaccompanied or with a male choir.

The Mikveh, purification Bath House, is maintained for use at prescribed times.

Strict adherence to the Dietary Laws and Laws of Shechitah and Kashruth. This precludes the Orthodox Jew from eating in public restaurants unless the food is prepared under rabbinic supervision or in accordance with the laws of Kashruth. A stamp of approval must be placed by rabbis on all products sold under the "Kosher" label.

Marriage rites require the reading of the ancient Kethubah (Marriage Contract). Extreme Orthodox practice requires the bride to cut her hair and wear a wig, "Sheitel." The ring is placed on the forefinger of the right hand. A glass is broken at the conclusion of the ceremony.

Funeral rites follow strict rules of washing and shrouding the corpse, simple caskets, broken shard on eyes and lips, pieces of wood in hands to expedite resurrection, a bag of earth in the casket symbolizing the soil of the Holy Land, the cutting of the outer garment as a sign of mourning, the required period of mourning, and abstention from worldly pleasures.

Circumcision rites and the Pidyon Haben ceremony for the newborn male child.

Separation of sexes. Men and women are not permitted to sit together during public worship. Women sit in balconies or in partitioned sections.

Belief in the doctrines of Revelation, Personal Messiah, Resurrection, and the rebuilding of the Temple.

Some Leaders of Orthodox Jewry

Isaac Bernays — (1792–1849). Chief Rabbi of Hamburg. First Orthodox rabbi to preach in German and to use German in Talmud Torah instruction. Opposed to religious reform.

Samson Raphael Hirsch—(1808-1888). German leader of Orthodoxy. Under his leadership Frankfort became center of Judaism in Germany. Antagonistic to Reform, claiming it would lead to degeneration and emptiness. Tried to fuse European culture with traditional Judaism.

Moses Sopher (Schreiber)—(1762–1839). Known after his most distinguished work as Hatam Sopher. Founded Yeshivah at Pressburg. Authority on Halachah. Bitter opponent of Reform.

Seligman Baer Bamberger—(1807–1878). Battle of Orthodoxy against Reform should be fought in the community. Rabbi at Wurzberg, where he founded a Yeshivah that exercised great influence in Germany.

Gershom Mendez—(1745–1816). Headed Sephardic Congregation in New York for fifty years.

Azriel Hildesheimer—(1820–1899). Founded Berlin Rabbinical Seminary to combine traditional Judaism with European culture. Neo-Orthodox.

Rabbi Meir Bar-Ilan (Berlin) — (1880–1949). Founder of the Teachers' Institute, now a part of the Isaac Elchanan Theological Seminary. Active in Mizrachi Zionist Groups.

Rabbi Samuel Belkin—(1911–). President of Yeshiva University. The growth and expansion of the Yeshiva, under his direction, is reflected in the strength of Orthodoxy in the United States.

Rabbi Bernard Revel—(1885–1940). Great influence on the development of modern Orthodoxy. Organized Yeshiva College and introduced arts and sciences. As a University, the Yeshiva operates a medical and dental school.

Rabbi Isaac Elchanan Spektor—(1817–1896). Founder of the first Yeshiva in the United States (1896). Besides training of rabbis and teachers, the Yeshiva has become the center of Jewish culture and learning.

Rabbi Faivel Mendelowitz—(1886–1948).Founder of the Torah and Umasorah movement (1944) and under whose leadership many Day Schools now flourish in the United States.

Rabbi Saul Silber—(1881–1946). Founder of the Chicago Hebrew Theological Seminary (1921). In addition to training young men for the Orthodox Rabbinate it offers degrees of Doctor and Master of Hebrew Literature.

Rabbi David de Sola Pool—(1885–). Since 1907 has been the rabbi of the Spanish and Portuguese synagogue in New York. Recognized leader of Sephardic Orthodox Jewry.

Rabbi Leo Jung—(1892–). Prominent Orthodox leader and author. Professor of Ethics at Yeshiva University.

REFORM JUDAISM

Reform or Liberal Judaism is a movement of protest and modernization. As a protest it is directed against the authority and legalism of Rabbinic Judaism and is a departure from strict traditionalism in Jewish life. As a progressive movement it seeks to adapt the Jewish religion to modern conditions and environment and its emphasis is on the ethical and moral teachings of Judaism rather than its rituals and ceremonials.

Reform Judaism began at the start of the 19th century in Germany. It followed closely after the French revolution of 1789, and meant the end of the ghetto and the Jewish badge. The Emancipation that came to Europe enabled the Jew to travel and live where he wished. His new freedom opened for him opportunities to enjoy long-desired privileges and benefits in social, political, economic, and cultural pursuits. The Jew suddenly found himself in the universities and professions. He copied the manner, dress, and language of his neighbors.

In this process of assimilation he was slowly but surely losing his Jewish identity. He was removing himself from the credal Orientalism that marked his life for so many centuries. He resented the peculiarism and isolationism that stamped him as a Jew. The Jew of Germany wanted a shortcut to escape his past. He resorted to the simple expedient of becoming a Gentile by completely assimilating the Christian way of life or changing his religion.

It was this new freedom that was responsible, in a large measure, for the beginnings of Reform Judaism—a religious movement against irreligion, assimilation, and estrangement from Judaism. The leaders of Reform did not attempt to change the Jewish religion. They wanted to modernize Jewish life, to make it more impressive, practical, and beautiful. The changes that were introduced were not in opposition or contrary to tradition, since the pioneers of Reform found precedent for new laws, prayers, and modes of worship.

On the theory that God reveals himself to the human conscience in all ages, Reform Judaism attempted to reinterpret tradition in modern terms, yet, at the same time, to retain the spirit and the essence of the heritage of Israel. Reform maintains that growth and change are necessary to life. Religion, therefore, with its dogmas and institutions, must conform to the changing conditions of life if it is to have a dynamic influence upon its adherents and engender the kind of commitment that is emotionally satisfying.

Philosophy of Reform Judaism

The philosophy of Reform Judaism rests on nonacceptance of dogma and creed and upholds the validity of modern interpretation of theological concepts. It refuses to accept rabbinical authority as the absolute criterion for living a Jewish life. Following are the more important attitudes of Reform Judaism pertaining to practice and belief :

Revised Prayer Book—Many prayers have been abbreviated or eliminated; new prayers have been added and services varied.

Language of the Vernacular—Prayers should be offered in the language best understood. The Reform Prayer Book is composed primarily of English prayers.

Organ and Instrumental Music—Since the fall of the Temple (70 CE), instrumental music has been barred from Jewish religious services. Reform Judaism sees no justification for this rule and has re-introduced this music as part of its regular service.

Mixed Choirs—Reform Judaism not only permits mixed choirs, which are forbidden in Orthodoxy, but also allows non-Jewish personnel to sing with the choir.

The Wearing of Hats—The covering of heads has no basis in Jewish law. Hence Reform Judaism discards this custom, which is based on tradition, and makes no demands upon its adherents to cover their heads during worship services.

Tallith and Tefillin—The Praying Shawl and Phylacteries, ritual symbols, are not necessary for the fulfillment of the obligation of prayer.

Sunday Schools—Religious education in Reform Judaism is conducted primarily on Sunday mornings. Some schools hold Sabbath and mid-week classes. The Cheder, or week-day Hebrew school, is not in the general program of Reform education, although Hebrew is included in the curriculum.

Late Friday Evening Services—This is an innovation of Reform Judaism and has been adopted by Conservative and Orthodox congregations. In many communities the late Friday evening service is the chief service of the week.

Minyan—A quorum of ten males is not essential to the performance of religious ceremony or prayer service in the Reform worship. Where such quorum is desired, women are accorded equal rights and can be counted as minyan members.

Sunday Services—Some Reform congregations conduct their main religious service on Sunday morning. At this service, as on Friday evening, a Torah service may be held. There is nothing in the spirit of Judaism or its laws to prevent the holding of worship services on any specific day of the week.

Bar Mitzvah—This ceremony is observed in many Reform congregations, although it may take place on occasions other than Saturday mornings. Girls may be accorded the same privileges as boys and

may be inducted into the rights of Judaism with a ceremony called
Bat Mitzvah— בת מצוה —a Daughter of the Commandment.

Confirmation—This is the religious graduation ceremony of boys and
girls. It takes place at the annual observance of Shebuoth—Feast of
Weeks. Reform Jewry accords the girls and boys equal honor and
consideration. Confirmation may take the place of the individual
Bar Mitzvah of a boy.

One-Day Holiday Observance—Reform Judaism does not observe the
extra day for a holiday as do Orthodox and Conservative Judaism.
The second-day observance is custom and not law.

Dietary Laws—Strict adherence to the eating of Kosher food and the
separation of forbidden foods is not observed by Reform Judaism.
Reform does not say that it is permissible to eat forbidden foods.
Rather it maintains that it is not a sin to eat such foods.

Marriage—Reform Judaism departs from the traditional celebration
of the Marriage ceremony in the following observances :

No Minyan (assembly of ten males) is required at the wedding.
The Kethubah (Marriage Contract) is not used because as a religious
contract of marriage it has no validity in modern times.
The ring may be of any choice and is placed on the proper ring
finger during the ceremony.
The breaking of glass is optional and is often omitted from the
marriage rite.
Fasting is not imposed upon the bride and groom on the day of
their marriage.
The Chuppah (Marriage Canopy) is not essential to the solemniza-
tion of the marriage.
Obstructive days, such as the weeks between Passover and Shebuoth,
and the three weeks preceding the 9th of Ab, are disregarded by
Reform Judaism.

Divorce—The rabbinical GET or divorce decree is not essential for
re-marriage in Reform Judaism. A civil divorce is the law of the
land and supersedes a religious divorce.

Intermarriage and Proselytes—Intermarriage requires conversion but
Reform Judaism does not impose conformity to ancient practice and
custom, such as circumcision for males and ritual purification for
women. This also applies to the admission of proselytes and adopted
children.

Funerals and Burials—Reform Judaism departs from many of the
traditional customs and ceremonies pertaining to the dead :

The traditional shroud is arbitrary. The deceased may be interred
in any appropriate suit or dress.

The ritual cleansing of a corpse by the Chevrah Kedushah (Holy Fellowship) is not followed, since the undertaker prepares the body for the funeral.

Embalming, forbidden by Orthodoxy, is sanctioned by Reform, as is the performance of post mortem.

Sitting up with a corpse all night and the reciting of Psalms are not necessary.

Flowers are permitted at funeral services and at the grave.

The casket is carried directly to the grave, without pauses for special prayers.

The casket is not opened at the grave, symbolically to prepare the body for the next world.

The casket may be left on top of the grave until all the mourners have departed.

The ceremony of "Keri'ah"—rending or tearing an outer garment—has been discarded.

Covering of mirrors and pictures and "sitting Shiva" is not a part of the home observance.

Personal Messiah—Reform Judaism does not accept the belief in a personal Messiah, hence all such references are eliminated from prayers. Instead, the goal is a Messianic age for all peoples.

Revelation—The Torah is not the literal or complete word of God as given to Moses at Sinai. Revelation is a continuous process as man seeks to understand the will of God.

Resurrection—The doctrine of Resurrection or Rebirth belongs to the realm of mystical belief and has no validity in modern Jewish life.

Aaronite Priesthood—The Biblical caste system of Priest, Levite, and Israelite is not recognized by Reform Judaism, since it went out of existence with the fall of the Temple.

Zionism—The destiny of the Jewish people does not depend upon any particular place for its survival. Reform Jews may or may not be Zionistically inclined.

Reform Judaism is represented by the *Union of American Hebrew Congregations,* founded in 1873 by Isaac Mayer Wise. On a national level it co-ordinates the activities of reform congregations through Sisterhoods, Men's Clubs, Youth Groups, and Religious Education. It serves American Reform Jewry through its Commissions of Justice and Peace, Social Action, and Church and State. It sponsors the Jewish Chautauqua Society through the Men's Clubs and conducts a weekly "Message of Israel" radio broadcast.

Reform rabbis receive their training at seminaries such as the Hebrew Union College—Jewish Institute of Religion located in Cincinnati, New York City, Los Angeles, and Jerusalem. The alumni association of Reform rabbis is called the Central Conference of American Rabbis.

The World Union for Progressive Judaism, organized in 1926, promotes and coordinates Liberal Judaism on a worldwide basis.

EARLY REFORM LEADERS

Moses Mendelssohn (1729–1786)

Leader of the Enlightenment movement that came to Germany, and advocate of Jewish emancipation. He made it possible for Jews to know more about their religion, history, and people through his translation of the Bible into German and through the study of the Hebrew and German languages. He paved the way for the reform that was soon to come in Germany.

Israel Jacobson (1768–1828)

First pioneer in Reform Judaism. Founded the first Reform Temple at Seesen, Germany, in the year 1810. He introduced many changes in the services, such as anthems, prayers, and sermons in the German language. He dignified the worship service through order and decorum. Many Reform congregations were organized subsequently, but Orthodox opposition induced the government to close them.

Leopold Zunz (1794–1886)

Founder of "The Society for the Culture and Science of Judaism." His historical and literary writings paved the way for a new approach to the knowledge and understanding of Judaism.

Solomon Judah Loeb Rappaport (1790–1867)

One of the foremost rabbis and scholars of his time. A contemporary with Zunz, he pioneered in modern Jewish learning through critical investigation.

Samuel Holdheim (1806–1869)

Outstanding leader of the German Reform movement. He sought to abolish old laws pertaining to Jewish life and to separate Biblical religion from Talmudic interpretation. He advocated the separation of nationalism from Judaism and maintained that intelligence, not tradition, must be the guide to Jewish living. He followed the Christian pattern of his day by conducting religious services on Sunday.

David Einhorn (1809–1879)

German and American leader in the Reform movement. In opposition to Rabbi Isaac Mayer Wise, he organized and led an extreme Reform wing. He was known for his radical views on religion and as a strong opponent of slavery.

Abraham Geiger (1810–1874)

He advocated the theory that Judaism was a theological system not to be chained by forms and rituals, but renewing itself in every age and under changing conditions. He was a student of Biblical criticism and established a scientific theological seminary. He is called the "Philosopher of Reform Judaism."

Isaac Mayer Wise (1819–1900)

Leader and founder of Reform Judaism in the United States. In 1873 he organized the Union of American Hebrew Congregations, now the parent organization of Reform congregations. In 1875 he founded the Hebrew Union College at Cincinnati, a theological seminary for the training of Reform rabbis. In 1879 he convened the Central Conference of American Rabbis. A prolific writer and an outstanding scholar, he has been termed "The Master Builder of American Judaism."

Joseph Krauskopf (1858–1923)

Prominent rabbi and civic leader in Philadelphia. Introduced many Reform innovations, including Sunday morning services in addition to regular Sabbath services. In 1894 he established and directed a National Farm School at Doylestown, Pa.

Stephen Samuel Wise (1874–1949)

Founder of the Free Synagogue in New York City for the purpose of making the pulpit a place for the liberal expression and teaching of Judaism. He was a national figure in the cause of liberal Judaism and among the first of Reform rabbis to espouse the cause of Zionism. In 1922 he founded the Jewish Institute of Religion as a seminary to train rabbis in the spirit of a changing Judaism, political liberalism, civic leadership, and Zionist ideologies. He organized the American Jewish Congress and until his death was a dynamic force in the Reform movement.

CONSERVATIVE JUDAISM

Conservative Judaism is primarily an American movement, although its beginnings may be traced to Rabbi Zacharias Frankel (1801–1875), of Germany, who sought to establish minor changes in Orthodoxy in opposition to the Reform movement. At the Historical School for Jewish Learning, which he founded in 1850, Frankel established the structure for Conservative Judaism, which maintains that traditionalism and historical development were both necessary to create a vital Jewish life. Thus was laid the groundwork for a middle course between Orthodox and Reform Judaism.

The popular notion about Conservative Judaism today is that it is a compromise or middle-road approach between the old and the new Judaism. Actually, Conservative Judaism is Orthodoxy in transition, without resorting to the drastic changes introduced by Reform Judaism.

Conservative Judaism had no philosophy or program until the extreme pronouncements of Reform Judaism in 1885 stirred it to action. These pronouncements rejected many basic tenets of Orthodox Judaism and claimed the right to make changes and modify the Jewish law and ceremonies according to its needs.

When Reform Judaism went so far as to hold services on Sunday and admit proselytes without circumcision, the reaction of many Orthodox rabbis led to the establishment of a rabbinical school for the training of Conservative rabbis. This school was called *The Jewish Theological Seminary of America* and was headed by its founder, Dr. Sabato Morais (1832–1897).

The purpose of Conservative or historic Judaism differed from Orthodox only in the form of the synagogue worship service. Like Reform, the rabbis desired more decorum and dignity at public worship, and resorted to the English language for the sermons. Aside from such external changes, Conservative Judaism continued much along the same lines as Orthodoxy and it was difficult to distinguish between the two.

With the rapid growth of the Conservative movement and the establishment of a Union of Conservative Congregations in 1913 (United Synagogue of America), many innovations that followed the pattern of Reform Judaism were introduced.

Late Friday evening services in addition to the regular sunset Minchah and Maariv services
Organ and instrumental music permitted in some congregations, as well as mixed choirs

Recitation of prayers in English
Sunday schools added to the Hebrew School program
Confirmation exercises
Men's Club, Women's Auxiliaries, and Youth Groups
Men and women allowed to sit together

Philosophy of Conservative Judaism

Like Orthodoxy, Conservative Judaism stresses Jewish nationalism. The Hebrew language and Palestine as a Jewish national homeland are essential to the life of the Jewish people. It stresses Jewish people-hood, Torah study, and adherence to, and the validity of, Halacha. In spite of this, Orthodox adherents criticize the Conservative movement as a departure from tradition. The principles of Conservative Judaism are stated in the Preamble of the Constitution of the United Synagogue of America :

To assert and establish loyalty to the Torah and its historical ex-position;

To further the observance of the Sabbath and the dietary laws;

To preserve in the service the reference to Israel's past and the hopes for Israel's redemption;

To maintain the traditional character of the liturgy, with Hebrew as the language of prayer;

To foster Jewish religious life in the home as expressed in traditional observances;

To encourage the establishment of Jewish religious schools, in the curricula of which the study of the Hebrew language and litera-ture shall be given a prominent place, both as the key to the true understanding of Judaism and as a bond holding together the scattered communities of Israel throughout the world.

Modern Trends in Conservative Judaism

In recent years leaders of the Conservative movement have recom-mended changes in certain Jewish traditions and observances that would ease the rigid adherence to ancient customs and practices. The United Synagogue of America, however, has given no sanction to any change that would depart from the strict acceptance of the Mosaic law. Conservative Judaism is nevertheless aware that between the law and its observance are to be found many breaches. Following are some problems facing Conservative Judaism today :

Sabbath Day Observance

There is no strict observance on the part of Conservative Jewry of the Sabbath day by refraining from work. Most Jewish business establishments are open. Men and women employed in gainful occupation work on the Sabbath where required.

Riding on the Sabbath and Holidays

Some conservative leaders have advocated a change in the rule that would make it possible for worshipers to ride to services on the Sabbath and Holidays. This would legalize a practice that is widespread in many communities and do away with the subterfuge of parking cars within convenient walking distance to the synagogue.

Dietary Laws

While the Mosaic law is regarded as obligatory toward the fulfillment of the complete Jewish life, Conservative Jews are inclined to be lax in its observance outside the home. Eating in public restaurants is a violation of this law, unless the restaurant conforms to the strict ritual regulations in the preparation and serving of food. Many homes keep "Kosher" in spirit but do not retain the separation of meat and dairy dishes.

Synagogue Services

The practise of holding late Friday evening services, started by Reform Judaism, has been adopted by the majority of Conservative congregations. Many of these services employ the use of the organ as well as mixed choirs. For the sake of uniformity, skull caps are worn by the male worshipers, as well as Prayer Shawls on Sabbaths and holidays. A number of congregations have done away with the segregation of sexes, permitting husbands and wives to sit together during services.

Early Leaders of Conservative Judaism

Zacharias Frankel (1801–1875)

Founder of the Conservative movement in Germany. He advocated a historical approach to the traditional acceptance of Judaism. He strongly opposed the changes introduced by Reform.

Dr. Sabato Morais (1823–1897)

Scholar, professor, and author. Organizer and first president of the Jewish Theological Seminary of New York City, a training school for Conservative rabbis.

Marcus Jastrow (1829–1903)

Vigorous advocate for a middle path between Orthodox and Reform Judaism. Proposed the use of prayer books with modified services.

Solomon Schecter (1847–1915)

Leader and spokesman for the American Conservative movement. President of the Jewish Theological Seminary and founder of the United Synagogue of America, he maintained that Judaism was absolutely incompatible with any abandonment of Torah.

Cyrus Adler (1863–1940)

Acknowledged leader of Conservative Judaism until his death. He was president of the Jewish Theological Seminary and prominent as an educator and orientalist. He was a founder of the American Jewish Committee and the Jewish Welfare Board, and was non-Zionist co-chairman of the Jewish Agency.

RECONSTRUCTIONISM

Reconstructionism is a Jewish religious movement founded by Rabbi Moredcai M. Kaplan of New York City in 1934. More correctly, Reconstructionism is a school of thought, since its adherents are found in all divisions of Jewry. Its philosophy is based on a synthesis between Orthodox and Reform, taking the maximum from the former toward the fuller Jewish life, and, from the latter, the progressive element of change and adaptation to modern life.

The philosophy of Reconstructionism holds that Judaism is more than a religion; it is a civilization, and embraces everything that goes with the life and culture of a people, such as its past, its language, its history, and its country. In this philosophy of religion, active participation in the total Jewish life becomes the essence of Judaism.

The Nature of Judaism

1. It is a civilization and not a religion in the denominational sense, because it includes language, literature, law, folkways, arts, etc., as well as religious beliefs and practices.
2. It is a religious civilization because it is dominated by the goal of making Jewish life supremely worthwhile or holy.
3. It is an evolving civilization, growing out of the life experiences of the Jewish people as they reacted to the changing circumstances of life. No belief in the miraculous is necessary to explain its development.

4. It is a civilization of the Jewish people and hence the common bond that unites Jews throughout the world.

Reconstructionism and Religious Progress

1. Tradition must not be viewed as authoritarian and prescriptive, but as the stored-up wisdom of the past. Jewish traditional beliefs must be re-evaluated from the standpoint of their application to contemporary life.
2. Changes in religious ideas call for changes in forms of worship that will make worship a sincere expression of Jewish ideals and sentiments.
3. Judaism should be brought into harmony with the world of to-day. Miracles that contradict natural law make our ideas about God inconsistent with other ideas of what is true about nature and the world in which we live.
4. The denial of the miraculous origin of Judaism involves a rejection of the traditional belief that the Jews are God's chosen people. God is equally accessible to all peoples and has no favorites.
5. The sacred conception of Torah and Talmud Torah must be modified and extended to include all study that is motivated by the desire to sanctify life by improving the human personality and human relations.
6. It is a vitalization of religion as a live and developing force, instead of being the preservative of ancient dicta and rites.

The Principles of Reconstructionism

1. Judaism as an Evolving Religious Civilization
   Judaism is not only a religion; it is an evolving religious civilization. During the course of its evolution, it has passed through three distinct stages, each reflecting the conditions under which it functioned.
2. What the Present Stage Calls For
   During those stages the Jews constituted a people apart. Now, the Jewish People, like every other, must learn to live both in its own historic civilization and in the civilization of its environment. That will usher in the democratic stage of Judaism, during which the reconstitution of the Jewish People, the revitalization of its religion, and the replenishment of its culture will be achieved.
3. Unity in Diversity
   Jewish unity should transcend the diversity among Jews which

is the result of geographical dispersion and of differences in cultural background and world outlook.

4. The Renewal of the Ancient Covenant

Jews the world over should renew their historic covenant, binding themselves into one transnational people, with the Jewish community in Israel as its core, henceforth to be known as "Zion."

5. Eretz Yisrael the Spiritual Homeland of World Jewry

Eretz Yisrael should be recognized as the home of the historic Jewish civilization.

6. Outside Israel, the Foundation of Organic Communities

Outside Israel, Jewish peoplehood should lead to the establishment of organic communities. All activities and institutions conducted by Jews for Jews should be interactive and should give primacy to the fostering of Jewish peoplehood, religion, and culture.

7. Prerequisites to the Revitalization of Religion

The revitalization of religion can best be achieved through the study of it in the spirit of free inquiry and through the separation of church and state.

8. How the Belief in God Is to Be Interpreted

The revitalization of the Jewish religion requires that the belief in God be interpreted in terms of universally human as well as specifically Jewish experience.

9. What Gives Continuity to a Religion

The continuity of a religion through different stages, and its identity amid diversity of belief and practice, are sustained by its *sancta*. These are the heroes, events, texts, places, and seasons which that religion signalizes as furthering the fulfillment of human destiny.

10. Torah as Synonymous with Ongoing Jewish Culture

The traditional concept of Torah should be understood as synonymous with Jewish religious civilization and should therefore embrace all the ongoing ethical, cultural, and spiritual experiences of the Jewish people.

Mordecai M. Kaplan

JEWISH SCIENCE

This religious movement was founded in New York City in 1922 by Rabbi Morris Lichtenstein. Its purpose was to appeal to and secure the support of Jews who were looking to the Christian Science Church for spiritual healing. Like its counterpart, Jewish science lays emphasis on Scripture, which is the source of spiritual help and healing. As a movement it has made little progress in touching the lives of American Jews. Its adherents are to be found mostly in New York City and Los Angeles.

LANGUAGES
Hebrew

The Hebrew language, which is called LASHON HA-KODESH—לשון הקדש —THE HOLY SPEECH or TONGUE, is the first language of the Jewish people. It is the language in which the Bible and most of the great kindred Jewish literature is written. It is the language of worship and prayer in the synagogue and home. It is the national spoken language of the State of Israel.

Hebrew belongs to the Semitic language group of which Aramaic, Arabic, Assyrian, and others are a part. Originally it was one of the dialects of the early Canaanite people. The word is not certain in its derivation. It may stem from the Hebrew root AYVER—עבר—which means FROM OVER or BEYOND. The first mention of the word is found in the Bible in connection with the Patriarch Abraham. As he was migrating to Palestine from Ur of Chaldee, the Canaanites greeted him with the phrase HO-IVRI—העברי—HE WHO CAME FROM BEYOND.

With the creation of the Jewish people as a nation, the Hebrew language became firmly established as Israel's national tongue. Despite the fact that Hebrew gave way at times to other popular languages, it has remained to this day the language of the Jewish people in classic and modern form.

The Hebrew alphabet is written in square or block-shape characters and conforms to definite rules of syntax and grammar.

Letters		Name	Sound	Number	Script
א	א	Aleph	Silent	1	lc
ב	בּ	Beth	B	2	ə
	ב	Veth	V	2	
ג	ג	Gimmel	G	3	₫
ד	ד	Daleth	D	4	ₔ
ה	ה	Hay	H	5	ꜝ
ו	ו	Vav	V	6	/
ז	ז	Za-yin	Z	7	ƕ
ח	ח	Cheth	Ch	8	n
ט	ט	Teth	T	9	ℓ
י	י	Yod	Y	10	,
כ	ךּ כּ	Kaf	K	20	ɔ
	ך כ	Chaf	Ch	20	
ל	ל	Lamed	L	30	ſ
מ	ם מ	Mem	M	40	N
נ	ן נ	Nun	N	50	J
ס	ס	Sa-mech	S	60	o
ע	ע	Ai-yin	Silent	70	ɤ
פ	ףּ פּ	Pay	P	80	ə
	ף פ	Fay	F	80	
צ	ץ צ	Tzadie	Tz	90	₴
ק	ק	Koof	K	100	₱
ר	ר	Resh	R	200	℩
ש	שׁ	Shin	Sh	300	e
	שׂ	Sin	S	300	
ת	תּ	Tav	T	400	n
	ת	Sav	S	400	

The Hebrew Alphabet

The Hebrew alphabet contains twenty-two letters and is written from right to left.

Some letters have a double pronunciation. They are marked by a dot in the center of the letter.

Five letters have two forms. The longer form is used at the end of a word.

Two letters—Aleph and Ai-yin—are silent. Only the vowel is sounded.

The Alphabet consists o n l y of consonants. Vowels, seven in number, are represented by a system of signs in the form of dots or dashes affixed below, above, or adjacent to the letters.

The first two letters— Aleph and Beth—are called Alpha and Beta in Greek. From these letters are derived the English name "Alphabet."

The Hebrew Vowels

Ah	‾
Awe	⊤
Ee	·ꞁ
Oh	
Ooh	ꞁ
Aye	..
Eh	.·.

Additional Numbers

תק	....	500
תר	....	600
תש	....	700
תת	....	800
תתק	....	900
א	....	1,000

THE HEBREW LANGUAGE TODAY

The language of world Jewry is polyglot. Wherever the Jews made their residence, they adopted the language of the country. Their own language, Hebrew, was always retained in the worship service of the synagogue and in the instruction of children and adults in their schools of learning. Whether or not Hebrew was in use as a spoken or literary language, it always remained the spiritual and holy tongue of the Jewish people.

Today Hebrew is the national language of the newly established State of Israel. In the diaspora many cultural groups have sprung up to revive Hebrew as a spoken and literary language. In the 18th century the Haskalah or Enlightenment movement resulted in the revival of the Hebrew language and literature. Today, an international organization, BRITH IVRITH OLAMITH—ברית עברית עולמית—WORLD FEDERATION OF HEBREW CULTURE, functions for the purpose of teaching and spreading Hebrew among the masses.

The Aramaic Language

Aramaic was the popular language of the Jewish people in Palestine during the second commonwealth. Though Hebrew was the national tongue of Israel, Aramaic was the language of the street. It was also the first language into which the Hebrew Bible was translated. This Aramaic version is known as TARGUM. In many versions of the Pentateuch the Targum appears alongside the Hebrew text. Several books of the Bible, like Ezra and Daniel, contain portions written in Aramaic.

After the destruction of the Temple (70 CE), Aramaic was still widely used by the Jews of Palestine and Babylon. Much of the Talmud was written in Aramaic by the Babylonian scholars, and many prayers were composed in that language. The traditional Jewish prayer recited for the dead, the "Kaddish," and the famous "Kol Nidre" prayer are recited to this day in their original Aramaic form.

Aramaic as a language is not generally used by the Jewish people today, although there are national Jewish groups, such as the Kurdistan Jews, who still speak the language.

The Greek Language

There was a time when the Greek language touched the lives of the Jewish people. With the settlement of many Jews in Egypt, the conquest of the world by the Greeks, and the rise of a large Jewish community in Alexandria, the Greek language made quite an impact as part of the expanding Hellenistic influence. The Hebrew Bible was translated into Greek and was called the Septuagint. Many Greek words and phrases crept into the Hebrew language. Greek-speaking Jews were found in large numbers in Jerusalem and Palestine. But the influence of the Greeks upon the Jews was of short duration. With the decline of Hellenism and the rise of the Roman empire, the Greek language fell into disuse.

Judeo-Persian

This dialect was used by the Jews of Persia in the fourth century BCE. It was called Grush or Parsi-Tat. It was popular for a time, but with the decline of the Persian empire this tongue disappeared. It is interesting to note, however, that the Jews of Bokhara, in central Asia, use this Judeo-Persian dialect.

The Arabic Language

When the crescent of the Mohammedan religion dominated the world, a Judeo-Arabic dialect arose among oriental Jews. During a period of Arab intellectualism many rabbis and scholars resorted to the Arabic language in producing great Jewish works in religion, philosophy, and poetry. Particularly in the "Golden Age" of Spain were a large number of famous works written in Arabic.

Ladino

Ladino is a Spanish-Hebrew dialect. It is Castillian Spanish mixed with Hebrew, Arabian, and Turkish words. It is written with Hebrew letters and is used by Sephardic Jews to this day. With the expulsion of the Jews from Spain went, also, the Ladino language. In Morocco, Ladino-speaking Jews created an extensive Ladino literature that flourished for a time. Refugee Sephardic Jews brought Ladino to Europe. The Bible was translated into Ladino in 1547 and a number of books were printed in that language. Though still in limited use, Ladino is slowly disappearing as a language of the Jewish people.

The Yiddish Language

The widest and most popular dialect language among the Jewish people is Yiddish. As Hebrew is called LASHON HAKODESH— לשון הקדש —the HOLY TONGUE, so Yiddish is known as MAMEH LASHON-מאמע לשון

—the MOTHER TONGUE. Another name for Yiddish is IVRE TEITSCH, the HEBREW EXPLANATION.

Yiddish stems from the German language and came into use in the 15th century. Its name is derived from the German word "Judisch," which means Jewish. Like Ladino, the Yiddish language is about 85 per cent German, with words and phrases borrowed from countries where Jews resided, particularly from Slavic peoples. The alphabet of Yiddish is written in Hebrew characters and reads from right to left.

Yiddish has often been referred to as a jargon dialect. Though it may have started in such a manner, it has nevertheless developed into a language firmly established on principles of syntax and grammar.

Within the Yiddish dialect are to be found many variations and differences in the pronunciation of words. These differences are owing to location and environment. Just as there are marked differences in Bostonian English and Southern English, so are there differences in Lithuanian Yiddish, Polish Yiddish, and Galician Yiddish. In the United States many English words have crept into the Yiddish language.

Yiddish lays claim to an extensive literature. The Bible and its kindred literature have long been translated into this tongue. Many writers, to name but Sholem Aleichem, and Peretz, rose to fame in the field of Yiddish literature. Yiddish daily and weekly newspapers, magazines, and periodicals flourish throughout the Yiddish-speaking world. Organizations have been established to promote Yiddish as the language of the Jews, especially YIVO (Yiddish Scientific Institute), which now has its headquarters in New York City, with branches in thirty countries of the world.

8

The Jews of the World.
Outline History of the Jewish People

PALESTINE AND ISRAEL

From Creation to the Exile

The story of the Jewish people, according to tradition, began in the year 3760 before the Common Era (BCE). The five books of Moses called the Pentateuch, relate the saga of the Jewish people from the time of the creation of the world to the death of Moses. Students of Bible chronology are not in agreement as to the exact dates in this period.

3760—Creation of the world.

2830—Death of ADAM at age of 930 years; first man to be created. His wife, Eve, bore two sons— Cain and Abel.

2704—Death of NOAH, aged 950 years. He and his family survived the flood. This event is associated with God's covenant with mankind.

1812—Birth of ABRAHAM. In 1737 he migrated to Canaan from Ur of Chaldea (Babylonia). He is the first Patriarch and founder of the Jewish religion. He had two sons. ISHMAEL was born of his handmaiden, HAGAR, and ISAAC was born of

his wife SARAH. He died in 1637 at the age of 175.

1532—Death of ISAAC, second of the Patriarchs. His wife, REBECCA, bore twins, Esau and Jacob.

1505—Death of JACOB, third and last Patriarch. The Twelve Tribes of Israel are named for some of his sons and grandsons.

THE TWELVE TRIBES OF ISRAEL

Reuben	Simeon	Issachar
Judah	Dan	Benjamin
Gad	Naphtali	Zebulun
Manasseh	Asher	Ephraim

1561–1451—JOSEPH, one of the younger sons of Jacob, was sold into slavery and taken to Egypt. Later he became governor in charge of Pharaoh's storehouses.

1578–1456—AARON, oldest brother of Moses, who became the first High Priest of Israel.

1572–1452—MOSES, Israel's greatest prophet, led the children of

Israel out of Egyptian bondage (1492) and brought them to Mt. Sinai to receive the Revelation from God.

1492–1452—The period of forty years of wandering in the wilderness; the first observance of the Passover; the building of the Tabernacle.

1522–1412—JOSHUA, successor to Moses, led the Israelites into Canaan. The land was divided among the tribes.

Essentials of Judaism Developed During This Period

The Name of God
(Yahweh) .... Ex.   3 : 13
The Passover Festival ... Ex.   12
The Ten Commandments .... Ex.   20
The Priesthood .... Ex.   25–29
The Dietary Laws ...... Lev.   11
The Day of Atonement Lev.   16
The Covenant of Holiness .... Lev.   17–20
The Jewish Holidays ... Lev.   23
Sabbatical–Jubilee Years Lev.   26
Redemption of First
Born .... Num.   3
The Priestly Blessing ... Num.   6
The Law of Fringes ...... Num. 15
Sacredness of Human
Life .... Num. 35
Declaration of Faith
(Shema) .... Deut.   6
Doctrine of Justice.........Deut. 16–21

THE PERIOD OF THE JUDGES
1370 – 1029

The period from the death of Joshua to the establishment of the Monarchy was marked by internal strife and conflict between the tribes. Israel's infidelity to God, her transgressions, her repentance,

and her redemption form the theme for this portion of history.

The Judges of Israel

Othniel   .... 40 years
Ehud   .... 80 years
Shamgar   .... 1 year
Barak and Deborah ... 40 years
Gideon   .... 40 years
Abimelech   .... 3 years
Tolah   .... 23 years
Jair   .... 22 years
Jephthah   .... 6 years
Ibzan   .... 7 years
Elon   .... 10 years
Abdon   .... 8 years
Samson   .... 20 years
Eli   .... 40 years
Samuel, the Seer ...... 11 years

THE KINGDOM OF ISRAEL
1028–933 BCE

Under the leadership of the kings of Israel the tribes were first united and the nation rose to glory and fame.

1053–1013—SAUL, son of Kish, was anointed first king of Israel by Samuel. He took his own life after being defeated by the Philistines.

1013—ISHBOSHETH, Saul's son, proclaimed King by Abner, the general.

1012–973—DAVID, second King of Israel. His father, JESSE, was the grandson of RUTH, the Moabitess, and BOAZ. David was a gifted poet and musician. Under his leadership Israel expanded in power and territory. He began the construction of the great Temple at Jerusalem but did not live to see its completion.

973–933—SOLOMON, son of David, who was famed for his wisdom, led the Jewish nation to its greatest power. In the year 962 he completed the Temple, but his rule was so unsatisfactory that at his death a civil war broke out that divided the country.

THE DIVIDED KINGDOM
933 – 586 BCE

After Solomon's death (933) the Kingdom was divided because of civil war. The northern ten tribes, under the leadership of Jeroboam, established the Kingdom of Israel with their capital city at Shechem (Samaria). Their history continued until the year 722, when they were conquered by the Assyrians. The two southern tribes, under the leadership of Rehoboam, son of Solomon, formed the Kingdom of Judah, with Jerusalem as the capital. Their history ended in the year 586, when they were conquered by the Babylonians.

The years of the divided Kingdom are centered around many kings and prophets who were instrumental in molding the destiny of the Jewish people. This period is characterized by the strong influence of Baalism or Calf Worship. The northern Kingdom, Israel, which lasted 210 years, rose to its greatest power under King Omri and his successors. For over 100 years Israel was at war with her sister state, Judah.

The Kings of Israel
933 – 722 BCE

933–912	Jeroboam
912–911	Nadab
911–888	Baasa
887	Elah
887	Zimri
887–876	Omri
876–853	Ahab
853–852	Ahaziah
852–843	Jehoram (Joram)
843–816	Jehu
816–800	Jehoahaz
800–785	Joash (Jehoash)
785–745	Jeroboam II
744	Zechariah
744	Shallum
744–737	Menahem
737–736	Pekahiah
736–734	Pekah
733–722	Hoshea
722	Fall of Israel

875–854—King Ahab of Israel married Jezebel of Tyre, who introduced Baal-worship in place of Yahweh religion.

843–816—King Jehu destroyed Baal-worship and instituted reforms.

722–At the fall of the Kingdom of Israel, Sargon, the Assyrian conqueror, forced the people into captivity, thus beginning the saga of the lost Ten Tribes of Israel.

The Kings of Judah
933–586 BCE

933–917	Rehoboam
917–915	Abijah (Abijam)
915–875	Asa
875–851	Jehoshaphat
851–844	Jehoram (Joram)
843	Ahaziah
843–837	Athaliah
837–798	Joash (Jehoash)
798–780	Amaziah
780–740	Uzziah (Azariah)
740–736	Jotham
736–720	Ahaz
720–692	Hezekiah

692–638 .... Manasseh
638 .... Amon
638–609 .... Josiah
609 .... Jehoahaz
608–598 .... Jehoiakim
598 .... Jehoiachin
598–587 .... Zedekiah
586   Fall of Jerusalem

The southern Kingdom, Judah, which lasted 345 years, followed the line of the royal house of David throughout its history. Its fall closed the period known as the "First Jewish Commonwealth."

621—The Book of the Law (Deuteronomy) was found in the Temple. King Josiah instituted a religious reformation. All worship was centralized in the Temple at Jerusalem.

597—Jerusalem was besieged by Babylonia and many leaders were taken into exile, including the prophet Ezekiel.

586—The fall of Judah, which ended the first Jewish Commonwealth, occurred when Nebuchadnezzar captured Jerusalem. The Temple was destroyed and the people were forced into exile. The ancient city of Tel Aviv along the Banks of the river Chebar became the temporary center of Jewish civilization.

THE PROPHETS OF ISRAEL
874–c.400 BCE

During the period of the Divided Kingdom the people often turned to the idol-worship of their neighbors. Some rulers misused their office and many people suffered from poverty and mistreatment.

At this crisis in the political and economic life of the people, there appeared men called Prophets (Nebi'im), who denounced evil and corruption and voiced the message of justice and righteousness. Many of them acted as political advisers to the rulers, but primarily they preached righteousness and urged the people to save themselves by turning back to God and His ways.

The Prophets in Chronological Order

874–840—ELIJAH, champion of God against Baal, or idol-worship. He opposed Jezebel, foreign wife of Ahab, who introduced Baal-worship in Israel.

840–800—ELISHA, successor to Elijah. He played an important role in the revolution against Ahab.

785—JONAH made his famous trip to Nineveh to prophesy its doom. Modern scholars place the writing of this book in the fourth century.

780–740—AMOS, prophet of justice, who preached the restoration and future glory of the Davidic kingdom.

750–722—HOSEA, prophet of love and forgiveness, whose messages contain the doctrine of a universal God for all nations.

738–700—ISAIAH, the statesman prophet, who described the ideal state and the golden age of man. Israel is the "Suffering Servant" and the "Remnant of God."

God's will, who urged every
735–700—MICAH, the interpreter of

man to do justice, to show mercy, and to live humbly.

630–623—ZEPHANIAH lived in the days of King Josiah's reformation. He condemned the idolatrous nations and threatened God's impending judgment.

625–608—NAHUM foretold the destruction of Sennacherib's army.

626–586—JEREMIAH, prophet of sorrow and doom, was witness to the fall of Jerusalem and the destruction of the Temple.

600–590—HABAKKUK preached the message of faith. God's punishment of Israel teaches the lesson that "the righteous shall live by faith."

586—OBADIAH's story is the shortest book of the prophets. It is directed against Israel's enemy, the nation of Edom.

597–571—EZEKIEL was the leader and comforter of Israel in exile. He laid the foundation of the Jewish religion as it is known today.

586–534—DANIEL, the prophet of exile, foretold the restoration of Israel and the coming of God's universal kingdom.

520–516—HAGGAI returned to Palestine from Babylonia and urged the rebuilding of the Temple.

520–516—ZECHARIAH, together with Haggai, dedicated the Second Temple as a spiritual house of God.

445–432—MALACHI prophesied that Elijah would announce the coming of God's Messiah. His is the last book in the canon of the prophets.

c.400—JOEL. His time of activity is uncertain. He lived during a plague of locusts, which he interpreted as God's divine justice.

The Post-Biblical Period

THE PERSIAN PERIOD
538–331 BCE

Jewish history during this period is strangely lacking in source material. Except for a few scattered accounts found in the Bible concerning the return from Babylonia, little information is available about Jewish life under Persian rule. Even the story of Purim, which describes an episode of Jewish life in the Persian city of Shushan, is not authenticated. It is claimed that the Book of Ruth, the Book of Job, and the Book of Chronicles were written during this period.

538–529—CYRUS conquered Belshazzar and ended the power of Babylonia. He permitted the return of the first group of exiles to Palestine, now to be known as Judea.

520–516—ZERUBBABEL was appointed governor at Jerusalem by Darius, King of Persia. The rebuilding of the Temple was completed under him.

485–465—King XERXES is said to be the King AHASUERUS who saved the Jews of Shushan from extermination by Haman. The story is related in the

Book of Esther and is commemorated by the holiday called "Purim." Some historians place this in the reign of Artaxerxes III (359–336).

459–EZRA, called "The Scribe," led the second return of exiles to Jerusalem. He assembled the people and instructed them in the Law of Moses. To him are credited the beginning of the Knesseth HaGadolah, The Great Assembly, and the institution of the synagogue.

444–NEHEMIAH was named governor of Judea after he led a third group of exiles back to Palestine. In cooperation with Ezra he instituted many reforms. The Temple was rededicated.

499—The SAMARITANS who had refused to approve the building of the Second Temple in Jerusalem, built their own Temple on Mount Gerizim. To this day there exists a small number of this sect.

338—Judea was made a tributary nation to Persia.

336–323—ALEXANDER THE GREAT appeared on the scene of history as a world conqueror.

335–331—The defeat of DARIUS III by Alexander ended Persian power and put Jewish life under Greek influence.

THE GREEK PERIOD
331–165 BCE

With the conquest of Palestine by Alexander the Great in 331 BCE, there began a new era in Jewish history, in which the Jewish people were strongly influenced by Hellenism or Greek culture. Many Jews adopted Greek names, dress, and manners. There was considerable assimilation resulting in divisive political activity.

Within the household of Judea there was a struggle for power. The central authority of the Priesthood was undermined by those who resorted to bribery and intrigue in order to win favor with the Greek rulers.

Hellenism and Chassidism

In opposition to the Hellenists, who sought assimilation with their Greek neighbors, there arose a group called *Chassidim* meaning *"Pious Ones."* These people were extremists, interpreting Jewish law in its strictest sense, without compromise.

From these two groups, the Hellenists and the Chassidic Jews, two major parties developed known as the Sadducees and the Pharisees.

331—Palestine came under the domination and influence of Greece.

323—Alexander died and his empire was divided among his generals:
Seleucus was given Syria and Eastern Asia.
Ptolemy ruled Egypt.
Antigonus (Lysimachus) took over North Asia Minor.
Cassander ruled over Greece.

Palestine, situated between Syria and Egypt, was claimed by the rulers of both countries. At first, it was controlled by Egypt but in 198 BCE Antiochus Epiphanes of Syria took it and held it until 164 BCE.

c.333—SIMON THE JUST. He was a High Priest and the last member of the Great Assembly, founded by Ezra the Scribe. He was the recognised spiritual and secular head of the Jewish people. The office was hereditary.

c.250—The BIBLE was translated into Greek. Its Greek name, SEPTUAGINT, means "Seventy," so called because of a legend that seventy Jewish scholars were invited to come to Egypt where they made identical translations of the Bible.

c.209—The book SONG OF SONGS, which is ascribed to Solomon, is considered one of the most beautiful of love poems.

MACCABEAN OR HASMONEAN PERIOD
168–37 BCE

Antiochus Epiphanes, eighth King in the Seleucid line, sought to impose Hellenistic religion and culture upon the Jews of Palestine. His severely oppressive measures led to revolt and the Jewish people obtained a short period of independence from Syria under Maccabean or Hasmonean rule.

This episode in Jewish history, which is commemorated by the observance of the Chanukah holiday, is recorded in the Apocryphal "Books of the Maccabees."

175—The Jewish struggle against Syrian-Greek oppression began.

168—Jerusalem taken by Antiochus and the Temple desecrated.

168–165—The Jews of Palestine revolted against the Syrians. Despite their small numbers they won major battles.

165—Under the leadership of Judah Maccabeus and his brothers, the Syrians were driven out of Jerusalem and the Temple was rededicated. Complete independence of the country was not achieved until the year 142.

161—Judah Maccabee, High Priest, killed in battle.

162—A Temple for Jewish worship, known as the Onias Temple, was built in Egypt.

143–135—Simon, brother of Judah, became religious and civil leader of Judea. Under him complete independence was regained after 600 years of foreign rule.

BEGINNINGS OF THE SANHEDRIN

When Ezra (444 BCE) established the institution of the *"Men of the Great Assembly,"* he laid the foundation for Jewish study and learning that was to continue throughout the centuries of Jewish history.

After the death of Simon the Just, individuals rose to prominence as rabbis and scholars. These men became leaders and teachers in the Pharisaic movement and their influence continued to the end of Herod's rule. They served in pairs and, accordingly, were called ZUGOTH— זוגות —which means PAIRS. Heading the list at this time of Judah's independence were YOSE BEN YOEZER and YOSE BEN YOCHANAN. These men presided over the academy of learning as NASI (Prince or President of the Sanhedrin) and AB BETH DIN (Father of the House of Judgment or Vice-President) respectively.

SADDUCEES AND PHARISEES

The Sadducees, deriving their name from TZADOK—צדק—meaning RIGHTEOUS, represented the priests, the nobility, and the wealthy landowners. They considered themselves the aristocracy of the land. They were used by occupying powers for the collection of taxes. Through their connections they exercised important controls over the Jewish community.

While the Sadducees were the strong assimilationists of their time, they were nonetheless loyal to the Mosaic law. They refused, however, to abide by the interpretations of the rabbis and scribes and observed the law of Moses in the strict sense of the word instead.

The word Pharisee comes from the Hebrew PARASHIM—פרשים—which has two meanings, SEPARATISTS and LAW EXPOUNDERS. This group represented the masses of the common people. Their leaders were the rabbis and scribes who interpreted the Law of Moses more in accordance with tradition and reason. In their opposition to assimilationist Hellenism, they emphasized the difference of the Jew by virtue of his religion, study, and service to God.

The conflict between the Pharisees and Sadducees for power and control continued to divide the people of Judea until the fall of the Temple in the year 70 CE.

135–106—JOHN HYRCANUS I, High Priest and King of Judea. He conquered Edom and Samaria and forced the inhabitants to adopt Judaism. In the struggle between the Pharisees and Sadducees he favored the former, but at the close of his life he gave support to the Sadducees. During his reign lived JOSHUA BEN PERACHYAH and NITTAI the ARBELITE, the second pair of scholars to head the academy.

104–79 — ALEXANDER JANNAEUS. During his reign, a rebellion broke out against his oppressive rule, which resulted in the death of many of the people. In this period the Zugoth were JUDAH BEN TABBAI and SIMEON BEN SHATACH.

78–69—SALOME ALEXANDRA, wife of Jannaeus. She became the second woman (Athaliah was the first) to reign as queen. Her favor was turned to the Pharisees, whose leader was Simeon ben Shatach, her brother.

69–63—HYRCANUS II and ARISTOBULUS II. These brothers fought for the throne left by their mother, Salome. Civil war resulted and each sought Roman intercession. As a result, Judah became a tributary state of Rome after 79 years of independence.

Palestine Under Rome
63 BCE—425 CE

63–43—ANTIPATER the Idumean, was appointed by Pompey to be the first foreign ruler over Judea, thus breaking the line of hereditary succession of the Hasmoneans. The Idumeans had been among those forcibly converted to Judaism under Hyrcanus I.

During this period there arose a party called the ZEALOTS, guerrilla fighters who swore destruction and death to the Romans. The Zealots were a nationalistic, militant group stemming from the Pharisees. After the fall of the Temple (70 CE) they disappeared as a party.

Jewish learning during these troubled times was carried on by the pair of scholars, SHEMAYAH and ABTALYON.

Roman Rulers

106–48 BCE	...	Pompey
46–44	...	Julius Caesar
31–14	...	Augustus
14–37 CE	...	Tiberius
37–41	...	Caligula
41–54	...	Claudius
54–68	...	Nero
68–69	...	Galba
69	...	Otho and Vitellius
69–79	...	Vespasian
79–81	...	Titus
81–96	...	Domitian
98–117	...	Trajan

THE HERODIAN DYNASTY
37 BCE–70 CE

37 BCE–4 BCE—HEROD, son of Antipater, was known as "The Great" because of his excessive cruelty and tyranny. He tried to make the people forget his non-Jewish descent by rebuilding the Temple. Upon his death the Kingdom of Judea was divided among his three sons.

4 BCE–6 CE—ARCHELAUS, appointed Ethnarch of Judea, Samaria, and Idumea.

4 BCE – 37 CE—HEROD ANTIPAS became Tetrarch of Petrea and Galilee. He built the city of Tiberias.

37–44—HEROD PHILLIP became Tetrarch of the northern provinces. Built the city of Caesarea.

37–44—AGRIPPA I made ruler of Judea by Emperor Claudius.

44–48—HEROD II

49–70—AGRIPPA II. Last ruler of the Jewish people. The revolt against Rome took place during his reign. Judea was besieged by Vespasian, who was proclaimed Emperor. His son, Titus, completed the conquest in the year 70 CE. The Temple was destroyed and the people sent or taken into exile. AGRIPPA II was allowed to retain his possessions and to live in Rome under the favor of Emperor Titus.

70 CE—End of the Second Jewish Commonwealth.

Under Julius Caesar the land had been divided into five districts governed by ETHNARCHS, a Hellenistic title used by both Greeks and Romans to designate the ruler of a country under their authority, and by TETRARCHS, the title given to Jewish princes under Rome who ruled over a part of the country.

The name PALESTINE now came into use to designate the land known as Judea. Originally, the

Greeks used it to denote the land of the Philistines, but after the fall of the Temple, the Romans imposed it upon Judea.

In general, the policy of the Romans was not to interfere with the religious affairs of the Jewish community. The country, however, was under the military jurisdiction of Roman Procurators, whose powers included capital punishment, the appointment of High Priests and state officials, the collection of various taxes and the keeping of law and order.

Fiscus Judaicus

This Latin phrase means "Jewish Fund." It refers to the annual poll tax levied by Rome in place of the "Half Shekel," which all male Jews over twenty years of age had been required to pay for the support of the Temple. The tax collectors visited each town annually at a fixed time and place, even in foreign countries where Jews lived. This money was converted to the use of the Temple of Jupiter at Rome until the fourth century. It was resumed by the Holy Roman Emperors as the "Opferpfennig."

The Procurators of Judea

6– 9 CE	...	Coponius
9–12	...	Ambivius Marcus
12–15	...	Rufus Annius
15–26	...	Gratus Valerius. He appointed four High Priests in succession.
26–36	...	Pontius Pilate, by whose order Jesus was crucified.
36	...	Marcellus
37–44	...	Marullus
44–48	...	Fadus Cuspius. Beheaded Theudas, a

		self-proclaimed prophet.
48	...	Tiberius Alexander. Son of the Jewish Alabarch of Alexandria.
48–52	...	Gumanus
52–60	...	Felix
60–62	...	Festus
62–64	...	Albinus
64–68	...	Florus Gessius

JEWISH LIFE IN PALESTINE

The religious life of the Jewish people underwent little change during this period. It centered around the Temple and the synagogues that existed in the country.

The Torah was still the text book and the authority for Jewish life. To its regular reading in the synagogue was added selections from the prophets, called HAFTOROTH.

Hebrew was the Holy tongue, but the language of the street was Aramaic. The Bible was taught in Aramaic and its translation, written next to the Hebrew text, was known as TARGUM. The Greek language was popular among the upper classes, particularly with the members of the Sadducee Party. During this period were written the Greek works known as the APOCRYPHA. The more important of these books are the Maccabees, Ezra III, Tobias, Judith, Sirach, Jeremiah's Letters and Additions to Daniel and Esther.

Jewish learning was carried on by the rabbis and scribes, who functioned in the SANHEDRIN as a rabbinical body. This assembly of scholars had its origin in THE MEN OF THE GREAT ASSEMBLY, which began during the time of Ezra the Scribe (444 BCE). The head of the Sanhedrin was called PATRIARCH or NASI meaning "Prince." The office of the Patriarch was often hereditary, but learning and scholarship were the chief factors in determining the appointments.

The Patriarchate

70–80	...	Jochanan ben Zakkai (Zaccai)
80–110	...	Gamaliel II
110–136	...	Simeon ben Gamaliel II
136–217	...	Judah HaNasi ben Simeon
225–255	...	Judah II ben Gamaliel
255–275	...	Gamaliel IV ben Judah
275–320	...	Judah III ben Gamaliel
320–365	...	Hillel II ben Judah
365–385	...	Gamaliel V ben Judah
385–400	...	Judah IV ben Gamaliel
400–425	...	Gamaliel VI ben Judah

End of Patriarchate

The Jewish inhabitants who remained in Palestine after the fall of the Temple, were now considered only a religious community. Yochanan ben Zakkai was their recognized leader. He convened the Sanhedrin at Jamnai and reorganized the religious life of the people, substituting the synagogue and the study of Torah for the worship of the Temple and its sacrifices.

The Sanhedrin was composed of seventy-one scholars chosen on the basis of moral and intellectual qualities. Money lenders, kings, young men, and unmarried men were ineligible. It was the privilege of the Nasi to bestow "Semicha," "Ordination," upon members elected to the Sanhedrin.

The men of the Sanhedrin became responsible for the canonization of the Bible in the form in which it is used today. They engaged in the study of Halachah and Haggadah, the legal and narrative interpretation of Jewish law.

Personalities

HILLEL, one of Israel's outstanding rabbis. He is said to have been the instructor of Jesus. Among his many famous sayings is that of the golden rule : "Do not unto others as you would not have others do unto you."

JOSEPHUS, also known as Flavius Josephus. He was in command of a fortress during the Roman conquest of Judea and surrendered to the Romans. Vespasian conferred Roman citizenship upon him. In Rome he wrote the following historical books : *The Jewish Wars, The Antiquities of the Jews,* and *Defense Against Apion,* which are the only sources for details concerning these times.

PHILO (First century.) This Bible interpreter and philosopher founded the Jewish-Alexandrian system of philosophy. He was also a spokesman for his people.

THE MISHNAH

The result of the literary labors of the scholars of this period was a literature known as the MISHNAH —משנה—which means TO TEACH BY REPETITION. These students of the Torah received the name TANNAIM —תנאים —TEACHERS or EXPOUNDERS of the Law. They functioned until about the year 220, when the Mishnah was put into written form under Judah HaNasi. Following are the more important Tannaim who were active in this period.

YOCHANAN ben ZAKKAI (70–80)

He was a disciple of Hillel. After the fall of the Temple he established the seat of Jewish learning at Jamnai or Jabneh, as it is sometimes called.

GAMALIEL II (80–110)

This Patriarch introduced the prayers for the Shemoneh Esreh, Eighteen Benedictions, and its thrice-daily recitation. He was responsible for the custom of simple and inexpensive funerals.

ELIEZER ben HYRCANUS (first century)

He was a contemporary of Zaccai and founded an academy at Lyddia.

JOSHUA ben CHANANIAH (95–131)

He represented the Jewish people before the Roman authorities during the reigns of Trajan and Hadrian. He was Ab Beth Din to Gamaliel II's Nasi.

ISHMAEL ben ELISHA (117–138)

He was a contemporary of Akiba and is said to be the author of MECHILTA, a commentary on the Book of Exodus. He was one of the ten martyrs killed by the Romans.

AKIBA ben JOSEPH (95–135)

This man rose from obscurity and poverty to become the foremost scholar in the land. He established principles and methods for the study of the Bible and laid the foundation for the compilation of the Mishnah. He supported BAR COCHBA in the revolt against Rome (135) and was among ten prominent rabbis to die a martyr's death.

RABBI MEIR (135)

He was a disciple of Akiba, and as "Chacham," wise in Jewish law, he was next in authority to the president of the Sanhedrin. He was noted for his keen wit and ability as a raconteur.

SIMEON ben YOCHAI (second century)

He was a disciple of Akiba. To him is ascribed the authorship of *Sifra,* a commentary on the Book of Numbers and Deuteronomy. Tradition has it that he wrote the *Zohar,* a mystical work.

JOSE ben CHALAFTA (135)

He was a pupil of Akiba and author of *Seder Olom,* the first Jewish history from Creation to the time of Alexander the Great, with notes concerning the destruction of the Temple and the revolt of Bar Cochba.

JUDAH ben ILLAI (second century)

He was one of the martyrs during the Roman persecution. To him is ascribed the authorship of *Sifre,* a commentary on the Book of Leviticus.

JUDAH HA-NASI ben SIMON (136–220)

He was known in Jewish history as RABBI. To him is credited the compilation of the Oral Law into a work called the "Mishnah," thus marking the first written form of the traditions of Judaism. Nasi means "Prince." He was also called "Judah Ha-Kodesh," "Judah the Holy One." Tradition holds that the "Written Law" and the "Oral Law" have existed side-by-side since the revelation to Moses at Sinai.

The Written Law, the "Torah," also known as the "Five Books of Moses," was arranged and classified in the following orders in the Mishnah :

Zeraim— זרעים —Seeds
Ritual laws relating to cultivation of the soil, husbandry, etc.

Moed—מועד—Festival-Season
Ritual laws dealing with festivals, feasts, and holiday observances.

Nashim— נשים —Women
Ritual laws concerning marriage, divorce, and domestic relations.

Nezikin— נזיקין —Damages
Laws relating to civil and criminal matters and rights of persons.

Kodashim—קדשים—Holy Things
Laws concerning clean and unclean things; Temple services and sacrifices; holiness.

Tohoroth—טהרות—Purity
Ritual laws of purity and defilement, and personal hygiene.

THE FORMATION OF THE TALMUD

In the centuries that followed the death of Judah HaNasi a number of prominent schools of learning began to flourish in Babylonia. Leading scholars left Palestine to continue their studies in Babylonia. The seat of Jewish authority, however, remained in the Holy Land. The rabbis and scholars of both countries carried on the work of expounding the laws of the Bible and Mishnah. These men received the title AMORAIM—אמרים—meaning INTERPRETERS.

The Gemara. For three centuries the scholars concentrated upon analyzing the Mishnah. They produced an extensive literature called the GEMARA—גמרא, the purpose of which was to throw more light and understanding on the decisions of the Tannaim. The word "Gemara" means "completion."

The Palestinian Talmud. The Mishnah and the Gemara were combined into the TALMUD—תלמוד —which means TEACHING. The exact date of its compilation (about the year 350) is uncertain.

To distinguish this work from a similar one in Babylonia, it is called "Talmud Yerushalmi," the Jerusalem or Palestinian Talmud. This Talmud is not complete, lacking commentaries on the fifth and sixth orders of the Mishnah.

Talmudic schools were also located at Sepphoris, Tiberias, Usha, and Lydda. After the Romans ended the Patriarchate (425), Palestine lost its importance as the center of Jewish life and learning.

Tosephta and Baraitha
The Amoraim were also concerned with the laws not included in the Mishnah. They compiled their interpretation of these laws under the title of TOSEPHTA—תוספתא—which means ADDITIONS or SUPPLEMENTS. The Tosephta followed the same arrangement of orders and subjects as the Mishnah.

The *Baraitha* —ברייתא—consisted of opinions, interpretations, and decisions that were incorporated into the Tosephta.

NOTABLE AMORAIM OF PALESTINE
220–425

CHANINAH bar CHAMA
One of the first Amoraim of

Palestine. He was a strict adherent of tradition.

JOCHANAN bar NAPPACHA

Founder of a school at Tiberias and renowned leader of his time. He maintained that Oral Law was as holy as the written law. He is credited with laying the foundation for the Jerusalem Talmud.

SIMEON ben LAKISH

A leading scholar at the school of Tiberias and a master in the use of logic. He opposed the Nasi for his anti-liberal views.

ELAZAR ben PEDATH

He was called the "Authority of the Holy Land," and succeeded Rabbi Jochanan as head of the academy.

RAV ASSI and RAV AMMI

These two scholars came from Babylonia to study at Tiberias. They became the co-heads of the academy and were known as the "Judges of Palestine." They were advisers to the Patriarch, Judah III.

OSHAIYA RABBA

He was referred to as the "Father of the Mishnah," since he was one of the first commentators on the Mishnah and the compiler of numerous Baraithoth.

CHIYA bar ABBA HA-COHEN

As his name implies, he was a priest. He studied in Palestine and Babylonia and was a renowned interpreter of Halachic law.

SIMLAI bar ABBA

He was a master of Haggadic interpretation and represented the Jews in a debate against the "Minim," Christian-Jews.

HILLEL II

As Nasi, about the year 350, he arranged a fixed calendar for Jewish holidays and observances. This calendar has remained authoritative for all Jewry to this date.

GAMALIEL VI

Last Patriarch in Israel. After his death the office of Nasi was abolished by the Emperor Theodosius II in the year 425.

ROMAN EMPERORS

The early rulers of Rome, with few exceptions, were favorably disposed toward the Jews. Aside from taxes and military control, the Jews of Palestine enjoyed comparative peace until the reign of Hadrian. They were permitted religious autonomy, which meant that they could live in conformity with their tradition.

HADRIAN (117–138)

He imposed repressive measures against the Jews. His severe oppression resulted in a rebellion headed by Bar Cochba and supported by the famous Rabbi Akiba. The rebellion failed and many prominent rabbis suffered martyrdom. Hadrian's revenge was to forbid the Jews to enter Jerusalem, which he renamed "Aelia Capitolina."

CONSTANTINE THE GREAT (306–337)

This Emperor was at first favorable toward the Jews. In the year 312 an edict of toleration was issued giving religious freedom to all people of the Roman empire.

In the year 325 he embraced Christianity, thus making it the official religion of all Rome. Under the influence of the Church fathers, he imposed severe restrictions upon the Jews.

He set up the capital of the Roman Empire in Constantinople, which was the ancient site of the city of Byzantium, which was founded in 658 BCE.

JULIAN (361–363)

Julian is called an "Apostate" by the church fathers because he was favorably disposed to the Jews. He was very friendly with Nasi Hillel II and considered plans to rebuild the Temple at Jerusalem.

THEODOSIUS THE GREAT (379–395)

The principle of toleration for all religions was embodied in his rule. Against the threat of the church he protected the Jews.

Theodosius divided the Roman Empire between his two sons, thus creating an Eastern or Byzantine Empire, with its capital at Constantinople, and a Western Empire, with its capital at Rome.

THEODOSIUS II (408–450)

This ruler of the Byzantine Empire enacted a law known as the "Code of Theodosius." It contained a list of severe and oppressive measures against the Jews, most of which had been practiced in many lands. Jews were forbidden to intermarry with Christians, to own Christian slaves, to build synagogues, and to exercise any kind of authority over non-Jews.

Basically, these laws were intended to make all Jews second-class citizens. The church elaborated on these disabilities, compelling Jews to live in segregated areas, to wear humiliating distinctions in dress, and to attend conversion services.

In the year 425 Theodosius abolished the office of the Patriarchate and ended Jewish autonomy in Palestine. In the same year, Rome was sacked by the Vandals, and the Byzantine Empire became the dominant power in the East.

Nations Over Palestine

UNDER BYZANTINE RULE
425–635

The Byzantine Empire is also known as the Eastern or Greek Empire. Its largest city, Constantinople, the former capital of Turkey, is one of the oldest cities in the world.

When the Vandals destroyed Rome (425) Palestine came under Byzantine rule and suffered almost complete destruction. The Jews hoped to better their lot by joining forces with the Persians against the Romans in 622, but they paid a bitter price when the armies of Roman Emperor Heraclius I prevailed. Although the Emperor granted them amnesty, the hostile Christian clergy persecuted them.

UNDER MOSLEM RULE
638–1098

The Moslem victory over Byzantium resulted in the fall of Jerusalem in 637. During the rule of the Mohammedans, the Jews were treated well and permitted to retain their religious autonomy, although they had to pay heavy taxes. The city of Jerusalem, which had been barred to them after the Bar Cochba rebellion (135), was again opened.

Literary activity flourished throughout the Islamic provinces and in Palestine. The rabbis and scholars reached out into new fields of Bible study and interpretation.

Midrash—Poetry—Cabala

During this period of Moslem rule, scholars concentrated on the study of the non-legal portions of the Bible, the Haggadah. They created the Midrash, which sought to amplify the Bible text through stories about the ethical and moral conduct of man.

The prayer service of the synagogue was augmented by "Piyutim," poetry, utilizing Scriptural quotations expressing adoration for God. Among the first scholars to write poetry in Palestine were Jannai and Eleazar HaKalir. In the year 1140 Judah HaLevi, the gifted poet of Spain, came to Palestine to make his home.

The literature of Cabala dealt with mystical interpretations of the Bible. Around it developed a religious cult that influenced the Jewish people for many centuries.

In addition to the above literature, the renewed study of the Bible, which followed the rise of the Karaite movement, led to the standardization of the Bible text, its vocalization, and its accents for cantorial singing. This fixing of the Bible text is called "Masorah," meaning "Tradition."

Palestine Under the Crusades (1096–1291)

With the endorsement of Pope Urban II, French and Norman nobles embarked upon a holy Christian war known as the "Crusades" or "Followers of the Cross." These soldiers were recruited from the religiously inspired as well as misfits and malcontents, with the avowed purpose of ridding the Holy Land of Moslem infidels. The Jews were the innocent victims of these crusading hordes. Some escaped to neighboring countries. Those that remained were killed or forced into baptism. When Jerusalem fell in 1098, the Jewish population of Palestine was reduced to about fifteen hundred souls.

The rule of the Crusaders lasted but a few years. In 1187 they were defeated by the Moslems under Saladin, who welcomed the return of the Jews. Jewish life was insecure and the people suffered from the many attacks of repeated invasions of Christians, Mongols, and Mohammedans.

For the next three centuries the fate of the Jew in Palestine was subject to the successive Moslem dynasties of the Omayads, the Abassids, the Fatimids, and the Seljuks. The results were the extreme impoverishment of the Jews and the reduction of their population.

Personalities and Events

The plight of Palestine Jewry became the concern of the rabbis and scholars of the Diaspora. Some decided to migrate to the Holy Land with the hope of putting new life into the dying communities. Others came in large numbers to settle there, as did three hundred rabbis from England and France in the year 1210.

NACHMANIDES (1194–1270)
This famous scholar of Spain came to Jerusalem at the age of 70 to reorganize the Jewish community. He also encouraged Jewish learning at Acre and Safed.

JECHIEL OF PARIS (1200–1286)
He was a renowned teacher and chief rabbi of Paris. He came to Palestine and settled at Haifa.

HAFARHI (1235)

Physician and scholar of France. In Palestine he wrote the first Hebrew geography of the Holy Land.

OBADIAH OF BERTINORA (c.1450–c.1510)

He came to Palestine from Italy and was responsible for the reorganization of the Jewish community in Jerusalem.

UNDER TURKISH RULE
1517–1917

In the year 1517 Palestine was conquered by the Ottoman Turks. They ruled almost uninterruptedly for four hundred years, until Palestine was taken by the British in World War I.

Jewish life under Turkish rule was marked by economic insecurity and political disorder. Though comparative peace prevailed, Jewish life was quite dormant. To escape the harsh realities of life the people delved more and more into the study of Cabala.

Outside of Palestine, however, Jewish eyes turned to the land of the Bible. The oppressed and persecuted of Europe yearned for Palestine as a haven of refuge and the fulfillment of God's promise. The expulsion of the Jews from Spain (1492) brought many Sephardim to Palestine. The Chmielnicki pogroms in the Ukraine (1648) started migrations of refugees to the Holy Land. Messianic movements and would-be messiahs were responsible for large-scale pilgrimages to Jerusalem. The Chassidim of Poland and Russia (1750) were among the new settlers in Palestine. And later, their opponents, the Mithnagdim, also migrated to the Holy Land.

PERSONALITIES AND EVENTS

ISAAC HA-KOHEN SHOLAL (d. 1525)

He was the chief rabbi in Egypt and left for Palestine to foster Jewish study at Jerusalem. He solicited support of Jews in the Diaspora.

JACOB BERAB (1474–1546)

A Spanish refugee who settled in Safed. He failed in his attempt to reestablish the Sanhedrin, but succeeded in reinstating the rite of Semicha or Ordination.

LEVI ben CHABIB (c. 1480–1545)

As a leader of the Jerusalem community, he opposed Jacob Berab because of his messianic speculations. His father, JACOB ibn HABIB was the author of EN YAACOB—עין יעקב, *The Well of Jacob.*

JOSEPH KARO (1488–1575)

Author of the famous codification of Jewish law known as the SHULCHAN ARUCH—שלחן ערוך, *The Prepared Table,* which became the authority for observance and tradition in Jewish life. It was printed in the year 1564.

ISAAC LURIA (1534–1572)

He is known as ARI and as the founder of the mystical movement called Cabala. He was the first to attempt to systematize the Zohar, the classic book on Jewish mysticism. He taught the doctrine of transmigration of souls and proclaimed himself a messiah.

CHAYIM VITAL CALABRESE (1543–1620)

Most renowned disciple of Luria. Claimed to possess mystical powers. He wrote ETZ CHAYIM—עץ חיים, *The Tree of Life,* in which he presented the teachings of Luria.

ISAIAH HOROWITZ (c.1555–1625)

Former chief Rabbi of Prague. He was imprisoned and held for ransom. He wrote *Sh'nay Luchoth Ha-brith* — שני לחות הברית, *The Two Tablets of the Covenant.*

MOSES CORDOVERO (1533–1570)

Wrote a compendium on Cabala known as *Pardes Rimmonim*— פרדס רמנים, *The Garden of Pomegranates.*

SOLOMON ALKABETZ (c. 1050–1584)

Cabalist and poet. Wrote LECHA DODI—לכה דודי, "Come my Friend," a mystic song of welcome to the Sabbath, which is still used in the liturgy of the Sabbath eve.

JOSEPH NASI (1520–1579)

He was made Duke of Naxos by the ruler of Turkey. He attempted to settle Jews in Tiberias.

SABBATAI ZEVI (1625–1676)

Israel's famous claimant to messiahship. He came to Jerusalem to proclaim his holy office. He failed his followers by converting to Mohammedism.

NATHAN GHAZZATI (1643–1680)

This man from Gaza was an influential follower of Shabbatai Zevi. He claimed to be the prophet Elijah, who was to announce the coming of the Messiah.

MOSES CHAYIM LUZZATTO (1707–1747)

Poet and Cabalist. He came to Safed to follow the teachings of Luria. Wrote *Mesillath Yesharim*—מסלת ישרים, *The Path of the Upright.*

Migrations and Zionism

The early Jewish communities that existed in Palestine during this period depended upon aid from their co-religionists in the Diaspora. The Crusades had left Palestine barren and desolate. Most of those who came to the Holy Land, Jews or Christians, were pilgrims. The Christians came to build churches and monasteries. The Jews came to pray and to hope for the fulfillment of the Messianic promise of restoration, and to die.

After 1799, Napoleon conquered and controlled the coastal plain. Jewish hopes rose, only to fall with this episode of history. In 1832 Palestine reverted to Egypt, which was under Turkish control. During this period an earthquake destroyed the city of Safed and some two thousand Jews lost their lives.

Among the Jews of Europe, the determination grew to go to Palestine despite government restrictions and bans. Anti-Semitic persecutions and pogroms, particularly in Russia and Poland, created the climate for a "Back to Palestine" movement that also had its counterparts in other countries.

ZIONISM

Zion is the Biblical and poetic name for Palestine, and Zionism is the modern name applied to the movement to fulfill the desire of the Jewish people in exile to return to Palestine.

The primacy of Palestine as the homeland of the Jews was transmitted from generation to generation through its literature, through the messianic spell of redemption, through abortive efforts to resettle the land, through the despair and suffering brought about by persecution, the Inquisition, the Crusades, and anti-Semitism in its most virulent forms. In the never-ceasing prayer of the Jew could be heard the plaintive r e f r a i n, B'SHANAH HABAH B'RUSHALAYIM בשנה הבאה בירושלים —NEXT YEAR, IN JERUSALEM.

EARLY CULTURAL THEORISTS

RABBI ZVI HIRSCH KALISCHER
(1795–1870)

During the 19th century, owing in large part to the prevailing anti-Semitism and persecution of the Jews, the idea of a rebirth of Jewish life and nationhood first developed along philosophical lines. It did not assume an urgent political direction until 1897 when Theodor Herzl called the World Zionist Congress into being. Before that time, in Germany, Rabbi Zvi Hirsch Kalischer advanced religious justification for the restoration of Palestine as not inconsistent with the messianic redemption. In his pamphlet *Derishat Tzion*—דרישת ציון —*Demands of Zion* (1862), he said that the Jews should not wait for a Messiah but should start going to Palestine as tillers of the soil to rebuild the land.

His idea of migrating to Palestine caught the interest of many people and resulted in the first ALIYAH — עליה—GOING UP to colonize the land. It was further accentuated by the Russian persecutions of the 1880's, which caused about 25,000 Jews to leave for Palestine.

MOSES HESS (1812–1875)

At about the same time, also in Germany, Moses Hess, who had worked with Karl Marx, became a leading pioneer Socialist theoretist

of Zionism. Shocked by the Damascus "Blood Libel," he wrote *Rome and Jerusalem* (1862) in which he expressed the idea of the fusion of Zionism and social idealism which was later to develop into the labor Zionist movement. He maintained that a national movement to colonize Palestine would lead to a normal life for the Jews and would create new social values for humanity. He anticipated Herzl when he suggested that a congress be convened to further this aim.

LEO PINSKER (1821–1891)

Born in Poland while it was under Russian domination, Pinsker became one of the fore-runners of political Zionism. At first he advocated assimilation as the solution to the problems faced by Russian Jewry, but the anti-Jewish riots of 1881 turned his attention to the widespread disease of anti-Semitism, which he called "Demon-apathy."

In 1882, he wrote his famous *Auto-Emancipation,* in which he argued that the salvation of the Jewish people was to be found in their self-emancipation in their historic homeland, Palestine. He joined the CHIBBAT TZION—חבת ציון —LOVE OF ZION, a movement that spread throughout E a s t Europe. Later, he became one of the founders of CHOVEVEI TZION— חבבי ציון —LOVERS OF ZION, an organization to further the settlement of Jews in agricultural colonies in Palestine.

ACHAD HA-AM *(Asher Ginsberg)*
(1856–1927)

One of the leading Jewish philosophers of the time, Achad Ha-am criticized the activities of the Chovevei Tzion and objected to their political Zionism. He advocated Cultural Zionism because he insisted that the Hebrew cultural survival and development of the Jewish people were most essential and that the first thing to be secured was a strong center in Palestine, which would cause a Jewish revival in communities all over the world.

In his essay, "Lo Zeh Ha-Derech"— לא זה הדרך —"This Is Not The Way" (1889), he advanced the idea that the Jewish state was the end and not the beginning of Jewish national creativeness. Many secular leaders found expression for their cultural Zionism in the B'nai Moshe Society which he founded in 1889. He participated in the World Zionist Congress and in the negotiations leading to the Balfour Declaration.

THEODOR HERZL
(1860–1904)

Zionism as a political movement became galvanized when Theodor Herzl (Benjamin Zeev), the Hungarian-born Paris correspondent for the Vienne Neue Freie Presse, became interested in the Jewish problem. His tendencies were assimilationist until he reported the Dreyfus trial, after which he wrote *Der Judenstaat, The Jewish State,* in 1895. He declared that assimilation for the Jewish people was an impractical solution to their problem and that only the founding of a Jewish state by international agreement would enable them to keep their social and economic position from further deterioration.

The First Zionist Congress

Favoring Palestine as the home-

land for the Jews, Herzl rallied the Hibbat Zion followers, the youth, and many influential men to his support. Despite the opposition of assimilated Jews as well as orthodox, he set out to influence European statesmen in favor of his cause.

In August of 1897, he convened the first Zionist Congress in Basle, Switzerland, out of which grew the World Zionist Organization, attended by 204 delegates from many countries. They adopted what came to be known as the "Basle Program." Its aim was to create a publicly recognized and legally secured home in Palestine. Its principles were :

1. To promote, through effective means, the settlement of Palestine by Jewish agriculturalists, artisans, and tradesmen.

2. To organize and unify the whole Jewish people by means of local and general institutions suitable for the purpose.

3. To strengthen and augment Jewish self-consciousness in the individual and in the community.

4. To take proper preliminary steps toward securing the concurrence of the powers, insofar as their assent may be necessary for the attainment of the Zionist goal.

The World Zionist Congress

This body grew out of the first Zionist Congress convened by Herzl in 1897. It met annually for four years, developed a shekel-paying membership, and outlined a campaign to win adherents to the cause of Zionism. It created the following organizations :

The Jewish Colonial Trust (1899)

A financial institution for the purpose of raising capital and making investments. In 1934 it was taken over by the Anglo-Palestine Bank to become a holding company.

Keren Kayemeth LeYisroel —קרן קימת לישראל— THE JEWISH NATIONAL FUND (1901)

This organization was started by Professor Hermann Schapira of Heidelberg as a land-purchasing agency. Its purpose was to acquire land in Palestine to be held in perpetual trust for the Jewish people. One of its chief functions today is to raise money for the reforestation of Israel.

Herzl's Dream

Among his first efforts was an unsuccessful attempt to persuade the Sultan of Turkey, who controlled Palestine, to legalize free mass Jewish immigration. He also failed to interest heads of other governments to bring pressure to bear upon the Sultan.

In 1903, after the Kishinev massacres in Russia, the British Colonial Office offered Uganda in East Africa as a temporary solution. It was opposed at the sixth Zionist Congress in Basle by a group headed by Ussishkin, Tschlenow, and Achad Ha-am. In order to prevent a split in the World Zionist Organization, Herzl had to reaffirm the primacy of Palestine as a Jewish homeland.

But the controversy affected his heart, already weakened by his strenuous intercessions, and he died in 1904. His remains have been brought from Vienna to Jerusalem, where they rest on Har Herzl (Mt. Herzl). Within eight years he had created a dynamic Zionist movement and the institutions to carry on its activities. He died in the firm belief that Palestine would become a reality for the Jewish people.

Max Nordau (1849–1923)

One of the many influential men who rallied to Herzl's support was Max Nordau (Sudfield). He was Hungarian by birth, practiced medicine in Paris, and achieved a reputation as an author. He drifted from Judaism, but, largely because of Herzl's magnetic personality, he became one of the first Zionists, addressing the opening session of the Zionist Congress in 1897. He participated in all the meetings until 1911, when he maintained that the World Zionist Organization had abandoned Herzl's ideas. He remained with the organization as adviser to David Wolffsohn (1856–1914), who took over the presidency of the Zionist Organization when Herzl died. Wolffsohn was succeeded by Otto Warburg (1859–1938), a leader of the Practical Zionist faction, who retained his office until 1920.

Nahum Sokolow (1860–1936)

This Polish-born Hebrew journalist and editor of a Hebrew weekly "HaOlom" came into the movement because of the influence of Herzl. He was general secretary of the World Zionist Organization from 1905 to 1910, traveling extensively on its behalf. He resigned because he supported the *practical* and not the *political* Zionists. He was active in the negotiations leading to the Balfour Declaration and from 1921 to 1931 was chairman of the Zionist Executive Committee. He succeeded Chaim Weizmann as president of the World Zionist Organization and the Jewish Agency.

Chaim Weizmann (1874–1952)

Although Polish-born, he pursued his chemical studies at German and Swiss universities before assuming a post in biological chemistry at Manchester, England, in 1904. He held this position until 1916, when he became director of the British Admiralty Chemical Laboratories. Deeply influenced by the HIBBAT TZION and by the Haskalah movement, he became associated early with Herzl through the group led by Ussishkin and the democratic faction.

Weizmann was more a cultural than a political Zionist, proposing the foundation of a Hebrew University as early as 1902. In 1907 he propounded what he called "synthetic" Zionism—a combination of political colonization and cultural activity. He moved into leadership during World War I and was largely responsible for the Balfour Declaration, its implementation through the San Remo Conference, and the financing of colonization through the "Keren Ha-Yesod," the "Foundation Fund" established by the Zionist Organization in 1921.

Weizmann was chairman of the Jewish Agency in 1929, when it included non-Zionists, and was the president of the World Zionist Organization from 1935 to 1946, when he resigned because of disillusionment by the refusal of the British government to honor its

pledges. He retired to Rehobot in Palestine to work at the Weizmann Institute, which he helped to form. In spite of failing health he assumed the presidency of the new state of Israel in 1948. He died in 1952 and his burial plot at Rehobot is a national shrine.

The Jewish Territorial Organization

Following Herzl's death, dissident groups seceded from the World Zionist Organization. Israel Zangwill (1864–1926) and those who favored the Uganda project, along with the Socialist Zionist group led by Nachman Syrkin (1867–1924), formed the Jewish Territorial Organization. An investigating commission was sent to Uganda and its findings were so negative and unfavorable that the Uganda project was eliminated completely. The commission reaffirmed the original program of promoting Jewish culture and economic penetration through land purchase and colonization of Palestine.

The Second Aliyah (1905–1913)

This migration to Palestine started during the pogroms in Tsarist Russia. Most of the people were young workers, liberals, and labor Zionist. They remained true to their philosophy in their approach to the rebuilding of their homeland. An office was established in Jaffa, under Arthur Ruppin (1876–1942), to help settle the newcomers. He was a German Zionist leader, an economist and sociologist. The Palestine Development Company and a number of small settlement companies were founded to purchase and develop the land.

By World War I there were 43 colonies in Palestine.

The Second Aliyah is known chiefly for two things. First was its cultural achievement. Hebrew gained ground as the vernacular and as the language of instruction, mainly through the efforts of Eliezer ben Yehuda (1858–1922). After his arrival in 1903 he established the VA-AD HA-LASHON, ועד הלשון —COUNCIL FOR THE DEVELOPMENT OF HEBREW, which was a language academy to make Hebrew the living language of Palestine. To further this project he wrote a Hebrew dictionary. In recognition of his pioneering work, two principal streets, one in Jerusalem and one in Tel Aviv, are named after him.

The second achievement was the development of the collective colony on a cooperative pattern. The first colony was started at Degania on the Sea of Galilee in 1909 on Jewish National Fund land. It was called a KEVUTZAH— קבוצה — literally, GATHERING, in which land, building, and all basic property is owned jointly. By 1914 a number of these were in operation, owing in large part to the efforts of Aharon David Gordon (1856–1922), who came from Russia in 1904. He exerted a great influence upon the Palestine labor movement with his theory that socialism had to merge with nationalism in order to have a viable society.

During this period, the World Zionist Organization, with headquarters in Cologne, was meeting biennially with not too many measurable achievements to its credit. The Jewish Territorial Organization, with its avowed purpose of settling Jews in other parts of the world, had the support of the wealthy Baron de Hirsch, but not the backing of the masses. It did,

however, manage to settle a number of Jews in Argentina and Brazil. Also, during this period, Hadassah, the Women's Zionist Organization of America, was started in 1912 by Henrietta Szold. They pioneered a health and welfare program for Palestine, and were the founders and builders of the Hadassah hospital in Jerusalem.

The Balfour Declaration

The 11th Congress in Vienna was the last one held before World War I, which divided the Zionists into three camps, one in each of the two belligerent areas and one in the neutral states, with an international office in Copenhagen. The Central European group worked at getting pledges from Turkey, but in England, Nahum Sokolow, Jehiel Tschlenow, Chaim Weizmann, and Ahad Ha-am formed a de facto executive committee that carried on correspondence and negotiations with the British government. Here the atmosphere seemed favorable for reasons that served British policy, and after considerable negotiations, the Balfour Declaration was issued. It came in the form of a letter to Lord Rothschild on November 2, 1917, from the Secretary for Foreign Affairs, Arthur James Balfour, and said :

His Majesty's government view with favour the establishment in Palestine of a national home for the Jewish people and will use their best endeavors to facilitate the achievement of this object, it being clearly understood that nothing shall be done which may prejudice the civil and religious rights of existing non-Jewish communities in Palestine, or the rights and political status enjoyed by Jews in any other country.

The Balfour Declaration was a powerful incentive to the growth and activity of the Zionist movement. The membership increased five-fold by 1921. There was an intensive program of recruiting and training Chalutzim to go to Palestine, in which all political parties cooperated. Private enterprise in industry and commerce was encouraged.

The period that followed the Balfour Declaration is known as the Third Aliyah (1919–1924). It brought about 35,000 Jews from Russia and neighboring countries. The HISTADRUTH—הסתדרות—FEDER-ATION OF JEWISH LABOR was established, which, in time, became the most influential organization in the country.

Nahum Sokolow secured endorsements of the Balfour Declaration from France and Italy. In the United States, Zionists Julian Mack, Louis D. Brandeis, and Stephen S. Wise obtained agreement from President Wilson. The United States Congress adopted a resolution on June 30, 1922, "favoring the establishment in Palestine of a national home for the Jewish people."

The British Mandate

The world soon learned that there was a wide gap between a statement and its implementation. The British had also made promises to the Arabs, which involved the creation of a number of free Arab states in the area. Great Britain also made a secret agreement with France to divide up the area so as to put most of Palestine under international administration (Sykes-Picot Treaty of March 1916)

On April 24, 1920, at the conference in San Remo, it was decided by the Supreme Council of the principal allied powers that Britain should be given the mandate to carry out the Balfour Declaration. The most important provisions were that a Jewish national home should be established and self-governing institutions be developed; the civil and religious rights of all the inhabitants be safeguarded; a Jewish Agency was to be established to take part in the development of the country; Jewish immigration should be facilitated; English, Arabic, and Hebrew were to be recognized as official languages of Palestine.

In the partitioning of Palestine, the Mandate gave recognition to Transjordan as an independent Arab country. Despite the fact that the Mandate obligated Britain to facilitate immigration, she refused a request to admit 60,000 Jews annually. The Mandate failed to carry out the essential provisions that would benefit the Jews and this policy remained in effect until the creation of the State of Israel in 1948.

The Third Aliyah (1919–24) and Arab Riots

The Third Aliyah, which mushroomed after World War I, saw about 48,000 pioneers come to drain swamps, build roads, and establish new KEVUTZOTH—קבוצות—COLLECTIVES with the aid of the KEREN HA-YESOD—קרן היסד—THE JEWISH FOUNDATION FUND. They also established colonies, partly capitalistic and partly cooperative. HECHALUTZ—החלוץ, an international labor-orientated organization, established HACHSHAROTH—הכשרות—TRAINING CAMPS to prepare CHALU-

TZIM—חלוצים PIONEERS vocationally, culturally, and socially for life in Palestine.

The military government, dominated by Turkish officials and Syrian Christians, was a source of great irritation to the YISHUV—ישוב—THE JEWISH COMMUNITY. It interfered with the functions of Jewish institutions, curtailed local elections, proscribed public use of the Hebrew language, and ordered the disbanding of the Jewish Legion that had helped General Allenby take Palestine from the Turks. Resentment against this unilateral discrimination was so strong that Lord Curzon, the British Foreign Secretary, openly reaffirmed the Balfour Declaration and sought to ease the tensions.

Nonetheless, the hostility of the Arabs, to the Jews in general and the Zionists in particular, led to riots during the Passover in 1920. The government refused to intervene and did not permit the Jews to aid the defenseless. In June of the same year, the Chalutzim at the colony of Tel Hai in northern Palestine were outnumbered and murdered by a large force of Arabs. Their leader, Joseph Trumpeldor, was killed in its defense.

The San Remo conference, which awarded the Mandate to Britain, met during this time. The discredited military regime was replaced by a civil one and Sir Herbert Samuel, a Jew, was sent by Britain to be the first High Commissioner of Palestine. He appointed as General Mufti of Jerusalem a member of a feudal family opposed to Zionism.

The continued hostility of the Arabs resulted in more riots in May of 1921. The Commissioner closed the door to further Jewish immigration. The Haycroft investigating Commission was sent from London and the first of a series of White Papers was issued in 1922 in which Churchill asserted "that the terms of the (Balfour) Declaration do not contemplate that Palestine as a whole should be converted into a national home, but that such a home should be founded in Palestine."

The Jewish homeland was meant to be merely a structure within an Arab land and the Zionist organization should have no part in ruling Palestine. The Zionists were willing to accept this interpretation, but the Arabs rejected it because they claimed that it favored the Jewish homeland too much.

The Jewish Agency

After World War I, the Zionist Organization was represented by the Jewish Agency in accordance with the provisions of the San Remo treaty. Under Article IV of the Mandate, the Agency was empowered to deal with all matters pertaining to Palestine. Its primary purpose was to advance the economic and cultural upbuilding of the country. Its general activities included :

Organization of immigration

Bringing immigrants to Palestine

Settling newcomers on the land

Helping immigrants to become farmers

Aiding cultural projects

Supporting institutions of higher learning

Fostering Hebrew education in the Diaspora

Guiding and assisting Zionist youth groups

Raising funds through voluntary contributions from world Jewry.

Maintaining a political department for representation before the Mandate Committee of the League of Nations, and before the United Nations prior to statehood.

Since its inception, the Jewish Agency was involved with the following matters pertaining to the land of Palestine and Israel.

1929—The Agency agreed to enlarge its scope of activity to include non-Zionist representatives of the principal Jewish communities in the world. The non-Zionists, headed by Louis Marshall (1856–1929), concluded this agreement with Chaim Weizmann, the president of the World Zionist Organization. Weizmann was to serve also as president of the Jewish Agency.

1939—The MacDonald White Paper, which in effect amounted to a nullification of the rights of the Jewish people to re-establish a national homeland, resulted in a statement tantamount to a declaration of war by the Jewish Agency: ". . . . The Jews will never accept the closing against them of the gates of Palestine. . . . Jewish pioneers will defend Jewish immigration, the Jewish home, the Jewish freedom."

1942—The Agency, as the official spokesman for World Jewry, called for the establishment of Palestine as a Jewish commonwealth. In spite of restrictions on immigration and settlement imposed by Great Britain, it initiated the formation of a "Rescue Committee" to aid the victims of Nazism. At the Biltmore Conference in New York the Agency

was voted control of all immigration into Palestine and given complete authority for building up the country.

1944—The British government authorized the Agency to form a Jewish brigade to operate within the framework of the British army.

1945—The Jewish Agency began operation "Aliyah Bet"—bringing in "illegal immigrants" to Palestine.

1946—June 29th became known as "Black Sabbath," because the British government outlawed the Agency, arrested them, and interned its leaders.

1947—The Jewish Agency operated under a policy of restraint in the case of the "Exodus 1947" incident in which 4,500 refugees were not permitted to enter Palestine. Dissident armed groups (Irgun and Stern members) were rejected and proscribed. Instead, the Agency supported the disciplined actions of Haganah.

Violence and tensions were so strong in Palestine that Great Britain was forced to refer the matter to the United Nations. The Jewish Agency became the spokesman for the Jewish people at all the assembly sessions. On November 29, the General Assembly voted in favor of a Jewish state in partitioned Palestine.

1948—On April 22, the Jewish Agency informed the United Nations Organization that Jewish statehood would be proclaimed. On May 5th, Ben Gurion, as the first Prime Minister of the new state, now named Israel, read the proclamation of independence.

1951—The functions of the Jewish Agency after statehood continued, with the approval of the government :

To assume responsibility for Jewish immigration,

To receive and assist new immigrants and settle them,

To care for the children and youth,

To engage in land amelioration and afforestation,

To stimulate Jewish interest in Israel throughout the world, and

To promote cultural and spiritual association of Jews with Israel.

1954—A formal covenant between the government of Israel and the Jewish Agency was signed. This covenant gave recognition to the Agency as representative of World Jewry in relation to the practical functions of Jewish immigration, reception and settlement of immigrants to Israel.

1966—Today the Jewish Agency concentrates on immigration, housing, jobs, and settlement. It is concerned with the regional development of areas for new settlements and with helping small businesses to get started.

Fund-Raising Arms of Zionism

In 1920 the World Zionist Organization created the KEREN HA-YESOD — קרן היסד —FOUNDATION FUND as its financial arm, based on the idea of a fixed obligatory annual tax (shekel tax) to be contributed by every Jew to-

ward the building of Palestine. Until the establishment of the State of Israel, the Keren HaYesod financed all the activities of the Jewish Agency in Palestine. Since then, it has concentrated on financing immigration, settlement, and absorption. Operating under the aegis of the United Jewish Appeal, it is active in over seventy countries.

In 1925, in the United States, the Keren HaYesod pooled fund-raising activities with the KEREN KAYEMETH L'YISROEL — קרן קימת לישראל —THE JEWISH NATIONAL FUND, but four years later they separated and the Keren HaYesod assumed the name of the American Palestine Campaign. In 1930 it joined with the Joint Distribution Committee and became the United Jewish Appeal.

For the next few years there were joint drives with other fund-raising agencies, but since 1939, when it merged with the American Joint Distribution Committee and the National Refugee Service, it has been identified with the United Jewish Appeal. Over the years the United Jewish Appeal has broadened its scope to include local and world-Jewish needs.

Education and Culture

A complete educational network has been built up in Israel from kindergarten to university. Primary education is free and compulsory between the ages of five and fourteen; scientific research has attained high standards and culture abounds in music, the theater, and the arts and letters.

THE HEBREW UNIVERSITY

The Hebrew University was founded in Jerusalem in 1925. It was first proposed by Professor Hermann Schapira at the early Zionist congresses. Land was secured on Mt. Scopus in 1914 and the university was officially dedicated in 1925. Rabbi Judah L. Magnes, an American Reform rabbi, became its first president.

In the war of Independence (1948) Mt. Scopus was cut off by the Arabs and became inaccessible to the Jews. A new campus was started at Givat Ram in the west suburbs of Jerusalem. The Hadassah medical and nursing schools were added to it. The new Hebrew University, the finest of its kind in the Middle East, has been in operation since 1958.

Its scope of education covers Jewish studies, Oriental history, general humanities, and sciences, which include the Einstein Institution of Mathematics and Physics, the Weizmann School of Chemistry, the Department of Botany, Zoology, and Geology, School of Agriculture, and Laboratories of Meteorology and Climatology.

THE HAIFA INSTITUTE OF TECHNOLOGY (TECHNION)

This technical university was founded in 1912 but was not in official operation until 1924. Its campus is located on Mt. Carmel and it is rated as the best engineering college in that part of the world. It also operates a Nautical School. Its growth has been so great that a new campus, "Technion City," is now being built.

WEIZMANN INSTITUTE OF SCIENCE

This school for fundamental and applied research in the exact sciences is an extension of the Daniel Sieff Research Institute, which opened in 1934 under the direction of Chaim Weizmann. It is located at Rehobot and includes the residence and grave of Dr. Weizmann.

BAR-ILAN UNIVERSITY

This religious institution was named for Rabbi Meir Bar-Ilan (Berlin), a noted Mizrachi leader. It is located at Ramat Gan, near Tel Aviv, and provides instruction in Jewish and general subjects.

TEL AVIV UNIVERSITY

This school is operated by the city of Tel Aviv. It offers degrees in Natural Science, Humanities, and Arts. There is a department of Pedagogy and Postgraduate Medical Studies.

PRIMARY AND SECONDARY SCHOOLS

The first modern Jewish school in Palestine was opened in Jerusalem in 1867; in 1870 the Alliance Universelle Israelite established the first Jewish agricultural school. In 1906, the first secondary school, Herzliah, began classes in Tel Aviv.

GENERAL SCHOOLS

These are maintained by the Zionist Organization to create a synthesis between Jewish culture and general subjects.

MIZRACHI SCHOOLS

Emphasis is placed on religious observance and the study of religious works.

PRIVATE SCHOOLS

These are maintained by the Women's International Zionist Organization, the Agudath Israel, the Alliance Universelle Israelite, the Anglo-Jewish Association, a n d others.

PUBLIC SCHOOLS

Operated by the Department of Education of the State of Israel. Primary school is eight years and secondary school is five. Common to all schools in Israel is instruction in Bible and English.

BOOKS AND LITERATURE

According to UNESCO releases, Israel ranks second in the world for the number of titles published in proportion to the population. An annual publication of some two thousand books includes translations of world classics and outstanding contemporary works.

THEATER

There are four repertory companies engaged in the dramatic arts —Habimah, Ohel, the Kameri (Chamber) Theatre and the Haifa Municipal Theatre.

THE DANCE

The Inbal Dance Theatre was founded in 1949 to preserve the folk art of the Yemenite Jews. Another popular group is the Batsheva Dance Company.

THE PRESS

There are 23 morning and two afternoon newspapers, with more than half published in Hebrew. There are about 340 periodicals, including 50 Government publications.

SPORTS

All sports in Israel are amateur. Every four years the Maccabiah Games for Jewish sportsmen are held under the auspices of the Maccabi World Union.

Commissions and White Papers

New Aliyahs (1924–31) from Poland numbered about 82,000. Most of the newcomers lived in the cities, worked in factories and entered the field of merchandising. The country was at comparative peace. Lord Plummer, an elderly conservative military man became High Commissioner in 1925. He was succeeded by Sir John Chancellor in 1928 and from then on the relations between the Jews and the Arabs worsened.

The new Commissioner was highly unsympathetic to Zionism. Tension between the Arabs and Jews mounted because of the strong influence of the Revisionists and the consolidation and successes of Zionist efforts. Rumors and warnings that there would be an Arab uprising in August of 1929 went unheeded by the British government. On the target date, Arabs attacked the Jews throughout the country. Many lives were lost and considerable property was destroyed. Britain delayed action by calling for a review of the entire question of a Jewish homeland.

THE SHAW COMMISSION
(1929)

The investigating Shaw Commission concluded that the Jews were to blame because of the increase in their numbers, their rapid and extensive acquisition of land, and their general prosperity. It was recommended, therefore, that Jewish immigration be drastically curtailed until the "landless Arab" population could be settled. The League of Nations Mandates Commission refused to accept the Shaw report and condemned the Mandatory administration.

THE PASSFIELD WHITE PAPER
(1930)

In 1930, the British government sent Sir John Hope Simpson to head a commission to investigate the economic conditions and potentials in Palestine. The report said that land purchase by Jews should be restricted and immigration cut down. Lord Passfield, the Colonial Secretary, issued a White Paper in October of the same year, accepting the Simpson report in its entirety and saying, "The Jewish National Home is not meant to be the principal feature of the Mandate," as Zionists claim.

Dr. Weizmann, who had always cooperated with the Mandatory power, resigned from the presidency of the World Zionist Organization in protest. Prime Minister Ramsay MacDonald retracted to some extent, and gave some assurance of cooperation that caused Weizmann to return to his office.

THE PEEL COMMISSION
(1937)

The prosperity of Palestine, the purchase of the Huleh swamp district in Upper Galilee, and the immigration of over 130,000 Jews following the rise of Nazism were seized upon by Arab nationalist leaders to instigate attacks of terrorism on outlying villages. Fields and factories were set afire, trees uprooted, buses ambushed, and people killed. The government was aware of this Arab rebellion against the Mandatory, but did little to interfere or stem it.

Strong protests at home and abroad caused Britain to send a Royal Commission, headed by Earl Peel, to investigate the trouble. Its report, issued in July, 1937, blamed the British government for the riots, which could have been halted. It recommended the end of the Mandate and the partitioning of Palestine into three parts: A Jewish state (Galilee, the Emek, and the coast), an Arab state (to be joined to Transjordania), and a permanent mandated territory under Great Britain (a strip from Jerusalem and Bethlehem to the coast).

The British Parliament opposed the report as being unfair to the Jews and a retreat for Britain. The Zionists were divided and the Arabs were against it. The Permanent Mandates Commission did not oppose partition, but felt that the country was not yet ready for independence. It felt, also, that further immigration should be based on the absorptive capacity of the land after March, 1938. It reminded the Arab powers that the Jews had no place but Palestine to which they could go, whereas the Arabs had the entire Near East open to them.

THE WOODHEAD COMMISSION
(1939)

To ease the tensions in Palestine, the British deposed the Grand Mufti, but permitted him to escape to Lebanon. New Arab disorders, however, started again. High Commissioner Wauchope was replaced by Sir Harold MacMichael.

Terrorism and disorder continued and this time it was the Woodhead Commission that was sent to Palestine to investigate the workability of the Partition plan. Again, the report was unfavorable. Prime Minister Chamberlain called a meeting in London in February, 1939, of an Arab delegation that was controlled by the Mufti, and a Jewish delegation with whom the Arabs refused to sit at the conference table. The two delegations had to meet separately, and nothing was accomplished. In March, Colonial Secretary MacDonald presented a plan for an Arab-controlled Palestine in which the Jews would be a permanent minority. This was rejected by both parties.

THE MACDONALD WHITE PAPER
(1939)

In May, 1939, the MacDonald White Paper was issued, stipulating that Jewish immigration would cease after 1944, until which time 75,000 Jews could enter. Land sales were to be prohibited and Palestine would become an independent state within ten years.

The Permanent Mandates Commission of the League of Nations considered it a breach of the Mandate, but Britain proceeded to put it into effect, nevertheless. The first reaction was on the part of the Arabs, who protested because they could not sell land to the Jews. The Zionist reaction created a Jewish resistance movement that caused general unrest and rioting. Before the Mandates Commission could vote on it, World War II engulfed the world.

The Beginnings of Statehood

THE HAGANAH—DEFENDERS

In spite of Britain's restrictions, Jews continued to come to Palestine. Nearly all of the 85,000 people who comprised the sixth Aliyah were "illegals" from Europe. They were skilled technicians, cultured and artistically creative.

Most of this immigration was made possible through the activities of the HAGANAH— הגנה —DEFENSE organization. It was an outlaw group, which succeeded HASHOMER—השומר—THE GUARDIANS, which was founded in 1920. Its primary activity was to circumvent British restrictions on immigration and their interference in local affairs.

Other dissident groups, like the Revisionists, the Irgun, and the "Stern Gang," resorted to terrorist retaliation tactics against the British and the Arabs.

THE FATE OF REFUGEES

The countries of the world were as callous as England in the face of the misery of thousands of refugees who braved the dangers of unseaworthy craft, of other hazardous means of transportation, of detention camps, of brutal treatment, and death in their attempt to escape from Hitler's hordes.

The overcrowded ship PATRIA blew up with 1,770 refugees

aboard, all of whom had been ordered deported from Palestine as illegal immigrants. The STRUMA carried 769 refugees from Rumania and when proven unseaworthy, the Turkish government refused it entry. Subsequently, the STRUMA sank with all but two of its passengers going to the bottom.

WORLD WAR II

The ruthless Nazi destruction of the European Jewish community ended Zionist activity in the conquered lands. Russia's antagonism to Jewish nationalism finished all such activity in the communist-dominated countries. But in America, all this served to broaden the sphere of Zionist work and inspire the Jews in the free world to unparalleled efforts, especially financially and politically.

The most impressive change was the development of the YISHUV in Palestine. It gave large numbers to the Allied fighting forces and it became the Middle East arsenal of the allies. Toward the end of the war, England reluctantly agreed to the formation of the Jewish Brigade, which fought so successfully in North Africa and Italy.

During this period Great Britain refused to alter its policy of restricting immigration or to permit the normal development of Palestine as the Jewish homeland.

THE BILTMORE CONFERENCE

In May, 1942, the American Zionists called a special conference at the Hotel Biltmore in New York City. Out of its deliberations came the "Biltmore Platform."

1. An affirmation that the intent of both the Balfour Declaration and the Mandate was to establish Palestine as a Jewish state.

2. That the Jewish Agency should be granted authority to control Jewish immigration and to develop the country.

3. That complete self-government and equality should be given to all inhabitants of Palestine in local municipal affairs, both Arab and Jewish, and the autonomous management of all their educational and religious matters.

This platform was reaffirmed at the Zionist Conference held in London in 1945 and, later, at the Zionist Congress held in Basle in 1946.

PALESTINE BEFORE THE UNITED NATIONS

With the coming to power of the Labor Party in England, the Jews expected a more cooperative mandatory policy. Instead, they found that the repressive measures continued unabated; that thousands of Jews including members of the Jewish Agency executive, were being imprisoned without trial.

The resistance of the Yishuv manifested itself in violence and terrorism throughout the land. The repercussion in England caused an upsurge of anti-Jewish feeling. Turning back ships packed with refugees and interning them in Cyprus brought an avalanche of protests upon the government. Demands were made that Britain withdraw from Palestine.

In April, 1947, the British government submitted the Palestine question to the United Nations at a special session of the Assembly. A United Nations Special Committee on Palestine was appointed by the Assembly. It was ordered to make a thorough on-the-spot study, not only in Palestine, but even in displaced persons' camps in Germany and Austria. The majority report of the committee recommended the termination of the Mandate and the evacuation of the British, partition of the country into an independent Arab state and an independent Jewish state with close economic union, and the internationalization of Jerusalem.

On November 29th, this proposal was accepted by the General Assembly. Thirty-three nations voted for it, 13 against, and ten abstained. Great Britain, however, refused to implement the decision and did everything possible to prevent it from becoming effective. She encouraged Arab defiance, opened the frontiers to armed Arab bands, attempted to get the United Nations to abandon the partition plan, and made no move to set up any kind of self-government machinery.

THE WAR OF LIBERATION

The birthday of the State of Israel on May 4, 1948, found the British gone, but they left a state of disorder and they destroyed or impounded assets that could have been used by the Jews. A full-scale military offensive by seven surrounding Arab nations was launched against Israel. The Arab Legion from Transjordan was completely equipped, financed, and officered by the British.

The war that ensued is known as the "War of Liberation." The little country of Israel, with a total population of 650,000, found herself pitted against overwhelming forces of Arabs, drawn from a population of over 30,000,000. There were more than 400,000 Arabs in Israel, before the war began. All but 60,000 fled the country, hoping to return with the victorious Arabs.

Despite initial attacks, setbacks, and heavy losses, Israel was able to stem the tide of the Arab invaders. The United Nations tried to impose periodic truces without success. Count Folke Bernadotte, United Nations mediator in Palestine, was assassinated by extremists while trying to negotiate a truce. Dr. Ralph Bunche, a Negro representing the United Nations, was able to effect an armistice on February 24, 1949, between Egypt and Israel. The Arabs of Israel who left of their own accord were not permitted to return. Israel had won her war of liberation and gained additional territory in her struggle. She was now a free and independent state.

The New State of Israel

Organization of the new state of Israel was rapid. An election was held on January 25, 1949, with the Mapai party, the moderate Socialists, polling about 34% of the total vote. This determined the social and economic philosophy of the country. David ben Gurion, head of the Mapai party, became the first Prime Minister and Minister of Defense. In order to govern the country he had to form a coalition government.

Unlimited immigration started at once and every year since has seen the influx of thousands of Jews from all corners of the world. Capital poured in to help absorb the immigrants and settle them. West Germany granted reparations in the form of machinery and money for the numberless Jewish families that had been destroyed by the Nazi holocaust.

DAVID Ben GURION
(1886—)

David Green (his family name) was born in Plonsk, Poland. In 1906 he went to Palestine to work in a Kibbutz and later changed his name to Ben Gurion, which means "Son of a young lion." He was a militant labor Zionist and became the General Secretary of this Histadruth—the Zionist Federation of Labor.

From 1935 to 1948 he was chairman of the World Zionist Executive and also the chairman of the Jewish Agency. Following the establishment of the State of Israel and Israel's Declaration of Independence, which he helped to draft, he became head of the provisional government as Prime Minister and also carried the portfolio of Minister of Defense. As Commander-in-Chief of the army, he was responsible for the successful Sinai Campaign against Egypt in 1956.

After two years of retirement (1953–55), he was returned to office which he held until 1963 when he was succeeded by Levi Eshkol.

THE SINAI INVASION

The bitterness of the Arab nations found expression in the activities of the Arab League with recurring threats of attack and an economic boycott. With the overthrow of the Royal House in Egypt by the Free Officers movement, Colonel Gamal Abdul Nasser rose to power in July, 1952. He was successful in mobilizing the masses and was able to secure arms from Russia in exchange for cotton. In defiance of an earlier treaty with Britain he seized the Suez canal and closed off all shipping by the Israeli government.

Nasser proclaimed to the world his intention of destroying Israel. He executed border attacks, sending FEDAYIN, raiders, across the frontier, terrorizing and killing many Israelis. The country of Jordan, too, was restless. General John Glubb, the British commander of her army, was dismissed. The country, subject to anti-Israel propaganda, became anti-British, anti-Western, and pro-Nasser. Syria, too, was spurred to mobilize upon the urging of Nasser. Israel's Arab neighbors were ready to attack.

With some modest help from abroad, in the form of planes, tanks, and mechanized equipment, Israel decided to attack first. Starting on October 29, 1956, she penetrated deep into the Sinai Peninsula and was on her way to the canal zone, where she had reason to believe that the British and French would be attacking to regain control of the canal. But the United States interfered and compelled all the aggressors to withdraw. Though Nasser was badly defeated his prestige remained untarnished. However, Israel did end the Fedayeen raids; she secured control of Aqaba, thus giving her an outlet on the Red Sea.

THE SIX DAY WAR

On June 5, 1967, Israel became engaged in a war against Egypt, Jordan, and Syria that lasted six days and ended with the complete collapse of the Arab armed forces. It began with a series of events based on the announced Arab determination to destroy Israel.

Syria openly called for a war of national liberation. The months before the war were marked by shelling of Israeli settlements from the Syrian Golan heights, sabotage raids by Arab terrorists, and border incidents that took the lives of many Israelis.

On May 18, Egypt demanded the immediate withdrawal of the United Nations Emergency Forces stationed on its borders and UN General Secretary U Thant complied. On May 22, a blockade began in the Tiran Straits with Egypt occupying Sharm el Sheikh and cutting off Israel's water passage by the way of the Gulf of Aqaba. On May 29, a statement was issued by the Arab countries saying that the "ultimate object of the Arabs was the destruction of the State of Israel." On June 4, Syria joined Egypt and Jordan in a defense pact putting all troops under Egyptian command.

On June 5, the war began with a surprise attack by Israel on the Egyptian forces threatening her western border. Jordan rejected an appeal by Israel to stay neutral. The war lasted six days and resulted in the complete vanquishment of the combined Arab forces. The Sinai penisula to the shores of the Suez canal, the Gaza strip, the entire west bank of Jordan, Jordanian Jerusalem, and the Golan heights were in the hands of Israel.

The UN Security Council was called into session. A cease-fire was voted and the debates that followed were full of accusations by Russian and Arab representatives pointing to Israel as the aggressor and demanding a return of all occupied territory. A resolution was passed incorporating this demand among others.

Israel refused to comply on the grounds that negotiations for a peace settlement must come about through direct confrontation between Israel and the defeated Arab countries, which would have to recognize that Israel is a sovereign nation. Free access to the Suez Canal and the Tiran Straits, as well as guarantees for border controls were demanded. Also asked was UN cooperation in the resettlement of refugees and the unifying of Jerusalem under Israel with the holy sites safeguarded and accessible to all. As of this date a stalemate, marked by terror and guerilla warfare, exists between Israel and the Arab countries with no immediate solution in sight.

The Political Structure of Israel

Israel is a parliamentary democracy, patterned after that of Great Britain. Her President is a figurehead and her supreme authority is vested in the KNESSETH (Assembly), a unicameral legislature with 120 seats or representatives elected by the various political parties in the country. The majority party or coalition elects the Prime Minister, who appoints the Cabinet, which must resign if it loses its vote of confidence.

The Knesseth, which is elected by universal suffrage, approves the annual budget and keeps the Cabinet under constant scrutiny. Electors choose between lists of candidates prepared by the party, not between individuals. The 120 seats are allocated in proportion to the number of votes obtained by each list.

In the first election held after Statehood was declared, the Mapai party held only 46 seats, which lacked 15 of being a majority. Ben Gurion, their choice for Prime Minister, had to form a coalition with other parties in order to govern. To date, no single party has been able to secure a majority, so coalitions have been the rule. There have been as many as 28 political parties seeking representation. The 1966 Cabinet, with Mapai holding 45 seats, consisted of the following alignment : UNITY OF ISRAEL'S WORKERS (Mapai and Achdut Ha-Avodah-Poalei Tzion), THE NATIONAL RELIGIOUS PARTY (Mirachi Ha-Poel Ha-Mizrach), UNITED WORKERS' PARTY (Mapam), THE INDEPENDENT LIBERAL PARTY and WORKERS' ASSOCIATION OF ISRAEL (Poalei Agudath Yisroel).

The political complexion of Israel reflects ideologies of the people who settled the country. The religious groups run the gamut from those who practice the strictest forms of orthodoxy to those who refuse to recognize the State of Israel because Zionism contradicts the ordained Messianic redemption of the country. Com-

munist anti-Zionists are to be found on the far left, and on the far right are the volatile freedom activists.

The November, 1965, election results give the statistical strength of the major parties.

	Seats
Mapai & Achdut Ha'avodah—Alignment	45
Gahal—Herut Liberal Bloc	26
National Religious Party	11
Rafi—Israel Labor List	10
Mapam—United Workers' Party	8
Independent Liberals	5
Agudat, Israel	4
Arabs—Affiliated to Mapai	4
New Communist List	3
Poalei Agudat Israel	2
Ho-olam Hazeh—New Force	1
Israel Communist Party	1
	120

General Zionists

This middle class, non-socialist, Center Party was composed of two elements. One, which was represented by Chaim Weizmann, cooperated with the labor group; the other, the middle-of-the-road Progressives, was not so disposed. In 1946 a world confederation of General Zionists was created, with Rabbi Israel Goldstein serving as its president. It tried to maintain a balance between the extremes of Socialism and Capitalism, maintaining that the country needed private enterprise. They advocated a national nonpolitical labor union, national arbitration in labor disputes, civil service reform, a unified school system, and respect for Jewish traditions.

SEPHARDIM

A minor "communal" faction representing groupings of oriental Jews in Israel. It has aligned itself with the General Zionists.

ALIYAH CHADASHAH—עליה חדשה—
THE NEW IMMIGRANTS PARTY

This middle-class group is composed primarily of German and Austrian settlers who had difficulty in adjusting to the new land. Within this organization is a workers' group called ALIYAH CHADASHAH OVEDET—עליה חדשה עבדת—THE NEW IMMIGRANT WORKERS' PARTY. It is associated with the Histadruth, but is conservative in politics and economics.

THE LIBERAL PARTY

In 1961, the Progressives, who had broken away from the General Zionists in 1948, rejoined the group, resulting in the formation of the Liberal Party. Its platform included the enactment of a written constitution, advocacy of a free enterprise economy, removal of political influence from civil service, and electoral reform.

HA-OBED HA-TZIONI העובד הציוני —
LABOR YOUTH ZIONISTS

This group is composed of younger immigrants more oriented to labor.

THE INDEPENDENT LIBERAL PARTY

Members stand for freedom of the individual and social justice; national unity and priority for national interests; equal rights for all economic sections; a Welfare State; the enactment of a Constitution, and National Health Insurance.

Religious Zionism

MIZRACHI—מזרחי—EASTERN

The word MIZRACHI is actually a combination of two words, MERKAZ RUCHANI— מרכז רוחני — SPIRITUAL CENTER. The movement was started in Europe in 1902 for the purpose

of bringing the Orthodox concept of Zionism into building the new land. The Palestine Mizrachi organization, which came into existence in 1918, tends toward the right. Its statement of principles is as follows:

Mizrachi strives for the upbuilding of the Jewish National Home in Palestine on the basis of Israel's religious traditions in the belief that Eretz Yisroel was not intended to be merely a dwelling place of the Jewish people, but also the abode of the Jewish spirit.

The Mizrachi party is concerned with religious education, supports its own network of schools, and exercises complete control of religious affairs in the state. It advocates middle-class religious colonization as distinct from labor colonization.

HA-POEL HA-MIZRACHI-הפועל המזרחי
RELIGIOUS WORKERS PARTY

This left-wing group, composed of religious Socialists, was founded in 1921. Its slogan is TORAH v'AVODAH— תורה ועבודה —RELIGION AND LABOR. They observe orthodox tradition and practice socialism in the communal settlements and cooperatives. In the government they have joined with Mizrachi (1956) to form the National Religious Party, known as MIZRACHI – HA-POEL–HA-MIZRACHI —המזרחי – הפועל – המזרחי, and stands for the religious administration of Israel.

AGUDATH YISROEL—אגודת ישראל—
ASSOCIATION OF ISRAEL

This ultra-Orthodox party, founded at Kattowitz in 1912, stands for the strictest observance of the Torah in the administration of the State, with jurisdiction entrusted to rabbinical authorities. It demands the speeding up of the ingathering of the exiles, and State control of the Sick Funds. Originally it was opposed to Zionism as a denial of the Messianic return.

POALE AGUDATH YISROEL— פועלי אגודת ישראל—WORKERS ASSOCIATION OF ISRAEL

This religious workers' movement, a branch of the Agudath Yisroel, was founded in 1924. Its aim is the upbuilding of the State in the spirit of the Torah, protection of workers' rights, settlement, and pioneering.

Labor Zionism

HA-POEL HA-TZAIR-הפועל הצעיר— THE YOUNG WORKER

This, the first Jewish labor party in Palestine, was founded in 1906. Originally this group was known as ZEIRE TZION-צערי ציון —THE YOUNG OF ZION. It was strongly Socialistic and fostered the Hebrew language, culture, and traditions. One of the chief supporters of this group was Aharon D. Gordon, a champion of the Jewish return-to-the-soil movement. In 1930 it merged with Achduth Ha-Avodah to form the Mapai party.

POALE TZION— פועלי ציון—WORKERS OF ZION

This movement started soon after the first Zionist Congress in 1897 and came to Palestine in 1907. It was a leftist-radical group and attempted to reconcile Zionism with Socialism. It advocated the establishment of cooperative agricultural workers' associations. As the Labor Zionist Party of Palestine, it created collective settlements and the Histadruth, the General Labor Federation.

HA-SHOMER HA-TZAIR-השומר הצעיר— —THE YOUNG GUARD

This party, founded in 1913, started as a Marxist-Zionist youth movement and was responsible for many settlement projects. It became a political party in 1946, before statehood was declared, and favored bi-nationalism with the Arabs. Their strict party discipline made them an influential factor. In 1948 it merged with other parties to form Mapam.

ACHDUTH HA-ABODAH-אחדות העבודה— —UNITY OF LABOR

The membership of this Socialist Workers' party is concentrated in the Kibbutzim. It was inspired by Marxism and founded in 1919, emphasizing agricultural pioneering. It has a marked tendency toward activism in foreign affairs. In 1930 it joined with Ha-Poel Ha-Tzair to form the Mapai party. In 1944 its leftist faction broke with Mapai and together with HaShomer HaTzair and the leftwing Poalei Tzion formed the more radical group, Mapam. Ten years later (1954), the same faction seceded from Mapam and formed a new party called ACHDUTH AVODAH— אחדות עבודה פועלי ציון — POALEI TZION THE UNITED LABOR ZIONISTS.

THE MAPAI PARTY— מפאי—

In 1930 the Ha-Poal HaTzair and the Achduth HaAvodah parties merged and took the name of MAPAI, which is derived from the initial letters of MIFLEGETH POALEI ERETZ YISROEL—מפלגת פועלי ארץ ישראל—PARTY OF THE WORKERS OF THE LAND OF ISRAEL. Its program, which is left of center, is based on a combination of Socialism and Zionism and results from the amalgamation of several labor parties with varying ideologies. It has been the largest single party in Israel and the dominant power in successive government coalitions.

It is devoted to making the Jewish people in Israel a free working people, rooted in agriculture and industrial economy and developing its own Hebrew culture; to cooperating in the struggle to abolish class subjection and establish social justice; to nationalizing natural resources and means of production; to building a commonwealth of labor, equality, and freedom; and to furthering peace and cooperation with all the countries in the Middle East.

THE MAPAM PARTY—מפם

The initial letters of MIFLEGETH HA-POALIM HA-MEUCHEDETH B'ERETZ YISROEL—מפלגת הפועלים מאוחדת בארץ ישראל—forms the w o r d MAPAM and stands for the UNITED WORKERS PARTY OF ISRAEL. It came into existence in 1948, when the leftist group of Achduth HaAvodah broke away from Mapai and joined with the left-wing groups of the Poalei Tzion and the HaShomer HaTzair. Mapam is a proletarian, anti-capitalistic party based on Marxist and Zionist principles. Its platform calls for an independent nation

To forge its "Socialistic future" in conjunction with the working Arabs of Israel.

To create a revolutionary workers' movement against capitalist-imperialist tendencies.

To correlate its activities with worldwide revolutionary movements, especially with the Soviet Union.

To effect complete equality and cooperation with the Arab masses.

To pursue permanent peace in the Middle East based on the neutrality of the whole region.

ACHDUTH HA-ABODAH — POALEI TZION — אחדות העבודה – פועלי ציון –LABOR UNITY AND LABOR ZION PARTY

In 1954, the Achduth HaAvodah party broke away from Mapam and united with the Poalei Tzion party. It stands for a planned economy, widespread agricultural settlements, an activist defense policy, a foreign policy of non-identification, and friendship with all peace-loving peoples, particularly in Asia.

ISRAEL LABOR PARTY (1968)

This party was formed by the merger of MAPAI, ACHDUTH HA-AVODAH, and RAFI.

THE HISTADRUTH

This is an arm of the Mapai party, organized in 1920. The HISTADRUTH —הסתדרות— GENERAL LABOR FEDERATION embraces about 75% of all wage-earners in Israel and exercises almost complete control over the economy and politics of the country. Its members belong to different political parties, but by its numerical strength it dominates the Knesseth. It is frequently referred to as a "State within a state."

Its basic principles are non-exploitation, self-help, and mutual aid. It directs most of the trade unions, sponsors collective farms and labor settlements; operates KUPAT CHOLIM (Workers' Sick Fund), which is the largest health organization in Israel; provides unemployment, old-age, and other forms of social security; operates an extensive adult education program; has its own publishing house; sponsors choirs and orchestras; manages cooperative housing, and consumer and producer projects; and operates a workers' bank.

The influence of the Histadruth extends into almost every facet of the life of Israel. It is the greatest single employer and controls many holding companies. It operates all the transportation in the country. Among the largest institutions under its control are SOLEL BONEH, a building and contracting society; SHIKUN, the cooperative housing authority; NACHSHON, the Jewish shipping industry; TNUVA, Agricultural and dairy marketing cooperative; HA-MASHBIR, a consumer's cooperative; and KUPAT CHOLIM, a cooperative medical system.

Activist Parties

REVISIONISTS

Vladimir Jabotinsky, founder of the Jewish Legion in World War I, organized the Revisionist Party in 1924. Basically it was a movement of protest against the official Zionist policy towards G r e a t Britain.

The program of the Revisionists was strongly against any partition of Palestine between the Jews and the Arabs. It operated unilaterally on militant and politically aggressive lines. It formulated the following aims :

To establish a Jewish state in the land of Israel with a Jewish majority on both sides of the Jordan.

To encourage, through mass immigration, middle class colonization and development of private enterprise.

To create a Jewish Legion for public security.

To outlaw strikes and substitute

compulsory arbitration during the period of national up-building.

In 1935, Jabotinsky withdrew from the World Zionist Organization and created the "New Zionist Organization." Its objectives were somewhat moderate but still characterized by extreme nationalism and activistic methods. In 1946, the party merged into a new group, United Zionist Revisionists, and rejoined the World Zionist Organization.

IRGUN Z'VAI LEUMI— **ארגון צבאי לאומי**—THE NATIONAL MILITARY ORGANIZATION

This party (ETZEL) was an outgrowth of Revisionist ideology. During the Arab riots (1936–1939) it resorted to terroristic reprisals against the Arabs. It was an underground organization and retaliated against the British government with violence and sabotage because of its White-Paper policy of restricting Jewish immigration to Palestine.

Under the leadership of Menachem Beigin it carried out repeated attacks on Arab villages. In 1947, the Irgun joined with the HAGANAH— **הגנה** —the Israel DEFENSE organization. After the proclamation of Israel's statehood, it disbanded as an independent organization and became a security arm of the government.

BEITAR— **בתר** —(*Brith Yosef Trumpeldor*) — REVISIONIST YOUTH ORGANISATION

This rightist group was named for Joseph Trumpeldor, the hero of the Tel-Hai massacre. He worked with Jabotinsky and organized volunteers to defend unprotected Jewish settlements against Arab attacks. He was killed in the defense of Tel-Hai. The movement was started by the Revisionists in 1923 and it is now a part of the Herut party.

T'NUATH HA-CHERUTH HA-IVRITH — תנועת החרות העברית –HEBREW FREEDOM MOVEMENT (HERUT)

This nationalistic freedom party was created by members of (1) the Revisionist Party, (2) the Beitar Youth Movement, and (3) the Irgun Tzvai Leumi (Etzel) in 1948. It is strongly militant, demanding an aggressive policy against the Arab countries, and agitates for territorial expansion. It advocated private initiative in the economic structure of Israel as well as the maintenance of geographic entity of Israel as consisting of all land east and west of the Jordan river; the guarantee of equal rights, regardless of origin, religion, or sex to every citizen. It maintains that Hebrew foreign policy must be based on reciprocity; friendship for friendship, enmity for enmity.

In the Knesseth the Herut party is aligned with the Liberal Bloc and is known as the "Gahal." The moving spirit of the Herut party, Menachem Beigin, announced in June, 1966, that he would like to join forces with Rafi, David Ben Gurion's new party.

LOCHAME HERUT YISROEL— לוחמי חרות ישראל FIGHTERS FOR THE FREEDOM OF ISRAEL (LEHI)

This terrorist organization left the Irgun in 1940 and under the leadership of Avraham Stern, engaged in revolutionary activities. The members became known as the "Stern Gang" and were said to be responsible for the assassination of Lord Moyne and Count Bernadotte. With the creation of the State of Israel in 1948, the organization disbanded.

RAFI — THE ISRAEL LABOR LIST

This party was founded by David ben Gurion in 1965 in opposition to the Mapai party. It stands for self-reliance in matters of national security; electoral reform action; peace with the neighboring countries; universal secondary education; modernization of the economy; and a democratic society with division of powers and social justice. It holds ten seats in the Knesseth. In 1968 it merged with Mapai and Achduth Ha-Avodah to form the Israel Labor Party.

Other Parties and Movements

THE COMMUNIST PARTY OF ISRAEL

This party demands equal rights for the Arab minority; peace between Israel and the Arab countries; friendship between Israel and the Soviet Union and the other Socialist countries; and it aims at Socialism in Israel. It works for Israel's independence and neutrality.

COOPERATION AND FRATERNITY

An Arab party representing Druzes and Moslems in the Carmel area, Western Galilee, and the central area. They are affiliated with Mapai and hold four seats in the Knesseth.

PROGRESS AND DEVELOPMENT

This party represents mainly Moslems and Christians in Central Galilee.

HA-OLAM HA-ZEH—העולם הזה—NEW FORCE

This is a non-party reform movement founded in 1965. It stands for democratization, a written Constitution, separation of religion and State, equality for the Arab minority, neutralism in foreign relations, and peace based on cooperation between the Arab and Hebrew national movements. It holds one seat in the Knesseth.

ICHUD—אחוד—UNITY

This small party favors the binational solution for Palestine.

NATUREI KARTA—נטורי קרתא—
GUARDIANS OF THE CITY

This small orthodox sect refuses to recognize Israel's official institutions or representatives, claiming that the state came into existence without the sanction of God and that Zionism displaces the Messianic redemption of the country. Its members live in the MEA SHEARIM section of Jerusalem and speak Yiddish, reserving Hebrew only for prayer and religious study.

Aliyahs—Immigration to Palestine

FIRST ALIYAH (1882–1903)

Aliyah means "Going Up" or "Migration." The first pioneers, about 25,000, came from Russia. Part of this Aliyah was known as the "Bilu."

SECOND ALIYAH (1904–1914)

This group, numbering about 40,000 was known as Socialist Zionists. They came from Russia, founded the city of Tel Aviv, and established Deganiah, the first collective settlement.

THIRD ALIYAH (1919–1923)

About 35,000 young people from Russia, imbued with Labor Zionism, comprised this group, following the establishment of Palestine as a Mandate under Great Britain. They founded the Histadruth and sought to industrialize the land.

FOURTH ALIYAH (1924–1931)

This was a middle-class group of about 82,000 that came from Poland. They settled in the cities, worked in factories, and entered the field of merchandising.

FIFTH ALIYAH (1932–1940)

Most of these immigrants (225,000) were refugees from Germany. They brought with them the skills of Western civilization and became influential in the trades and industries. A large number were professionally trained.

SIXTH ALIYAH (1941–1947)

Nearly all of the 85,000 immigrants were "illegals" from Europe. They were the homeless and displaced of World War II.

SEVENTH ALIYAH (1948)

With the establishment of the State of Israel, over 1,600,000 Jews from European and Oriental countries came to rebuild their lives in the new state.

Movements and Settlements

MIKVEH ISRAEL—מקוה ישראל—HOPE
OF ISRAEL

This was the first Jewish agricultural school in Palestine. It was founded by Carl Netter in 1870, with the help of the Alliance Israelite Universelle. It became a government school in 1956 and has achieved eminence in research and development in the field of agriculture.

PETACH TIKVAH—פתח תקוה—GATE
OF HOPE

After an unsuccessful attempt to settle a colony in 1878, the Chovevei Tzion pioneers founded the present town with the aid of Baron Edmond de Rothschild. It became a center of both citriculture and industry.

CHOVEVEI TZION— חבבי ציון —
LOVERS OF ZION
Originally, the movement was known as HIBBAT TZION— חבת ציון
LOVE OF ZION and consisted of groups throughout Eastern Europe. After the pogroms of 1881, they united to promote immigration to and settlement in Palestine.

THE BILU MOVEMENT (1882)

"Bilu" is a word composed of the initial letters of the Hebrew phrase, BETH YA-AKOV LECHU V'NELECHA— בית יעקב לכו ונלכה—O HOUSE OF JACOB, COME AND LET US GO.
This Aliyah group was part of the Chovevei Tzion, which left Russia following the riots of 1881.

ZICHRON YA-AKOV— זכרון יעקב — IN
MEMORY OF JACOB
Concurrent with the Russian migration, there was a group of Rumanian pioneers that started Zichron Ya-Akov, a wine-producing village on Mt. Carmel, aided by Baron and Baroness Edmond de Rothschild, who are interred there.

RISHON L'TZION— ראשון לציון —
FIRST OF ZION
In 1882 the Chovevei Tzion established this wine-producing colony on the Judean coastal plane. After 1930 it also entered the field of industry and manufacturing.

CHEVER HA-KEVUTZOT—חבר הקבוצות
—FEDERATION OF COMMUNAL
SETTLEMENTS
This was an attempt to bring all the settlements in the land under a collective body.

HA-KIBBUTZ HA-MEUCHAD— הקבוץ המאוחד—THE UNITED GROUP
A federation of collective colonies. similar to the Chever Ha-Kevutzoth, except that individual colonies aimed at expansion and growth.

HITYASHBUT— התישבות —SETTLE-MENT
The act of colonizing or establishing a new colony in Palestine.

KEVUTZAH— קבוצה —G R O U P or
GATHERING — A COLLECTIVE
AGRICULTURAL SETTLEMENT
A cooperative association, working a common farm on national land. The economy is collective; economic principle based on one large family; a completely integrated communal settlement.

KIBBUTZ—קבוץ—GATHERING
A collective workers' group or farm; economy based on industry and agriculture; almost identical with KEVUTZAH, except that the Kibbutz is larger and more diversified.

MOSHAV—מושב—AGRICULTURAL CO-OPERATIVE
This is a small holders' settlement where individual farmers own home and land, but form a cooperative for their operations.

KIBBUTZ ARTZI—קבוץ ארצי—PALES-TINE GROUP
An association of collective settlements affiliated with Ha-Shomer HaTzair.

MOSHAVAH— מושבה — COLONY —
VILLAGE
A settlement of independent Jewish farmers owning private farms and operating on a capitalistic basis.

MOSHAV SHITUFI— מושב שיתופי —
COOPERATIVE SETTLEMENT

This kind of settlement is a combination of the Kibbutz and the Moshav. It features both cooperative and private ownership in that each family has a home of its own, and the principle of communal responsibility governs land, machinery, and general operation.

YISHUV—ישוב— SETTLEMENT

A term applied collectively to the entire Palestine Jewish community.

THE JEWS IN THE DIASPORA

The Jews of Babylonia

East of Canaan (Palestine) was the great Mesopotamian plain between the Tigris and Euphrates rivers and extending to the Persian gulf. It was divided into Assyria (Iraq) in the north and Babylonia (Iran) in the south.

Originally, this Mesopotamian area was the country of the Sumerian and Akkadian civilizations. It was the land (Ur of Chaldee) from which Abraham migrated to Canaan. The northern area (Assyria) conquered Samaria and Israel in 722 BCE. One of its famous cities (Nineveh) is the scene of the Biblical book, Jonah. The southern area (Babylonia) conquered Judea, destroyed the Temple, and exiled its people in 586 BCE.

The deity of the Babylonians was Marduk, the supreme god of the pantheon. He was also known as Bel, meaning Lord. The characteristic features of the Babylonian religion were, (1) magical practices, (2) divination, interpretation of omens (astrology), and (3) animal worship.

Successive invaders — Persians, Greeks, Romans, Moslems, and Turks ruled this country now known as Iraq.

JEWISH LIFE IN BABYLONIA

A number of Jewish communities flourished in the Mesopotamian valley—Apamea, Nares, Machusa, Nahardea, Pumbeditha, Firuz-Shabur, and Sura (Matha Mahasia). Many Jews settled there during Roman persecution and subjugation.

The religious and secular head of the Jewish people in exile was known as Resh Galutha, "Head of the Exile" or "Prince of the Captivity." As an official directly responsible to the ruling powers, he had the title of Exilarch.

The Exilarchs were also the supreme judges. Some of them distinguished themselves in the field of scholarship and attained prominence as heads of schools. Most of them, however, made little contribution to the development of Jewish life.

The Schools of Learning

After the death of Judah HaNasi (220 CE) the intellectual life of the Jews started to shift to Babylonia even though the Patriarchate did not end until 425 CE. Many prominent rabbis and scholars of Palestine moved to the new centers of learning. Some became heads of the academies by virtue of their scholarship and erudition.

Like their predecessors in Palestine, they continued the study of the Bible and Mishnah and created a Talmud of their own, which is called "Talmud Babli" — "The Babylonian Talmud." The compilation and arrangement of this gigantic work of the Babylonian Amoraim is credited to Rav Ashi of the Sura Academy.

The Babylonian Talmud differs from the Jerusalem Talmud in language and style. Much of its language is Aramaic, which was the popular tongue of the time. Like the Jerusalem Talmud, this work is also incomplete, lacking commentaries on portions of the first and last orders of the Mishnah. Because of the personalities associated with the Babylonian Talmud and the vast amount of study connected with it, it is considered a higher authority than the Palestinian Talmud.

Kallah—Rabbinical Assemblies

Twice a year, during the months of Adar and Elul, students and teachers met together to discuss special sections of the Mishnah. These conferences were known by the name KALLAH—כלה—a word derived from the Aramaic and meaning ASSEMBLY. The lecturers at these meetings were called ROSHE KALLAH—ראשי כלה—HEADS OF THE ASSEMBLY. The assembly places were called YESHIVOTH—ישיבות —SCHOOLS OF LEARNING. At these Kallahs new laws were enacted to meet the current needs of life.

The Saboraim (500–600)

After the completion of the Talmud, Jewish learning was carried on by scholars who were called SABORAIM— סבוראים —OPINIONISTS or PONDERERS. Though their individual contributions as scholars are not known, they are credited with arranging the final edition of the Talmud as it is now known.

Lesser Tractates of the Talmud

About this time were written several tractates on various subjects, which were later appended to the Talmud. These treatises deal with such subjects as Scrolls of the Law, Funeral Rites, Sayings of the Rabbis, etc. They are placed at the end of the fourth Order of the Talmud (Nezikin) and are referred to as the Lesser Tractates.

The Midrashim

Concurrent with Bible study in Palestine, there developed a body of rabbinic literature that was collected under the title of MIDRASH which means TO SEARCH OUT or TO INTERPRET. This literature is of two types—Halachic, or legal nature, and Haggidic, or narrative nature. They were collected anonymously during and after the Talmudic period and today we have a large collection of Midrashim on nearly all the books of the Bible.

The Halachah sought the meaning of all the legal portions of the Bible. Stories and illustrations supplemented the discourses on Jewish life. The Haggadah sought the meaning of non legal portions of the Bible. It dealt with legends, personalities, and folklore with the purpose of educating the people and strengthening them morally.

The Gaonim—(580–1038)

Oppressive measures of the Persian rulers caused most of the Jewish schools of learning in Babylonia to suspend their activities eventually.

When Persia succumbed to Moslem power in the year 642 the schools began to flourish anew. The leading rabbis or rectors of the academies received the title GAON— גאון —a term derived from the phrase THE EXCELLENCY OF JACOB. Gaon, hence, means EXCELLENCY, or THE GREAT ONE. As dean of the academy his official title was "Resh Yeshivah," "Head of the College."

Though the Gaonim were under the jurisdiction of the Exilarch, they were recognized as the supreme judicial authorities in all Jewish religious and secular affairs. They rendered decisions for far and near communities. They prepared prayers and arranged the order for synagogue worship. They convened the semi-annual Kallahs. They also had the honor of installing the Exilarchs in office.

Although the Exilarch was the head of the Jewish community, his power was limited and he could enforce his decisions only by the imposition of fines or religious bans. There was so much rivalry between the Exilarchs and the Gaonim that the Caliph would have to interfere. Meanwhile, new sects like the Karaites, Issawites, and Yudghanites emerged to further accentuate internal Jewish strife.

The Gaonim also codified the many laws of the Talmud into handy reference guides. Until the year 1038 the Gaonim remained the central authority in all Jewish life.

Responsa Literature

The decisions on or answers to the many questions submitted to the Gaonim and other accepted authorities by the Jews of the world, were embodied in a literature known as TESHU-BOTH — תשובות —ANSWERS. The Latin name is Responsa. This literature is a valuable source of information since it throws much light on the life of the Jewish communities in the Diaspora from which questions came.

NOTABLE GAONIM

YEHUDAI THE BLIND (760)
Codified Jewish law in a work called *Halachoth Pesukoth*— הלכות פסוקות —*Short and Established Practice.*

ACHAI (760)
Wrote a book called *Sefer Shealtoth*— ספר שאלתות, *A Book of Questions.*

NATRONAI II (853–869)
Known for his prolific correspondence with Jewish communities. He was bitterly opposed to the Karaites. Arranged a Prayer Book for synagogue services.

MAR AMRAM (856–874)
Compiler of the first complete liturgical order of the prayers, known as the *Siddur Rab Amram.*

ZEMACH ben PALTOI (872–890)
Compiler of the first Talmudic dictionary.

NACHSHON ben ZADOK (881–889)
Wrote a dictionary of the difficult words of the Talmud. Also arranged a key to the Jewish calendar.

SIMON OF CAIRO (900)
Compiled a code embracing all religious and ceremonial law. This work is called *Halachoth Gedoloth* —הלכות גדולות—*The Great Halachoth.*

KOHEN – ZEDEK (917–936)

Leader of opposition to the Exilarchate.

SAADIAH ben JOSEPH (882–942)

Under this foremost of all Gaonim, the Gaonate experienced its most flourishing period. Saadiah wrote the first philosophy of religion, known as *Emunoth V'deoth—* אמונות ודעות, *Faith and Creed.* He also wrote a commentary called *Sefer Yetzirah—* ספר יצירה *—The Book of Creation.* He translated the Bible into Arabic and was a leading figure in the opposition movement against the Karaites.

SHERIRA (906–1006)

Distinguished for his "Letter" (Iggereth), which gives a chronological account of the Talmudic, post-Talmudic, and Gaonic periods of Jewish history. He also wrote *Megillath Setarim—* מגלת סתרים *—on the secret meaning of the Haggadah.

HAI (939–1038)

He was the last of the Gaonim. Among his many writings was an exposition in Arabic on the Bible known by the name *Musar Haskal.*

In 948 four scholars left Babylonia for other parts of the world to secure financial support for the academies. These men were Shemaria ben Elchanan, Hushiel, Nathan ben Isaac Kohen, and Moses ben Chanoch, the last of whom became an outstanding rabbi in Spain.

FROM 637 TO THE PRESENT

After relief from Sassanid persecution, which followed the Moslem invasion in 637, Jewish life continued without change. But with the suspension of the Exilarchate and the closing of the academies of learning at Sura and Pumbeditha in 1040, Babylonia ceased to be the center of Jewish life.

A change in the social and economic structure, however, had taken place during these centuries. Jews tended to leave agricultural pursuits for urban advantages and occupations.

Despite discrimination and occasional repression, individual Jews were included in the courts of the Caliphs as physicians, advisers, and bankers. In the larger communities some became traders and craftsmen.

In the second half of the 13th century the Mongols invaded the land. Under their rule the Jews enjoyed religious freedom and some rose to high position. But when the Mongols converted to Islam, Jewish persecution followed and continued until the Turks took possession of the land.

1534—Turkish domination of the country continued for almost 400 years. There was little change in the condition of the Jews. They were concentrated chiefly in Baghdad where they were dominant in commerce and in the professions.

1917—Turkey was defeated in World War I by the Allies. The country of Iraq was created by the partition of Turkish possessions, and was mandated to Great Britain by the League of Nations.

1932—Iraq acquired her independence. Feisal, King of Iraq, was sympathetic to the Jews. About 88,000 Jews lived in the country. Over the centuries they had become oriental in character and speech.

1948—With the creation of the State of Israel and the establishment of the United Arab League, anti-Jewish measures in Iraq caused many Jews to leave the country. The Jewish population had increased considerably with European refugees.

1951—Because of the hostility of the Arab leaders, an air-lift operation was undertaken that enabled some 120,000 Jews to enter Israel.

1953—The threat of annihilation of the Jews by the Arab world, and border clashes between Israel and Iraq, placed the remaining Jews of Iraq in a precarious position. More succeeded in entering Israel.

1960—About 6,000 Jews still reside in Iraq. Most of them live in Baghdad. The remainder live in Basra, Mosul, and Iraqui Kurdistan.

The Jews of Syria

Syria, which was known as Aram in Bible times, is bounded on the west by Lebanon, on the south by Jordan, on the east by Iraq and on the north by Turkey. Its capital city is Damascus. Its association with Jewish history dates back to the reign of King David. Before Syria became part of the Persian Empire (538 BCE) it suffered invasions by Assyrians, Babylonians, and Egyptians.

332 BCE—After the conquest by Alexander the Great, Syria came under the rule of Seleucus I. A Jewish community existed at Antioch at this time.

168–165 BCE—The Jewish people of Palestine revolted successfully against the religious persecution by the Syrian King, Antiochus. The Chanukah holiday, ordained by Judah Maccabeus, celebrates this short-lived period of freedom.

63 BCE—Syria was conquered by Pompey and came under Roman rule.

67 CE—Many Jews suffered in retaliation because of the unsuc-

cessful Syrian revolt against Rome.

395 CE—The Roman Empire was divided and Syria became subject to Byzantine or Eastern rule.

408–450—Under Theodosius II, religious freedom was restricted. Many synagogues were converted to churches.

634—Syria was taken by Moslems and accepted the religion of Islam. Jews were granted religious autonomy but forced to pay taxes.

Ninth and Tenth centuries—The city of Damascus was known as an important Karaite center.

12th century—The traveler, Benjamin of Tudela, reported sizable Jewish communities in the cities of Aleppo, Damascus, and Palmyra. He noted that there were 3,000 Rabbinite Jews and 200 Karaite Jews in Damascus.

1492—Refugees from Spain settled in Syria.

1840—*The Damascus Affair.* This city of Damascus had a blood libel event that had wide repercussions. The disappearance of a Franciscan churchman and his servant raised the Ritual Murder charge and leading Jewish residents were arrested and subjected to extreme torture and forced confessions. Incited mobs threatened the safety of the Damascus Jewish community. World protests and the personal intervention of such men as Sir Moses Montefiore of England and Adolphe Cremieux of France resulted in the release of all Jews held suspect. Many Jews left the country after this affair.

1920—After World War I, France was given the Mandate over Syria by the League of Nations. Though Jews were granted equal rights, many decided to migrate because of intense Arab nationalism.

1941—Republic of Syria proclaimed. Following World War II many Jews migrated to Lebanon, Israel, and the United States.

1943—Jewish population estimated at about 30,000. Of the Arab countries in the Near East, Syria was most hostile and anti-Semitic.

1947—Zionism and illegal emigration to Palestine and Lebanon were banned on penalty of death. There were pogroms in Allepo and bomb attacks in Damascus. The government retricted Jews in public service and in economic pursuits.

1948—With the establishment of Israel, Arab aggression against it jeopardized the Jews of Syria. Of the 30,000 Jews in the country about 25,000 emigrated.

1958—About 3,000 Jews reside in the cities of Damascus, Aleppo, and Qamishleyeh. Legally, Jews cannot leave the country except for Lebanon.

The Jews of Persia (Iran)

The original inhabitants of Persia, the ancient Iranians, lived in the southwestern part of the great Mesopotamian plateau. Next to Egypt and China, it is the oldest country in the world.

Jewish history in the land of Persia began when Cyrus, King of the Persians and Medes, conquered the Babylonian empire in 538 BCE. This was the country that had destroyed Jerusalem (586 BCE) and had caused many of its people to go into exile. For the next two centuries, both the Jews in exile in Babylonia and the Jews in Palestine were under Persian rule.

King Cyrus was hailed as a great redeemer of the Jews, for he permitted a large number to return to their homeland. Jews were granted religious autonomy and were engaged in many economic activities. Little, however, is known about their history following the return of the exiles. The Book of Esther, which speaks of a Jewish community in the Persian city of Shushan (Susa), is not authentic. Some historians associate the story of Esther with the ruler Artaxerxes I Longamanus, and it is known that a

Persian Queen, "Shushan Dukht," was of Jewish faith.

UNDER PERSIAN RULERS
538–323 BCE

538—CYRUS THE GREAT founded the Persian Empire. He permitted Zerubbabel to lead a large number of exiles back to Jerusalem to rebuild the Temple.

521–485—DARIUS I. During his reign a second contingent of exiles returned to Palestine under the leadership of Nehemiah and, later, Ezra. The Second Temple was dedicated in 516. Establishment of the Zoroastrian religion.

465–424—ARTAXERXES I LONGAMANUS. His name is associated with Ahasuerus. The Purim story was supposed to have taken place during his reign.

336–330—DARIUS III. He was killed in Battle when Alexander the Great conquered Persia. From this time until the third century of the common era little is known about Jewish life in Persia. About a century after the division of Alexander's empire among his generals the country came under the rule of the Parthians, a people located southwest of the Caspian Sea.

FROM 226 TO 636 CE

226—End of the Parthian Empire. Beginning of Sassanid or Neo-Persian Empire.

226–241—ARDASHIR I. He was intolerant of religious minorities. He made Zoroastrianism the state religion.

241–271 — SHAPUR. Despite his friendliness, Jews suffered because of warfare. City of Nahardea, a center of Jewish learning, was destroyed.

438–457—YEZDEGERD II. He imposed severe restrictions against the Jews. Forbade observance of the Sabbath and festivals.

459–483—FIRUZ (PEROZES). He put to death half of the Jewish community of Isfahan and forced conversion of Jewish children. This city was supposedly founded by Jews.

485–531—KOBAD I. He favored Zendicism, a communist cult that shared property and wives. As a result of a revolt led by the Exilarch Mar Zutra (513), schools of learning were suspended. Mar Zutra suffered martyrdom.

531–579—CHOSROES I. He was favorably disposed toward the Jewish people but their lot remained unimproved.

579–590—HORMIZD IV. Jews joined in an unsuccessful rebellion against the King. Beginning of the Gaonic period. Invasion of Persia by Arabs, Khazars, and Turks.

632–636—YEZDEGERD III. Last Sassanid ruler to reign over Persia, which was conquered by the Arabs.

The Religion of Zoroastrianism

The religion of the Persian people is named after its founder, Zoroaster. It is also known as Mazdaism. It was a religion of dualism based on the belief in the existence of good and evil spirits, or forces of light and darkness. The God of good and light was called Ormuzd. The demon of evil and darkness was called Ahriman. Worship of Ormuzd was by the symbols of the sun and fire.

Mazdaism became the official state religion under Ardashir I (226–241 CE). The minority religious groups suffered persecution from time to time. Judaism did not fare too badly under Persian rule until the fifth century, when severe persecution caused many to migrate to neighbouring countries.

Persian Jewry

With the coming of Islamic rule to Persia (636), the Mohammedan religion became the dominant faith of the land. The new rulers were tolerant toward the Jews, and the Jewish communities and institutions of learning flourished under the Gaonate (580–1038). The communities were controlled by Exilarchs, and a number of sectarian movements, such as Karaism, developed. The language used by these Persian Jews was called Grush, a Hebrew-Persian dialect.

Conquests by neighboring nations usually affected the Jews adversely. Through the many centuries a number of Jewish communities were established by refugees seeking havens of refuge. The traveler Benjamin of Tudela, toward the end of the 12th century, wrote about a number of such flourishing communities. There was an interlude between the 13th and 15th centuries, when Persia was under Mongol rule. During this time the lot of the Jews was checkered.

From 1500 to the Present

1500—A new Persian dynasty, the Safavids, re-established Persian independence. Shiism became the state religion. It was a branch of the Moslem religion that rejected the body of tradition respecting Mohammed as any part of the law. Under these rulers and later the Shahs, Jewish life in Persia was severely proscribed. A distinctive dress was imposed and many Jews were converted by force.

1736–1747—NADIR SHAH. During his reign a Jewish settlement was created in his capital city, Meshed.

1795–1825—KADJAR DYNASTY. Discrimination and humiliating treatment of Jews caused disintegration of Jewish life.

1838—Nearly all the Jews of Meshed were forcibly converted to Islam. They became known as Djedid Al-Islam or New Moslems. Like the Marrano Jews of Spain, they secretly practiced their religion.

1871—World Jewry, through Alliance Israelite Universelle, attempted to intercede in behalf of Persian Jewry. Some Jewish schools were established and economic aid was given, but general depressive conditions remained the same.

1907 — Anti-Jewish riots caused many Jews to migrate to European countries.

1925 REZA SHAH PAHLEVI. Power of Mohammedan clergy broken. A new religion, Bahai—a mixture of Islam, Christianity, and Judaism—attracted many Jews.

1928—Arab opposition to Palestine as a country for all Jews caused hardships for the Jews of Iran.

1948–1953—With the establishment of the State of Israel, over 35,000 Jews left Iran to settle in Israel.

1960—It is estimated that about 75,000 Jews reside in Iran.

Jewish Communities

There is no central Jewish community in Iran. Teheran, with 40,000 Jews, is served by special committees. Rabbinical courts have jurisdiction in all Jewish matters.

Azerbaijan	Mosul
Hamadan (4,000)	Senne
Isfahan (8,000)	Semandej
Kermanshah	Shiraz (15,000)
(3,500)	
Kaswin	Tabriz
Kurdistan	Teheran (40,000)
Meshed (2,500)	Yezd

Personalities and Events

ANAN ben DAVID (c. 756)

Founder of a religious sect known as Karaism. This sect rebelled against the authority of rabbinic Judaism and created a "Back to the Bible" movement as the basis of the Jewish religion. The sect flourished in Palestine and was bitterly opposed by the Rabbinites. Subsequently, the Karaites lost their influence in Jewish life. The movement, however, produced many scholars in the field of Bible literature and was responsible for the masoretic structure of the Bible.

DAVID ALROY (1154–1160)

A messianic pretender. He started a revolt against Persian rule but was assassinated in the attempt. His followers continued as a secret sect known as Menahemites, and were once very active in Kurdistan.

SAAD ad-DAULA (1288–1291)

Jewish physician and statesman. He was appointed Vizier of the entire Mongol Empire under the ruler Arghun.

The Jews of Arabia

JEWISH ORIGINS

The vast Arabian Peninsula, southeast of Palestine, is situated between the Red Sea and Gulf of Aqaba on the west, the Persian Gulf and Gulf of Oman on the east. Its southern border is the Arabian Sea and Gulf of Aden. Jordan and Iraq are to the north.

The chief countries and protectorates in this 1,000,000 square mile area are Saudi Arabia, Yemen, Aden, Oman, Trucial Oman, Bahrein, Qatar, and Kuwait.

Historically, Arabia is the ancient cradle of the Semites. Assyrian, Persian, and Greek empires successfully engulfed this area at various times between 750 and 275 BCE. Scattered Jewish communities have existed in this desert wilderness from early Bible times. The Midianites and Ishmaelites, mentioned in Scripture, also lived here.

In 64 CE Rome began to divide the land into provinces and in the year 305 it became part of the Byzantine empire.

Persecution in Palestine caused

many Jews to seek refuge in Arabia. They established communities or tribes that bore such names as Banu-Bachdal and Banu-Kainuka. These tribes lived in cities or territories of Khaibar, Wadi al-Kura, and Yathrib (Medina). A large number lived in Mecca, the capital city of Arabia. Jews also migrated to Arabia in the fifth century when Persia imposed severe restrictions upon them. Their fortunes varied according to the ruler.

The Jewish religion appealed to many of the native Arabs and records show that tribes and even kingdoms embraced Judaism. One notable instance was the Kingdom of Yemen ruled by Abu Kariba Assad and later his son, Joseph. Another king to accept the faith of the Jew was Dhu Nuwas. When Islam conquered the land these people became Moslems.

The Arabs worshiped idols. Mecca was their holy city and the chief object of worship was a black stone shrine called the Kaaba, which they surrounded with figures.

The Arabs of this period looked upon the Jews as their spiritual brothers. They claimed a common ancestor, Ishmael, Abraham's son. Their language is Semitic, being basically similar to Hebrew.

MOHAMMED (570–632)

Jews in Arabia had an uneventful history until the rise of Mohammed in the year 610. This man, who created a new religion called Islam, borrowed from Hebrew teachers and the Jewish religion to write his Bible called the Koran.

In the year 622 Mohammed made his famous Hegira or Flight to Medina. This date marks the first year of the Moslem calendar and the beginning of the Mohammedan or Moslem religion. The fundamental belief of this religion is the Oneness of God called Allah and his chosen prophet, Mohammed. Like the Jewish religion it condemned idolatry, commanded prayer, and practiced charity.

Mohammed incorporated the black Kaaba stone shrine into his new religion. The Kaaba houses a black meteorite stone. It is venerated as a sacred symbol that was given to Abraham by the angel Gabriel.

Because the Jews denied Mohammed's claim to holy office, he turned against them, and commanded that the religion of Islam, which means "Submission," be spread among all unbelievers by sword. In the holy war against the Jews (625), the Jewish tribe of Banu-Kainuka was first to fall. In rapid succession the Jews of Banu-Nadhir, Banu-Kuraiza, and Banu-Khabar fell.

When Mohammed died in 632, his successors were the Caliphs, Arab kings. They were the spiritual and temporal rulers of the Moslem people and they followed the command of Mohammed to spread the religion of Islam by conquest. In the span of 128 years they had expanded Islam from Arabia into North Africa, Spain, and the Near and Middle East, and into the heart of Asia.

632—ABU-BEKR. Converted to Islam. First Caliph to succeed Mohammed. Kept Jewish people in a semi-servile position.

634–644—OMAR. Second ruler of the Arabs. He conquered Persia, North Africa, and the Byzantine Empire. This Caliph built the Mosque of Omar on the site of

King Solomon's Temple. He ordered the Jews to wear a badge as a mark of humiliation. He expelled the Jews from the cities of Khaibar and Fadak.

656—ALI. Jews regained their complete freedom under the Caliph. They occupied important state offices. Under his rule the Gaonate was established.

813—AL-MAMUM. Jews reached the height of their intellectual and economic prosperity.

The history of Arabia in the centuries that followed was overshadowed by the Moslem invasions of North Africa, Europe, and the Near and Middle East. This period is marked by the dynasties of the Umayyads, Abbasids, Fatimids, Sunnites, Mamelukes, and Ottomans.

1516—With the ascendancy of the Ottoman Empire, Turkey conquered Byzantium and so fell heir to Arabia.

ARABIAN JEWRY

Under the Caliphate the Jews retained their religious autonomy. They were responsible to an Exilarch appointed by the rulers as the political head of the Jews. This officer was responsible for the remission of taxes and had the power to make appointments of minor importance. Under favorable conditions the Jews maintained schools under the leadership of the Gaonate of Babylonia. The status of the Jews, generally, was not very good. In other countries, under Arab domination, Jewish learning flourished and many works were written in the Arabic language, but from Arabia itself nothing of importance was produced.

JEWISH COMMUNITIES

Jewish settlements were located in the following communities.

Adhruh	Jarba
Bahrein	Makna
Hejaz	Mecca
Medina	

MODERN ARABIA

1516—The Ottoman Empire (Turkey) controlled most of the Arab lands for almost 400 years.

1918—Turkey was defeated in World War I. Her Empire was dissolved.

1920—League of Nations partitioned Palestine and mandated Transjordan to Britain.

1921–1931—Ibn Saud consolidated north and central Arabia into the Kingdom of Saudi Arabia.

1945—Egypt initiated the formation of the Arab League for mutual benefit and in common antagonism to the existence of Israel. Saudi Arabia, Jordan, and Yemen joined Iraq, Lebanon, and Syria. The League has not endured as originally constituted.

1948—The newly established State of Israel was attacked by surrounding Arab states, but the war was won by Israel.

THE JEWS OF YEMEN

Yemen forms the southern tip of the Arabian Peninsula. Its water boundary is the Red Sea and the

Gulf of Aden. Jews have lived in Yemen from ancient times. Tradition suggests that a Jewish community flourished in Yemen prior to the Babylonian exile (506 BCE). The first real information dates from the first century CE, when it is claimed that there were about 3,000 Jews in the country.

Conversion to Judaism seems to have played an important role in Yemen. Imam Abu Kariba (390-420) converted to Judaism and propagated his adopted faith among his subjects. The dynasty of the Himyarites (sixth century) adopted Judaism but was unable to spread the new religion among the people. Imam Dhu Nuwas (d. 525 CE) was the last Jewish ruler of the Yemenite Kingdom. After his death, Judaism declined and lost its importance.

Yemen came under Mohammedan rule in 717. The Jews were assured protection and freedom of religion, but they were subject to severe restrictions applied to all non-Moslems. They were forced to wear different clothing and were not permitted to ride on animals. Moslem religious law taught that unbelievers and infidels should be degraded. Hence, Jews could not testify in a Moslem court, and were subject to extensive insults and abuses.

Yemenite Jews were susceptible to Messianic movements. In the 12th century a false Messiah proclaimed the merger of Judaism and Mohammedanism, which resulted in harrassment and persecution of the Jews. The incident elicited a letter from Maimonides to Rabbi Jacob ben Nathaniel, Chief Rabbi of the Yemenite Jews, which helped bolster their waning morale. The Sabbatai Zevi movement of the 17th century caused much suffering to the Jews of Yemen, who attempted to leave the country and join him for the return to Palestine.

The Jews of Yemen spoke Arabic Hebrew, and Aramaic. They were skilled artisans and renowned gold and silversmiths. They were creative in Jewish scholarship and wrote many Midrashim and Piyutim. They also contributed to the literature of Cabala.

The elected leader of the Jewish community was called the Nasi. Some Jews held high office under the ruling Imams. Economically, most Jews were very poor.

In 1882, during the first Aliyah to Palestine, a small number of Jews managed to migrate despite hardships and restrictive measures.

In 1948, when the State of Israel was established, the 50,000 Jews of Yemen were subject to extreme Arab hostility and vengeance. The Jewish Agency undertook to transfer the entire Jewish population to Israel by air. In two years "Operation Magic Carpet" brought over 47,000 Jews to Israel from the cities of San'a, Sa'da Shamar, Kaukauban, and Adan. There was continued emigration, and only about 600 Jews now remain in Yemen.

The Jews of Rome and Italy

Italy is the first of the European countries to which the Jews migrated. Records show that the Jewish people have lived in Italy from the time of the Hasmonean period (165 BCE to 4 CE). Jewish communities flourished in the city of Rome and on the banks of the Tiber river from pre-Christian times. Annually, they sent their Temple taxes to Jerusalem. Before the close of the Classical Period, Jews lived in at least forty places in the country. The Catacombs in Rome provide evidence of their cultural, social, and economic conditions.

UNDER PAGAN ROMAN EMPERORS

In the year 63 BCE, civil war broke out in Judea between the rival brothers Hyrcanus and Aristobulus. Pompey of Rome interceded and thus Palestine became a vassal state. During the next century, many Jews settled voluntarily in port cities and many reached Italy as captives.

The year 70 CE marks the end of the second Jewish commonwealth. The revolt against Rome was crushed and the Temple destroyed. Most of the inhabitants were exiled to Rome as captives and slaves. The same thing happened again in the year 135 during the Bar Cochba revolt. The Jewish population of Rome again increased.

Under the pagan rulers of Rome, the Jews, though denied citizenship, enjoyed freedom in their religious and economic life. The Roman government looked upon Judaism as a "permitted religion."

HADRIAN (117–138)

This emperor cruelly persecuted the Jews because they attempted to revolt against Roman rule.

CARACALLA (211–217)

In the year 212 he granted citizenship and equal rights to all subjects of Rome.

Judaism, in contrast to the Polytheism of Rome, was highly respected and its influence brought many prominent converts to its fold. At one time intermarriage became a prominent practice.

CONSTANTINE THE GREAT (306–337)

This Emperor was at first favorably disposed toward the Jews. During his early reign an edict of toleration was issued granting religious freedom to all.

Despite bans and proscriptions imposed at times by previous Emperors, their religion and life continued without any drastic interference until, in 325, the Roman Empire, through the conversion of the Emperor Constantine, embraced Christianity and proclaimed it the official religion of the land.

With this new power coming suddenly to the church, the edicts of toleration were soon forgotten. The rise of Christianity saw the gradual transfer of power from Emperor to the Pope—the Bishop of Rome. Christian Rome adopted a policy of religious persecution and church legislation against the Jews. With few exceptions this anti-Jewish policy continued throughout the centuries that followed.

JEWISH LIFE UNDER CHRISTIAN ROME

Little is known concerning the Jews in the early centuries of the Roman Empire. The Jews fared the same as the rest of the population with each new invasion or conquest. Although their position as Jews deteriorated, some Emperors and Popes were more kindly disposed than was the church proper. The Jewish people continued their livelihood as traders and merchants. They spoke a mixture of Greek, Latin, and Hebrew.

The history of Italy in these centuries is the history of Emperor and Pope striving for power and supremacy. The history of the Jew follows an uneven pattern—edicts of intolerance, political and economic restrictions, religious prohibitions.

JULIAN (361–363)

Julian is called an apostate by the church fathers because of his favorable treatment of the Jews. In defiance of the hostile church, he removed the poll tax and restrictive legislation. He made plans for the restoration of the Temple at Jerusalem, which was interrupted by his death.

THEODOSIUS THE GREAT (379–395)

Against the threat of the church, this Emperor protected the Jews. Theodosius divided the Roman Empire between his two sons, thus creating an Eastern or Byzantine Empire with its capital at Constantinople, and a Western Empire with its capital at Rome It was at this time that a Jewish community was established at Constantinople.

THEODOSIUS II (408–450)

The severe restrictions and oppressive measures that were enacted under Hadrian were revived under this Emperor in the "Code of Theodosius." New synagogues could not be built. Old ones were confiscated or burned. Marriage and fraternization with Christians were forbidden.

In the year 425 he abolished the office of Patriarch, thus breaking the ties that bound the Jews in exile with their homeland in Palestine.

It was during the reign of this Byzantine ruler that Italy was invaded by the Goths, who conquered Rome (410) under the leadership of Alaric. They later divided into two groups—Ostrogoths, rulers of Italy and the east, and Visigoths, rulers of Spain and the west. In the year 476 Vandals invaded the country and defeated the Goths.

THEODORIC (474–526)

This king of the Ostrogoths conquered Italy, took the title "Governor of the Romans," ruled beneficently and restored Jewish privileges.

JUSTINIAN I (527–565)

Under this Byzantine ruler all previous restrictions against the Jews were renewed and embodied in a decree known as the "Code of Justinian." His reign was a rebirth of imperial greatness.

The Lombards (568–574)

The reign of the Lombards paved the way for ducal and papal alliances with independent Italian cities. After this Germanic people invaded north Italy in 568, their conquest spread throughout most of Italy.

Charlemagne (800–814)

He was a Frankish king who invaded Italy to support Pope Adrian I. This papal ruler was under attack by Desiderius, the last of the Lombard kings. Charlemagne was the first Emperor of the Holy Roman Empire. He patronized the Jews and granted them freedom of worship, exemption from excise taxes, and security of life and property. His favors to the Jews are legendary.

JUDAISM UNDER THE CHRISTIAN CHURCH

The fall of the Roman Empire (476) did not destroy the power of the church, but rather added to it. The church adopted a policy of legislating against the Jewish rights and privileges granted by Emperors.

Persecution against the Jew was based on the belief that the Jew was the enemy of God. The church fathers regarded it as a God-given duty to preach against the Jews. Hence, the Jewish people were constantly subjected to burdensome taxes and threatened with baptism, death, or exile.

With the fall of the Roman Empire the Bishop of Rome, the temporal and spiritual leader of all the Christian people, was henceforth called the Pope, meaning Father.

The general policy of the Popes was to restrict and humiliate the Jewish people abroad, but to treat them favorably within the heart of the papacy. Local Jewish communities fared well and many individual Jews were employed as physicians and financial advisers to clergy and ruler.

Pope Gregory the Great (590–604)

His policy characterized the attitude of the church toward the Jews. They were to be tolerated and won over to Christianity. They were not to hold any office or authority over Christians. He strongly opposed compulsory conversions.

Pope Leo III (795–816)

He introduced public disputations between Jews and Christians, which usually ended against the Jews and resulted in forced conversions.

Pope Urban II (1088–1099)

This cleric put his blessing on the Holy war known as the Crusades, which turned out to be one of Israel's darkest hours at the hands of Christians.

Pope Innocent III (1198–1216)

Enforcing all the restrictions of his predecessors, Innocent III, through the fourth Lateran Council, added the disgraceful "Jew Badge" to the growing list of Jewish humiliations. In addition, he repeated the libel that Jews used Christian blood for ritual purposes. His toleration of the Jews was based on the assertion that they must be considered as the living witness of the Christian faith.

Pope John XXII (1316–1334)

He issued an edict to expell all the Jews from Rome. This decree was averted by King Robert of Sicily upon the payment of a large sum of money. There was a sizable Jewish community of manual laborers at this time.

Pope Benedict XIII (1394–1424)

He was the instigator of the famous Tortosa disputation, at which the Jews had to defend themselves against unjust Christian accusations in Spain.

Pope Clement VII (1523–1534)

He was known as "Prince gracious to Israel" because of his tolerance to the Marranos and his interest in the false Messiah, David Reubeni.

Pope Paul IV (1555–1559)

He invoked all former papal restrictions, which firmly established the ghetto life of the Jews. The Jewish people could not own property or engage in professions. They were compelled to wear yellow hats and to pay taxes for the maintenance of converts.

Pope Pius V (1566–1572)

His papacy was marked by the burning of Jewish books and the expulsion of Jews from the papal states.

Pope Gregory XIII (1572–1585)

He revived a papal decree making weekly attendance of Jews at Christian services compulsory. This became a common practice with succeeding popes.

Pope Pius VII (1800–1823)

He reinstituted the inquisition in papal states and deprived the Jews of the freedom obtained in the era of Napoleonic emancipation. He decreed their return to the ghetto.

JEWISH LIFE IN ITALY

Italian Jewry, throughout its history, escaped the bitterest forms of persecution and suffering that were visited upon European Jewry. They were more or less permitted to direct their own religious life and allowed to participate in cultural and economic pursuits.

Scholarship, though limited, was still the primary interest of the people, and schools were established in many Jewish communities. Newly founded universities of Italy opened their doors to Jews and attracted many students and professors in the field of medicine, science, and philosophy.

Medicine was always a favorite pursuit of the Jews and records show that as physicians their services were held in high esteem by Popes and rulers. Pope Boniface ix (1392) called his Jewish doctor Angelus Manuale, his "beloved son." Another Jewish doctor, Jacob Mantino, was physician to Pope Paul iii (1534–1549). Popes Alexander vi (1492–1503) and Leo x (1049–1054) used the services of Bonet di Lattes. Simon Tarfati attended Julius ii (1503–1513).

Many Jewish communities were established throughout Italy, particularly in the south. Jews settled in large numbers in Venice and Rome. Under the favorable disposition of King Roger, the city of Naples became a leading center for Jewish learning. Jewish scholarship took on a new lease of life when, in 1140, the renowned Spanish scholar, Abraham Ibn Ezra spread his influence among the Jewish communities.

When the Jews were exiled from Spain (1492), many of them found refuge in the Italian republics of Florence, Venice, Genoa, and Pisa In Venice the Jews were permitted to engage in banking. But there was persecution in Naples and Sicily, ending in expulsion from both.

Jews contributed to the Renaissance of Italy. Their social level was high and their services were recognized in many fields of endeavor. In the field of printing they were pioneers. The Soncini family (named after an Italian town) established printing houses in a number of communities.

It was not until the middle of the 16th century that ecclesiastical edicts deprived the Jews of their prestige.

PERSONALITIES AND EVENTS

SABBATAI ben ABRAHAM DONNOLO (913–984)

Wrote *Sefer Yetzirah, Book of Creation.* He is credited with being the first European Jewish author. He was also highly regarded as a medical authority.

PALTIEL (953–975)

He rose to prominence as the Vizier to the Caliph Muizz. Wrote a condensation of the history of Josephus known as *Jossiphon*.

AHIMAAZ (1054)

Wrote an historical account of two centuries of contemporary Jewish history, known as the *Chronicles of Ahimaaz*.

NATHAN ben YECHIEL (1035–1106)

Headed the academy at Rome. Wrote a dictionary of Hebrew and Aramaic words and called it the *Aruch*.

ABRAHAM ibn EZRA (1098–1164)

This Spanish scholar and poet came to Rome in 1140, where his influence became widespread. His Hebrew writings date from this period.

THE GOLDEN AGE OF ITALIAN JEWRY
(1230–1550)

During these two centuries the Jews enjoyed the fruits of culture and scholarship. While they did not keep pace with their co-religionists of Spain, they did produce a number of literary lights.

JACOB ANATOLI (1194–1246)

He settled in Naples from Provence and entered the service of Frederick II. He translated Arabic philosophy into Hebrew and was a popular preacher.

HILLEL OF VERONA (1220–1295)

Author of *The Recompense of the Soul*, a work on Jewish philosophy and tradition.

EMANUEL OF ROME (1270–1330)

Wrote a secular Hebrew volume of poetry called *Machbereth, Compositions*.

KALONYMOS b. KALONYMOS (1287–1337)

He came from France and was received with favor by King Robert of Naples. He translated many works into Hebrew and wrote a book called *Touchstone,* containing an account of his time.

ELIJAH del MEDIGO (1460–1497)

Philosopher, scientist, physician, and professor at the University at Padua. He wrote many works on scientific subjects and was widely known for his studies on mathematical astronomy. He also wrote scholarly articles on Rashi and Ibn Ezra. His book *Bechinath HaDaath, Examination of Religion,* explored religious and philosophical doctrine.

MOSES RIETI (1388–1460)

Wrote *Mikdash Me'ath, The Small Sanctuary,* an imitation of Dante's Divine Comedy. He was the first to introduce regular stanzas in Hebrew poetry. He served as rabbi in Rome and physican to Pius II.

ABRAHAM FARISSOL (1451–1526)

Wrote *Iggereth Orchot Olom, A Letter on the Ways of the World,* a geographical work in which the discoveries of Vasco de Gama are mentioned, as well as a chapter on the discovery of America. His other works include a commentary on Job and an account of a disputation at Ferrara.

DAVID ben JUDAH ben JECHEL (1471–c. 1526)

Also known as Messer Leon. He was a rabbi, Bible commentator, physician, and author of philosophical works. His dispute with Joseph Kolon, rabbi of Mantua, caused both to be banished from the city.

Printed Works

Rashi's *Commentary on the Pentateuch* is the earliest known printed work in Hebrew. It was published in 1475 in Reggio. About the same time there was also published the famous work of Jacob ben Asher, the *Arbah Turim—The Four Rows.*

DISCRIMINATORY MEASURES

The Jewish Ghetto

Venice was the first city in the Middle Ages to establish segregated living areas for its Jewish inhabitants in order to prevent their contact with Christians. The date was 1516 and this example of minority humiliation and restriction was followed by many other communities in Italy and other places in Europe.

The ghetto was usually a walled-in section of the city with its gates guarded by day and locked by night. In Venice, this section was located on the island of Lunga Spina, near an iron or cannon foundry called GHETA or GETO, from which some scholars think that the name "Ghetto" is derived. Other possible sources are BORGHETTO, a small burgh or quarter; GUITTO or GHITO meaning "dirty"; and GITTAR from the German meaning "Bars."

Upon the Christian church rests full responsibility for the establishment of the ghetto. From early times the church discouraged fraternization with Jews, and endorsed the ghetto as a means of cutting off social and economic intercourse. In 1550 Pope Paul IV issued the infamous Bull that established "The Jewish Quarter," Vicus Judaeaorum.

. . . In Rome and all other cities of the Papal States, the Jews shall live entirely separated from the Christians, in a quarter or a street with one entrance and one exit. They shall have but one synagogue, shall build no new synagogue, nor own real estate.

In some countries of Europe the Jews often found it to their advantage to live in ghettos, since they served as security and protection against hostile mobs.

The Burning of Books and Censorship

The Talmud was regarded by Christianity as the main core of Jewish resistance to conversion. Suppression of its study was periodically ordered by popes and rulers because they believed that it implied "Jewish contempt" for Christianity.

It was first in Italy and at the instigation of the heads of the church that the Jews were forced to watch the burning of their religious books. Their anguish was the greater because in most instances converts and renegades were the chief denouncers of the Talmud.

During the Papacy of Paul IV (1559), there were many such public bonfires. Those books that were not burned were subject to strict censorship. They were examined for slanders, insults, objectionable heretical statements, and offensive words and sentences. These would be deleted or forbidden in subsequent editions.

The papal office issued an index of forbidden books that included the Talmud. Jewish homes and synagogues were searched and books confiscated. Often the books were not returned, even though they were declared free of any offense.

Oath—(More Judaico)

The Latin phrase *"More Judaico"* means *"According to the custom of the Jews."* During the Middle Ages and continuing to the era of emancipation in the nineteenth century, the Jews were subjected to a special form of oath accompanied by unusual phraseology and ceremonials. The authorities in many European countries imposed degrading formalities, such as standing on the skin of a pig, demanding the oath be taken over the Torah, girding oneself with thorns, stepping into a container of water, spitting three times on his male member, or wearing the Tallith and Jewish hat.

Money-Lending

Christian and Jewish law were both opposed to the practice of usury, but restrictions and bans in so many other fields of endeavor forced the Jews into this despised occupation. It became one of the chief sources of income for the Jewish people and incurred the envy and hatred of Christian laymen. Even after the church did permit its adherents to enter the field, this hostility against the Jews continued unabated.

When the Jewish people were engaged in money-lending, the church condemned the practice and fixed the limit of interest at 5%. When Christians entered the field, the church called the practice "Mounts of Piety" and permitted interest charges as high as 40% on loans.

The Scourge of the Jews

John of Capistrano (1386–1456), with other church leaders, organized preacher friars from among the Franciscan and Dominican monks. These men of God went about the land inciting the people to riots and massacres against the Jews. John was the Papal Inquisitor and his organized system of disseminating anti-Semitism earned for him the title "The Scourge of the Jews."

The Yellow Badge

This degrading symbol, which was first decreed by the Moslems in the seventh century to distinguish Jews and Christians from "believers," was imposed upon the Jews by Innocent III at the Fourth Lateran Council (1215) The purpose of the badge or hat was to identify the Jews and set them apart as social pariahs. At times, the color and placement of the badges were changed or the details of the clothing were varied, but they all served the same purpose.

Compulsory Conversionist Sermons

Pope Benedict (1450) introduced this method of persuading Jews by force to attend church services and to listen to conversion sermons. This practice was carried on in many European countries for almost four centuries.

Running the Gauntlet

During the annual Roman Carnival, eight Jews were forced to run a foot-race to provide sport for the people. During this race and for the entire length of the course they were subject to jeers, interference, abuse, humiliations, and severe beatings.

Servitude of the Jews

Thomas Aquinas, the revered church dignitary (1225 – 1274), known as "The Angelic Father," established the doctrine of "Servitus Judaeorum," "The Servitude of the Jews." This church decision stated that on religious grounds the Jews should be held in perpetual servitude. In practice this doctrine resulted in making Jews throughout Europe "Chattels of the King."

The Mortara Case

Edgardo Mortara (1858–1940), a seven-year old Jewish boy, was forcibly abducted from the custody of his parents in Bologna. This came about because his Christian nurse had him baptized secretly four years earlier when he was critically ill. She confessed to her priest and the matter came to the attention of the Papal Inquisition. It was decreed that the child, by virtue of his baptism, was a Christian and that he be taken from his home and be educated as a Christian by the church.

Widespread protest and intercession were of no avail. The Pope refused audience to Jewish delegations and resented the unfavorable publicity that resulted. Mortara had an opportunity to return to Judaism at the age of eighteen, but chose to remain a Catholic. Subsequently he entered the priesthood, serving the church as a missionary. Because of this case and the involvement of many prominent Jews, the Alliance Israelite Universelle was formed in France for the purpose of championing and protecting Jewish rights.

Simon of Trent

In the northern Italian city of Trent there existed a small Jewish community, where, in the year 1475, the Jews were accused of killing a Christian child, Simon, for Passover ritual purposes. A Franciscan preacher, Bernardino de Feltre, aroused and agitated the populace against the Jews, which resulted in their extermination as a community. The child, Simon, was beatified in 1582, and was venerated until 1965, when the Catholic church announced that the accusation was false.

NOTEWORTHY PERSONALITIES

When the Jews outside of Italy were subject to persecution and expulsion, many rabbis and scholars found refuge in Italy, where they made notable contributions to the growing field of Jewish scholarship. The Spanish expulsion of 1492 brought many outstanding Jewish personalities to Italy. Some of them were mystics and succeeded in planting the roots for Cabalism. These, together with native scholars, made important contributions to Jewish literature.

DON ISAAC ABRAVANEL (1437–1508)

He came from Spain and entered the diplomatic service at Venice. He spread the belief in the coming of the Messiah. One of his sons, Joseph, was a prominent physician. Another, Samuel, was minister of finance to the Spanish Viceroy of Naples.

ELIAS LEVITA (1465–1579)

He came from Germany and was engaged as instructor of Hebrew to Cardinal Viterbo. Wrote many works on Hebrew grammar which were translated into Latin. He also compiled a Concordance containing every word of the Bible.

SOLOMON USQUE (16th century)

Came from Portugal and lived in several Italian cities. Author of a history book on Jewish persecution called *Consolation in Israel's Tribulations*. This was written to give courage and bolster the morale of Marranos.

JOSEPH HAKOHEN (1496–1575)

He wrote *Emek ha-Bacha, Vale of Tears,* a book describing the Jewish sufferings of his time. He also wrote a history of the rulers of France and Turkey.

SALOMONE DE ROSSI (1567–c.1628)

Instrumentalist and musical director at court of Mantua. Cantor in Venice synagogue. Composed many musical settings to Psalms and prayers for Sabbath and Holy Days.

AZARIAH DE ROSSI (1511–1578)

Renowned literary figure of his time. Used the scientific method in the treatment of Jewish literature. His book *Meor Aynaim, The Light of the Eyes,* contains an account of the great earthquake of his time. He also wrote essays on Philo and Bible translations. He was the author of poems written in Italian, Aramaic, and Hebrew.

DAVID DE POMIS (1525–1588)

Author of *Tzemach David, The Sprout of David,* a Hebrew, Latin, and Italian Dictionary. He also wrote a book in defense of Jewish physicians.

LEON DE MODENA (1571–1648)

A prolific writer in the field of diverse subjects. Despite his addiction to gambling he wrote a book strongly denouncing the evil.

LUZZATTO, SIMON ben ISAAC (SIMCHAH) (1583–1663)

He was a student of political economy and in his book *Discourse on the Status of the Jews,* he showed how the Jews were necessary to the well-being of a country.

GEDALIAH *ibn* YAHYA (1515–1587)

Wrote a history of Jewish tradition entitled *Shalsheleth HaCabal,* *The Chain of Tradition,* based on Jewish and non-Jewish sources.

ISAAC LAMPRONTI (1679–1756)

Rabbi and physician. Wrote *Pachad Yitzchak, The Fear of Isaac,* a Talmudic encyclopedia.

MOSES CHAYIM LUZZATTO (1707–1747)

He was a gifted poet and scholar who succumbed to the lure of Cabala. He was excommunicated and traveled extensively. Author of a morality play called *The Tower of Strength.* He also wrote *The Path of the Upright,* a work which is popular to this day. He died in Palestine.

ISAAC SAMUEL REGGIO (1784–1855)

Scholar, mathematician, and rabbi who wrote commentaries on the Bible with Italian translations. He labored for the establishment of a seminary to train rabbis and in 1829 the first rabbinical school was opened at Padua. Reggio was the first scholar to record medieval Jewish history. He is referred to as the Mendelssohn of Italy.

SAMUEL DAVID LUZZATTO (1800–1865)

Scholar of Hebrew and Aramaic grammar. He gave new impetus to the study of the Bible and the Hebrew language.

EMANCIPATION AND JEWISH LIFE

The first period of freedom, though of short duration, came with the French Revolution in 1789 and Napoleon's invasion of Italy. The liberating army opened the ghetto gates and ordered the removal of the Yellow Badge. In 1807 religious representatives of

Italian Jewry were invited to the Sanhedrin convened by Napoleon in Paris. After Napoleon fell, Pope Pius the VII reinstated the Inquisition and the Jews were again deprived of all their rights.

The revolution of 1848, under Mazzini and Garibaldi, brought new freedoms to the Jews, but it was not until 1870, and the end of Papal domination, that the ghetto walls were destroyed and full freedom was granted to the Jews throughout Italy.

With this new freedom, the Jews began to take on an Italian acculturation. The new generation wanted to be more Italian than Jewish. As they became prominent and influential in Italian life, assimilation began to take its toll. Intermarriage reached such sizable proportions that in some communities they exceeded the number of Jewish marriages.

Many Jews or persons of Jewish descent achieved fame as statesmen. Isaac Artom (1829–1900) was general secretary of the foreign office and the first Jew of Italy to become a senator. Luigi Luzzatti (1841–1907) was appointed Prime Minister and served on five occasions as Minister of the Treasury. General Giuseppe Ottolenghi (1838–1904) was Minister of War, and Sansone d'Ancona (1814–1894), Minister of Finance.

This era of freedom and equality ended with the rise of Fascism in 1922 under the dictatorship of Benito Mussolini. The Jewish population numbered about 40,000 and despite their participation in civic and political affairs, despite their record of loyalty and patriotism in World War I, they were subject to the anti-Semitism that accompanied the rise of Hitlerism.

When Italy became part of the Rome-Berlin axis in 1938, Jews were excluded from schools and dismissed from all official positions. Anti-Jewish legislation followed Hitler's pattern. Unlike their coreligionists in Germany, the Jews of Italy did not suffer the full brunt of extermination. A large segment sought to escape through conversion. Some 5,000, about 10 per cent of the Jewish population, including the chief rabbi, Ignazio Zolli, turned to the Catholic faith.

It is estimated that as of 1960 about 36,000 Jews lived in Italy. The main Jewish communities are Rome (12,000 Jews), Milan (5,000 Jews), and Turin (3,000 Jews).

JEWISH COMMUNITIES IN ITALIAN HISTORY

Alessandria	Padua
Ancona	Parma
Aquileia	Palermo
Bologna	Pompeii
Concordia	Rome
Firenze	Salerno
Ferrara	Sardinia
Genoa	Sicily
Gorizia	Syracusa
Mantua	Torina
Merano	Trent
Milan	Turin
Messina	Venice
Modena	Vercelli
Naples	Verona

The Jews of Spain

The Hebrew name for Spain is Sepharad (Obadiah 20). The Jews from Spain and Portugal are known as Sephardim.

Early Jewish migration to Spain began around the year 300 CE, although Jewish communities are not recorded until the ninth century. From 486 to 711, Spain was under Visigoth rulers, conquerors of Rome. It was during the Arab invasion (711–828) that large numbers of Jews settled there.

RICCARED I (590) made Catholicism the religion of Spain and sought to suppress all minority religions, regardless of how weak or few the adherents.

CHINTILLA (638) decreed that only professing Catholics could live in Spain. Few Jews, however, were forced to migrate because of this decree.

KING EGICA (639) attempted to proscribe the Jewish religion, but with little success. Christians were forbidden to fraternize with Jews.

SPAIN UNDER MOSLEM RULE (711–1031)

The Moslem conquest of Spain gave the Jews religious liberty and self-government. Large Jewish communities were established at Granada, Cordova, Seville, and Toledo. Jews became prominent in science, philosophy, poetry, and politics. Scholarship flourished and Jewish literature reached a "golden age" of achievement during the tenth and 11th centuries. Economically and politically the Jews fared well. Many occupied high government offices.

PERSONALITIES OF THIS PERIOD

MENAHEM ben SARUK (910–970)
Grammarian and lexicographer. He was first to distinguish pure roots in the Hebrew language. Other grammarians of note were Dunah ibn Labret (920–990) and Jonah ibn Janach (990–1020).

CHASDAI ibn SHAPRUT (912–961)
Adviser to Sultan Abdurraham III. He was a prominent physician, communal leader, and Nasi of all Jews in the Caliphate. As a patron of learning, he opened the first Jewish academy in Spain and supported many scholars in their studies. His letters referred to correspondence with the mythical Jewish King of the Khazars.

MOSES ben CHANOCH (c.960)
This man was one of four scholars who left Sura (Babylonia) in behalf of the academies of learning. Captured and sold into slavery, he was ransomed by Jews of Spain and subsequently became the leading Jewish scholar and authority of his time. Through him the study of the Talmud began to flourish in Europe.

SAMUEL HALEVI ibn NAGRELA (ibn Nagdela) (HANAGID) (993–1056)
Poet, grammarian, statesman, and Talmudist, he served as Vizier at Granada. In addition to his many poems he wrote a dictionary of Biblical Hebrew.

ISAAC ALFASI OF FEZ (1013–1069)
Famous Talmudist of his day. Wrote an important rabbinical compendium known as *Halachoth, —The Book of Laws.*

SOLOMON ibn GABIROL (1021–1069)
Poet and philosopher. Many of his religious poems are included in the liturgy of the Jewish Prayer Book. His philosophy of religion and life is contained in his book

Mechor Chayim, The Fountain of Life. This book, under the Latin name *Fons Vitae,* was popular with Christian scholars.

FROM END OF MOSLEM RULE TO EXPULSION FROM SPAIN
(1037–1492)

In the centuries that followed, Spain became a country of small provinces, each ruled by a Moslem Caliph or Christian King. In the struggle for power between these, the Jewish people were often the first victims and usually suffered the most. Each change of power revoked old privileges, imposed new restrictions, and decreed severe punishments, hardships, and expulsions. In the 13th century, the Moslems were defeated in most of Spain and Christian rule became dominant.

As Christianity gained power, the fortunes of the Jews grew worse. Often their choice was between enforced conversion or expulsion. A new and terrible device for the persecution of heretics was introduced by the Catholic church, called the "Inquisition."

The history of this period reads with monotonous routine of persecution, massacre, and expulsion. The long list of abuses and excesses might be condensed as follows:

Jews banished from Andulasia.

Jews forced to defend themselves in public disputation at Barcelona and Toledo.

Property of the Jews of Navarre confiscated.

Jews of Castile and Toledo subjected to badge of shame.

Ghetto imposed upon Jews of Castile and Aragon.

Jewish children seized by church and baptized into Christian faith.

Jews of Valencia wiped out by massacre.

Church edict forbade Jews to live in Christian quarters.

Papal decree forced Jews to listen to Christian sermons in synagogues.

Talmud ordered burned in many cities throughout Spain.

Torquemada appointed Chief Inquisitor of Spain.

Many Jews put to death at Auto-da-fe.

Jews confined to *Juderias,* areas completely enclosed by walls.

PERSONALITIES OF THIS PERIOD

BACHYA ben JOSEPH ibn PAKUDA (c.1050–c.1120)

A philosopher known for his work *Chovoth HaLevavoth, Duties of the Heart,* containing personal thoughts about ethical conduct.

JUDAH ben SAMUEL HALEVI (1086–1140)

The greatest poet of the "Golden Age." His two outstanding works are *Songs of Zion* and *The Kuzari.* The former concerns Jewish suffering and the eternal hope for Palestine. The latter, a philosophic work in dialogue form, exalts the moral truths of Judaism.

ABRAHAM ibn EZRA (1098–1164)

Scholar, poet, grammarian, and scientist. Wrote many Bible commentaries and was among the first to enter the field of Bible criticism. Traveled extensively.

ABRAHAM ibn DAUD (c.1110–c.1180)

Philosopher and historian. Author of *Sefer HaCabala, Book of Traditions,* and *Emunah Ramah, The Sublime Faith.*

MOSES MAIMONIDES
(1135–1204)

Known as the "Rambam," this man achieved fame in the field of medicine, philosophy, and Judaism. He wrote *Mishnah Torah,* the *Study of the Torah,* which contains a systematic arrangement and classification of all the Jewish laws. Another important work was his *Moreh Nebuchim, Guide to the Perplexed,* a basic philosophical study of Judaism.

MOSES ben NACHMAN (1194–1270)

Better known as Nachmanides, this man was a student of Talmud, Bible, and Cabala. He was one of the chief opponents of the teachings of Maimonides. He was chosen to represent the Jews at the famous Barcelona disputation in 1263 against the apostate Pablo Christiani.

SOLOMON ben ADRET (1235–1310)

Rabbi of Barcelona ("Rashba,"), known for his responsa and decisions. He forbade scholars under twenty-five to study philosophy and science. This marked the decline of Jewish scientific learning in Spain.

MOSES ben SHEMTOV de LEON
(1250–1305)

One of the reputed authors of the *Zohar,* the Bible of Cabalism. This book greatly influenced the mystical thinking of Jews in the centuries that followed.

JACOB ben ASHER (1280–1340)

Author of *Sefer HaTurim, The Book of Four Rows,* an important compendium of ritual and legal laws.

CHASDAI ben ABRAHAM CRESCAS
(1340–1410)

Philosopher and defender of the Jewish faith. Wrote *Or Adonoy, The Light of the Lord,* a work on logic. Engaged in a disputation with apostate Paul Burgos.

JOSEPH ALBO (c.1380–c.1435)

Participated in the disputation at Tortosa. Author of *Ikkarim, Principles* or *Fundamentals* of Judaism.

ISAAC ABRAVANEL (1437–1509)

Communal leader and statesman. Tried in vain to stop expulsion of Jews from Spain. In 1492 Ferdinand and Isabella issued the infamous decree expelling all Jews who refused to accept Christianity.

INSTITUTIONS AND EVENTS

Marranos

The word Marrano means "Swine." It was applied to the Jews of Spain and Portugal who were coerced into Christianity or embraced the religion as an expediency. The Jews called such converts "Anusim" — "Forced Converts." They became numerous after the 1391 massacre.

Outwardly these people professed to be Catholics, attended church services, and associated with Christians. Secretly, however, they adhered to Judaism, observing holidays, ritual, and ceremony at great risk to their lives.

The Inquisition

The word "Inquisition" means an act of inquiry, search, examination, and investigation. As used by the Catholic church, the Inquisition was the systematic pursuit of heresy against the church and the punishment of heretics by the general tribunal of the papal Holy Office. It was established by Pope Gregory IX in 1231 for the purpose of keeping converts from leaving Christianity.

Its operation, though widespread, was chiefly confined to Spain and Portugal and their dependencies in South America. It was abolished in France in 1772 and in Spain in 1834.

Originally, the Inquisition was directed against Christian offenders, with occasional charges against Jews for blasphemy, host desecration, and reversion from Christianity. Under the notorious Inquisitor-General, Thomas de Torquemada, who was appointed in 1483, the Inquisition was directed chiefly against Marranos (Secret Jews). These were Jews who underwent forced mass conversions to escape death. Outwardly they were Christian, but secretly they remained loyal to and practiced their Judaism.

Torquemada was a cruel and fanatic inquisitor. He devised ingenious forms of torture and employed the most barbaric methods in wringing confessions, even from the innocent. The Inquisition used informers to effect accusations and arrests of Judaizers. There were few acquittals and those who did not receive the maximum penalty of death were subject to heavy fines, confiscation of property, and sometimes banishment. Torquemada was responsible for the order of expulsion of all Spanish Jewry in 1492.

Auto-da-fé (Death by fire)

This is a Spanish term meaning an "Act of Faith." It was a solemn ceremony carried out by the Inquisition, in which those convicted of heresy were publicly burned at the stake. Marrano Jews, who were suspected or caught in the act of reverting to Judaism, were often victims of this form of execution.

It is estimated that in Spain, Portugal, and their colonies, between the fifteenth and nineteenth centuries, there were about 30,000 Auto-da-fés. Over 6,000 Jews were condemned by the Inquisition, about 3,000 with the penalty of death. The Auto-da-fé came to South America in 1569. It was not officially abolished by the church until 1834.

Proselytizing and Forced Conversions

Compulsory baptism is the forcible conversion of "unbelievers" to Christianity. The first large-scale conversion on record is by the Roman Emperor, Justinian I (527–565), who ordered the Jews of Borion, in Northern Africa, to embrace Christianity and had their synagogues converted into churches. In Visigoth Spain (eighth century), rulers gave their Jewish subjects the alternative of conversion or expulsion. Jewish children from the age of seven were forcibly taken from their parents and raised as Christians.

Papal edicts sought to convert Jews by "persuasion and gentleness," but when church leaders found this method to be ineffective, they usually resorted to more drastic measures. Pope Clement III (1080–1100) enjoined rulers from permitting baptized Jews to return to their faith. Pope Benedict XIV (1675–1758) declared that baptism, once performed, was forever valid, regardless of how improperly conferred.

In many instances the only alternative to enforced conversion was expulsion or death. In 1391, for the Jews of Spain and Portugal, it was only death. This resulted in a large segment of the Jewish population's becoming Marranos or crypto-Jews. Following the great expulsions of

1492, many Jews who were unable to leave were converted by threats of starvation or violence.

Public Disputations

Apostates and converts to Christianity added their voices to the false accusations and charges against the Jews. Following such charges, Jewish leaders were summoned to defend their people and their religion at public forums. These debates did the Jews little good. If they were successful in their arguments they usually incurred the hostility of the church.

One of the most famous disputations was held at Barcelona in 1263 between Nachmanides and Pablo Christiani, a converted Jew. The latter sought to prove, from the Torah, that Jesus, the predicted Messiah, had already made his appearance. Nachmanides maintained that the coming of the Messiah would mean peace, whereas the nations of the world were still engaged in war. As in most disputations, the protagonists were forced into exile.

Another disputation held at Tortosa (1413–1414) lasted one-and-a-half years and contributed to mass conversions and the deterioration of the Jewish community.

PREACHERS OF VIOLENCE

PABLO CHRISTIANI (d. 1274)

This Dominican agitator against the Jews forced them to engage in "Disputations" to defend themselves against his anti-Semitic accusations. One of these was held in Barcelona in 1263, resulting in the censorship and excision of many passages from the Talmud.

VINCENTE FERRER (1350–1419)

Also known as Ferrus Pedro Vin-

centi, this flagellant member of a Dominican order was possessed of an overwhelming desire to convert the Jews to Christianity. By church edict he forced them to listen to his preachments in the synagogue, which, by threat and coercion, often resulted in mass conversions.

FERNANDO MARTINEZ (Fourteenth century)

This high church dignitary planted the seeds of the Inquisition because he saw in Judaism the implacable enemy of Christ. He believed that the only way to make Jews convert to Christianity was through force and violence. Upon his appointment as Vicar General, he instituted a program of terrorism and malevolence with the sole purpose of exterminating all Jews. Thousands who refused to be baptized perished in the widespread riots that followed. In Seville, 6,000 Jews chose the alternative of baptism to death. In his zeal to stamp out every vestige of Judaism, he caused synagogues to be converted to churches and women and children to be sold into slavery. So popular was this high church cleric that he was worshiped as a saint.

RAYMOND (MARTI) MARTINI (1225–1284)

He was a Spanish Hebraist and became an anti-Jewish Dominican theologian. Because of his knowledge of oriental languages he attended "Disputations" that tended to prove the truth of Christianity from Jewish sources. He quoted the Talmud as giving credence to Jesus as the Messiah.

ALFONSO DE SPINA (Espina) (Fifteenth century)

He was a Franciscan monk and an inveterate enemy of the Jews, devoting his efforts to their destruction, whether converts or Marranos. He attempted to win others to his cause by amassing a collection of all the false accusations brought against them. He was one of the originators of the Spanish Inquisition and was responsible for many of the tortures inflicted upon the Jews.

Cabala

The word "Cabala" means "Tradition" and is a system of thought based on mystical speculation. It became popular at the time that Rabbi Aderet (1305) banned the pursuit of scientific studies. This form of mystical speculation was an attempt to know God through divine emanations revealed to man. It found support in the Bible, where every word and letter was given a mystical explanation.

The source book for Cabalistic teachings is the "Zohar," meaning "Splendor," and is said to be redacted by Moses de Leon in the late 13th century.

FALSE MESSIAHS

Mystical speculations gave rise to a number of individuals who laid claim to being Messiahs. Their delusions often brought tragedy to the Jewish people. Though they promised deliverance and return to Palestine in attracting the masses, they were nevertheless denounced as false Messiahs by the rabbis.

DAVID REUBENI (1491–1535)
He wanted the Pope and Charles v of Germany to approve an alliance against Turkey for the purpose of driving out the Moslems from Palestine. He was turned over to the Inquisition and brought to Spain, where he was imprisoned.

SOLOMON MOLCHO (1500–1532)
This Marrano of Portugal became interested in the messianic claims of Reubeni and followed his banner as an associate. He was arrested by the Inquisition and sentenced to death by burning.

THE GOLDEN AGE

With the closing of the great schools of learning in Babylonia, Jewish literary activity began to flourish in Spain. Poets, philosophers, and Bible and Talmudic scholars rose to great heights. The period in which they achieved their finest literary productivity, the tenth to the 12th century, is known as the "Golden Age" of learning in Spain.

CODES OF JEWISH LAW

Jewish scholars of Spain were among the first to arrange and classify the vast literature of Talmudic law. Their codes became the bases for many of the subsequent compendiums. Among these are:

Halachoth Gedoloth

This book of *The Great or Major Laws* was written by Isaac Alfasi (1013–1103). It was the main such compendium until the one produced by Maimonides.

The Sefer HaTurim

The "Book of Rows" was written by Jacob ben Asher (1280–1340). It is arranged in four rows or divisions.

Orach Chayim—Path of Life;
Yoreh Deah—Guide to Knowledge;
Eben HaEzer—Stone of Help;
Choshen Mishpat—Breastplate of Judgment.

The Mishnah Torah

This book, *The Teaching of Torah,* is also known as *Yad Chazakah, The Strong Hand.* Written by Moses Maimonides (1135–1204), it contains a complete and systematic arrangement of all the laws of the Talmud.

SPANISH JEWRY TO MODERN TIMES

From the writings of Isaac Abravanel (1437–1508) we learn that there were some 300,000 Jews living in Spain at the time of the Expulsion in 1492. Since that time, little has happened concerning the Jews. Marranos remained after the expulsion, but their number was negligible. Persecution in Russia caused a small group of Jews from there to migrate to Spain in 1882. The city of Madrid had a Jewish congregation but the law did not permit them to engage in public worship.

1492–1900—Jewish life all but disappeared following the great expulsion. Refugees settled in Portugal, Turkey, Italy, and North Africa.

1902–1913—Alfonso xiii permitted Jews to settle in small numbers.

1906—About 25,000 Jews living in Morocco came under the rule of Spain.

1914—There were approximately 4,000 Jews living in Spain, but by the end of World War i the number was considerably augmented by the influx of refugees.

1931—An edict of religious freedom was issued by the government. During the first years of Franco's rule the Jews of Barcelona suffered rampant anti-Semitism.

1940—Many German Jews who escaped to Spain, as well as other refugees, were rounded up and interned in camps.

1942—By order of the government all synagogues and Jewish centers were closed.

Since World War ii the condition of the Jews has greatly improved. The Jewish communities are tolerated but have no legal status. The old expulsion law has never been abrogated, although the decrees by Primo de Rivera (1924) and Franco (1948) are regarded by Spanish leaders as a cancellation.

In Spain today, all Sephardim may become citizens, but Ashkenazim cannot, unless they convert to Catholicism. There is a Hebrew chair at Madrid University headed by a Catholic professor. The birthplace of Maimonides at Cordova is a historic shrine maintained by the government.

In 1960 Barcelona had 2,500 Jews; Madrid 1,000; Seville 30; and Valencia 15.

JEWISH COMMUNITIES IN SPAIN

Avila	Lucena
Barcelona	Medina
Carrion	Pamplona
Catalonia	Perpignan
Catatayud	Segovia
Cordova	Saragossa
Cuenca	Seville
Estella	Soria
Gerona	Tarragona
Granada	Toledo
Leon	Tortosa
Lerida	Tudela

These communities are located in the provinces of Aragon, Castille, Leon, and Navarre.

The Jews of Portugal

The country of Portugal plays a

minor role in the history of the Jew. Its story is similar to that of Spain, though of shorter duration. Spanish persecutions sent many Jewish refugees to Portugal who found the same restrictions and hardships confronting them.

In 1492 John II permitted Jews to enter from Spain on payment of a special tax for eight months. Those who could not leave at the end of that period were sold as slaves.

In 1498, during the reign of Manuel, the Jews were expelled from Portugal. Many children were forcibly taken from their parents and baptized into the Christian faith.

Only a few names of Jews who contributed to Jewish learning can be mentioned. David ibn Biliah in philosophy; Joseph Sarco, Cabalist; Judah and Joseph ben Jachi; Isaac Abravanel; Gedaliah ibn David; Isaac Aboab; and Abraham Zacuto. The last moved to Tunis and in the year 1505 wrote a classic reference book called *Sefer Yuchasin.*

The Jews of Poland

There is evidence that small groups of Jews settled in Poland in early times, coming from the Byzantium Empire, the Moslem East, and the Khazar Kingdom. However, Polish Jewish history does not actually begin until the tenth century when refugees from persecution in Germany found a haven there. Mieszko I (960–992), who had converted to Christianity, welcomed them. He was among the many Polish kings who granted Jews the right to reside in Poland, to subsist as merchants and artisans, to protection of life and property, and to religious freedom.

Although the Jews achieved religious autonomy, politically they became wards of the crown and tools of the nobility.

BOLESLAV I, THE BRAVE (992–1025)

Under his reign Jewish immigration from the west increased. The Jews prospered and constituted most of the commercial class in a country of landlords and peasants. Religious intolerance started to make itself felt as the growing power of the church attempted to enforce anti-Jewish canon laws and as the German-Christian artisans and merchants agitated against them.

BOLESLAV III (1102–1138)

At the end of his reign the country was divided into five principalities, Silesia, Great Poland, Masovia, Sandomir, and Cracow. This division endured for about 200 years, during which time Jewish immigration from the west continued in large numbers.

BOLESLAV, THE PIOUS (1264)

This ruler of Kalisz (Great Poland) sought to shield the Jews from intolerance and prejudice by granting them a charter of "general privileges." This became the basis for subsequent Polish-Jewish legislation.

CASIMIR, THE GREAT (1333–1370)

Poland was reunified in 1320 under Ladislaus, the Short, whose enlightened son, Casimir, became known as the "King of the Serfs and the Jews" because he extended their charters of liberty. This encouraged more Jews from neighboring hostile countries to migrate to Poland, where they had some protection from the growing animosity of the church and the peasantry. It was during his reign in 1348–49 that Jews were blamed for the plague in Western Europe known as the Black Death. The massacres there caused large numbers of Jews to flee to Poland.

VLADISLAV V (JAGIELLO) (1386–1434)

By the 15th century there was a large, influential Jewish population engaged mostly in trade and money lending. As Polish rulers became less favorably disposed to them, anti-Jewish sentiment was frequently allowed to erupt into mob violence. There were blood libels and pogroms at Posen in 1399 and in Cracow in 1407. Jagiello refused to confirm the Jewish privileges that had been granted by his predecessors. His reign marked the beginning of religious persecution in Poland.

SIGISMUND I (1506–1548)

His policy toward the Jews was comparatively liberal, but under church pressure he approved certain discriminatory acts that jeopardized the Jews in business and commerce. During his reign attempts were made to restrict their residence to special quarters or ghettos.

SIGISMUND II, AUGUSTUS (1548–1572)

There was a short period of tolerance as the Protestant Reformation spread to Poland. This ruler defended the Jews against various church accusations. By this time Poland had become the center of a vigorous Jewish cultural life. The famous Jewish community organization, known as the Kahal, was established during this period.

STEPHEN BATHORY (1575–1586)

The "Golden Age" of Poland came to an end during his reign. Because of his interest and support, the Jewish people had prospered and had received increased protection against false accusations by the church and hostility of the peasants.

SIGISMUND III (1587–1632)

This ruler threw his entire influence on the side of the Counter Reformation. Under the increasing power of the church, an intense religious fanaticism developed and attacks on Jews became widespread.

JOHN II, CASIMIR (1648–1688)

His reign was marked by grave internal disturbances. Poland ceased to be a haven of refuge for the Jewish people. The Cossack uprising (1648–49) is one of the blackest chapters of mass murders of Jews.

BOGDAN CHMIELNICKI. As the Polish leader of the Cossacks, he was responsible for the butchering and slaughtering of an estimated 300,000 Jews in over 700 communities in Ukraine, Volhynia, and Podolia. While the revolt of the Cossacks was directed against Polish landowners and the Catholic church, the Jews felt the full brunt of the violence because many were agents and tax collectors for the nobility. In the city of Nemirov some 10,000 Jews were killed. In many instances entire Jewish communities were delivered to the Cossacks by the Poles. Baptism was the only means of escape and captured Jews were sold into slavery.

SIMON PETLURA (1880–1926)

Between 1918 and 1920, this nationalist Ukrainian leader personally organized and instigated pogroms against the Jews. These were comparable to the Chmielnicki massacres of 1848. It is estimated that over 16,000 Jews were killed in almost 500 separate pogroms. After World War I he fled to Galicia and then to Paris, where he was assassinated in 1926.

THE PARTITIONING OF POLAND

In 1772 the first partition of Poland took place. Greater Poland, including Posen with its Jewry, went to Prussia. Eastern Galicia, with its Lemberg Jewry, was taken over by Austria. A small portion, known as White Russia, became a province of Russia.

Two more partitions took place —one in 1793 and the other in 1795. The former gave most of Lithuania and the western Ukraine to Russia. The last partition marked the end of Poland's independence. Most of the remaining country came under Russian rule and approximately a million-and-a-half Jews were transferred to Russian despotism. The rest of Poland went to Prussia and Austria. Poland did not regain her independence as a nation until the end of World War I (1917).

In most of its history, Polish Jewry was subject to three forces : (1) the church, with its long history of anti-Jewish policies, (2) the nobility (Shlakhta), that used the Jew to further its own economic ends, and (3) artisans and burghers, many of German descent, who resented the Jews because of their economic success, their religious separatism, and the special privileges extended to them.

POLISH JEWRY UNDER THE CHURCH

Christianity came to Poland about the year 1000 and with it came the hostility of the church against the Jew. Church leaders ever reminded their adherents that the abject and miserable condition of the Jews was an example of the just chastisement of infidels by God. The principal argument of the church was the doctrine that the church tolerated the Jews for the sole purpose of reminding Christians of the torments of the Savior.

It was the church that forced the expulsion of Jews from Poland; that instigated ritual murder and host-desecration accusations, which resulted in mob violence, persecution, and massacre; that segregated the Jews in ghettos; that restricted their activities in trades and handicrafts; and that reduced them to a state of perpetual poverty. It was the church that openly incited the people to riots and pogroms against the Jews through its priests, theologians, students, and fanatics; that kept alive the anti-Semitism that was to endure for many centuries. It was the church that taught its children that it was a religious duty to hate and persecute the Jews.

The Kahal or Kehillah

Throughout history there have been various forms of community organization and self-government among Jews. But it was in Poland that they had their most extensive autonomy in the form of the Kahal or "Assembly of Elders." The Jewish people formed a class of their own, between the nobles and the masses, with which the Polish government found it convenient to deal as a group.

A Charter, issued by Sigismund Augustus in 1551, known as the "Magna Charta of Jewish Self-Government," gave the Jews the right to establish a Kahal, also known by its Ashkenazic term "Kehillah." This elected body regulated every aspect of religious life. It had the responsibility for collecting its own taxes, for administering all Jewish communal institutions, and for settling litigation.

The honorary head of the Kahal, the "Rosh HaKahal" or "Parnas," was assisted by three to seven advisers. He appointed all necessary committees and he represented the Jewish community vis-a-vis the Polish government.

Every Jewish community had its own Kahal. Annual elections were held during the Passover festival and representatives were chosen from among the rabbis, scholars, and business leaders of the community. The Kahals, in turn, belonged to district organizations called "Galiloth," which were combined into provincial organizations known as "Medinoth."

The Council of the Four Lands

Four Medinoth, or Provinces, existed in Poland : Great Poland, Little Poland, Volhynia, and Galicia, or Red Russia. In the year 1580 these four formed a Va-ad or Council known as the VA-AD ARBA ARATZOTH— ועד ארבע ארצות —THE COUNCIL OF THE FOUR LANDS. The chief cities in these provinces were Posen, Cracow, Lublin, Astrog, Ludmir, and Lemberg.

Twice each year they met as one body. The province of Lithuania had its own Va-ad and cooperated with the "big four" until 1623 when it withdrew. The Va-ad met in the cities of Lublin and Yaroslav with some thirty official representatives called Shtadlanim, in attendance. These elected a presiding officer, ROSH HA-KAHAL— ראש הקהל and a chief rabbi. They established a High Court known as the BETH DIN HA-GADOL—בית דין הגדל, which ruled on the decision of the local kahal courts, allocated local tax quotas, settled disputes between provinces and communities, and appointed Shtadlanim to speak for all the Jews in the Va-ad. They also had the power to amend old laws, enact new ones, supervise schools and charities, and to regulate every aspect of Jewish life.

When the Polish government decided to impose a direct poll tax in 1764, it abolished the Va-ad, which no longer served its need. Local community Kahals, however, continued their other functions until 1882, when Russia ended all autonomy for Polish Jewry.

Polish Jewry

During these centuries Jewish life in Poland existed on the perimeter of tolerance. Despite charters of protection and privileges, they were never totally free from anti-Semitism. The church, nobility, and peasantry pressed them into an economic class that left them landless and rootless.

Their chief source of livelihood was as merchants, traders, tax-farmers, money-lenders, and peddlers. Feudal lords and Polish-Catholic landowners employed them as supervisors of their estates. With few exceptions the Jews of Poland lived a precarious existence, segregated in ghettos in most places and uncertain of their fate.

The declared hostility of the church and the relentless hatred of the masses resulted in the Jews' enclosing themselves in a world of Talmud, Cabala, and Chassidism.

In the ghetto the rabbi, scholar, and learned layman were held in highest esteem. Torah was the chief matter of study. Every community had its outstanding Talmudists. Throughout Poland there were many famous YESHIVOTH— ישיבות —SCHOOLS OF LEARNING, which influenced Jewish thought in the Diaspora.

Polish Jewry produced a host of Talmudic and Chassidic scholars and also initiated several religious movements that were outgrowths of historic events. Scholars a l s o seemed to concentrate on codes of Jewish law, some of which survive to this day.

PERSONALITIES AND EVENTS

Poland's Jewry of the 18th and 19th centuries was subject to an existence of degradation and persecution. It was but natural that in this land ridden with anti-Semitism that the masses should look for redemption through individuals and movements. The hope for the coming of a Messiah received its greatest impetus in this country of misery and suffering.

SABBATAI ZEVI (1626–1676)

This self-proclaimed Messiah promised Jews release from suffering, salvation, and a new life in the Holy Land. Everywhere Jews flocked to his banner. Even though this false Messiah became an apostate to save his life, many hopeless, poverty-stricken Jews continued to believe in him. So strong were his faithful that the Rabbi of Nemirov decreed a ban of excommunication against them in 1772.

The Frankist Movement

YANKEV LEIBOVICZ (1726–1791)

This man from Podolia was another famous false Messiah. He changed his name to Jacob Frank when he proclaimed himself successor to Sabbatai Zevi.

The disillusionment that followed Zevi's false promises caused Frank to be denounced and rejected by Israel's leaders. He and his followers retaliated by bringing false charges against the Jews to the Church authorities. These accusations resulted in the burning of the books of the Talmud in 1757. The Frankists were discredited and many of them embraced Christianity. After duping the multitudes, Jacob Frank retired as a wealthy baron.

The Chassidic Movement

The plight of Polish Jewry at the start of the 18th century led to the establishment of a new movement known as Chassidism. The word CHASSID— חסד —means PIOUS ONE. Leaders of the movement came to be known as TZADAKIM— צדקים —RIGHTEOUS ONES, and were believed to be direct intermediaries of God.

Chassidim had its origin in Cabala, a mystical movement absorbed in speculative thought concerning life after death and the world of Paradise. Unlike Cabala, however, Chassidism was a revivalist movement, appealing to the masses to liberate themselves from the yoke of rabbinic Judaism.

ISRAEL ben ELIEZER OF MIEDZIBOZ (1700–1760)

He was the founder of Chassidism. The name BAAL SHEM TOV— בעל שם טוב —MASTER OF THE GOOD NAME was bestowed upon him. Its abbreviated form is BESHT. This pious leader taught that God understood joyous worship and that man could be free from the dreary legalism of Talmudic law because God did not require either great learning or adherence to man-made rabbinic edicts. He believed that the simple Jew could approach God through emotionalism, fervent prayer, and joy; that prayer should be an ecstatic experience accompanied by song and dance. He gained legendary fame as a miracle-worker.

The movement incurred the disfavor of the Talmudic Rabbinites and for almost two centuries there was a schism in Polish Jewry. Foremost among the opponents (Mithnagdim) was the renowned Rabbi Elijah Gaon of Vilna, who exercised his authority as Chief Rabbi by excommunicating many famous Chassidic leaders.

RABBI SHALOM SHACKNAH (1500–1559)

He was the Chief Rabbi of Little Poland and the father of Polish Talmudism.

SOLOMON LURIA (Maharashal) (1510–1573)

He was a famous Talmudic scholar and head of the Academy at Lublin.

MOSES ISSERLES (Rama) (1513–1572)

Rabbi of Cracow, who wrote *Mappah, Tablecloth,* an addition to Karo's *Shulchan Aruch* for Polish and German (Ashkenazim) Jews.

RABBI MEIR OF LUBLIN (Maharam) (1558–1616)

He was a leader of the Va-ad and a noted Talmudic scholar. His explanations of the Talmud appear under the name *Maharam, Our Master.*

MORDECAI JAFFE (1530–1612)

Wrote, *Lebushim, Raiments,* a rival code of law to the *Shulchan Aruch.*

SAMUEL EDELS (Maharsha) (1555–1631)

The commentaries of this famous Talmudic scholar and head of the Lublin Yeshivah are included in many editions of the Talmud, appearing under the title *Chiddushe Halachoth, Halachic Novellae.*

YOM TOV LIPPMAN HELLER (1579–1654)

This rabbi of Prague and Cracow wrote *Tosefoth Yom Tov* on the six orders of the Mishnah. He composed poems of courage and hope for his persecuted people.

SHABBATAI HAKOHEN (Shach) (1621–1662)

His commentary on the *Shulchan Aruch* is called *Siftai Kohen, Lips of the Priests,* and is classed among the great codes of Jewish law.

JEICHEL HEILPRIN (1660–1746)

He was the head of the Minsk Yeshivah and a forerunner of modern Jewish learning. His famous work *Seder HaDoroth, Book of Generations,* is a biographical and historical chronicle of the Jewish people.

DOV BAER OF MESERITZ (1710–1772)

He was the successor to the Besht. He popularized the Chassidic movement.

ELIJAH GAON OF VILNA (1729–1797)

He was known as the great Talmudist of Lithuania who opposed Chassidism and excommunicated its leaders. He created a new system of Talmudic study that departed from the Pilpul method.

ABRAHAM KALISHER OF KALISK
(d. 1810)
Noted Chassidic rabbi. In 1777 he emigrated to Palestine with 300 Chassidic followers.

SHNEOUR ZALMAN ben BARUCH
(1747–1812)
This scholar of Lyadi founded a splinter movement in Chassidism known as "Habad," formed from initial letters of three words meaning Wisdom, Understanding, and Knowledge. His movement attempted a rational rather than an emotional or mystical approach. His opponents (Mithnagdim) brought charges against him that resulted in a period of imprisonment by the Russian government.

ISRAEL MEIR KAHAN (1837–1933)
Known as "Chafetz Chayim," "Desirer of Life," he was an outstanding authority on law and ethics.

POLISH JEWRY TODAY

Poland regained her independence following World War i. In 1921 she was declared a republic and all minority groups were guaranteed constitutional protection and religious-cultural autonomy.

But anti-Semitism continued and all the old restrictions were introduced against the two million Jews. Economic opportunities were denied, a numerus clausus was introduced in the schools, ghetto benches were imposed in the classrooms, and pogroms had the tacit approval of the government.

What it lacked in privilege, Polish Jewry made up in religious zeal. Zionism and the training of Chalutzim for settlement in Israel gave meaning and direction to their lives. There was a revival of Chassidism and Talmudic Yeshivoth flourished.

With the invasion of Poland by Nazi Germany in 1939 the great reservoir of Judaism completely collapsed. Every vestige of Jewish life was destroyed. Some three-and-a-half-million Jews of Poland were exterminated or deported.

Poland today has but a remnant of Jews, approximately 35,000, in the land. Most of the refugees returning from Russia emigrated to Israel between 1946 and 1957. Since that time they have been locked in by the "Iron Curtain" of Russia.

JEWISH COMMUNITIES OF POLAND

Bar	Lublin	Sandomierz
Bialystock	Ludmir	Stolin
Brest	Mezeritz	Szczecin
Chelm	Mezibush	Tulchin
Grodno	Miedziboz	Uman
Kalisz	Minsk	Vilna
Kovna	Nemirov	Walbrzych
Kracow	Ostrog	Warsaw
(5,000)	Pinsk	Wroclaw
Lodz	Poznan	Yaroslav
(5,000)	Plotsk	Zamosc
Lvov	Radom	

The Jews of Russia

EARLY HISTORY—THE KHAZARS

Early Russian history speaks of a kingdom called Khazaria, in the Crimean region, which became converted to Judaism in the eighth century when their King, Bulan, embraced the faith. During the Byzantine persecutions, many Jews took refuge there.

In 955, Chasdai ibn Shaprut, the Jewish Vizier of Spain, was in correspondence with King Joseph of Khazaria. Nothing is known about this people except that in 986 they participated in a religious disputation held in the presence of Prince Vladimir of Kiev, and that in 1016 they succumbed to Russian forces. Many converted to Christianity; some migrated to Hungary and Poland; a segment settled in Kiev, which became the first Russian city to house a large settlement of Jews.

Later, Theodosius (1057–1074), the abbot of the monastery at Kiev, instructed his people to live in peace with all except the Jews and heretics. When Prince Gedymin of Lithuania occupied southern Russia in 1340, he found a considerable Jewish population there.

UNDER RUSSIAN RULERS

The Jews who lived in Russia from Byzantine times were subjected to varying forms of persecution, most of them instigated by the church, which very often was synonymous with the government. From the tenth through to the 16th centuries, there were a few attempts to restrict their freedom of occupation. Occasionally there were uprisings and lootings of Jewish property especially during periods of national crisis. But the Jewish population of Russia continued to grow, owing, in part, to the refugees from the Crusades in Central Europe.

There was little Jewish scholarship in a land that was not conducive to learning. Anti-Jewish sentiment was slow to develop, except in areas of Muscovy that despised any people of alien faith or stock. Jews were denied permanent residence there. By the 16th

century the rulers of Russia and the Eastern Orthodox church had made the Jews their victims, usually giving two reasons : (1) their religion, and (2) their economic pursuits.

IVAN THE TERRIBLE (1462–1505)

He was the first to favor complete exclusion of Jews from Russia. In his conquest of Poland, his brutality was so great that when he would conquer a town, he would order all Jews to be baptized or drowned. Despite restrictions and expulsions, a number of Jews managed to find their way to Moscow and even to achieve a certain measure of success in their chosen fields.

ALEXIS MIKHAILOVICH (1645–1676)

Owing to constant warring with Poland and Lithuania, under this Czar many Jews were among the captured. They could survive only by baptism. Such Jews established a sect similar to the Marranos or secret Jews of Spain. In time they rose to prominent positions and became completely assimilated. During the reign of Alexis, the Russian empire remained largely barred to Jews.

PETER THE GREAT (1672–1725)

He was known as a liberal, but not to the Jews. In 1722 the holy synod ordered the few Jews left in the province of Smolensky to be deprived of their leases, to have their synagogues destroyed and their books burned.

There was a Jewish community in little Russia (Eastern Ukraine) that had been conquered by Muscovy in 1667. Under this ruler, the Jews were expelled in 1721 and could re-enter only by submission to baptism.

CATHERINE I (1725–1727)

She was the wife of Peter the Great. One of her edicts was to banish Jews permanently from all Russian cities and to force them to exchange their gold and silver coins for Russian copper ones. This was not strictly enforced, because it went counter to the interests of powerful nobles in the area. Jewish merchants, however, were allowed to visit the fairs on condition that they sold their goods wholesale and bought local goods with the money.

EMPRESS ANNA (1730–1740)

In her reign, one Boruch Leibov converted a retired naval officer to Judaism, touching off an anti-Jewish campaign when the apostasy was discovered. Both men were put to death. The remaining 573 Jews in the Ukraine were ordered deported.

EMPRESS ELIZABETH (1741–1762)

She was an ardent and zealous supporter of the church. She ordered and carried out the expulsion of all unbaptized Jews, numbering 35,000 and closed the doors of the country to Jewish immigration. Only by special permission could a Jew enter the country.

CATHERINE II (the Great) (1762–1796)

It was during her reign that the partitions of Poland occurred, which gave to Russia a large Jewish population. It was she who coined the phrase "Kromye Zydov" —"Except the Jews," in a manifesto permitting foreigners to live and travel in Russia. However, she did allow a few Jews into proscribed vocations and attempted to attract them to the undeveloped southern province of New Russia, which needed industry and commerce.

The Pale of Settlement

In 1791 she established the "Pale of Settlement," limiting the places where Jews could reside. Special travel permits were granted and the provinces designated for residence were Kiev, Czernigow, Poltava, Minsk, Volhynia, Podolia, Lithuania, Courland, and Bessarabia. Only a few privileged Jews were allowed to dwell outside. Catherine recognized Jewish autonomy only in the form of the Kahal and used it to collect taxes. As of 1794 Jews had to pay double the taxes imposed upon Christian merchants.

ALEXANDER I (1801–1825)

At first this ruler made sincere efforts to improve the desperate situation of the Jews, partly because they had supported him against Napoleon. He tried, unsuccessfully, to assimilate them into the population, economically and religiously. Eventually he reverted to the historic pattern of forced conversion and expulsions. The Jews considered him a benefactor by comparison with his successors.

NICHOLAS I (1825–1855)

He was known as the "Iron Czar" and sometimes as the "Russian Haman," dedicating himself to autocracy, extreme nationalism and religious fanaticism. He considered the Jews as parasites and sought to destroy them because they were unassimilable.

The Canton System

In 1827 he instituted the "Canton System" of compulsory military service for all able-bodied Russians above the age of 18, for a period of twenty-five years. The quota was seven for each one-thousand Russians, but ten for each one-thousand Jews, for whom the period of service was increased by six years, with attendance at preparatory camps, called "cantons," from the age of twelve. This had the effect Nicholas desired because it resulted in a wave of conversions and the demoralization of the Jewish community.

Jewish children were kidnaped, baptized, and prepared for military life. The Kahal was mandated to supply the quota and this sometimes resulted in kidnapings of Jewish children by the Jewish "Livchiki" (catchers).

In 1844 Nicholas legislated against Jewish education, literature, customs, ceremonies, and religious laws. He abolished the Kahal and set up secular or Crown schools with the aid of Jewish intellectuals like Max Lilienthal of Germany. But the project was abandoned when the Jews realized that the Czar was not interested in their secular progress, but only in destroying their traditional autonomous system. In 1853 he narrowed the "Pale of Settlement" and forbade the use of the Hebrew language.

Intercession by Jews such as the English philanthropist, Sir Moses Montefiore, brought no change in his attitude. Even Russian novelists and poets joined the crusade against the Jews by caricaturing them as the most undesirable aliens. In all, about six hundred laws restricting Jewish rights were passed during this reign.

ALEXANDER II (1855-1881)
He was well educated and surrounded himself with enlightened statesmen. His reign of liberalism

started with a respite from persecution of the Jews. He ended the dreaded Cantonist system and allowed Jews to live in the cities and to attend schools and universities. A vigorous intellectual Jewish life developed in Russian as well as in Hebrew and Yiddish.

The liberalism of Alexander, instead of diminishing dissension, increased revolutionary zeal, which was shared actively by many Jews. Alexander then reverted to traditional repressive Russian policies, especially in the case of the Jews. In 1871, some Jewish schools were closed. Jews could no longer advance in the military. At the Congress of Berlin, Russia refused to grant legal equality to eastern European Jews. Ritual murder accusations began to crop up, to be accompanied by pogroms.

Pogroms

The word "Pogrom" is of Russian derivation and means "Destruction," "Disturbance," or "Riot." With Russian government collusion, it was primarily directed against Jews in the form of violence, pillage, carnage, massacre, destruction of property and violation of women. From 1881 on, these uncontrolled attacks were carried out with the knowledge and consent of local authorities, while police and soldiers looked on. Often a pogrom was instigated by corrupt government officials to divert the discontented masses or to counteract reactionary and revolutionary movements.

The Easter season was usually a period of great concern for the safety of the Jews. A number of pogroms occurred in various Russian cities, usually following blood libel accusations. The Kishinev pogrom (1903) was preceded by violent anti-Semitic attacks in the press. It lasted for three days and resulted in the death of 47 Jews; hundreds were seriously injured; and more than 1,300 Jewish-owned homes and shops were demolished. Another pogrom occurred there in 1905.

The government officially denounced the pogroms, but shirked responsibility by blaming them on anarchists or accusing the Jews of exploiting the peasants. One government official declared that "the riots were directed against the Jews because the population was convinced that there would be little or no punishment for crimes that were committed against Jews."

Reactionary groups, known as the Black Hundreds, were responsible for many brutal anti-Jewish outbreaks. Often they were aided and abetted by police and government officials. Few of their leaders were ever arrested or convicted. In many instances, when impending attacks were about to take place, the Jews were not permitted to organize for their self-defense.

ALEXANDER III (1881–1894)

The brutal assassination of his father reenforced his opposition to liberalism, including leniency toward the Jews. His reign was marked by unprecedented terror, pogroms, and massacres.

The May Laws

In May, 1882, he approved the enactment of "Temporary Rules" against the Jews. These "May Laws" remained in effect until the outbreak of the war in 1914. Jews could not own land outside the towns or hold civil posts. They could not travel freely and were restricted in pursuing their livelihoods and their education. Mortgages or leases in their possession were declared invalid. Those Jews who had settled in the empire during the reign of Alexander II were to be deported. Special taxes were imposed on Kosher meat and all ritual accessories. The security of entire Jewish communities was put in the hands of the police, who exacted exorbitant bribes for physical protection.

Numerus Clausus

In secondary schools and universities a quota of only 10 per cent of the Jewish population was allowed to be educated. In addition to these restrictions, barriers were set up in the professions. Protests of the civilized world went unheeded.

Alexander's former tutor, a reactionary by the name of Pobedonostsev, was made procurator of the holy synod. His idea of power was autocratic rule under the protection of the Orthodox Church. He became a "second Torquemada," and began a war on all minority groups. A series of organized anti-Jewish riots raged throughout the country. He offered to solve the Jewish problem by forcing one-third to migrate, another third into the church, and the remaining third to starve.

The pogroms, disabilities, and economic insecurities that followed in the wake of fanatic anti-Semitism gave a tremendous impetus to Jewish emigration and to the development of the Zionist ideology. Baron de Hirsch started Jewish colonies in Argentina; many families went to Israel. In the last decade of the 19th century more than 100,000 Jews came to the United States.

NICHOLAS II (1894–1917)

He was the last of the Russian Czars and the cruelest. This weak-willed, superstitious ruler inaugurated the bloodiest twenty years in the history of the Jews in Russia. Government-approved and militarily organized mass violence took place at least once a year. In 1903, one of the largest pogroms in history occurred during the Easter holiday in the province of Kishinev. Although world-wide indignation was aroused, the plight of the Jew in Russia remained unchanged.

The Black Hundreds

They were known as the "League of the Russian People" and were sponsored by the government. The violence and pogroms instigated against the Jews followed a calculated campaign of terror, exploitation, and massacre. Taking their cue from government officials, they held the Jews responsible for all of Russia's misfortunes.

During the revolution of 1905, unspeakable horror was visited upon Jews in more than fifty localities. The government could not satisfy the clamor of the masses. By 1907 a reactionary Duma was finally convened and ordered the hanging of all liberals implicated in the revolutionary movement, many of whom were Jews.

Ritual Murder Accusations

This was a claim that Jews used the blood of Christian children in the preparation of Matzoth for their Passover celebration. While the church branded such accusations as false, it did not raise its voice to prevent fanatical leaders from wreaking their hatred against innocent Jews, especially at the Passover season.

The Beilis Case

In 1911, the Mendel Beilis ritual murder accusation attracted world-wide attention. For two years the government tried to prove that he had killed a Christian child for Passover ritual purposes, despite valid testimony refuting the charge. The Russian government could not ignore the protest of the world and Beilis was acquitted, although the jury insisted that some other Jew was responsible for the act.

The Protocols of the Elders of Zion

In 1904 Nicholas II instructed his secret police to revise a book written by a Frenchman, Maurice Joly, in 1865, which was a vicious attack against Napoleon. The word "Jew" was substituted for "Napoleon," inferring that all the Jewish people were engaged in a great conspiracy to conquer the entire world.

The book served the purpose of drawing public attention away from needed reforms by making the Jew a scapegoat for all of Russia's troubles.

Though this scurrilous work has been discredited and its falsification exposed, it still receives world attention, especially from subversive and anti-Semitic organizations. In America it was published by Henry Ford under the title "The International Jew," and though he was forced to make a legal retraction, the damage done was extensive.

DEFENDERS AND FRIENDS

Only a few of Russia's intellectuals and liberals had the courage to come to the defense of the Jewish people. Although they were but a voice in the wilderness, they did lift the hopes of the Jews and inspired them in the struggle to cope with their hardships and to bolster their morale.

LEO TOLSTOY (1828–1910)

He denounced the pogroms and blamed the Czarist officials for their irresponsibility. He appealed to the conscience of Russia to accord humane treatment to the Jews. In his writings he wrote a beautiful description of what it means to be a Jew.

MAXIM GORKY (1868–1936)

One of Russia's foremost literary writers. He championed the cause of the Jews and vigorously opposed the anti-Semitic press.

The Haskalah Movement

The word HASKALAH—השכלה—from the root SECHEL—שכל—meaning INTELLIGENCE, is the term used for the Jewish enlightenment movement. It began in Germany, with Moses Mendelssohn (1729–1786) and spread to surrounding countries, reaching Russian Jewry in 1863.

The people who associated themselves with Haskalah were known as MASKILIM—משכילים—ENLIGHTENED ONES. They revolted against the narrow and rigid restrictions of Ghetto Judaism, which confined them to the traditions of the past. They broke with Orthodoxy and despite threats of excommunication, entered the field of secular learning. It was a form of assimilation in which Yiddish gave way to Russian and Hebrew. It also became the instrument for the dissemination of Western ideas.

The Haskalah movement was held suspect by the orthodox leaders who saw only assimilation and conversion through the new liberalism. In spite of this opposition the movement attracted many intellectuals who became prominent in the fields of literature and science. Weekly newspapers and magazines, written in Russian and Hebrew, contained poetry, stories, and scholarly articles. Some of these were "The Dawn," a Russian weekly; "HaMelitz" and "HaCarmel," Hebrew weeklies; and "Kol Mevasser," a Yiddish newspaper. In the city of Petrograd there was founded the Society for the Advancement of Haskalah.

While Haskalah raised the hopes of emancipation for the Jewish people, it did not stem anti-Semitism. This disillusionment caused them to turn to emigration to Palestine and the development of the Zionist ideology.

CHOVOVEI TZIYON—Lovers of Zion

This organization was founded in 1881 when the Russian pogroms began. Its goal was the development of a Jewish nationalist movement, starting with the colonization of Palestine. This became known as Zionism, with Moses Leib Lilienblum and Dr. Leon Pinsker as its first leaders.

The Bilu

This name is formed from the initial letters of the Hebrew phrase, "Beth ya-akov l'chu v'nelcho" — "O House of Jacob, come, let us go." The Bilu, a movement similar to the Chovovei Tziyon, enabled Russian Jews to migrate to Palestine to form some twenty colonies.

Colonization Plans

Baron Maurice de Hirsch, a German-Jewish philanthropist, sought in 1891 to resettle persecuted Jews in various countries of the world through the "Jewish Colonization Association" (ICA), which he set up with a capital of two million pounds. He negotiated with the government of Argentina and succeeded in bringing some 10,000 Jews to settle there.

Jews in Modern Russia

During the period of the civil war (1914–1917) the Jews were at the mercy of the Black Hundreds, the White Guardists, and anti-Bolsheviks. In the Ukraine, where the Jews were caught between the Red and White forces, it is estimated that some 200,000 were killed.

Following the revolution, Russia's new form of government, Communism, elevated the Jewish people (seven million in Russia, Poland, and Lithuania) to an equal status with all the people of the land. The "Declaration of the Rights of the People of Russia" gave recognition to all minority and ethnic groups. Anti-Semitism was outlawed as an act against the state. The new provisional government looked with favor upon the Jews and conferred leadership upon such individuals as Sverdlov, Trotsky, Kamenev, and Zinoviev.

But this new freedom and equality did not last long. Communism proscribed religion, and Judaism fell victim to an anti-religious government that fostered the propaganda that all religion was the opiate of the people. Under this repressive system, the teaching of religion was forbidden and nearly all synagogues were closed. Without a rabbi, a teacher, and a school, the Jewish community was placed in great jeopardy, especially after the government abolished the

Kahal, the only agency that had kept the Jews together.

The Jewish people were singled out from all the minority groups to feel the brunt of the Russian crusade against cultural and religious freedom. The Hebrew language, which flourished under Haskalah, was prohibited. At first Yiddish was encouraged and the government went so far as to establish an all-Jewish settlement at Birobidzhan in 1934. Only a small percentage of the Jewish people settled in this province. The Russian government admitted failure and abandoned this attempt to settle the Jews collectively. In 1948 cultural restrictions were extended to the Yiddish language.

Zionism, the hope of the oppressed Jew, met the same fate as religion. The government saw in Zionism a middle class threat to its own program of nationalism and refused to permit Jews to emigrate, even though it supported the statehood of Israel in 1947.

The invasion of Russia by the Germans in World War II resulted in the unprecedented extermination of more than a million Jews in the Ukraine and White Russia. The tragic fate of this hapless people did not abate the anti-Semitic campaigns of the government, which accused them of "Cosmopolitanism" and summarily dismissed them as government workers and university professors. Their cultural life ended in 1948 with the banning of Yiddish newspapers and theaters, the printing of Prayer Books, and the closing of literary and cultural research institutions. Doctors were accused of plotting against Russian leaders. The baking of Matzah for the Passover was proscribed. Hundreds of Jews were arrested and many were sentenced to death on charges of economic exploitation. The Jews were the only national group denied basic religious and cultural rights accorded to all other minorities.

Some three million Jews live behind the "Iron Curtain." Their identification cards designate them as "Jewish Nationals" and are stamped "Jew." The refusal of the government to permit Jews to migrate or rejoin their families, the open anti-Jewish press campaign against Zionism and the State of Israel, and the imposition of severe cultural and economic disabilities show that the basic attitude of Communist Russia toward the Jewish people is not a radical change from the historic pattern.

JEWISH PERSONALITIES

Russia, with her large Jewish population, did not produce a galaxy of great Jews, as occurred in some of the smaller countries of Europe. The Jews of Russia and Poland lived under the most repressive conditions and their economic status reflected their constant and bitter struggle for survival.

Religion was their only hope. In their schools, Torah and Talmud provided an intellectual outlet for the Jew and resulted in the emergence of some renowned Talmudists. During the Haskalah movement, men of letters and vision, who spoke a new language, offered new hope to downcast and oppressed Jewry.

ISAAC BAER LEVINSOHN (1788–1860)
He founded the Haskalah movement among the Jews of Russia. His mastery of the Russian language and his devotion to the educational needs of the people paved the way to the cultural development of Russian Jewry. Like Mendelssohn of Germany, he promoted Jewish scientific and philosophical studies.

His book *Tu-edah B'yisroel, Testimony in Israel,* was a call to his people to rebuild their lives on the basis of Hebrew study and productive occupations. In 1839 he published his chief work *Beth Yehudah, House of Judah,* concerning the Bible, the Talmud, and the study of languages and secular sciences.

ABRAHAM DOV LEBENSOHN (1798–1878)
Russia's first modern Hebrew poet was also an eminent Bible scholar. To him is credited the revival of Hebrew poetry and literature.

ABRAHAM MAPU (1808–1867)
He is known as the father of the Hebrew novel. *Ahavath Tziyon, Love of Zion,* was his first one.

DR. LEON PINSKER (1821–1891)
He was the author of the book *Auto Emancipation,* which called for the colonization of Palestine as the only solution to the Jewish problem. He was one of the founders and president of the *Chovovei Tziyon, Lovers of Zion.* When the "May Laws" of 1882 were enacted against the Jews, Pinsker advocated mass migrations to Palestine.

JUDAH LEIB GORDON (1830–1892)
He was the most representative Hebrew poet of his time and an outstanding leader of the Haskalah movement. He was opposed to "petrified rabbanism" and "fanatical Chassidism." He espoused a dualistic credo and coined the phrase "Be a Jew in your private life and a man in the outside world."

SHOLOM JACOB ABRAMOVITCH
(1835–1917)

He was known in the world of Yiddish literature as "Mendele Mocher Seforim, Mendel, the Seller of Books." He is considered "The Grandfather" of modern Yiddish literature and one of the greatest Yiddish story tellers.

PERETZ SMOLENSKIN (1842–1885)

This leader in the Haskalah movement published a liberal magazine called *HaShachar, The Morning,* in which he inveighed against Jewish assimilation. In his book *Am Olam, The Eternal People,* he maintained that the Jews must achieve political as well as moral independence.

MOSES LEIB LILIENBLUM
(1843–1910)

This Hebrew writer and poet wrote *Olom Hatohu, World of Chaos* and *Hatoth N'urim, Sins of Youth,* which depict the struggle of his people in the darkness and despair of Russian life. He believed that Zionism rather than liberalism was the solution of the Jewish problem. He was one of the founders and leaders of "Chovovei Tziyon," the movement to encourage Jews to prepare for and migrate to the Holy Land.

REUBEN ASHER BROYDES
(1851–1903)

In his novel, *Shetai Ha-Ketzavot, The Two Extremes,* he sought a middle road between the old form of ghetto-life and the extreme liberalism of Haskalah.

NAPHTALI HERZ IMBER (1856–1909)

Poet and author of the national song of Israel called *Hatikvah, The Hope.*

ISAAC LEIB PERETZ (1852–1915)

This dramatist, novelist, and poet pleaded the cause of the oppressed and poor and interpreted Chassidic life from the folkways of his people.

ASHER GINSBERG (1856–1927)

His pen name was "Achad Ha-Am," "One of the People." He advocated a cultural and spiritual Zionism in opposition to political Zionism as espoused by the followers of "Chovovei Tziyon." In his chief work *Al Parshat D'rachim, At the Parting of the Ways,* he conceived Palestine as a spiritual center that would stimulate Jewish creativeness and have world-wide influence.

SHOLEM RABINOVICH (1859–1916)

He used the pen name "Sholem Aleichem, "Peace unto You." This humorist is known as the Yiddish Mark Twain. His fame as a story-teller was unequaled.

Some Russian Jewish Communities

Baku	Leningrad
Birobidzhan	Lvov-Lemberg
Czerkassy	Minsk
Czernowitz	Moscow
Kharkov	Odessa
Kiev	Riga
Kishinev	Tashkent
Kovno	Vilna

The Jews of France

EARLY HISTORY

The first Jews came to France (Gaul) about 51 BCE with the Roman conquest. There is evidence that small Jewish communities existed in the cities of Arles, Narbonne, Lyon, Bordeaux, Marseilles, Toulouse, Beziers, and Paris.

When Constantine adopted Christianity as the state religion for the Roman empire in 325 CE, there were some restrictions placed upon the Jews, such as not marrying nor fraternizing with Christians, and not keeping Christian slaves. A century later anti-Semitism manifested itself when Jews were deprived of all public positions and honorary titles. But the impositions were not so drastic as to keep them out of agriculture, crafts, and commerce. In general their relations with their neighbors were tolerable.

CLOVIS I (481–511)

When the Franks conquered the Romans (481 CE) Gaul was incorporated into the new empire, along with Germanic tribes under Clovis, who earlier had converted to Catholicism.

THE BISHOP OF CLERMONT (576)

He imposed upon the Jews the alternative of baptism or expulsion. Those who left were usually forced into the same choices in their new communities. It was the practice of the church and state to cooperate in the forcible conversion of the Jews to Christianity.

KING DAGOBERT (628–638)

He followed the pattern of baptism or expulsion set by his predecessors. During his reign all the Jews of his province were forced to leave. They did not return in any significant numbers for one hundred and fifty years.

THE RULE OF CHARLEMAGNE (765–814)

Charlemagne is remembered by Jews for his tolerant attitude toward them. He resisted the pressure of the church by disregarding its decrees and punishing oppressors of the Jews. Jewish autonomy was completely restored and a government official, "Magister Judaeorum," was appointed to head all Jewish communities and to provide a liaison.

Charlemagne was deeply impressed by Jewish intellectualism and leadership. He respected and honored the Jewish Sabbath day. He employed Jewish ambassadors in his foreign service. One such Jew, Isaac, represented him in the court at Baghdad. At his request, the scholar Machir came from Babylonia to head the Jewish community at Narbonne. Meshullam of Italy was also persuaded to come to France. Economically the Jews of France thrived as merchants and traders throughout Europe and Asia at this period.

The Treaty of Verdun (843)

The golden era of peace for the Jews of France and middle Europe began with Charlemagne and continued until 843 when, at the Treaty of Verdun, the Frankish empire was divided among the sons of Charlemagne into the independent states of France, Germany, Lorraine, and Italy.

The Jewish people were again caught between the intolerance of the church leaders and the rivalry and avarice of the rulers and princes. The former, such as Bishop Agobard of Lyons sought to abolish all established privileges of the Jews. The latter regarded the Jews as property to be used for purposes of taxation and exploitation.

POPE GREGORY VII (1073–1085)

He prohibited Jews from holding any office in Christendom. The old restrictions against fraternization with Jews were revived.

POPE URBAN II (1042–1099)

In the year 1093 this prelate put his blessing upon the Crusades by authorizing a French Monk called Peter the Hermit to start a "Holy War" against the Moslem infidels in Palestine.

THE CRUSADES

The comparative peace and security of the Jews were shattered by a "Holy War" called the Crusades. In 1096 the first march to the Holy Land began. Some 200,000 volunteers, made up of peasants, knights, and adventurers, with crosses on their uniforms, assembled for this holy mission.

With the Crusades began the dark ages of persecution for the Jews. Although the war was directed against the Moslems, the Jews were the "unbelievers" who became the immediate victims in Europe. Jewish communities, particularly in Germany, felt the full force of massacres and economic ruin. The Crusaders knew no restraint as they killed, maimed, and pillaged in the name of God. The Jewish people were forced to establish segregated areas or ghettos for their mutual protection.

The Jews of France escaped the full force of destruction by the Crusaders. Except for the communities of Rouen and Blois, where Jews were burned at the stake, there was little bloodshed and violence in the country.

The economic life of the Jew, however, was deeply affected. In 1146 the church decreed that all Christians who volunteered for the Holy War would be released from Jewish debts.

POPE EUGENIUS III (1145–1153)

He was the instigator of the Second Crusade, which was aided and abetted by the kings of Germany and France. The battle cry of the mob was "Hep Hep," an abbreviation of a Latin phrase meaning "Jerusalem is Lost." In many communities the Jews purchased protection in fortified castles of barons and noblemen. In some instances they were betrayed to the ravaging mobs.

THE THIRD CRUSADE (1170)

During this period of violence the ritual blood accusation was revived and thirty Jews of Blois were martyred in the hysteria that followed. Philip Augustus (1182) forced the Jews of Paris to buy their freedom at an exorbitant price. Within the same year he ordered the expulsion of all the Jews from France. The decree was later revoked, but much of their property had been confiscated, their synagogues converted to churches, and the people forced to wear special badges.

THE AFTERMATH OF THE CRUSADES

The nightmare of the Crusades produced a social, moral, and intellectual degradation of the Jews in France. The proscriptive measures of the clergy and rulers crushed their dignity and deprived them of natural human rights. They were not allowed to own real estate nor engage in agriculture. Their form of livelihood was confined to the area of small merchants and minor tradesmen. They were stigmatized by the badge and forced to congregate in ghettos.

Few were the students and scholars of Jewish learning that

emerged in these tragic times. Those that did come out of the darkness of the Crusades, like Rashi and his school of Tosafoths, were fortunate in spreading enough light to illumine Jewish scholarship for many centuries that followed.

The aftermath of the Crusades did not ameliorate the condition of the Jews. Like their co-religionists in other countries, they were always on the defensive against accusations, distortions, and untruths leveled against them and their religion. Pope Innocent III (1198–1216), in promoting the Fourth Crusade, instructed Christian rulers to make Jews atone for their sin of deicide. They were to be segregated forever as pariahs. Persecutions in the year 1211 caused a large number of rabbis to migrate to Palestine.

KING LOUIS IX (1226–1274)

He demanded the baptism of all Jews and decreed the burning of twenty-four cartloads of the Talmud in Paris. This was carried out with the approval of Pope Gregory IX (1227–1241). In 1242 the Jews had to defend themselves in public disputation against the apostate Nicholas Donin and the Catholic church. Despite the testimony and refutation of the charges by such Jewish leaders as Jechiel of Paris, Moses of Coucy, Judah of Melun, and Samuel B. Salomo, the decision of the church went against them.

PHILIP IV, THE FAIR (1268–1314)

He expelled all the Jews from his kingdom. His example was followed by rulers, provincial heads, and clergy, but they usually disregarded such decrees upon payment of huge ransoms.

PHILIP THE TALL (1294–1322)

He brutally expelled some 100,000 Jews from France in order to seize their property. Some of them settled in other French territory, which, in later years, formed the basis for German and Italian Jewish communities. Some who left came back when a recall was issued. This process of expulsion and recall went on for some time.

City authorities, church clerics, and councils followed the pattern of discrimination and extortion. Jews were denied the right to hold public office, to keep Christian servants, to work or to eat meat on Christian holidays. Often mobs were incited to violence by false accusations such as the desecration of the Host. In 1321 they were accused of poisoning the wells and in the following year they were expelled. From 1322 to 1359 France was again officially without Jews, although a few communities under Papal rule remained.

A similar banishment took place in 1394 when Charles IV ordered the expulsion of all Jews from France, except Marranos who had escaped the inquisition of Spain and who were considered essential for the economy of the country. The period of banishment continued until the year 1759.

JEWS TO REMEMBER

RASHI (RABBI SOLOMON ben ISAAC) (Yitzchaki) (1040–1105)

This Rabbi of Troyes, France, was called the "Prince of Rabbinic Literature," because it is said that the Talmud could not be understood without his explanations and that the Bible became known to the people through his interpretations. He founded a school in the city of Troyes.

JACOB ben MEIR (1107–1170)

He was a grandson of Rashi and became known as "Rabbenu Tam." He founded the French school of Tosaphists and the first rabbinical conference in France. He wrote *Sefer Ha-Yashar, Book of the Upright,* which was an interpretation of the Talmud, with Tosaphoth and Responsa appended.

ABRAHAM ben DAVID (1125–1198)

Leading scholar of his time and one of the chief exponents of Cabala. In opposition to the works of Maimonides on dogma and creed, he wrote critical works on the "Mishnah Torah."

THE TIBBON FAMILY

These men are known in history as the "Fathers of Hebrew Translation." They were linguists and their skill enabled them to translate into Hebrew many important Arabic works written by Jews.

JUDAH ibn TIBBON (1120–1190)

Physician and scholar. Translated Bachyas' *Duties of the Heart,* Halevi's *Kuzari,* and Saadiah's *Beliefs and Doctrines.*

SAMUEL ibn TIBBON (1150–1230)

In addition to his many translations. Samuel wrote a number of commentaries on the Bible. His famous translation was *The Guide to the Perplexed* by Maimonides.

JACOB MACHIR ibn TIBBON (1236–1304)

He achieved fame as an astronomer as well as a translator of many important rabbinic works.

The Kimchi Family

JOSEPH KIMCHI (1105–1170)

He was the father of this famous family and was known in

the Jewish world for his translation into Hebrew of Ibn Gabirol's *Choice of Pearls* and Bachya's *Duties of the Heart.*

DAVID KIMCHI (1160–1235)

He was the son of Joseph and known as REDAK. He made his reputation in the field of grammar and Bible commentaries. The work that brought him fame was a Hebrew grammar called *Perfection.* To this he appended *The Book of Roots,* a dictionary of the Bible that served as a source book of Jewish and Christian scholars.

SERACHYA HALEVI GERONDI (1125–1186)

Leading Talmudist of his time. He supported the philosophy of Maimonides and was engaged in many controversies with his co-religionists.

JECHIEL ben JOSEPH OF PARIS (1249–1285)

Talmudist of note. He headed a religious disputation in opposition to the apostate Donin. He maintained that there are no references to Jesus in the Talmud. One of his distinctions was the writing of all the Tosefta from memory. Migrated to Palestine.

ISAAC OF CORBEIL (d. 1280)

Author of *Ammundeh Golah,* a treatise on the 613 commandments.

KALONYMOS ben KALONYMOS (1286–1328)

This scholar belongs to a family of famous translators. He rendered from Arabic to Hebrew some thirty scientific works on medicine, mathematics, and astronomy. His own writings were in the field of philosophy and moral teachings. He wrote "The Touchstone," an ethical story in which man gained eternal life by using the power of the touchstone, a symbol of good deeds.

LEVI ben GERSHON (1288–1345)

This renowned scholar was known by the following names: Ralbag—Gersonides— Leon de Bagnois—and Leo the Hebrew. He was a gifted scientist and wrote an astronomical treatise in Latin. He was also a religious philosopher who wrote his views in a book called *Milchomoth Adonoy, Wars of the Lord.* He differed with the school of Rashi and, as a rationalist, followed the school of Maimonides.

JOSEPH ben JOSHUA HAKOHEN (1496–1576)

Physician and historian. Wrote *Emek Habachah, Vale of Tears,* which was an Israel martyrology.

THE TOSAPHOTH LITERATURE

Tosaphoth means "Additions" or "Supplements" to the commentaries of Rashi. It began with the relatives of Rashi and continued with scholars in France, Germany, and Italy over several centuries. The Tosaphists attempted to evolve new principles of interpretation and to bring Jewish law up to date.

PREACHERS OF HATE AND VIOLENCE

AGOBARD OF LYONS (779–840)

This Archbishop of Lyons has been called the father of medieval anti-Semitism. His influential writings sought to set Jews apart from Christians and to forbid social fraternization with them.

EUGEN DÜHRING (1833–1921)

He was one of the founders of modern racial anti-Semitism, with a pathological hatred of Jews. He wrote a widely read book in which he attacked the Jews as undermining the social fabric of civilization.

JOSEPH ARTHUR GOBINEAU (1816–1882)

This French diplomat and traveler was the founder and expounder of pseudo-scientific race theories, many of them directed against the Jews. He taught that human races were unequal and that the Nordic-Aryan people were superior to all others. Although not an anti-Semite, his book has been used for racist ideologies.

EDOUARD-ADOLPHE DRUMONT (1844–1917)

He was a prolific writer who concentrated on vicious anti-Semitic publications that had extensive circulation, and prejudiced the minds of the French people against the Jews. The notorious Dreyfus case was, in some measure, traceable to his unfounded anti-Jewish diatribes, which were based on clerical sources and sociological theories that were economically motivated.

TRAGIC EVENTS

Massacre of the Lepers

In the year 1321 a large number of lepers were driven out of their settlement. Rumors spread swiftly that the Jews and Mohammedans had bribed the lepers to spread disease by poisoning the wells. The result was a wave of terror involving extortions of large sums of money for protection, as well as confiscation of property and expulsion of Jews from many communities.

The Dreyfus Affair

In 1894 a Jewish army officer, Captain Alfred Dreyfus, was falsely accused of betraying his country by selling military secrets. Tried by a military court he was convicted and sentenced to life imprisonment in exile. After serving for many years on lonely Devils Island off the coast of French Guiana, his case came to the attention of the noted French writer, Emile Zola.

Dreyfus was given another trial, which revealed that he was the victim of anti-Semitic officers who sought to make him a scapegoat for their own treachery. The affair attracted world-wide attention and brought to light the extent of anti-Semitism in Europe. Dreyfus was vindicated and restored to his office and rank in the army. By its effect upon Theodore Herzl, this trial gave tremendous impetus to the rise of the Zionist movement.

SOME FRIENDS OF THE JEWS

COUNT MIRABEAU (1749–1791)

He was a liberal who, influenced by Mendelssohn, denounced persecution of Jews and appealed to Christians for their equal rights.

ABBE HENRI GREGOIRE (1750–1831)

This Protestant churchman and deputy was an ardent advocate of Jewish emancipation. He headed a Jewish delegation from Alsace-Lorraine at a hearing before the National Assembly and played an important role in procuring equal rights for them.

STANISLAS CLERMONT–TONNERRE (1757–1792)

He was a nobleman and a vigorous champion of Jewish emancipation. He declared: "To Jews as human beings, everything; to Jews as a people, nothing!" He maintained that the Christian people owed the Jewish people reparation for the gross injustices inflicted upon them.

A GREAT JEWISH LEADER

ADOLPHE CREMIEUX (1796–1881)

Minister of Justice and champion of human rights. He was instrumental in having a law known as "More Judaica" declared unconstitutional. This law forced Jews to take a humiliating oath when they appeared before a court of justice.

In 1870, after the fall of Napoleon III, he became head of the provisional government of France. He was later made a life-long member of the Senate.

Cremieux became interested in Jewish affairs and founded the "Alliance Israelite Universelle" (1860), an organization to work for the rights and welfare of the Jewish people everywhere.

The Damascus Affair (1860) brought his name into prominence as a champion of human rights. Seven Jews of Damascus were arrested because of the disappearance of a monk. Despite their innocence, the government ordered sixty Jewish children to be taken forcibly from their homes. Aided by Sir Moses Montefiore of England, Cremieux argued the case before the Damascus authorities and succeeded in having all the Jewish people involved in the case released.

ORGANIZATIONS

The Grand Sanhedrin

This body of Jews came into existence at the time of Jewish emancipation. It was convened by Napoleon in Paris in 1807 and patterned after the Sanhedrin of Jerusalem, which consisted of 71 members, two-thirds rabbis and one-third laymen. Leaders of other countries were accepted into membership, since it was the desire of Napoleon that the decisions of the Grand Sanhedrin would be binding upon all Jewry.

Among the major decisions handed down by the Sanhedrin were the following:

Polygamy is forbidden to Jews.

Jewish marriage and divorce, to be valid, must be preceded by civil contract.

A religious ceremony was not necessary to validate mixed civil marriages.

It is the religious duty of the Jew to aid, protect, and love his non-Jewish fellow-citizens.

The Jew is duty bound to regard the country of his birth or of his choice as his fatherland and to love and defend it.

The Jew shall have the right to every occupation and profession.

Jews are urged to engage in agriculture, manual labor, arts, and crafts.

The practice of usury on Jew or non-Jew is to be prohibited.

Alliance Israelite Universelle

This philanthropic and political organization was founded in the year 1860 with the express purpose of championing the rights of oppressed Jews everywhere and of rendering financial assistance. It became the leading organization working for the welfare of the Jews throughout the world. One of its founders and promoters was Cre-

mieux. The Alliance also achieved prominence in the field of social service and established vocational and parochial schools in France, North Africa, and Asia.

MODERN FRANCE

Jews were not free from the many disabilities imposed upon them until the revolution of 1789 gave France the honor of being the first country of Europe to grant equal rights to minorities. In 1791 some 40,000 Jews were granted the privilege of full citizenship.

In 1806 an Assembly of Notables from France and Italy was convened by Napoleon to determine the status of the Jews and their loyalty to the French government. This Assembly or Sanhedrin, under the presidency of Abraham Furtago, consisted of 112 members. It defined the Jew and his religion, and affirmed the loyalty of the Jewish people to France.

Out of this Assembly developed the Grand Sanhedrin, which met in 1807 under the leadership of Rabbi David Zinzheim. One of the acts of this body was the sanction of civil marriage for Jews.

In 1808 the Jews were officially classed as a religious group by the government. In 1831 they received equality on the same basis as Christians, and the Jewish clergy became entitled to state subsidy. A rabbinical college was established at Metz and a Grand Consistory, headed by a chief rabbi, was empowered to regulate the religious life of the Jewish people. Jewish communities subsequently established their own consistories directed by rabbis and laymen.

At the turn of the century France extended its hospitality to world refugees of all creeds. Paris became a great cosmopolitan city. Many Jews from Russia, and later from Nazi Germany, found freedom and security in this land of tolerance. Their loyalty to the country was attested by the fact that some 60,000 Jews served in the armed forces during World War II.

When Nazism came to France in 1940 it spelled the complete loss of independence for the Jewish people. Those Jews who could not escape to other lands became the victims of the anti-Semitic Vichy regime. It is estimated that about 120,000 Jews were sent to annihilation camps.

Including refugees from North Africa, especially Algeria, there are about 500,000 Jews living in France. Many Jewish communities never recovered from the effects of the Vichy government because the Jewish population became concentrated in Paris.

Mertviller
Metz
Moissac
Montauben
Montbéliard
Mulhouse
Mutzig
Nantes
Narbonne
Nice
Niederbronn-
  les-Bains
Nimes
Obernai
Orléans
Paris
Pau
Périgueux
Perpignan
Poitiers
Pont-à-Mousson
Provence
Reichshoffen
Reims
Rennes

Roanne
Rouen
Saint-Etienne
Saint-Fons
Saint-Quentin
Saverne
Savoy
Sedan
Soultz-sous-
  Forets
Strasbourg
Tarbes
Toulon
Toulouse
Tours
Troyes
Valenciennes
Venaissin
Verdun
Versailles
Vichy
Villeurbanne
Westhoffen
Woerth

JEWISH COMMUNITIES

Amiens
Arles
Avignon
Bar-le-duc
Bayonne
Belfort
Besançon
Beziers
Bischwiller
Blois
Bordeaux
Caen
Cannes
Chalons sur
  Marne
Chateauroux
Chateau Thierry
Clermont-
  Ferrand
Colmar
Coucy
Dauendorg

Dijon
Dieppe
Elbeuf
Epernay
Epinal
Grenoble
Gundershoffen
Haguenau
Herrlisheim-
  Offendorff
Laferte-sous-
  Jouarre
Lauterbourg
Le Havre
Le Mans
Lens
Lille
Limoges
Lorraine
Luneville
Lyon
Marseilles

The Jews of Germany

FROM EARLY ROMAN TIMES TO THE FIRST CRUSADE

The first Jews arrived in what is now Germany with the Roman armies in the early centuries of the Common Era. In the year 321, records show that King Constantine issued regulations to a Jewish settlement in Cologne. The extent of their survival during the Barbaric invasions is open to question.

Little is known about the Jews in Germany until after the eighth century, when the area was ruled by Charlemagne. Under him, they enjoyed certain privileges and protection. In the centuries after his death, when Germany became an independent kingdom, the Jewish people founded many communities, such as Augsberg, Metz, Worms, Mainz, Magdeburg, Speyer, and developed a vital intellectual life. Talmudic studies were pursued, especially in schools founded by Rabbenu Gershom ben Judah (965–1028). He became the "Light of the Exile" and was the recognized religious authority of his time, rivaling the Gaonim.

Conditions of life were not generally unfavorable. The Feudal system made it impossible for Jews to own land, but there were ample opportunities for merchants and artisans to engage in their trades. The country was not a unified nation, since it was composed of lesser princedoms or duchies.

OTTO I, THE GREAT (936–973)

He succeeded his father, Henri I, as King of Germany and was crowned as Emperor of the Holy Roman Empire by Pope John XII in 962. During his reign, synagogues and schools were opened in many German cities.

THE FIRST CRUSADE (1096) TO 16th CENTURY

The favorable atmosphere of tolerance changed with the advent of a series of Crusades. Wherever there was unrest or excitement, Jews were certain of attack. The political fragmentation of the country made it impossible for unified action to defend the Jews or to stem the onslaught of the Crusaders. Driven from one area, another would receive them. Expulsions were local and sporadic, but the situation of the Jews kept deteriorating with the growing fervor of the Crusading movement.

The first Crusade, which was started in France, was authorized by Pope Urban II (1042–1099) to retake the Holy Land from the Moslem infidels. As the Crusaders wended their way across Europe, in too many instances the Jews became their victims en route. In their wake the Crusaders left ravaged Jewish communities that had been plundered and the inhabitants brutally exterminated.

In some communities the entire Jewish population went to their martyrdom. In numerous instances the Jews were given the alternative of choosing between Christianity and death. Occasionally some church official offered them protection and usually for an exorbitant price. The position of the Jews became untenable and many sought refuge in neighboring countries.

The Second Crusade (1146), sponsored by Pope Eugenius III (1145–1153), witnessed a repetition of persecution, blood ritual accusations, and mass expulsions. The economic ruin of the Jews was intensified because of a decree absolving Christians from all Jewish indebtedness. At this time many Jews migrated to south and east Europe, particularly to Poland.

During the next two centuries the plight of the Jew continued without radical change. Restrictions were removed and then renewed. Conrad III (1093–1152) classed the Jews as *Servi Camerae,* Servants of the Crown. While this status gave them some degree of protection against mob violence, they were virtually deprived of all freedom. The Jews paid a great price for this protection. While one ruler like Frederick I interceded for the Jews and confirmed privileges granted by city rulers, another king, Rudolph of Hapsburg (1273–1291), extorted large sums of money from them.

For centuries locally inspired

massacres repeated the pattern set by the Crusades. By the 16th century, most of the large German cities, except Frankfort-on-Main, had banished Jews. Settlements did exist, however, in many of the smaller towns. A new era began in Europe in which there was to be no security, no tolerance, and no welcome for the Jewish people.

With the ascendancy of the church, the Jews were more and more degraded in body and in spirit. Only Jewish intellectual life seemed to remain sturdy. In isolated instances a few Jews who were useful to the rulers were accorded privileges and protection at court. Sometimes they were able to use their position as "Court Jews" to help their co-religionists.

CIVIL AND RELIGIOUS PERSECUTION

Servi Camerae or Servants of the Chamber or Crown

This was imposed by Conrad III and renewed by Frederick I. The Jews were made wards or personal servants of the Emperor. This act robbed them of their freedom and reduced them to the status of bondsmen or chattels to be sold or traded at the whim of the ruler. The Golden Bull of Charles IV (1356) put the Jews under the ownership of electors, princes, and city rulers. This imperial prerogative continued until the dissolution of the Reich in 1806.

The Blood Libel

This old and untruthful charge was first raised by the church, accusing the Jews of using the blood of a Christian child in the preparation of their Passover Matzah (Un-leavened Bread). Despite the fact that Jewish law specifically forbade the use of blood under any circumstances, the Jews became the victims of horrible massacres provoked by fanatical Christian leaders. These religious excesses continued, despite the fact that Emperor Frederick II declared the libel to be unfounded ana Pope Innocent IV ruled against the persecution of Jews on such grounds.

Desecrating the Host

In the Christian Church, the Host or Wafer symbolized the body of Christ. This doctrine ot Transubstantiation was accepted by the Church in 1215. The Host was usually carried in church processions through the streets and even though the Jews were forbidden to witness the processions, they were nevertheless accused of desecrating the symbol of the Host in various ways. Like the Blood Libel, this unfounded accusation resulted in open violence against the Jews.

Jewish Badge and Dress

To mark the Jews apart from the rest of the population, they were compelled to wear a yellow badge on their outer garment. Special hats were also imposed upon them in some places. The pointed top and twisted rim was to suggest horns.

Flagellants

The Flagellants were a Christian brotherhood of the Middle Ages, who practiced self-inflicted bodily torture as a means of attaining salvation. During the period of the Black Death they wandered as bands throughout Western Europe, inciting persecution of the Jews, whom they accused of being responsible for the pestilence. Their exhortations usually caused a large death-toll among the Jews, as well as expulsions and expropriation of their property.

Armleder

A systematic campaign of murder and robbery of Jews (1336–1338) by organized bands of peasants in Alsace and in the Rhine country resulted in the annihilation of many Jewish communities. The name "Armleder" refers to a leather band worn as a badge on the arm of each member of the gang. Their campaigns were carried on without interference by the ruling powers.

Fettmilch Riots

Vincent Fettmilch, a demagogue baker and soldier, was the cause of an instigated riot against the Jews of Frankfort in May, 1614. He accused them of a list of undocumented atrocities and demanded their expulsion from the city. In spite of the Emperor's rejection of these accusations, Fettmilch and his followers would invade the Jewish quarter, pillage, and destroy property. It is reported that 1,380 Jews were forced to leave the city without their possessions. Two years later, Fettmilch was arrested and executed, and the Frankfort community was ordered to reimburse the losses of those Jews who returned.

Synagogue Destruction

The desecration and burning of synagogues was regarded by some Christian leaders as an act of special piety. This usually happened in connection with other forms of violence against Jewish communities. During the Crusades, synagogues were set on fire, completely destroyed, or converted into churches.

The greatest outburst of synagogue destruction took place during Hitler's reign of terror. Every form of vandalism was freely committed. In November, 1938, nearly every synagogue in greater Germany suffered bombing, burning, razing, or some form of desecration.

Cemetery Desecrations

A popular form of activism against the Jews, and still recurrent in modern times, was the desecration of Jewish graves. Tombstones were broken, marred, or stolen. The aftermath of many persecutions found some cemeteries completely destroyed and the land confiscated by the government.

The Ghetto—Judengasse

The idea of keeping the Jews apart from the rest of the community originated in Italy. This enforced isolation compelled the Jews to live in segregated areas of the city behind walls and guarded gates. These restricted areas were "Judengasse" or "Judenstadt" — Jews' street or Jews' place.

Inside these areas the Jews lived under the most crowded conditions. Dwellings were built side-by-side and several stories in height. The streets were narrow and dirty. On Sundays they could not leave the boundaries of the enclosed area and on holidays the ghetto gates were closed so that none could enter or leave.

Under such conditions the Jews had to develop a complete community life of their own, social, spiritual, and educational.

The Black Death (1348–1349)

This plague is so called because it caused its victims to turn black. It ravaged the countries of Europe and caused the death of about one-third of the population.

Because of the Jewish laws of cleanliness and sanitary precautions, particularly in the ghettos, the Jewish people suffered less in proportion to their Christian neighbors. This seeming immunity from the epidemic led to the belief that the Jews poisoned the wells to spread the disease. The result was the widest visitation of barbarism known up to that time. Over 350 Jewish communities were affected, with about 200 completely wiped out.

Mobs known as "Flagellants" moved without restraint. In Strausberg alone, some two thousand Jews were killed. Emperor Charles IV even guaranteed city elders against imperial punishment for the murder of Jews.

Extortion by Taxation

Many devices were employed by rulers and petty princes to extort money from the Jews. A tax had to be paid to travel, to enter or leave a city, to get married, to bear children, and to be buried. The privilege of being a tolerated or protected Jew was also subject to taxation. Life and livelihood were denied as natural rights for the Jew. These had to be purchased over and over again.

The Golden Penny Tax

This was an annual tax of one florin levied against every Jewish person above the age of twelve. It started with Louis the Bavarian in 1342 for the purpose of giving the Jewish people protection.

The Community Tax

A capital levy ranging from one third to one half was occasionally levied against all Jewish capital and resources, individual or group.

Ransoms and Extortions

Prominent rabbis and leaders were sometimes arrested and imprisoned without charges. The Jewish community was forced to raise the ransoms for their release.

The privilege of fleecing the Jews was sold to prince and nobleman, who extorted large sums of money under threat of depriving them of their livelihood or of expulsion from the city.

Expulsions

Germany was a country of hundreds of independent kingdoms, dukedoms, bishoprics and self-governing cities. When a ruler found it expedient to his interests, he would order the expulsion of all his Jewish inhabitants. They usually went to a neighboring area or migrated to another country. For a fixed price they were often invited to return only to be the victims of subsequent expulsions. This repeated pattern meant economic ruin and social deterioration. In many instances their property was confiscated and their children forced into baptism.

Doctrine of Servitus Judaeorum

This church doctrine, "Servitude of the Jews," elaborated by Thomas Aquinas, held that the Jews must always occupy a status inferior to the Christian.

SCHOLARS AND SAINTS

RABBENU GERSHOM ben JUDAH (965–1028)

This rabbi of Mayence was known as MEOR HAGOLA— מאור הגולה —THE LIGHT OF THE EXILE. He established schools and was recognized as the leading Jewish authority of his time. He changed many laws to meet the needs of the times.

He was the author of TAKANOTH —תקנת, a book of regulations pertaining to Jewish life and practice. One of his important rulings was to prohibit polygamy among Jews. He endeavored to make lenient the return to Judaism of those who were forced into Christianity. His son was forcibly baptized in 1012, an event for which he composed penitential prayers expressing his grief.

JUDAH ben SAMUEL HECHASID (d. 1217)

This scholar of Regensberg introduced Cabala into Germany. His book *Sefer Hachassidim*— ספר החסדים—*Book of the Pious*, ranked him among the great Jewish mystics of his time.

MEIR ben BARUCH OF ROTHENBURG (1215–1293)

This outstanding authority of his time was known as "The Great Light." On his way to Palestine he was imprisoned and held for exorbitant ransom. He refused to allow his people to pay for his liberty and subsequently died in prison.

ELEAZER ben JUDAH OF WORMS (1176–1238)

This renowned scholar and author achieved prominence in the field of mysticism and ethics. He was also distinguished in the field of science. He wrote *Rokeach*, a book on moral virtues.

MEIR HALEVI OF VIENNA (1394–1408)

He introduced the title "Morenu"—מורנו—"Our Teacher" and compiled a book of customs of the Jews.

KALONYMOS ben JUDAH (12th century) (Mainz)

Many prayers of our present-day liturgy are attributed to this man. His family name is also well known in the history of the Jews in Italy.

RABBI YOMTOV LIPPMAN MUHLHAUSEN (1410) (Prague)

He was an outstanding Talmudist and the author of *Nitzachon* —נצחון, a defense of Judaism against Christianity. After participating in a disputation at Prague against a converted Jew, who claimed that Jews blasphemed against Christianity, he wrote more polemical works in defense of Judaism.

JACOB ben MOSES HALEVI MOLLN (1360–1427)

Known as "Maharil," he composed German synagogue prayers and melodies. He was also a codifier.

ISRAEL ISSERLEIN (1390–1460) (Marburg)

He was the authority on Jewish law and revived the study of the Gaonic and Talmudic research. Published *Terumat haDeshan* — תרומת הדשן, a collection of decisions and responsa.

DAVID ben SOLOMON GANS (1541–1613)

He was a historian, Talmudist, mathematician, and astronomer.

Wrote a history of the Jewish people called *Zemach David*— צמח דוד, *The Shoot of David*.

JACOB JOSHUA FALK (HIRSCH) (1680–1756)

As chief rabbi of Metz and Frankfort, he was considered one of the great Talmudists of his time. He wrote *Pene Yehoshuah*, a commentary on the Talmud.

JONATHAN EIBESCHUTZ (1690–1764) (Metz)

He headed the famous Yeshivah at Prague. He was a student of Cabala and was called a "Miracle Worker." In a disputation with Rabbi Emden he was accused of being a follower of Sabbatai Zevi. He wrote many annotations on the *Shulchan Aruch* and a number of articles on Cabala.

JACOB ISRAEL EMDEN (1697–1776)

This rabbi was a bitter opponent of the movement that hailed Sabbatai Zevi as the Messiah. In a dispute with Rabbi Eibeschutz he had to flee for his life. His polemical writings were directed against false Messiah movements. He wrote *Megillath Sefer*—מגלת ספר, a work on contemporary Jewish life and thought.

DAVID FRANKEL (1704–1762) (Dessau)

Teacher of Moses Mendelssohn. He popularized the study of the Jerusalem Talmud. His work *Korban HaEdah* is a commentary on the lesser known Jerusalem Talmud.

EZEKIEL LANDAU (1713–1793)

As chief rabbi of Prague, he tried to mediate the quarrel between Emden and Eibeschutz. A staunch Halachist, he denounced Chassidism. His major work is *Noda Biye-*

hudah, a collection of Responsa. He objected to Mendelssohn's translation of the Bible into German.

DEFENDERS AND DEFAMERS

Each of the hundreds of kingdoms, provinces, and independent city governments of this period had its own rules and regulations concerning its Jewish subjects. Many vied with each other in restricting their rights and exploiting their resources. The Jews developed a horror of Christianity, which to them was a religion of hate and oppression, a religion steeped in the superstition of monks and the licentiousness of the clergy.

Time and again they were betrayed by the brutality of the nobles and the avariciousness of the people. They resigned themselves to the ghetto and to the distinctive dress and the yellow badge. They sought their livelihood from petty commerce, since they were systematically excluded from other work. And they always paid dearly for the privilege of survival.

Europe eventually started to emerge from the darkness of medievalism to the slow but gradual dawn of the era of political emancipation. While the Jew may have benefited in some instances from these changes, he continued to be classed as alien and undesirable.

Out of the organized opposition of the church to Judaism arose both defamers and defenders of the Jews; the former to burn new scars into the soul of the Jew and the latter to raise his hopes and bolster his morale.

DEFAMERS

MARTIN LUTHER (1483–1546)

This religious leader of the Protestant or Reformation movement was at first favorably inclined toward the Jews and sought to win them to his new church. Failing in his efforts, he turned against them and in his sermons he sanctioned their persecution and expulsion.

RINDFLEISCH (Thirteenth century)

This nobleman claimed to have received a vision that the Jews were responsible for the desecration of the Host and that he was selected by God to avenge this sacrilege by exterminating the "accursed race." His fanaticism caused many Jews to be burned at the stake in Rottingen. He led mobs through towns, killing Jews at random and causing the annihilation of the entire Jewish community of Wurzburg. Some 120 synagogues were desecrated and over 100,000 Jews killed.

JOHN CAPISTRANA (1453)

He was known as the "Scourge of the Hebrews." He instigated the burning of hundreds of Jews and the expulsion of entire Jewish communities.

JOSEPH PFEFFERKORN (John) (1469–1521)

He was a Jewish convert to Catholicism, who revived the blood libel accusation and sought unsuccessfully to have the church destroy all the Prayer Books and the Talmudic literature of the Jews. He wrote many pamphlets of a defamatory nature.

HOUSTON STEWART CHAMBERLAIN (1855–1927)

He was the son-in-law of the great German musician, Wagner, who was also strongly prejudiced against the Jews. He wrote a pseudo-scientific work called *Foundations of the 19th Century*, in which he created and developed anti-Semitic pseudo-racial theories that permeated and poisoned the German mind and which later became the basis for the Aryan claim to superiority. The theories were embodied in the philosophy of Nazism, under the leadership of Adolph Hitler.

OTTO HAUSER (1876–1932)

He was a prolific writer and given to virulent Jewbaiting. He maintained that the Jews were an inferior race and that Germany should set the example of eliminating them by persecution and expulsion.

ADOLF HITLER (1889–1945)

This Nazi leader was responsible for the destruction of more than six million Jews in Europe. He was a supreme racist and under his maniacal rule anti-Semitism reached its highest inhuman state. The story of the Jews during World War II is told in the deportation of men, women, and children, the erection of slave labor camps, and the horrendous extermination by gas and crematoria.

PAUL DE LA GARDE (1827–1891)

He was a skilled philologist who became increasingly virulent against Jews and Jewish literature as he grew older. He was usually engaged in some scholarly conflict that involved Judaism, the Bible, the Talmud, or Jewish individuals, while refusing to listen to any refutation.

JOHANN ANDREAS EISENMENGER (1654–1704)

This Christian scholar of Hebrew studies used his knowledge purposely to distort and falsify rabbinical texts. His anti-Semitic book was confiscated and banned for a number of years, but subsequently went through a number of editions and is still used as authoritative background material by anti-Semites.

AUGUST ROHLING (1839–1931)

This Catholic theologian wrote and agitated against Protestantism and Judaism. His attacks were vicious, unfounded, and full of forgeries. When Rabbi Joseph Samuel Bloch publicly accused him of being ignorant of Judaism and Hebrew, there was a trial that left Rohling branded as an ignoramus and a perjurer. Despite this, his anti-Semitic works were used by others as source material.

WILHELM MARR (b. 1819)

In his anti-Jewish writing he coined the word "Anti-Semitism." While the term has reference to all non-Aryan people, he applied it specifically to the Jews.

DEFENDERS

JOHANN REUCHLIN (1455–1522)

This foremost Christian scholar and student of Hebrew was called a traitor and a "baptized Jew" by Pfefferkorn, because of his defense of the Jews against Jew-baiting attacks. Although he was accused of heresy and declared guilty by the Pope, no action was taken against him because of his popularity among the people.

GOTTHOLD EPHRAIM LESSING (1729–1781)

He was one of Germany's great authors and playwrights, and was a champion of toleration and freedom of thought. In his writings he demanded equal rights for oppressed minority groups. He was a personal friend of the philosopher Mendelssohn and many of his works were written in the defense of the Jews, among which was the widely acclaimed "Nathan the Wise."

CHRISTIAN WILHELM DOHM (1781)

He wrote a challenging work on *The Civic Improvement of the Jews,* in which he asked for civil rights and religious liberty and blamed Christianity for its harsh treatment of the Jews.

THE BEGINNING OF EMANCIPATION

FREDERICK WILLIAM I (1620–1688)

Known as the "Great Elector," this ruler tolerated all religions and was the first to give legal protection to the Jews. During his reign, the Thirty Years' War (1618–1648) took place between the Protestants and Catholics. Again the Jewish people were the innocent victims. Their situation was not helped by the return of large numbers of Jews who had fled to Poland in earlier times and who were now fleeing the Polish massacres of 1648.

After the war, competition between the petty states opened opportunities for employment of Jews, with some rising to privileged positions as court Jews. These men serving as military purveyors, factors, and financiers for rulers and noblemen, were often instrumental in averting decrees of expulsion and extortion leveled against their co-religionists. They were permitted special privileges and exempted from ghetto restrictions. They contributed to the development of free trade and business enterprise. Sometimes they acted as intercessors (Shtadlanim) between Jews and government officials. Though some became highly assimilated, others were devoted to Jewish culture and became patrons of libraries and collectors of ceremonial objects later found in museums.

Shtadlanim, who were appointed by the Jewish community to speak and act on its behalf, were often court Jews because of their privileged positions. Some court Jews of prominence were :

Josel of Rosheim (1510–1554)
Michel Jud of Derensberg (1563)
Samuel Oppenheim (1635–1703)
    Financial agent of Austria
Samson Wertheimer (1658–1724)
    Chief rabbi of Hungary; served as banker and financial agent.
Jost Liebmann (c. 1704)
Elias Gompertz of Brandenberg
Behrend Lehmann (1661–1730)
Joseph Suss Oppenheimer (c. 1730) Cabinet minister

FREDERICK II, THE GREAT (1740–1786)

Despite his reputation as Europe's most enlightened ruler, he imposed severe restrictions upon the Jews. In spite of these disabilities, Jews began to reach out in the fields of German culture and secular science. One such Jew, Moses Mendelssohn, was instrumental in opening the door of the modern world to the Jew.

THE YIDDISH LANGUAGE

The base for the Yiddish language is German, augmented by words and phrases borrowed from all countries where Jews established residence. The name is derived from the German word "Judisch" and the language is written in Hebrew characters to read from right to left.

As Yiddish developed into a folk language, it opened the doors of Jewish literature to those unlearned in Hebrew. An anthology of moral and ethical teachings, taken from the Talmud and Midrash, was specially prepared for women. This book was called *Tzeenah Ureenah* meaning "Go forth and see ye daughters of Jerusalem" (Song of Songs 3 : 11). Prayer Books called "Techinnoth," "Supplication Prayers" were also made available to women.

As the Jews spread throughout the Jewish world, their language, Yiddish, became known as "Mameh Lashon"—"The Mother Tongue," even as Hebrew was always considered to be the "Lashon HaKodesh"—"the Holy Tongue."

FORERUNNERS OF EMANCIPATION

MOSES MENDELSSOHN (1728–1786)

Mendelssohn, the father of "Haskalah" (Enlightenment) and of Jewish emancipation, rose from the poverty of the ghetto to become the foremost Jewish intellectual in modern Jewish history.

He opened the doors of secular learning for the Jewish people by translating the Bible into German (*Bi-ur*), in spite of bans and protests by the rabbinate. He helped to start a parochial school for Jewish children where German and manual trades were also taught. He cooperated in the preparation of a common-sense commentary on the Bible. He rejected Talmudic religious law as being too restricted, obstructive, and often repressive. He encouraged a group of Jewish scholars to start a Hebrew magazine called "Ha-Meassef"—"The Gatherer." When the belief in immortality was being questioned, he wrote *Immortality,* a work that stamped him as an outstanding religious teacher.

Physically, Mendelssohn was a hunchback, but mentally he was a giant. In competition with the great philosopher Emanuel Kant, he won the Royal Academy of Science award. He was a personal friend of Lessing, Germany's foremost literary genius and defender of the Jews.

Mendelssohn came into conflict with Orthodox Judaism because he criticized the power of the rabbis in his book *Jerusalem, or the Civil Emancipation of the Jews.* While observing tradition himself, he insisted on freedom of conscience. As a representative of his people he became the champion of Jewish rights and was instrumental in alleviating their lot. Even as he opened the doors of the outside world to the Jew, so also did he open the doors of the Jewish world to the Christians.

His Chief Writings

Phaedon—A scholarly treatment of the subject of immortality of the soul

Jerusalem—A case for Jewish rights based on the ecclesiastical powers of Judaism

Morning Hours — A dialogue about God and the influence of religion upon man

NAPHTALI HERZ WESSELY (1725–1805)

This pioneer in the Haskalah movement collaborated with Mendelssohn in the translation of the Hebrew Bible into German. Following the Edict of Toleration issued by Joseph of Austria, he wrote the provocative book *Divre Sholom Ve-emeth*—דברי שלום ואמת, *Words of Peace and Truth,* in which he advocated the modernization of

Jewish education. He urged that Jews study the sciences and modern languages.

SOLOMON DUBNO (1738–1837)

He was a Bible commentator, a student of Masorah, a Hebrew poet and grammarian. He became a close friend of Mendelssohn while tutoring his son in Hebrew. He contributed to the translation of the Bible into German and wrote many Bible commentaries. One of his many books was *Kontres Aharon,* on the geography of Palestine.

HERZ HOMBERG (1749–1841)

This leading educator and author was instrumental in improving the school system for the Jewish people throughout Austria. He contributed a commentary on Deuteronomy to Mendelssohn's *Bi-ur.*

DAVID FRIEDLANDER (1750–1834)

Unlike Mendelssohn, with whom he was closely associated, Friedlander opposed ceremonial law and rabbinical tradition. He championed Reform in religious services and wrote many works to encourage emancipation of the Jew from his ghetto environment. In 1778 he opened the first free school for the education of Jewish boys and girls in German and Hebrew.

SOLOMON MAIMON (1753–1828)

He was an associate of Mendelssohn and among his many writings is an autobiography in which can be found valuable historical data concerning Polish Jewry and the Chassidic movement.

MARCUS HERZ (1747–1803)

This philanthropist, philosopher, and physician was an intimate friend of Mendelssohn. He was appointed permanent physician to the Prussian ruler. His correspondence with Kant, his philosophy teacher, casts much light on Kant's work. As a humanitarian he endeavored to improve the social and cultural conditions of the Jews and encouraged them to participate in German culture.

ISRAEL JACOBSON (1768-1828)

He was a Westphalian Court banker and a prime mover in the Reform movement. He founded a boarding school for Jewish and Christian children and introduced the organ, hymns, and German sermons in the first Reform synagogue established in Seesen in 1810. He advocated the elimination of all prayers and customs not in accordance with modern times.

SOLOMON JUDAH RAPPAPORT (1790–1867)

This foremost rabbi wrote *Bikkure Ha-ittim* —בכורי העתים, *First Fruits of our Time,* an anthology pertaining to the history and personalities of the Talmud. His enlightened approach to learning caused him to be attacked by the ultra-orthodox and the Chassidim.

ISSAC MARCUS JOST (1793–1860)

He was the first great Jewish historian of Germany. He wrote *The General History of the Jews,* which was later superseded by Graetz's work.

LEOPOLD ZUNZ (1794–1886)

Known for his scholarship, he founded the "Science of Judaism" and organized the "Society for the Culture and Science of Jews." By Orthodox standards he was a liberal. His chief contribution was in the field of historical Judaism. He used every known source to build his philosophic and scientific foundation of Judaism.

In his book *Chapters on the Divine Services of the Jews* he traced the history of the Prayer Book. In his *Literature and History of Synagogue Poetry* he gave a chronological account of the hundreds of men who contributed to the liturgy and poetry of the Prayer Book.

Besides his activities as a scholar, Zunz was also a champion of Jewish rights. His scholarly research on the subject of oaths resulted in the abolishment of the Jewish oath in Prussia. Zunz maintained that self-respect for the Jew can be attained not from enlightenment from without, but rather from light from within.

HEINRICH HEINE (1797–1856)

One of the greatest lyric poets of Germany. He submitted to baptism in order to gain admittance to the practice of law. At the close of his life he returned to Judaism, which in his heart he never forsook.

GABRIEL RIESSER (1806–1863)

He championed equal rights for all Jewish citizens in Germany. He coined the phrase "German Citizens of the Mosaic Faith." He stated that Jews were not a national group, but natural-born citizens. Riesser was appointed a judge to the highest court in the land (1859).

MOSES HESS (1812–1875)

A product of the emancipation, Hess sought the solution to the Jewish problem by creating a Jewish state. In his book *Rome and Jerusalem* he proposed the rebuilding of Palestine not only as a Jewish national homeland, but as an ideal social order. Hess became a forerunner of the Zionist movement by proclaiming that the Jewish people could win the respect of the world only if a nation of Jews existed.

SAMUEL HOLDHEIM (1806–1860)

He was a leader and exponent of Reform Judaism, who instituted Sunday worship services and did away with many traditional ceremonies. He maintained that marriage and divorce laws had nothing to do with religion. He also drew a distinction between Biblical and Talmudical Judaism and sought to separate the former from the latter.

SAMSON RAPHAEL HIRSCH (1808–1888)

This Orthodox rabbi opposed the Reform movement. He stated that Jews, not Judaism, needed reforming. His neo-orthodox theory was that it is necessary to know Judaism, not to follow blindly. He claimed that one could become active in national and political affairs without forsaking tradition.

ABRAHAM GEIGER (1810–1874)

Known as the philosopher of Reform Judaism, he believed that the moral law was more important than ritual observances. His central thought was that Judaism was a theological system. In his book *Judaism and History* he explains his theories concerning Reform Judaism. In 1837 he convened the first meeting of Reform Rabbis.

LUDWIG PHILIPPSON (1811–1899)

This rabbi and scholar labored for the political and spiritual emancipation of the Jew and pointed out the inseparable relationship between Judaism, Christianity, and Islam. It was said of him that he was the most dynamic personality of his time, as he dedicated himself to the advancement of his people in Germany. He founded a German-Jewish newspaper, established an Institute for Jewish Literature, initiated several rabbinical conferences, and published many books.

HEINRICH GRAETZ (1817–1891)

He is known for his outstanding history of the Jewish people, which is based on all known sources of his time. It is one of the most remarkable single contributions in the history of Jewish literature.

ALBERT EINSTEIN (1879–1955)

This world-renowned physicist had to flee Germany because of Hitlerism. He was awarded the Nobel Prize in 1922 for work on photo-chemical equivalents, that helped lay the foundation for the quantum theory. He developed the theory of relativity, which in turn led to the splitting of the atom and the construction of the atom bomb. He was an active Zionist supporter.

THE AGE OF REASON

Napoleon's conquest of Europe (1806–1812) gave impetus to the emancipation movement. Though it had a slow start, it ultimately broke the ghetto walls and ended in the granting of citizenship to the Jews. King Frederick William III (1812) issued an edict of civil rights for his Jewish subjects, but full emancipation was yet to be achieved. Though the Jews fought for their fatherland, their newly found freedom was taken from them soon after the defeat of Napoleon in 1813.

But the Jew of Germany had tasted of this short-lived freedom and enlightenment and wanted to become a part of European civilization and culture. One thing only stood in his way—his Jewishness. This barrier was hurdled by baptism. By 1846, thousands of Jews, including prominent intellectuals, escaped the restrictions of second-class citizenship by embracing Christianity. It became fashionable for wealthy and influential Jewish converts to entertain statesmen, scientists, musicians, philosophers, and even royalty.

Haskalah—Jewish Enlightenment

This "Age of Reason" produced Jews who believed that the key to Jewish enlightenment was through complete assimilation. It had a counterpart in Jewish life called "Haskalah" — השכלה — "Intelligence." At first it took shape by breaking with the narrow forms and disciplines of Orthodoxy. Followers of Haskalah were known as "Maskilim"— משכילים —"Enlightened Ones." Not only did they grasp at the culture of European civilization, but they wanted their co-religionists to benefit by it.

The Maskilim published a Hebrew journal called "Ha-Measif," containing articles on German culture, history, philosophy, drama, poetry, etc. Later the magazine gave way to a German periodical called the "Allgemeine Zeitung des Judentums."

Thus began a new era in Jewish life. The Haskalah movement attracted brilliant men to its ranks. It enabled Jews to rise to prominent positions as statesmen, philosophers, scientists, and writers. It became the forerunner of another movement that was to be called Reform or Liberal Judaism.

Emancipation and the German Empire

As the surge for liberalization of laws swept through Europe, Jews were an integral part of the struggle. The revolutions of 1848 caused kings and princelings to grant constitutional rights. These were annulled during the reaction that followed. Ultimately, the unification of Germany helped to erase distinctions between races and creeds. After 1871, the end of the Franco-Prussian war, equal rights to citizenship were granted to all. Since that time, Jews might be considered emancipated, but they still suffered disabilities resulting from discrimination and anti-Semitism.

Reform Judaism

The age of reason or enlightenment paved the way for the rise of Reform or Liberal Judaism in Germany. Mendelssohn and his followers opened the doors to a world of science, literature, and culture for the Jews. They came into contact with European civilization and broke the ties of their ghetto life. Yiddish, the mother language of all Jews, gave way to German. Secular study displaced the Bible and Talmud, and Judaism as a religion and culture was deserted by many educated Jews.

Reform Judaism came into existence not only to stem the rising tide of apostasy, but to bring the Jewish religion into line with emancipation and reason. To break completely with the ghetto and Orthodoxy was the goal of Liberal Judaism.

The early pioneers of Reform, following their brethren of France, maintained that Jewish law must conform to the law of the land and that its literature and faith must be in harmony with the spirit of modern life. Hence, references to Zionism, resurrection, and the Chosenness of Israel, were deleted from the Prayer Book. The revolt against orthodoxy and Rabbinism was marked by the opening of a Reform synagogue in Hamburg in 1818.

The changes introduced by Reform Judaism were radical. The first concern was with prayer, ritual, and ceremony. Instrumental music, forbidden in the synagogue, now found its place through the organ. The devotions were modernized and shortened. Sermons were delivered in German. There was a strong resemblance to the Protestant type of service.

Some of the leading exponents of Reform Judaism were David Friedlander, Israel Jacobson, Abraham Geiger, and Ludwig Philippson.

ANTI-SEMITISM

Wilhelm Marr erroneously has been claimed to be the son of a Jewish actor, and is said to have introduced the term "anti-Semitism" in connection with the activities of the Christian Socialist Workers Party which was founded in 1878. Today the name is used to describe active dislike and intolerance of the Jew. It became more accentuated in Germany toward the end of the 19th century. The great economic crash of 1873 stirred up a rash of vicious and irresponsible writings citing the Jew as the scapegoat for Germany's troubles. Educated Germans, resentful of the new freedom accorded the Jews and of their appointments to important educational and cultural positions, started a systematic campaign to undermine them by branding them an inferior race of parasites. Thus began a system of anti-Semitic propaganda that subsequently affected the lives of the Jews throughout the world.

Prominent German intellectuals attempted to prove in their writings and speeches that the Jews were an undesirable people; that they were directly responsible for the country's depression; that they were a danger and menace to the welfare of German culture and society; that as anti-Christs they should not be tolerated. Men like the historian Chamberlain and the musician Wagner were instigators of the German brand of Aryanism and its counterpart, anti-Semitism. It was the subject of conversation among the elite. It was preached in the church and disseminated in learned articles by responsible leaders. It was given a pseudo-scientific basis by Heinrich von Treitschke, Hitler's arch-propagandist of hate.

The seeds of anti-Semitism found fertile ground in Germany and the masses were taught to think of the Jew as the great misfortune of Germany. The story of German anti-Semitism is long and tragic. It culminated in the destruction of six million Jews under Nazism. As long as Germany remained the superior nation of Europe, the Jews were tolerated. After World War I, the prestige of Germany was at a very low ebb. Who but the Jew could be responsible for Germany's defeat and humiliation? In such a climate of hate and defeatism, Hitler rose to power. Under Nazi domination was written the cruelest chapter of genocide ever to blot the pages of history.

Hitlerism and the Jews

The World War of 1914 found a population of 600,000 Jews in Germany. Of this number 100,000 served in the armed forces, with some 12,000 giving their lives in the service of their country.

With the end of the war, which was followed by economic chaos, the Jews again became the scapegoat for Germany's internal troubles. They were accused of being disloyal to the country and labeled war-mongers. The inequalities of the Peace Treaty were blamed upon them. Based on documents many times proved to be forged, the preposterous claim that they were organized under the "Elders of Zion" to conquer the world became widely publicized.

In 1922, anti-Semitism reached a new high with the assassination of Walter Rathenau, the Jewish Minister of Foreign Affairs. The world was shocked, but for the German people who believed that the influence of the Jew was pernicious and was a prelude to the rise of Hitler and his destruction of the Jewish people. Many Jews fled in anticipation of a holocaust. The year 1933 marked the beginning of Nazism under Hitler. It resulted in a Second World War, which Germany lost.

In 1935, the infamous Nuremberg laws deprived Jews of their citizenship and made them an outcast people. It meant a systematized inhuman plan for their complete isolation and extermination. A nation-wide boycott of all Jewish business was undertaken. It was followed by burning of books, deprivation of citizenship, confiscation of business, property, money, and inheritance. It saw the burning of synagogues, deportation of men, women, and children, the erection of slave-labor camps, and the extermination of human beings by gas and cremation. These and other indescribable horrors tell the story of the Jews under Nazism. When the final chapter of Hitlerism was written, there remained some 15,000 Jews of the original 600,000, who had found refuge outside the country. After the war many of these returned. A 1959 estimation gives the number of 2,000 Jews living in East Germany and 22,000 in West Germany.

In 1952 reparations were offered to survivors and to Israel, which were paid by West Germany. In 1965 West Germany and Israel established diplomatic relations.

JEWISH COMMUNITIES

Aachen	Hannover
Berlin	Herrne
Bielefeld	Kiel
Bochun	Koblenz
Bonn	Koehn
Bremen	Krefeld
Dortmund	Landau
Dresden	Leipzig
Duisberg	Mainz
Dusseldorf	Mannheim
Erfurt	Minden
Essen	Muehlein-
Frankfort	Ruhr
Frieburg	Muenchen-
Gelsen-	Gladbach
kirchen	Muenster
Hagen	Oberhausen-
Westfalen	Wesel
Hamburg	Rheydt
Hamm	Trier
Heidelberg	Wuppertal
Herford	

The Jews of Great Britain

Legend has it that the first Jews came to England in the time of King Solomon, with the Phoenicians who sailed from the Near East. Centuries later Jews accompanied the Roman conquerors of England.

The first Jewish community of record was established in 1066, when William the Conqueror brought over the entire Jewish community of Rouen, France, to start a commercial middle class. After that, many small Jewish settlements made their appearance. There are laws to be found in eighth- and ninth-century statute books that concern Jews, but it is not known whether these laws were copied mechanically from the laws of other parts of Europe.

Like Jews in other countries, English Jewry was subject to discriminatory pressures from the church, the peasants, and the nobility. However, they did not suffer the humiliation and degradation of their brethren in other European countries. They were segregated but did not live in ghettos. Under rabbinic authority they were permitted communal self-government. Because many occupied positions in the economy of the land that were closed to Christians and that needed protection, like that of money lending, they were declared to be the king's "Chattel," both in person and in possessions. They were made to pay special taxes and were exempt from the authority of the church and the nobles.

During the first two Crusades, under Henry II (1154–1189), the Jews were not physically molested. However, they were forced to contribute large sums of money toward the Crusades. In 1144 there occurred a blood accusation in Norwich. This superstitious belief that Jews used the blood of Christians for the baking of their Unleavened Bread set a precedent for violence and bloodshed that was repeated many times, over the years, under the instigation of the church. It was also encouraged by the nobility and an emerging Christian merchant class.

The accession of Richard I (1189–1199), the Lion-hearted, brought a century of oppression which included forced baptism. Although he did not approve of the fanaticism of the Church, his absence on the Third Crusade made it impossible to prevent the recurring persecutions in many cities, including London and York, where many Jews were massacred and all signs of indebtedness to them were destroyed. When he returned he ordered an inquiry at York and the prime instigators were punished.

RICHARD I inaugurated the "Exchequer of the Jews," a systematic regulation of their lives and their property that put them at the mercy of succeeding monarchs and nobles. When King John needed money in 1210, he imprisoned all the Jews until he collected a huge ransom. Despite the Magna Charta (1215), in 1218 all Jews over seven years of age had to wear a distinctive white badge (tabula), which was changed to yellow at a later date. The pattern of extortion and collection of debts assumed various forms, sometimes including ritual murder accusations, such as that brought by Hugh of Lincoln in the thirteenth century, and the confiscation of synagogue buildings, which were turned over to the church.

Burgesses in various towns petitioned successfully to have the Jewish population removed. By 1245, places of residence were greatly restricted and the Jews were practically drained of all resources. In 1255, they asked the King for permission to leave the country, which he refused. In 1252, during a civil war, the Jews of London were pillaged and murdered. In 1269 they were disqualified from holding land.

EDWARD I (1272–1307), issued "De Judaismo" or "Statute of Judaism," which further limited their ability to earn a living. The masses of poor Jews were forced into questionable practices, such as clipping coins, which resulted in the arrest and execution of 239. In 1282 all synagogues were seized by the order of the Archbishop. Six years later Jews were proscribed from practicing medicine.

The clergy and baronage, realizing that King Edward retained the Jews only as a source of revenue, voted him one-tenth of their movable property if he would expel them from the country. This he did on July 18, 1290. About 16,000 were forced to leave with what little they could salvage. Most of them found homes in Germany, France, and Spain.

Although for 350 years there was no organized Jewish communal life, small numbers of Jews, most of foreign birth, were able to enter England secretly as Marranos. They were primarily professional people, such as physicians who ministered to kings, queens, and religious dignitaries. There must have been a number of such Jews because a census was ordered in 1542 by the Privy Council and their colony was broken up in 1609.

It was MANASSEH BEN ISRAEL (1604–1657), a Marrano Jew of Amsterdam, who was largely responsible for the re-admittance of the Jews to England. He appealed to Oliver Cromwell to permit them to enter England on the ground that they would be fulfilling the prophecy of Daniel, that the Jews would have to be liberated and scattered all over the world before the Day of Judgment would come. While no formal admission was proclaimed, because of the strong objections of merchants and clergy, Jews were admitted to the country without fanfare in 1656.

They established a new Sephardic (Marrano) community in London in 1664 and lived without civil rights and privileges for almost a century. An Ashkenazic congregation also was formed in London in 1690 and in time their influence spread throughout the country, challenging and surpassing that of the Sephardim. During this period there was no ghetto or overt hostility. Although the Jews maintained a secure position from the time of Charles II (1660–1685), they were subject to heavy taxes and were forced to contribute to the DOMUS CONVERSORUM, a home for poor converted Jews.

Jews lived in an intellectual climate of freedom but often at the expense of conversion. In an attempt to give sanction to Jewish equality, to facilitate naturalization and encourage immigration, a "Jew Bill" was passed in 1753, but artificially stimulated hostility of the people forced its withdrawal. In 1830 another attempt to repeal the civil disabilities of the Jews failed. In 1847, Lionel de Rothschild became the first Jew to be elected to Parliament, but he refused to take the Christian Oath and therefore could not be seated. Eleven years later the oath was removed and he was officially installed. Jews benefited by the era of liberalism, which was influenced by John Locke's "Letter Concerning Toleration." (1869)

JEWISH LIFE

Before the expulsion in 1290, there were about 5,000 Jews in England, most of whom were of Sephardic origin. From 1290 to 1655, no Jews as such lived in the country. The first influx of Ashkenazim (German Jews) occurred in 1692. The Polish and Russian Jews started to come in the 1870's and 1880's as refugees from persecution.

English Jewry was free from imposed ghettos and discriminatory restrictions. However, they tended to live together and "Jew Street" became well known. They were allowed liberty of worship and exercised self-government in their communal affairs. They had a "Beth Din" (Court of Law) for adjudication of such controversies as those arising in marriages, divorces, business transactions, and religious matters. The King appointed a Chief Rabbi, who was the liaison between him and the Jewish community. Women had equal rights and were active in business. Complete equality was granted to Jews in 1890 after much prolonged debate in Parliament.

At the founding of Oxford University, Jews contributed rare Hebrew books and manuscripts and were generous in their support. They began entering the university as students in the 1850's. Their enrollment increased after religious tests were removed in 1871.

The Board of Deputies of British Jews was organized in London as a representative body of both the Sephardic and Ashkenazic Jewry in 1760, at the accession of George III, to represent them at court. By the 19th century it included provincial and overseas communities. At first only synagogues were represented, but later secular organizations were admitted to the Board. By 1959 it had 450 members. It followed British parliamentary procedure and received its finances by assessment of its constituent bodies. Over the years it has reflected the changing current in Jewish life, being strongly Zionistic in modern times. It has been active in the defence of political and civil rights in England and abroad.

A federation of Ashkenazic synagogues was established in London in 1870 by Act of Parliament and is known as United Synagogue. Originally there were five synagogues, but now there are twenty-five, with a membership of 19,000 in the city. There are 21 "District" and 33 "Affiliated" synagogues representing about 110,000 individuals. The United Synagogue is the main support of the office of the Chief Rabbi and of the London Beth Din. It is also a primary source of support for many religious and charitable institutions.

In 1926 the World Union for Progressive Judaism was founded to coordinate the activities of liberal Jewish groups and to establish new liberal congregations throughout the world. In 1955 the Union established a theological seminary for training progressive rabbis in Paris. At the present time there are 23 countries with affiliated constituents in the Union. In 1960 the headquarters of the World Union were moved to the UAHC House of Living Judaism in New York. The organization is accorded a consultative status by the United Nations in the non-governmental category.

From 1933 to 1939 there was an influx of refugees from Nazi Germany, which stimulated organized anti-Semitic movements similar to those in many other countries of the world.

British Jewry, and especially one individual, Chaim Weizmann, who later became the first president of Israel, played a vital role in influencing the British government to assume the Mandate over Palestine after World War I. Sir Herbert Samuel, a Jew, was the first of the series of high commissioners sent to govern Palestine. The Mandate ended with the creation of the

State of Israel by the United Nations Organization in 1948.

By 1964 the Jewish population of Great Britain was 450,000. The large Jewish communities are London 280,000, Manchester, 30,000, Leeds, 30,000, Glasgow, 15,000, and Liverpool, 7,500. Some communities of early Jewish history are

Cambridge	Norwich
Birmingham	Oxford
Edinburgh	Plymouth
Lincoln	York
Lynn	

NOTABLE JEWS

BENJAMIN DISRAELI (1804–1881)

This statesman and author is also known as the Earl of Beaconsfield. He was elected to Parliament in 1837 and rose in the Conservative party to become the "Favorite Prime Minister" of Queen Victoria. He succeeded in enlarging the British Empire to include countries in Asia and Africa.

As an author he wrote a number of works on social and political affairs. Though he was baptized by his father at the age of 13, Disraeli did not cut off his identity with the Jewish people. He visited Palestine and remained proud of his Jewish origin throughout his career. He was an outspoken proponent of Jewish emancipation in Parliament. His writings include *Vivian Grey*, a social satire, *Alroy, Coningsby*, and *Tancred*, novels on Christianity as a development of Judaism, and *The Voyage of Captain Popanilla*, a political satire.

SIR MOSES MONTEFIORE (1784–1885)

He was a communal leader and philanthropist, whose place in history is owing to his tireless efforts on behalf of his oppressed people everywhere. In 1840, with Cremieux of France, he successfully interceded in gaining the freedom of innocent Jews in the Damascus Blood Libel. On two occasions (1864 and 1872) he visited Russia and obtained assurances of fair and better treatment of Russian Jewry. In 1858 he went to Rome on behalf of Edgar Mortara, a Jewish boy who was kidnaped and baptized in the Catholic religion. He was received in the court of the Sultan of Morocco, Prince Carol of Rumania, and other men of state, where he pleaded the cause of his people. He visited Palestine seven times, the last at the age of 90. He organized the first agriculture settlements there.

Montefiore founded the Bank of Ireland and was prominent in the industrial world. His benefactions were widespread, aiding every worthwhile cause that might help his people. Nor did he neglect the tradition of Jewish learning. He founded a theological school and always remained a Jew of staunch principles and deep piety.

ISRAEL ZANGWILL (1864–1926)

He was born of poor Russian parents in London. His first recognition as an author came in 1892, while teaching at the "Jews Free School." His classic, *Children of the Ghetto,* was followed by many books based on East End Jewish life. Dramas, essays, and particularly translations of liturgical poetry brought him further literary recognition.

In 1895 he was influenced by Theodore Herzl to become an active Zionist. He also joined forces in securing voting rights for women and in promoting pacifist movements.

RUFUS DANIEL ISAACS (1860–1935)
MARQUESS OF READING.

This outstanding jurist entered Parliament as a Liberal, (1904), serving as solicitor general, attorney general and lord chief justice respectively. He represented his country as ambassador to the United States and viceroy of India. In 1931 he became Foreign Secretary. He was not an observant Jew but was strongly pro-Jewish in behalf of his people. He was the only Jew to be created a peer and a Marquess, (1926).

The Jews of Ireland

The first Jews to settle in Ireland (1232) were Marranos from Spain and Portugal. Though few in number, they were expelled from the country in 1290, at the time that England ordered all the Jews to leave. In 1661 Oliver Cromwell permitted them to return. They established a Jewish community and founded a house of worship in the city of Dublin. There is no marked history about the Jews for the next two centuries. In 1860, discriminatory measures forced Jews to wear a distinctive badge and dress.

Jewish life in Ireland was directed by a chief rabbi. Several Jews achieved prominence in industry and politics. The Belfast ship industry was developed by a Jewish settler. In recent times, Robert Briscoe was twice elected to the high office of Lord Mayor of Dublin.

The present population is about 5,500. Most of the Jews live in Dublin and Cork.

The Jews of Scotland

The first records of Jews in Scotland are dated in the seventeenth century, when there was a small community in Edinburgh. There was one in Glasgow in 1823 and now there are about 16,000 in these and other places in the country as of 1964.

The Jews of Austria

FROM EARLY TIMES

It is thought that Jews came to the Danube area with the Roman legions and that some settled in Austria, which was originally a part of Charlemagne's empire. In 955 this country was known as Oesterreich. Records indicate that Jews resided in the realm as early as 906. The first synagogue was built in Vienna in 1204.

The story of the Austrian Jew follows the pattern set in Germany. They were subject to innumerable pressures and their status as "Servi Camerae" — "Property of the Crown," left them at the mercy of rulers, bishops, and noblemen. The Christian church would not let them forget that they were the killers of Christ, a crime for which they were to be bound in everlasting servitude.

FREDERICK II (1238)

He labeled the Jews "Chattels of our Chamber," thus to be sold or held at the whim of the ruler. He did this under the guise of granting them a charter and taking them under his "protection." When Rudolph of Hapsburg took Austria (1876) he, too, claimed all the Jews as his personal property.

PERSECUTIONS

The persecution of Jews in Austria followed a monotonous routine between the 13th and 15th centuries. The Black Death accusation (1338–1345) caused the spilling of much Jewish blood. In 1420 they were charged with aiding the Hussite heresy and accused of the ritual murder crime. As a result, all the Jews of Austria were either imprisoned, deprived of their property, burned, or expelled. In spite of these persecutions, they did not disappear as a people. In 1451 they were allowed to establish residence again.

FERDINAND II (1619–1637)

Hungarian domination in 1438 and Maximilian's reign (1493–1519) did not alter the miserable plight of the Jews. In 1625, Ferdinand II granted them a place of residence in a suburb of Vienna, which subsequently became known as Leopold Stadt. Imperial policy varied with localities. Some tolerated them as convenient scapegoats; some permitted them privileges at a stipulated price; some allowed them to acquire money, only to take it away at a later time; some expelled them and then invited return on payment of large sums of money. After another period of excessive persecution, a general expulsion for the whole country was decreed by Margaret Theresa in 1670. A number of individual Jews were excepted, although they were subject to major restrictions.

MARIA THERESA (1740–1780)

The war of succession brought this woman to power. She was bitter in her attitude toward the Jews and brutal in her treatment of them. She ordered them expelled from Bohemia, Silesia, and Moravia. In the large cities of Vienna and Prague she imposed limitations of population and residential restrictions. She decreed that all beardless Jews must wear badges. She boasted that she had but one interest in the Jews and that was to see that they always decreased in population.

JOSEPH II (1765–1790)

Though he was the son of Maria Theresa he became known as the "Lover of Mankind." He was responsible for the famous "Edict of Toleration," which granted civil liberties to the Jews of lower Austria. With assimilation as his goal, he abolished Jewish poll taxes, distinctive dress, and the Jewish badge. After his death these privileges were withdrawn until the Constitution of 1848 restored them. But all limitations were not removed until 1867, after which Jewish communities were permitted to settle in all parts of the country.

At one time or another Austria ruled over the Jews of Bohemia, Moravia, South Poland, Lombardy, Venetia, Carniola, Istria, Dalmatia, Hungary, Croatia, Slovonia, Transylvania, Galicia, and the Kingdom of Italy.

FRANCIS JOSEPH I (1848–1916)

This Emperor was the most tolerant of all the Hapsburg rulers. Under his regime many Jews became prominent and successful in the field of letters, medicine, and industry. Old discriminatory measures, however, continued unofficially in many areas.

In 1867 the Republic of Austria-Hungary was established. With it came gradual emancipation, which prevailed until 1914 when the Republic allied itself with Germany and was defeated in World War I. The collapse of Austria-Hungary in the postwar years left the Jews in a precarious position. There was little relief until the revolution of 1918, which lasted ten years. During this brief period the Austrian Republic extended full equality to the Jews.

JEWISH LIFE

Until 1421, a central organization of Jewish communities existed in Austria. Assimilation and conversion brought a number of Jews into prominence, but, for the masses, Jewish life remained the same. The Jew could engage in handicraft, trade, and the arts, but he could never rise higher than his master. He was not permitted to become a landowner and his livelihood was restricted in accordance with the general European treatment of the Jew. A large number of Jews, between three and four thousand, paid a special tax for the privilege of living on the estates of the aristocracy.

After 1867 Jews participated in the founding of many industries and attained positions in government service, legislative bodies, the army, and the universities. Learning flourished. The wave of enlightenment, Haskalah, resulted in the establishment of printing presses and the spread of Jewish literature in Hebrew and Yiddish.

The law of March 21, 1890, set up Jewish communities called "Locally Limited Territories." All Jews in a specified area were compelled to belong to the one religious community, served by a board of directors that had the power to levy taxes and to control all religious institutions.

World War I involved the Jewish population as it did all citizens. It also created many problems for them because of the great influx of refugees from surrounding countries. After the war, under pressure of local anti-Semitic measures, most of them returned to their homes. Although excesses were first directed against the refugees, all Jews became victims after Austria-Hungary collapsed.

Anti-Semitism subsided following the revolution of 1918 when the Austrian Republic extended full equality to the Jews and a Jewish National Council was formed to serve their political and educational purposes. During the life of the Republic, Jews produced a number of political figures, artists, authors, and scholars, among whom were Sigmund Freud, Arthur Schnitzler and Stefan Zweig.

Jews emerged as publicists, critics, bankers, statesmen, and industrialists. Many joined the Social Democratic party, which became known all over the world for its housing programs. When the party declined in 1927, Jewish energy turned to the support of Zionism.

After the defeat of Germany in 1945, only 29 Jewish children were left in Vienna. Before the war about 20,000 Jews (10 per cent of the total Jewish population) lived in Vienna. In 1953 there was one Jewish afternoon school and six centers of religious instruction, with five teachers for a total of 246 pupils.

FROM HITLERISM TO THE PRESENT TIME

The rise of the Christian Socialist Party to power forced the Jews to adopt a defensive position. The Osterreichisch-Israelitische Union was formed to combat attacks on the Jews and Judaism.

The economic crisis starting in 1929 brought an upsurge of anti-

Semitism. The collapse of the Viennese branch of the Rothschild bank caused havoc in the lives of the Jews. These conditions made it easy for Hitler to establish Nazi branches in Austria. The constitution of 1934 curtailed the rights of Jews in schools. The Numerus Clausus was introduced into the universities. Jews were dismissed from government positions. Boycotts and a host of economic disabilities left them impoverished. From 1934–1938 the government made a vain attempt to check the rising tide of anti-Semitism that erupted in anti-Jewish riots and demonstrations.

Austria was annexed by Germany when Hitler's armies bloodlessly took over the country in March, 1938. For two years, those who were able to obtain visas left the country. The rest of the Jewish community was exterminated by 1943. Of 250,000 Jews only 6,000 remained alive when World War II ended. In the 20 years that followed, a few Jews returned to salvage what they could. Recent estimates show the population to be about 12,000, with only 680 of them living outside Vienna. Some 3,000 Austrian Jews have settled in Israel since 1948. There are remnants of prewar parties, such as Socialist and Zionist, but there is not much vitality in Austrian Jewish life.

JEWISH COMMUNITIES

Innsbruck
Graz
Linz
Salzburg
Vienna

The Jews of Czechoslovakia

Jews have lived in Bohemia, one of the many provinces of Czechoslovakia, since the Crusades (1096). Since this area was at one time part of the Austro-Hungarian empire, their fate was very similar in pattern to that of the Jews of Austria. The city of Prague was one of the greatest Jewish centers prior to Hitlerism, and the repository of the oldest and richest tradition in European history.

During the Crusades, the Jews bore the marks left by persecution, forcible baptism, and pillage. Their situation improved and worsened as the several waves of Crusaders swept through their communities. For a time, in the 13th century, under Ottocar II, a favorable climate prevailed, but in the 14th century King Charles IV (1347–1379) proclaimed the Jews to be his "imperial serfs." His successor, Wenzel IV, (1378–1419) seized the property of all Jews killed in a massacre in Prague, without prosecuting the murderers. The Jagellons (1471–1526) undermined the economic position of the Jewish population. By the end of the 16th century, there had been several expulsions, particularly from Prague.

In 1625 Bohemia was conquered by the Hapsburgs of Austria and their unfortunate lot was aggravated by the imposition of heavy taxes. During the Chmielnicki massacres in Poland (1648) many Jews migrated to this area. The Jewish population increased again in 1670 as a result of the expulsion of Jews from Vienna. By 1708 their number had grown to over 12,000. They were restricted to ghettos and because of a special "Familianten law" the number of marriages was kept at a minimum.

In 1744 Maria Theresa ordered their expulsion, but the decree was not fully carried out. The history of Czech Jews actually merged with that of the Jews in other parts of the Austrian empire, when Joseph II in 1871 issued his "Edict of Toleration." They were not fully emancipated, however, until 1867.

The Czechoslovakian Republic was constituted as a nation in 1919 at the end of World War I. It included the provinces of Bohemia, Moravia, Silesia, Slovakia, and Ruthenia, with a total estimated Jewish population of 357,000.

Under the Republic Jews were given full equality of citizenship, which remained in effect until the country was conquered by Hitler in 1939. At the end of World War II there were 35,000 left, of whom 24,000 emigrated to Israel from 1945 to 1953.

JEWISH LIFE

In 1938 about 105,000 Jews in Czechoslovakia lived in Ruthenia, where they formed over 15% of the population. Until World War I this area was part of Hungary and many Jews worked in rural sections as farmers and forest workers. The province of Mukacevo had the largest Jewish population.

Of the 150,000 Jews in Slovakia, Bratislava had the most important Jewish community and boasted of having one of the most prominent Yeshivoth in Europe. Jews of Bohemia and Moravia numbered about 80,000 and in 1938 were considered to be the most progressive of all Czechoslovakian Jewry.

The political status of the Jewish population was favorable. Until Nazi Germany occupied the country, Jews were represented in all phases of public life. Their fate followed that of all Nazi-occupied countries.

After World War II, when the country was under Communist control, a relatively large number of Jews held positions as officials and directors of nationalized enterprises.

In 1950–1951 the Joint Distribution Committee and the Zionist organizations were banned. In 1952 there was a purge in the Communist party resulting in an anti-Semitic trial of Rudolph Slansky and his "associates." There were 14 in the Group of whom 11 were Jews. Slansky was General Secretary of the Czech Communist Party and Vice Premier of the country. He was charged with Trotskyite-Titoist-Zionist activities and found guilty. He was executed along with seven other Jews.

This trial and the resultant feeling against "intellectualism" and "cosmopolitanism" hurt the Jews severely. Many lost their jobs and the condition of the Jewish community began to deteriorate.

The religious life of the Jews in Czechoslovakia has not been very vital since World War II. The number of rabbis dwindled from 300 before the war to four in 1959. There are few synagogues functioning and the seized property of the Jewish communities has not been returned. The people subsist on small allowances from the government and no Jewish schools are in operation.

In November, 1953, a congress of Jewish religious communities was held by permission of the communist government. The constitution, which limited their activities, provides that a Kehillah may be established wherever there are ten persons who are living in accordance with Jewish religious tradition. Supreme authority is vested in the "Council of Jewish Communities," which appoints rabbis and teachers. Provision is made for a chief rabbi and a council of rabbis.

JEWS TO REMEMBER

ISAAC ben MOSES OF VIENNA
(c. 1180–1260)

He was born in Bohemia, studied in France and Germany with the Tosaphists, and died in Vienna. His Talmudic commentary *Zarua, Light Is Sown*—contains codifications and responsa as well as material concerning the life of medieval Jews in Germany, France, and Italy.

ISAAC ben MORDECAI (RIBAM)

In the 12th century he was recognized as an outstanding rabbi in Prague and Regensburg and was called the "chief and first man" among the sages of the time. His Tosaphoth and decisions are found in the collections of other authors.

LOWE JUDAH ben BEZALEL (1529–1609)

Although born in Posen, he became known as "Der hohe Rabbi Lowe," or Maharal of Prague. He served as Rabbi in Nikolsburg, Moravia, from 1553–1573, after which he became the religious head of the Prague community. Many famous rabbis were among his pupils and he was highly esteemed among non-Jews. Among his numerous works on religious subjects are a commentary to Rashi on the Pentateuch. He opposed excess casuistry (Pilpul) in Talmudic study, was somewhat hostile to Cabala, and insisted that the Talmud and not the Shulchan Aruch was the primary authority for Jewish life. Legends clustered about

his life, especially that he created the Golem, a huge clay image, which protected the Jewish community from imminent danger. When the ghetto was torn down, a statue of this rabbi was placed before the new city hall.

MORDECAI MARCUS MEISEL
(1528–1601)

He was a great benefactor to the Jewish community in Prague, where there is a synagogue named after him. Although he was a court-banker to the rulers, his estate was confiscated upon his death.

YOMTOV LIPMANN MUHLHAUSEN
(14th–15th centuries)

Known as a polemicist, he was compelled to defend Judaism in a disputation in Prague in 1399 against the apostate Peter (Pesach). He was subsequently released but 80 other Jews were killed. He wrote about the disputation in his famous anti-Christian work, *Sepher Nitzchon, Book of Triumph.*

DAVID ben SOLOMON GANS
(1541–1613)

This historian was also an astronomer who worked with Kepler and Tycho Brahe in Prague. He is best known for his *Tzemach David, The Branch of David* (1592), a short chronicle of Jewish life down to his own time. It was translated into Latin and Yiddish.

ISAIAH HOROWITZ (c. 1556–1630)

This man is known by the initials of the name of his chief work, *Shene Luchoth HaBrit, Two Tablets of the Covenant,* which forms the word SHELOH. It is a Cabalistic work on Jewish laws and customs and strongly opposed the pilpul method of study. The book advocated the study of Hebrew grammar. Sheloh as rabbi, scholar, and Cabalist, officiated in several Polish and German communities before coming to Prague in 1615. From there he went to Palestine (1621) where he lived out his life.

JOSEPH PERL (1773–1839)

He was a Hebrew author and a MASKIL—AN ENLIGHTENED ONE, as well as a wealthy merchant. He founded the first modern Jewish school and a Reform synagogue in Galicia. He sought to liberate his people from Chassidic influences.

NACHMAN KOHEN KROCHMAL (1785–1840)

He lived as a merchant in Galicia, which was part of Austria during his lifetime. This great philosopher-historian attracted many pupils. His most famous book is *Moreh Nebuche Haz'man, Guide to the Perplexed of the Time*. It illustrated his talent in the field of religious history. As a leader of the Haskalah, he stressed the spirituality of the Jewish people.

SOLOMON JUDAH RAPPAPORT (1790–1867)

He was a leading rabbi, historian, and biographer. Born in Galicia, he served there as Rabbi before he went to Prague in 1840. Here he was attacked by the Chassidim and the ultra-Orthodox for his liberal approach to Jewish history and religion. He wrote on Jewish chronology and formulated scientific principles that helped to lay the foundations of modern Jewish scholarship. He also compiled a biography of Talmudic personalities. He and Krochmal influenced each other.

ZEBI HIRSCH CHAJES (1805–1885)

This Galician rabbi worked with Krochmal and Rappaport as a pioneer in the scientific study of Judaica, although he was more traditionally inclined than either of them. He wrote on the principles of the written and oral law, on the Targums and Midrash, and contributed an introduction to the Talmud. He was the recognized spiritual leader throughout Europe.

JEHIEL SACHS MICHAEL (1808–1864)

He was a famous preacher and rabbi in Prague and devoted much of his time to counteracting the spread of Reform Judaism. He translated the liturgy and parts of the Bible into German.

ADOLF J. JELLINEK (c.1821–1893)

He was born in Moravia and served as a Rabbi first in Leipzig (1845) and then in Vienna from 1856. He was famous as a preacher, philosopher, and bibliographile. He wrote and edited noteworthy works in the fields of Cabala and Jewish philosophy. His *Beth Ha-Midrash* is a work on the minor Midrashim and it comprised six volumes.

THEODORE HERZL (1856–1904)

This journalist and founder of the World Zionist movement was born in Budapest, but received his education in Vienna. He was the Paris correspondent for the Vienna *Neue Freie Presse* when he was stirred by the anti-Semitism of the Dreyfus affair to such an extent that he dedicated the remainder of his life to trying to establish a Jewish homeland where Jews could live free and secure. In his book *Judenstaat* he proposed a world Zionist organization and a political movement that he launched in Basle, Switzerland, in 1897. He is credited with being the father of the Jewish state in Israel.

COURT JEWS OF NOTE

Kaiser Juden—Emperor Jews
  Baron von Arnstein
  Michael Lazar Biedermann
  Issachar Baruch Eskeles
  Ritter Honig von Honigsberg
  Baron Salomon Rothschild
  Joseph von Sonnenfels
  Ritter von Wertheimer

JEWISH COMMUNITIES

1935—Jewish population 357,000
      Ruthenia 105,000
      Slovakia 150,000
      Bohemia–Moravia 80,000
1945—Estimated Jewish
      population of Buko-
      vina, Prague, Lem-
      berg, and Galicia 42,000
1964—Estimated Jewish
      population 18,000
Other communities
      Brno
      Bratislava
      Moravska
      Mukacevo
      Ostrava

The Jews of Hungary

From a memorial tablet in Dunopentele, erected by Cosmos, a Palestinian, containing the word "sinagogae," and from early Jewish gravestones dated about the second century CE, the presence of Jews in Hungary is indicated as far back as the destruction of the second Temple (70 CE). Their troubles began in 325 with the triumph of Christianity and the imposition of various forms of restrictions and disabilities. It is documented that there was a Jewish cemetery in Sopron, which was even before the Hungarians conquered the land in the ninth century.

The Jewish population was augmented about 970 by the influx of the Jewish Khazars from Russia and by co-religionists fleeing from other countries. The Crusades struck Hungary about 1072, bringing some suffering and hardship. During the next three centuries, although the attitude of the ruling Arpads was generally benevolent, and the Jews were able to live in comparative freedom and rise to high economic and social positions, there was a gradual erosion of their rights.

After the first Crusade, a law prohibiting the Jews from having Christian slaves was enacted. In the 13th century, the Lateran Council decreed that Jews should be separated from their neighbors and should wear a distinctive badge. Bela IV (1235–1270) made Jews his personal property. In 1349 they were expelled for the first time; in 1360, for a second time. When the edict was revoked in 1364, many Jews immigrated from surrounding countries.

The office of "Judge of the Jews" was created in 1365 for the purpose of collecting taxes and protecting their interests. The last judge was appointed in 1440, after which time debts to Jews were canceled by decree. Ritual murder accusations kept recurring, which brought death to many Jews and frequent anti-Jewish outbreaks throughout the 15th and 16th centuries.

UNDER TURKISH RULE

In 1526 the Turks wrested control of Hungary from Ladislaus of Bohemia. In 1541 the Jews were caught between the hostility of the Cross and the Crescent. Ottoman rule, for about 150 years, gave the Jews some religious liberty and civic equality. They were forced, however, to wear badges and were subject to heavy taxation.

HUNGARIAN SOVEREIGNTY

In 1686 Hungarian sovereignty was restored and the Jewish people were faced with renewal of old exclusions and disabilities. King Lipot (1657–1705) wanted to make Hungary a purely Catholic state. Systematic persecutions and expulsions from royal cities were directed against the Jews. They were excluded from the guilds, from agriculture, and from the professions. Exceptions prevailed only when some nobles offered special protection.

The Jewish people earned their living mainly by small trade and money transactions. In the northeast there were Jewish peasants and serfs working on large estates. The Jewish population of Hungary was very poor and their economic distress was heightened by the influx of refugees from Vienna, Moravia, and Poland. The latter, however, brought with them the study of the Talmud and the accompanying institutions of education. According to statistics, there were 11,621 Jews in Hungary in 1735. By 1840 there were about 200,000.

MARIA THERESA (1740–1780)

In 1726 Charles III decreed that only one male member of a Jewish family could marry and settle in his home community. This resulted in a wave of migration of Jews to Hungary. During the reign of Maria Theresa new methods were designed for extracting increasingly large sums of money from them. In 1760 she imposed a new tax called a "Toleration Tax" in the sum of 20,000 gulden, annually. She also decreed badges for beardless Jews.

JOSEPH II (1780–1790)

The rule of this tolerant emperor of Austria brought a great improvement in the condition of Hungarian Jews. They could establish schools or attend public schools; they could settle in royal cities that had been closed to them; they could lease land and engage in all trades and professions; they no longer had to wear badges, but they had to adopt German surnames.

All these privileges were nullified upon Joseph's death, when all efforts were made to force assimilation upon them. They were deprived of their religious freedoms and under Ferenz I (1806) there were forced conversions. In spite of their unfavorable situation, and risking severe reprisals, Jews became part of the great struggle for human rights that was developing throughout Europe, culminating in the revolution of 1848. Hungary became independent of Austria and Louis Kossuth, a national hero, urged the National Assembly to grant equality to the Jews. Ferdinand V (1830–1848) granted them freedom of residence, the right to own property, and permission to join the army.

THE REPUBLIC OF AUSTRIA-HUNGARY

In 1867 the Republic of Austria-Hungary was established and the new constitution granted equal rights to Jews. But Judaism, as a religion, was not recognized legally on a par with Christian denominations until 1896.

During the period between 1867 and 1896, Jews were integrated rapidly into the life of the country. As this occurred, Hungarian Jewry became divided into two opposing groups—the Orthodox and the Liberal—with the latter group finally establishing a seminary in Budapest in 1877.

Along with this development came a period of anti-Semitism, which culminated in the TISZA-ESZLAR ritual murder libel in 1882. Tisza-Eszlar is a Hungarian town in which 15 Jews were accused of the murder of a 14-year-old Christian girl for ritual purposes. This set off a wave of anti-Jewish agitation that led to prolonged mob violence and rioting. When the innocence of the prisoners was established after 15 months in prison, they were released amid additional anti-Jewish outbreaks in various parts of the country.

After this period, the lives of the Jews proceeded without major incidents for a brief period. They were prominent in Hungarian cultural, military, and economic life. Thousands of Jews served and died during World War I. Hungary was an ally of Germany. There was a disproportionate number of them who participated in the communist revolution of 1919, and as a result, suffered heavily after the collapse of the Bela Kun regime. Discriminations of various kinds were instituted against them by Admiral Horthy in a new wave of anti-Semitism, which kept on unabated for twenty years and which was aided and abetted by government officials. There were economic boycotts, social and political discrimination, riots, and a numerus clausus in universities. Jews were barred from veterans' organizations and public offices. There were anti-Jewish leagues and a white terror was unleashed.

By 1931, there were outspoken anti-Semites in the Hungarian cabinet. The number of conversions of Jews increased; the birth rate declined; German and Jewish names were Hungarianized. At this time there were about 450,000 Jews in the country.

The scope of anti-Jewish measures enacted by the government followed the Nazi pattern in Germany. When the Nazi hordes overran Hungary in 1939, it became a simple matter to create ghettos and extermination camps, and to deport Jews to forced labor and concentration camps. The death toll started to rise as thousands of refugees were stranded. As many as 600,000 of Hungary's 725,000 Jews were killed.

At the time of the liberation there were Jews only in Budapest, approximately 119,000. By the end of 1946 there were about 180,000. The fragments of families, all pauperized, set to work to rebuild their shattered lives. All prewar national Jewish organizations were re-established. Of former 473 Jewish communities, 266 resumed their activities. The Rabbinical Seminary in Budapest started training young rabbis to fill the places of those who had been martyred. The Budapest congregation established a free university and reopened the Jewish museum. Twenty-three elementary schools and eight high schools were put into operation. Some lost or confiscated properties were recovered. The 50,000 needy orphans, aged, invalids, and widows were cared for by the Joint Distribution Committee, HIAS, and the World Jewish Congress.

Anti-Semitism had by no means disappeared. In 1945 a pogrom occurred in Hunmadaras. Because of the unstable conditions in the country, most Jews indicated a desire to emigrate.

In 1948, the communist party seized power and Hungary became a vassal state of Russia. Many Jews lost everything they had so recently re-acquired, because all industries, trade organizations, and retail stores were nationalized. All Jewish organizations, Liberal and Orthodox, were put under one authority. Congregations could not tax their members, although the government agreed on subsidies for 20 years at a declining rate. There could be but one congregation in any city or town. Many social and cultural Jewish organizations were disbanded. The American Joint Distribution Committee subsidized religious and cultural institutions and philanthropic agencies until 1953, when it, along with other American Jewish agencies, was closed by the government.

In May, 1949, about 5,000 Jews fled through Czechoslovakia before the government interfered. Three thousand Jews were permitted to go to Israel, although ten Zionist leaders were arrested, of whom seven were sentenced to long terms. In 1951 about 6,000 Jews were arrested on a mass scale and shipped to villages or farms as servants and to forced labor camps in Russia. A wave of protest from the United States, Britain, France, and church dignitaries put an end to the deportations and in 1953 some of them were released.

In 1954 there were 150 synagogues in Hungary, of which 50 were in Budapest. The government still sought to interfere with religious observance. Before the 1956 rebellion there were 89 rabbis in the country, with the chief rabbi residing in Budapest. The Hungarian Jewish Synagogue is the name of the present central religious body.

In 1955 there were about 500 children attending the Budapest Talmud Torah. Of the 70,000 Jews in Budapest, 4,000 are orthodox.

From October 23, 1956, when Russian tanks rolled into the land to quell a revolt, at least 25,000 Jews fled Hungary, including many rabbis, cantors, and other religious functionaries. The estimated Jewish population today is about 100,000.

JEWISH COMMUNITIES

Cities and Towns

Baja	Mateszalka
Balassagyamat	Miskolc
Bekescsaba	Nagykanisza
Berettyoujfalu	Nyirbator
Bonyhad	Nyiregyhaza
Budapest	Oroshaza
Csepel	Papa
Debrecen	Pecs
Gyongyos	Rakospalota
Gyor	Satoraljaujhely
Eger	Salgotarjan
Hajdunanas	Szeged
Hodmezovasarhely	Sopron
Kecskemet	Szombathely
Karcag	Tisza Eszlar
Kisvarda	Vasarosnameny
Mako	

The Jews of the Balkans

The Balkan Peninsula derives its name from the Balkan Mountains, which run from the Adriatic Sea to the Black Sea. It was once a part of the Roman Empire and later, the Byzantine Empire. In turn it was occupied by Goths, Huns, Magyars, Serbs, Bulgars, and others. In 1453 the Peninsula came under control of the Turks.

Many different nationalities lived in the Balkans. The religion of the people was divided among Greek Orthodox, Roman Catholic, and Mohammedan.

Jewish people arrived in the Balkans during the Roman conquest. Many notable communities were established. Their history follows the same pattern as in the other countries of Europe and Asia.

NATIONAL GROUPS OF THE BALKANS

Albania	Rumania
Bosnia	Serbia
Bulgaria	Slovakia
Croats	Slovenes
Czechs	Thrace
Greece	Turkey
Macedonia	Yugoslavia
Montenegro	

The Jews of Bulgaria

EARLY HISTORY

The ancient name of this country was Moesia. Jews settled in this area about the second century CE. During the Roman Emperor Hadrian's reign it is reported that a Jewish community existed in the city of Nicopolis. The decline of the Kingdom of Khazars brought more Jews to the country. Others came with the Byzantine conquest in the tenth century. In the early period of Bulgaria's independence there was an important Jewish community in the capital city of Trnovo.

In 1367, following excessive oppression in Hungary and a decree of expulsion by King Louis the Great, many Jewish refugees came to Bulgaria. With few exceptions conditions were favorable for the Jews. There was an incident in which the church council was responsible for the destruction of the Trnovo congregation. The first rabbinical school was founded in 1370 at Vidin, which became the center of learning and the seat of authority. Legend has it that in this century a Jewish girl became the wife of the Tsar Ivan Alexander.

UNDER OTTOMAN RULE

In 1396 the Ottoman Turks captured Bulgaria. Under them Jewish communities grew and prospered. Trade brought Italian and French Jews to the country. Their numbers were again increased by Sephardic Jews after the Spanish and Portuguese expulsions. With them came Joseph Karo of Shulchan Aruch fame. German Jews who came from Bavaria brought Rabbi Benjamin ben Meir Halevi, who prepared the Ashkenazi Machzor. For centuries Bulgarian Jewry was more or less a typical Sephardic community. In 1660 the false messiah, Sabbatai Zevi, made a deep impact upon the Jewish people in the country.

THE BALKAN ERA

When the country was liberated by the Russians from Turkish rule (1877–78), Jews were granted equality with the Christian population under a treaty enacted at the Congress of Berlin.

Jewish participation in the Serbian-Bulgarian war of 1885 was marked by outstanding bravery and received national recognition. However, anti-Semitism became rife in the years following the enactment of the Russian May laws. The years 1884, 1890, 1895, and 1903–04 were marked by ritual murder accusations, mob rioting, pillage, and destruction of Jewish communities. During this period many Jews migrated to Anatolia.

During the Balkan Wars (1912–13) and World War I, 5,000 Jews fought on the battlefields in Bulgaria's struggle for freedom. But official anti-Semitism persisted. In the professions not one Jew has ever taught in any primary school nor acted as a judge, and since 1898 no Jew has been nominated as a professor at the university. Discrimination kept recurring and in 1925, a communist who happened to be a Jew was accused of exploding a bomb. This started a wave of Jew-baiting by a Fascist organization called "The Home Guard," with its demand that all Jews be expelled from the land. The officials tried to suppress demonstrations and to curb the movement, but its influence was too strong. When the Hitler scourge reached Bulgaria it found a ready ally in the "Home Guard." The government, however, refused to carry out the policy of the Nazis except in minor matters. The Jews of Bulgaria and Finland were the only groups in occupied territory that escaped the horror of extermination.

The Zionist movement, which was spreading throughout Europe, developed a large following. Bulgarian Jews established an agricultural colony in Palestine—Har Tov —in 1896.

PRESENT-DAY JEWRY

Before the war there were 48,000 Jews in the country. Most of them emigrated to Israel when statehood was declared in 1948. Because they were never encouraged to assimilate, their economic level was generally low. About three-fifths of these people lived in Sophia. Their affairs were regulated by a Central Jewish Consistory headed by a Grand Rabbi. The close of the war found about 7,000 Jews left in the country, practically all of them living in Sophia. Small businesses and commerce comprise their livelihood.

A law passed in 1951 converted all Jewish organizations to lay institutions. Jewish libraries became municipal facilities. The ORT school was converted into a model technical school named after a communist leader. The Bulgarian Academy of Science took over the Jewish Scientific Institute in Sophia. There are very few Jews in government or military positions, most having been ousted in 1953.

JEWISH COMMUNITIES

Burgas	Samacoff
Kazanlik	Shumla
Kolarovgrad	Silistria
Kyustendil	Sofia
Lom	Stalin
Nikopolis	Stanke Dimitrov
Philipopolis	Stara
Plevin	Tatar-Bazarjik
Plovdiv	Trnovo
Ruse	Vidin
Rustcoff	Yambol
	Zagora

The Jews of Greece

EARLY HISTORY

Jewish settlements in Greece started at least three centuries before the beginning of the Christian era. The Book of Maccabees mentions the renewal of an alliance between Sparta and Palestine. Philo, the Jewish philosopher who wrote in the first century BCE, mentions Jews living in Greece. Jewish communities have existed in the following provinces or kingdoms for over two thousand years.

Athens	Morea
Corfu	Salonika
Corinth	Thessaly
Ionia	Thrace
Larissa	Volvos
Macedonia	

Jewish life flourished under the Greeks and Romans, but when Byzantium became Christian, restrictions and persecutions were imposed. Papal decrees sought to convert Jews by force. Marriages between Jews and Christians were forbidden.

Other than Papal pronouncements from Rome concerning fraternization with Jews, there were no overt acts of discrimination. Benjamin of Tudela (c. 1165) reported on his travels in Greece that he found Jews in many parts of the country prosperously engaged in silk-weaving and in agriculture.

UNDER OTTOMAN RULE

When the Turks established the Ottoman Empire throughout the Balkans in 1453, Greece was included. The toleration of the Mohammedans for minorities attracted many Jews to Greece. The Spanish expulsion of 1492 sent many Jews to settle in Salonika and Larissa. The position of the Jews improved and Jewish scholarship flourished. The language of the Jews varied. Italian Jews who settled at Corfu retained Italian as their mother tongue. Ladino (Judeo-Spanish) was used in Macedonia and Thrace. In Athens and Crete they spoke Greek.

The Greek wars of liberation from the Turks started in 1821 and subsequently resulted in an end to Ottoman rule. The revolution caused frequent hostile outbreaks against the Jewish communities. One especially severe incident occurred when the Patriarch Gregory was murdered by the Turks. Several Jews were forced to throw his body into the sea. All the Jews became the scapegoat for this incident and were subject to anti-Jewish excesses that wiped out the entire Jewish community in Morea, and continued through the years to cause many thousands to leave the country.

JEWISH LIFE

In 1891, a repetition of a ritual murder charge in Corfu resulted in pogroms that caused some 1,500 Jews to leave for Egypt, Turkey, and Italy. Anti-Jewish riots occurred in 1898, when Jews were accused of siding with the Turks.

In 1912 Salonika was occupied by Greece, but it was not legally awarded to her until the Treaty of Versailles in 1919. Sixty thousand Jews, who had come because of the friendliness of the Turks, became subject to Greek prejudice. They swelled the total Greek Jewish population to 125,000. But even though the Jews had lived in Greece for over 2,000 years, they were not considered Greeks. The Greek nationalist movement provoked harassments aimed at emphasizing the distinction between Greek Christians and Greek Jews. Jews were forbidden to wear a fez. Even Jewish cemeteries were ordered destroyed.

In 1922, a great economic dislocation took place when 1,500,000 Greeks returned to the mainland. Competition in commerce and in the trades became so severe that the Jews found themselves deprived of a livelihood. By 1935, one-fifth of them were subsisting on charity. There was a steady stream of emigration until World War II.

The Nazi invasion of Greece resulted in the liquidation of 75,000 Jews, leaving 11,000 by 1944. By 1960, this number had dwindled to below 6,000. There are no viable Jewish communities in Greece today.

The Jews of Rumania

EARLY HISTORY

Historians have recorded that Jews lived wherever Rome had conquered, so they must have lived in what is now Rumania since the fourth century. The country came into being when the Congress of Paris united Wallachia and Moldavia in 1856 under Turkish overlordship. The history of the Jews in these principalities goes back to the 14th century.

When Joseph Nasi (c. 1520–1579) and Solomon Ashkenazi (1520–1600) lived, this area was under Turkish rule. Nasi was appointed governor of Wallachia in 1571 by the Sultan. At this time, Jews had no civil status, other than that conferred upon them as a special favor. One hundred years later this recognition was granted by the princes of the land. References to Jews are found in numerous documents involving special regulations concerning them. There is mention of a Jewish synagogue and cemetery in Jassy in 1678, and of blood accusations (1726) in the village of Onitzvani, which was used as a means of extorting money by landowners and princes.

OPPRESSIVE LAWS

Legally constituted Jewish communities were organized in the second half of the 17th century. They were granted religious autonomy and directed by a chief rabbi. The government exercised secular supervision by appointing a "Starostes of the Jews" who was responsible for the collection of taxes and assessments imposed upon the Jews.

In 1740 the important Jewish communities were Bacau, Barlad, Galatz, and Roman. The Jews suffered from both sides in the various Russo-Turkish wars between 1769 and 1812, and also from the peasant and ruling classes in their local struggles. Excesses in Bucharest (1801) took the lives of 128 Jews and further depressed the economic conditions of the Jewish people.

Under Russian occupation (1828–1834), anti-Semitism became a government-directed program. The peasants, who were about 80% of the population, were not basically anti-Semitic. They were duped by the government, which frequently resorted to the stratagem to divert the population from the bad social and economic conditions that frequently prevailed.

In 1834 the "Organic Law" was passed, which included many repressive measures. This law stipulated that Jews were parasites; that they had no useful trades and therefore should be classed as "vagabonds." As such, they could be arbitrarily expelled from the country. The only way they could remain as citizens was to accept Christianity.

The city of Galatz made world headlines when a large number of Jews were forced to leave as "vagabonds." They were ferried across the Danube to Turkey, but the

Turkish authorities promptly sent them back. Back and forth they were ferried until the Rumanian government literally flung them into the river. They were finally rescued by sympathetic Turks.

The revolution of 1848 and the Congress of Paris (1858) provided a short liberal era favorable for the Jew. In 1850 the ruler eased the requirements concerning business and trades. Expulsions were not enforced except in cases of recent indigent immigrants. They were permitted to keep inns in villages and could own vineyards. Their most favorable era was under Cuza, who promised them gradual emancipation in 1864. With his abdication, however, anti-Semitism again became official government policy.

JEWISH LIFE

Upon invitation of the boyars (landholders), large numbers of Russian and Polish Jews came to Moldavia in the middle of the 18th century and modernized the feudal economy. They received exemptions from taxes, free cemetery sites, and complete community autonomy. Before the migrations ceased in 1860 they had founded 63 towns and villages. This influx changed the pattern of Jewish life. All Jews now wore the garb of Eastern Europe. Their principal language was Yiddish.

In practice, the government was compelled to differentiate between those Jews who were native-born and therefore could ask for protection, and those Jews who had come to the country as immigrants and could not receive protection. This distinction served the government well in stirring up the population against all Jews, because they were caricatured as conniving for special privileges that were not accorded to ordinary citizens.

THE BRATIANU GOVERNMENT

John Bratianu (1864–1927) became Prime Minister of Rumania and began a systematic attack against the Jews. He classed them as "vagabonds," "lepers," and "social disease." For this affliction to his country he demanded retribution before Parliament. Anti-Semitism took on various hues. Religion became another hazard for the Jews and for the third time in Rumanian history the profession of the Christian religion became a prerequisite for citizenship. Anti-Semitism became so virulent that it attracted the attention of the Western world. In the United States, President Grant received official protestations.

There was no apparent change in the treatment of the Jews even though the Congress of Berlin (1878) provided equal status for Rumanian Jewry. These provisions were evaded on the old pretext that Jews were not citizens. As such, they were excluded from all sources of livelihood and the terror of starvation resulted in mass emigration to the United States at the turn of the century.

Anti-Jewish nationalism was the platform of Ion Bratianu. Like his brother John, he could not and would not tolerate Jews. In 1900 the attention of the world was turned to the plight of Rumanian Jewry when a volunteer mass exodus of 4,000 Jews trudged through Europe on foot seeking havens of refuge. Protests by the United States government were ignored. Between 1900 and 1906 about 125,000 Jews left the country. Those who remained were excluded from the villages and forced to live in city ghettos.

Rumania emerged from World War I with her land area and her population more than doubled. Bratianu was willing to grant citizenship to those Jews who could prove before a court that they had been born in the country and that their parents had never been under the protection of a foreign power. About 25% were too poor and too ignorant to establish such qualification and remained persons without a country. Following the Treaty of Versailles (1919) Bratianu resigned his office because he refused to accept the provisions granting full recognition and equality to all minorities, particularly the Jews.

As citizens, the Jews started to participate in political life, in the economic upsurge, and in the industrialization of the country. But this equality did not last long. Land reform failed; universal suffrage was revoked; fascism emerged and the universities became the centers of anti-Semitic agitation. From 1920 on, the National Christian League for Students clamored for a numerus clausus and barring Jews from academic advantages. Jewish medical students were not permitted to dissect a Christian corpse. Anti - Jewish demonstrations increased as vandals broke up Jewish meetings, smashed windows in Jewish homes and shops, and pushed Jewish passengers off moving vehicles. In the process of rioting, pillaging, and murdering, the vandals became national heroes. During this period notorious demagogues organized the Iron Guard, which later became the counterpart of Hitler's Storm Troopers.

KING CAROL II (1893–1953)

During this ruler's reign there was a brief period of remission for the Jews, but an upsurge of nationalism that was aided by Hitler's advent to power made conditions worse. By the end of 1937 the anti-Semitic National Christian Party was able to sponsor and have enacted a series of decrees depriving Jews of citizenship, banning the Hebrew and Yiddish press, and making it virtually impossible for them to practice their professions. Laws patterned after the infamous Nuremberg Laws came into effect in 1940, with ensuing massacres of Jews.

With King Carol's abdication in September, 1940, the Fascist Iron Guard regime took over. Hitler's army entered the country in October. There followed a period of horror for Jews that surpassed all previous episodes. Collaboration between Nazis and Rumanians resulted in the activating of a concentration camp at Transdniestria. Of the nearly 800,000 Jews in Rumania when World War II broke out, 385,000 were dead before liberation.

After the war, some deportees returned from the Auschwitz and Transdniestria concentration camps. About 50,000 came from Soviet-annexed territory, bringing the total Jewish population to about 400,000. The first task of the Jews was to revive their communal life. The central religious body was again organized. The Jewish Party and the Zionist organizations resumed their activities. Parochial and Hebrew schools were reopened. Jewish weeklies and periodicals made their reappearance.

Communist domination in 1946 put an end to all Jewish organizational life. Those not liquidated were taken over by the regime. Trade and industry were nationalized, depriving many Jews from making a living. About 37,000 left the country in 1946–47. Two years later most of the Yiddish elementary and high schools were closed. All hospitals and homes for the aged were nationalized. By 1952 there were only three Jewish elementary schools left.

THE DECLINE OF RUMANIAN JEWRY

Following the abdication of King Carol, a violent anti-Zionist campaign was started, with leaders being arrested and some sentenced to life imprisonment. Until 1952 emigration to Israel had been permitted. About 247,000 left the country, legally or otherwise.

Under Communist domination thousands of Jews were deported from cities to remote rural districts and to labor camps. There was a gradual purge of Jews from government offices, from the army, and from the many nationalized industries. In January, 1953, there was a pogrom at the University of Jassy, in which 60 Jewish students were injured.

In 1957 there were 190,000 Jews left in the country, with Bucharest (60,000), Botosani (7,000), Suceava (18,865), and Jassy (18,000) having the bulk of them.

All the Jewish religious groups in the country have been merged into one national federation, headed by a Supreme Council of Rabbis. There is a rabbinical seminary but few students are enrolled. Jewish community life is steadily deteriorating. In 1959 there was only the Great Synagogue and three other houses of worship in Bucharest and 32 rabbis throughout the country as compared with 92 at the end of World War II. Most of the synagogues in Transylvania have been closed for lack of congregants.

JEWISH COMMUNITIES

Alexandren	Jassy
Arad	Onitzvani
Bacau	Oradea
Baia-Mare	Piatra-Neamt
Barlad	Roman
Bessarabia	Satu-Mare
Bostonis	Suceava
Bucharest	Stalin
Cluj	Timisora
Galatz	Transylvania
Isai	

The Jews of Turkey

EARLY HISTORY

Historically there have been three groups of Jews in Turkey: (1) those who had lived in the Byzantine Empire and became part of Turkey when Byzantium fell; (2) Sephardim from Spain and Portugal; (3) and Ashkenazim from Eastern and Western Europe.

During the first centuries of the present era, the small Jewish communities fared badly under the Christian Byzantine emperors. Before the fall of Jerusalem (70 CE), the city that became Constantinople (also known as Stambul, Istanbul, Byzantium, Rhoun, and New Rome) was the contact point for the Jews of Alexandria. In 330, Emperor Constantine made the city his eastern capital. Documents relating to Jews, dating back to 390, are known to exist.

THE OTTOMAN DYNASTY

In the 14th century, Byzantium was conquered by Mohammedan

Turks. Jews were accorded the same rights and religious freedom as all non-Moslems. They could own land and were encouraged to settle at Brusa on the peninsula of Anatolia and in Adrianople. Here they set up Jewish community organizations, including schools and seminaries under the authority of a chief rabbi. Salonika, which had been Greek, became part of Turkey in 1430 and flourished as a center of Jewish life.

BAYAZID II (1481–1512)

This ruler induced thousands of Jewish merchants and traders to come to Turkey, because he wanted to develop his country economically and culturally. Marrano Jews had started to come in large numbers after their expulsion from Spain and Portugal. They settled in Constantinople, Salonika, and Smyrna. Because of their experience as military men in the Spanish Army, and their knowledge of gunpowder and the manufacture of cannons, the Sultan used them to train his officers and to modernize his war machine.

SELIM II—SULEIMAN, THE MAGNIFICENT (1520–1574)

The brightest chapter in the annals of Turkish Jewry was written during the reign of Selim II. His friendly attitude toward minorities caused many Jews to come to Turkey, with a resultant vigorous Jewish life. Ashkenazic groups added to the Sephardic influx and by the end of the 16th century there were as many as 13 synagogues in Salonika, alone. The tolerant sultan surrounded himself with many Jews in his court, such as Don Joseph Nasi, who became his Foreign Minister; Hamon, who was his personal physician; Solomon Ashkenazi, who was one of his financial advisers; and Esther Kiera, who was a court aid.

DECLINE OF TURKISH JEWRY

Jewish cultural and social life flourished in the 16th and 17th centuries but started to lose their vigor with the rise of Cabala and its mysticism. The community was further weakened in 1655 by the false Messiah, Sabbatai Zevi, who failed to live up to his promise to lead the Jewish people to Palestine.

Until the 19th century, the position of the Jewish community remained fairly stable. After that, autocratic sultans and wars against Egypt, Palestine, and Crimea reduced the Jews to great poverty. Even though paper equality was granted to them following the Russo-Turkish War in 1878, they were restricted in employment, in government, and in industry.

As the Turkish Empire disintegrated, the position of the Jews kept deteriorating. World Jewry, too, was in a depressing state. In 1898, Theodore Herzl, the leading Zionist figure, negotiated with the sultan for territory for a Jewish nation, but this failed to materialize. By 1901, the fifth of a series of Blood Accusations occurred, causing undue hardships to the Jewish population. Refutation and protests did not guard against the repetition of this unfounded libel. With the fall of the Sultanate in 1908, conditions continued to worsen for the Jewish people. In 1912, when Salonika again became part of Greece, many of its 80,000 Jews emigrated. By 1918, there were no more Jewish deputies in Parliament, and the Jewish Community Council of 60 members, which represented the Jewish people and the

Rabbinate, were no longer recognized.

In 1923 Kemal (Ataturk) Pasha (1880–1938) brought an era of nationalism to Turkey that made it difficult for all minorities. Hebrew instruction was repressed; Ladino was discouraged; Zionism was outlawed. The government refused to recognize the minority rights treaty of Lausanne after World War I. Of the 400,000 Jews in Turkey in 1912, only 79,000 were left by 1927.

During Word War II there was a special tax, known as VARLIK, and great rigor was applied to its enforcement on minorities, especially the Jews, but there has been no overt discrimination since that time. All Zionist organizations went out of existence because no Turkish citizen was allowed to maintain a relationship with organizations with foreign centers. While there was martial law, the authorities would consider and act in cases of anti-Semitism, but in 1955 and 1956 there were some attacks in the press by individuals. Slanderous articles appeared as late as 1961.

With the establishment of the state of Israel in 1948, some 37,000 Jews were permitted to migrate there. What little is left of the golden age of spiritual and cultural distinction is found in Constantinople. And in recent years there has been a migration of about 7,000 Sephardim to Uruguay.

JEWISH LIFE

Most of the Jewish population of Turkey were Sephardic, although a few of the prominent leaders and rabbis were of Ashkenazic background. Cabala, the mystical movement in Jewish life, had a large number of adherents following the 17th century. Its sacred book the Zohar, was used with the Talmud, the chief book of study in most communities.

In recent times there is a Grand Rabbi, and a Rabbinical Council that has constituted a Beth Din. There is a seminary for the training of teachers and rabbis and a lay administrative council in which the Ashkenazim and the Sephardim cooperate.

The Jewish community of Istanbul maintains five schools, four elementary and one secondary, with an enrollment of about 2,000 Jewish children, which is about 50% of all. Izmir has two schools, one of which is their own, and one of which belongs to the Alliance Israelite Universelle. There are synagogues in all Jewish settlements with a cantor in each one. Before 1963, the Jewish press consisted of a weekly Turkish newspaper, which still exists, and a Ladino (Spanish-Jewish) newspaper which ceased publication.

The 1960 census showed an estimated Jewish population of about 43,000, of whom most are Sephardic, and that number has since declined. Jews participate in all phases of Turkish life and experience no undue hardships.

JEWS TO REMEMBER

DON JOSEPH NASI (1520–1579)

This banker, philanthropist, and statesman left Portugal before the Inquisition, established a banking business in Constantinople, and became financial minister to the Sultan. He was the nephew of Gracia Nasi Mendes (1510–1569), who preceded him to Constantinople and who had become an outstanding leader in commerce and in philanthropy.

Don Joseph also became a patron of Jewish learning and gave his personal support to rabbis, scholars, and academies of learning.

In 1566, he was made Duke of Naxos by Selim II. He became interested in the problems of his people and sought, vainly, to establish a settlement for them in Cyprus. And even though he could not persuade the Sultan to restore Palestine to his people, he did succeed in settling large numbers of them in the land, which was then under Turkish rule. Selim did grant him a lease on Tiberias and an adjacent area, which he hoped to develop into an autonomous Jewish center.

Partly responsible for a break with Venice and a disastrous war with Cyprus from 1570–73, his influence waned. After his death, his widow established a Hebrew printing-press at her palace, where several works were printed from 1592–99.

SABBATAI ZEVI (1626–1675)

This false prophet was born in Smyrna. After studying the writings of Luria and becoming convinced that he was God's messenger to redeem the Jewish people, he proclaimed himself to be the Messiah (1648) and sought to lead the Jews of Europe back to Palestine. In his travels he allied himself with Nathan of Gaza who became his "prophet." Nathan propagandized the Jews of Europe to prepare for the coming of the Messiah, Sabbatai.

European Jewry, suffering under the full impact of anti-Semitism and persecution, was ready to accept the claims of Sabbatai. Many sold their possessions to join the march to the Holy Land.

Sabbatai had many opponents. One of them, a Cabalist, Nehemiah Cohen, labeled him an imposter and informed the Turkish authorities that he was planning a revolt. Sabbatai was imprisoned. To escape punishment he and his wife embraced the Mohammedan religion. Though the Jewish people were greatly disillusioned, many of them believed that Sabbatai was the true Messiah and they formed a sect to continue his work.

ISAAC AKRISH (1489–1578)

Author of *Kol Mebassar, The Voice of Good Tidings,* a work about the Ten Tribes of Israel and other historical documents.

MOSES ALMOSNINO (c.1510–1580)

Author of a book of sermons, *Meametz Koah, The Power of Strength;* also scientific commentaries on astronomy.

CHAIM BENVENISTA (1603–1673)

Wrote *Knesseth HaGadolah, The Great Assembly,* a supplement to Karo's *Beth Joseph.*

JOSHUA RAPHAEL BENVENISTA (1595–1670)

Rabbi, liturgical poet, and physician. Author of many commentaries, sermons, and liturgical prayers.

JACOB ben SOLOMON CHABIB (1460–1516)

Spanish Talmudist. Wrote *En Ya-cob, Well of Jacob,* a collection of the Haggadic portions of the Talmud.

MOSES CAPSALI (c.1420–1495)

Appointed "Chacham Bashi" — Chief Rabbi—by Mohammed II. He was included in high rank among the "Mufti" of the court of the Caliphs.

MOSES HAMON (1490–1565)

Physician to the Sultan. Succeeded in having the Sultan try every case of blood accusation personally. Published a Persian translation of the Pentateuch. Established a Yeshivah at Constantinople.

DONNA GRACIA MENDES (c.1510–1568)

Mother-in-law of Don Nasi. Wealthy and cultured, she returned to her Jewish faith and became a benefactress to Jews and championed Jewish rights.

ELIAS MIZRACHI (1455–1526)

Renowned rabbi of Constantinople. Talmudist, mathematician, and Rashi commentator.

SOLOMON MOLCHO (c.1500–1532)

His Marrano name was Diogo Pires. He was a false messiah, who fired the imagination of the Jewish people. He published works on Cabala and the appearance of the Messiah. He was burned at the stake.

ESTHER KIERA (c.1520–1593)

She became a court adviser and exercised great influence on state policy. She was a patroness of Jewish learning.

DAVID REUBENI (1491–1535)

A self-styled ambassador of a non-existent kingdom, he proclaimed himself a messiah. With Solomon Molcho he wandered through Turkey exorting the Jewish people to follow him.

SOLOMON ibn VERGA (1460–1554)

Wrote *Shevet Yehudah, The Rod* of *Jacob,* a history of the Spanish Inquisition and religious disputations of his time.

JEWISH COMMUNITIES

Adrianople	Izmir
Ankara	Salonika
Brussa	Smyrna
Edirne	Sofia
Constantinople (Istanbul)	

The Jews of Yugoslavia

Since Roman times Jews had lived continually in Dalmatia, which is part of the area now called Yugoslavia and which was then known as Illyria. Synagogue inscriptions and relics reveal that another part of this territory, Slovenia, had Jews since the 12th century. Little is known about the conditions existing under the Serbians in medieval times. Jewish settlements are attested to in some places by folk tradition and rabbinic literature.

The largest Jewish community was in the city of Belgrade. Refugees from Germany and Hungary augmented the Jewish population. Later, the Spanish inquisition brought more Jews to the country. Sephardic congregations flourished in both Belgrade and Sarajevo.

Before Serbia re-established her independence in the 19th century, the Jewish situation was not good. After the Balkan War of 1912–1913 and World War I, religious equality was extended to all the conquered territories. This added a new Ashkenazic element to the Jewish community. According to the census in 1921, Yugoslavia had 64,746 Jews which increased to 76,654 by 1931. Most of them were concentrated in large cities.

The Yugoslavian state came into existence in 1918. By natural division the Jews fell into four geographic and cultural groups : (1) Serbia, (2) Croatia and Slovenia, (3) Bosnia and Herzegovina, and (4) Macedonia. Zionist, literary, and intellectual activity was encouraged by the government. Full autonomy was granted in religious matters, including the establishment of a Theological Seminary and Teacher's Institute.

Anti-Semitism in Yugoslavia is of recent origin, owing almost entirely to the Nazis, who exterminated 55,000 Jews when they overran the country. They were aided by local collaborators and sympathetic Bosnian Moslems. It is the only communist country that allows Jews to keep in touch with world Jewry, affiliate with the World Jewish Congress, and to emigrate to Israel.

The present Jewish population is about 6,500. About 8,000 of the Jewish survivors of World War I have gone to Israel.

JEWISH COMMUNITIES

Backa Palanka	Pancevo
Bajmok	Pristina
Banjaluka	Sarajevo
Becej	Sento
Belgrade	Somber
Bjelovar	Sibenik
Bosnia	Subotica
Djakovo	Travnik
Dubrovnik	Tuzla
Hercegovina	Vinkovci
Jajce	Virovitica
Koprivnica	Vrbas
Mostar	Zagreb
Nis	Zavidovici
Nova Gradisna	Zemun
Novi Sad	Zenica
Objlin	Zrenjanin
Osijek	

The Jews of the Netherlands (Holland)

EARLY HISTORY

Holland records settlements of Jews in the southern part of the country as early as 1290, as a result of the expulsion from England. In 1306 Count William permitted French exiled Jews to enter the country. A century later (1492), the great expulsion from Spain and Portugal brought a steady stream of Marranos into the land. In 1550, Charles v expelled all Marranos, but with the successful rebellion against Spain in 1579, the Dutch Republic was established and all Jews were made welcome.

At this time there was no uniform rule concerning the status of the Jews. The cities had the right to accept or exclude them. Antwerp, Alkmaar, Haarlem, and Rotterdam gave them the right of citizenship. Wherever they were permitted to settle, they organized autonomous Jewish communities, printed books without censorship, established schools, and were free from wearing any distinguishing badge or dress.

In 1614, after Holland broke from the authority of the Catholic church, the government published the tolerant "39 rules pertaining to the treatment of the Jews."

DUTCH COLONIES

With the establishment in 1640 of colonies in South America, some 600 Jewish families migrated to Brazil under the leadership of Saul Mortiera, Isaac Aboab, and Moses Aguilar. When Portugal regained control of Brazil many Jews returned to Holland. Dutch Jews played an important role in the establishment of the communities of London and New York.

EMANCIPATION

By 1657 Jews became subjects of the State and were granted equal rights, although there were still some places where they could not practice their Judaism or carry on a trade. Throughout the 17th century there was considerable migration to the Netherlands from Germany and Poland. In 1795, when the country came under the rule of the French Republic, the Jews of Holland were fully emancipated. Two Jews were elected to the national assembly. Holland became the first country in the modern world to admit Jews to its Parliament.

From 1815, when Holland regained her freedom, until 1940, Jews held favorable positions and distinguished themselves in all walks of life. Rabbis were maintained by the State as were the Christian clergy. A central commission administered all the Jewish communities except the two Sephardic communities in Amsterdam and the Hague.

Although in the 18th century most of the Jews were of Sephardic origin, their percentage of the Jewish population and their influence declined in the course of the 19th century. Most of them lived in the cities, especially in Rotterdam. Because of the favorable treatment accorded them, they prospered and proved themselves loyal subjects.

When Hitler came to power in Germany in 1933, the Dutch people were active in aiding German Jewish refugees. Many continued this activity even when the Nazis occu-

pied the country in 1940. Before World War II, about 150,000 Jews lived in Holland. The Jewish population in 1960 was about 26,000, of whom 6,000 were returnees.

JEWISH LIFE

The Jews of Holland were not subjected to the same degree of persecution as existed in most other countries. They enjoyed freedom and a large measure of civil rights. Jewish life was governed by a college of rabbis, which had the power of excommunication. They exercised this power in the cases of Uriel Acosta and Baruch Spinoza.

The Jews played an important economic role in the development of the Dutch East Indies colonies in the western hemisphere. In their homeland, they were prominent as physicians, artists, writers, journalists, in the theater, and in national affairs. The principal occupation of Jews was the diamond industry. They helped to establish Holland as the chief exporter of diamonds to all parts of the world.

Organized Jewish education, today, is to be found only in Amsterdam. Elsewhere, instruction is provided by visiting teachers. The Jewish Agency sponsors a Hebrew Seminary and ORT offers vocational training in some cities.

JEWS TO REMEMBER

URIEL ACOSTA (1594–1640)

Acosta was a Portuguese Marrano, trained as a Catholic clergyman. At the age of 30, he decided to live openly as a Jew. Because he did not believe in the authority of the Talmud and refused to observe all the ritual and customs of his people, he was excommunicated by the College of Rabbis. Unable to face the consequences of this ban, he recanted and was forced to make a public apology. The humiliation was so great that he took his life.

BARUCH SPINOZA (1632–1677)

Spinoza is called the "Father of Modern Philosophy." He incurred the displeasure of the Jewish authorities because he expounded a theory of God that is called PANTHEISM—a belief that God is a part of everything that exists. He further believed that all religions are good that lead to a good life.

Because he would not retract his rationalistic and unorthodox beliefs, he was excommunicated. Unlike Acosta, he accepted the bans without protest or bitterness. He lived outside the Jewish fold and earned his living as a lens grinder.

In his pursuit of philosophical studies, he wrote two books that earned for him a place among the great scholars of his time. One was his *Ethics,* principles of his philosophic thinking, and the other, *Theological-Political Tractate,* theories on the Bible and Jewish Christian developments.

Spinoza never returned to his people nor did he ever deny his Jewishness. He lived and died a simple man.

MANASSEH ben ISRAEL (1604–1657)

This outstanding Jewish scholar of Amsterdam wrote many religious and philosophic books in Hebrew and other languages. He believed that the Messianic promise of redemption could not be fulfilled unless the Jewish people were scattered all over the earth.

It was on the basis of this belief that he succeeded in gaining permission from Oliver Cromwell to allow the Jews to resettle in England in the 17th century after their expulsion in 1290.

In his book, *Defense of the Jew,* he refuted the charge that the Jews used the blood of Christian people for their Passover. He also pointed out that wherever Jews were allowed to live in freedom and to engage in business, they exemplified the highest ethics.

JOSEF ISRAELS (1824–1911)

He was a painter and etcher, whose portrayal of fishermen and peasant folk brought him recognition as one of the most popular artists of Holland. His chief literary work, *Spain: The Story of a Journey,* is considered one of the most significant Dutch works on painting of the 19th century.

TOBIAS MICHAEL CAREL ASSER (1838–1913)

Professor of international law, member of the International Arbitration Court at the Hague, and co-recipient of the Nobel Peace Prize in 1911.

JEWISH COMMUNITIES

Before the advent of Hitlerism there were 156,817 Jews living in Holland. In 1951 there were approximately 27,000, most of them living in Amsterdam.

Alkmaar
Amsterdam
Arnhem
Groningen
The Hague
Haarlem
Rotterdam
Utrecht

The Jews of Belgium

EARLY HISTORY

History for Belgian Jewry began as early as the fourth century. The small population was relatively free from the usual discriminatory measures against Jews. Until the middle ages they enjoyed full rights and privileges.

But in the following centuries their situation became similar to those of their people in neighboring countries. Heavy taxes, Black Death accusations, provoked rioting, and massacres dot the pages of their history.

It was not until the 19th century that conditions improved. Under Dutch control (1815) they were granted full civil rights. When Belgium regained her national independence (1830) the constitution guaranteed Jews religious freedom and permitted them self-rule.

JEWISH LIFE

When the French annexed Belgium in 1797, they instituted the Consistorial system for the organizational life of the Jewish people. All the Jewish communities were under the supervision of a Grand Rabbi in Brussels. Like other religious denominations, the Consistory received government support. The only exception to complete Jewish autonomy was the prohibition against Jewish cemeteries. Burial could take place only in a Christian cemetery or outside the country. In the business world, Jews were dominant in the diamond-jewelry industry and in the leather and garment trades.

Prior to Hitler's conquest of the country, a large number of refugees came to Belgium. It is estimated that about 100,000 were there, with about half living in Antwerp. This number was considerably diminished with the Nazi occupation.

JEWISH COMMUNITIES

The Jewish population of Belgium is about 35,000. Most of them are of East-European extraction.

Antwerp	Liege
Arlon	Louvain
Brussels	Mons
Charleroi	Ostende
Ghent	Tournay

The Scandinavian Countries

The Jews of Denmark

Jewish history in Denmark began in 1662 when King Christian iv (1577–1648), on the advice of his Jewish physician, Dr. Jonah Charizi, invited the Marrano Jews of Holland to come to Denmark to engage in commerce.

In 1657, King Frederick iii gave permission to all Sephardic Jews to settle in Denmark without the requirement of special passports, which were required of German Jews. Later, with the influx of German and Polish Jews, the Jewish community became firmly established.

ENLIGHTENMENT AND ASSIMILATION

The Enlightenment movement of the 18th century, linked closely to the Haskalah of Europe, brought a number of Danish Jews to the support of Mendelssohn in Germany. Denmark was dominantly a

Protestant country. There was religious tolerance under the Lutheran Church and many Jews enjoyed social and cultural equality. There were no restrictions on general education.

In 1814, some civic but not political rights were granted. Full rights to higher education and livelihood did not come until 1849. The age of Enlightenment, however, took its toll of Jews through assimilation and conversion. The young people and many careerists in the arts and sciences were lost to Judaism. This wave was checked by a resurgence to Judaism under the leadership of the Chief Rabbi, Abraham A. Wolff (1801–1891). He introduced changes similar to those of the German Reform movement.

THE JEWISH COMMUNITY

The Jewish population of Denmark has never been large. At the turn of the 20th century there were about 3,500 Jews in the country. The present population is estimated to be 6,500. During the Nazi invasion the Danish people, led by Christian x, made it possible for nearly all the Jews to escape to Sweden and to be repatriated after the war. Copenhagen is the center of all Jewish life in Denmark.

The Jews of Sweden

Swedish-Jewish history began in 1774, when a German Jew, Aaron Isaac, came to Stockholm and was granted religious liberty by King Gustav III. In 1779, the right to residence was extended to the cities of Gothenburg and Norrkoping. In 1880, twenty families erected a synagogue in Stockholm.

Jews of Sweden suffered only slight disabilities as compared with most other countries. There was a period of gradual emancipation from 1838 when King Karl XIV repealed some restrictions, until 1870, when full equality was granted.

Because Sweden is a Protestant Church-State, all vital statistics must be officially recorded by the church, including Jewish births, deaths, and marriages. No Jew or Catholic may be a teacher in any state school. A Jewish couple can be united in marriage by a rabbi only after their names have been announced in a Protestant Church for three successive Sundays.

The incidence of intermarriage is very high in Sweden. Children of these marriages belong to the Protestant church. It is estimated that some 10,000 Jews have forsaken their religion by this route.

Hitlerism caused many refugee Jews, including those from Denmark, to go to Sweden for protection and hospitality, which was extended in full measure.

The present Jewish population is between 12,000 and 13,000. They enjoy complete emancipation and are totally integrated into Swedish life.

JEWISH COMMUNITIES

Boras
Gothenburg
Halsingborg
Karlstad
Jonkoping
Kristianstad
Malmo
Stockholm
Sundsvall
Uppsala

The Jews of Norway

There is no record of Jews establishing residence in Norway before the seventeenth century. Some Danish kings granted permission to small groups of Sephardic Jews to settle in the country. When Norway succumbed to Swedish rule, all Jews were excluded until the year 1851. Norway's Jewish population was never large. In 1891 they were granted emancipation and a year later were permitted to establish a Jewish community at Oslo. Ritual slaughter was prohibited in 1930.

When Nazism prevailed in Germany, some 2,000 refugees came to Norway, more than doubling the Jewish population. Under Nazi occupation the Jews were subject to the Nuremberg laws and threatened with extermination. The government sought to protect its Jewish subjects, but did not have the same success as in Denmark.

Present-day population is estimated to be about 1,000 Jews, living in Oslo, Trondheim, and Bergen.

The Jews of Switzerland

Jews lived in the German part of what is now Switzerland in the Middle Ages, holding the same status and suffering the same treatment as in Germany. In 1294, there was a Ritual Murder accusation followed by expulsion from Bern.

Other Jewish residents came from Alsace and France. They lived under the protection of city rulers and paid high taxes (The Golden Pfennig). Their primary livelihood was money-lending, because they were excluded from commerce and handicraft.

Because they were held responsible, the Black Death of 1348–49 brought persecution to the Jews. Burning at the stake, periodic expulsion from various cities, and excessive forms of discrimination were common practices. By 1622 nearly all the Jews were expelled from the country, at which time the Diet excluded them in perpetuity. However, Jews lived in cantons that did not join the Swiss Confederation until 1803, and there were Jews in Carouge (1780), a suburb of Geneva ruled by the dukes of Savoy.

In 1744 Jews began to arrive from Germany and Poland. There were periods of segregation and anti-Jewish measures that restricted their civil rights. The majority of Swiss cantons excluded Jews up to the 19th century. Pressure from England, the United States, and France was exerted on behalf of their Jewish citizens, who were entitled to rights of trade and residence in Switzerland. Gradually, individual cantons removed their restrictions against Jews. Although full emancipation was achieved in 1874, ritual slaughter is forbidden, ostensibly on humanitarian grounds.

With the advent of Hitlerism, thousands of Jews escaped to Switzerland, where they received the right of asylum. The present population is about 20,000.

COMMUNITIES

Baden	Lugano
Basel	Oberdendigen
Bern	Schauffhausen
Biel	St. Gall
Fribourg	Waadt
Geneva	Winterthur
Lausanne	Zurich
Lengnau	Interlochen

The Jews of North Africa

EARLY HISTORY

Africa is a vast continent embracing many ancient civilizations. With the exception of Egypt, which reached its zenith in the period of the Pharaohs, Africa has been characterized as the land of the black man, the jungle, the slave market, and diamond mines.

All the early history of African Jewry takes place in the northern countries bordering the Mediterranean Sea. Middle Africa has no Jewish history at all. In South Africa Jewish history started in the 15th century.

JEWISH SETTLEMENTS

The first record of Jews in North Africa is the Biblical account of how Joseph caused his father, Jacob, to settle in the land of Goshen. In other countries of North Africa, Jews lived from early times as cave-dwellers and nomads. In Ethiopia they are known as Falasha Jews; in Tripoli, Mountain Jews; in Morocco, Berber or Daggutun Jews. Some called themselves Black Jews or Negro Jews.

In the fifth and sixth centuries North Africa was occupied by the Vandals and Byzantines. The latter, during the reign of Justinian, vigorously persecuted the Jews.

UNDER MOSLEM RULE

The Arab conquest, following the death of Mohammed (632), brought all of North Africa under the banner of the Crescent, territorially and religiously. The Jewish communities were allowed religious autonomy and were in touch with the great academies of Jewish learning in Babylonia.

Under the fanatical rule of a Berber Moslem sect known as the Almohades, the Jews suffered persecution, forced conversion, and martyrdom.

Beginning with the expulsions from Spain and Portugal (1492), many Sephardic Jews settled in the North African countries. Their conditions of residence depended on the tolerance of the respective ruler. In the 16th century the Mellah (the Jewish ghetto) was frequently attacked and sacked. Jews were sometimes massacred or forcibly converted. Entire Jewish communities, like the Sephardic settlements in Fez, Morocco, were destroyed. In the 17th century Italian Jews from Leghorn settled in Tunis.

The past few centuries brought European influence to the area, that of the Dutch, the Spanish and especially the French. The 20th century brought to North Africa Nazism, rising nationalism, and freedom from colonialism. These changes placed the Jews in an untenable position, with citizenship denied to them, their education and employment limited, and their areas of habitation restricted.

The Jews of South Africa

Jews are comparatively recent settlers in South Africa. Some Spanish and Portuguese Jews are said to have come to the Cape in the 16th century as traders. In 1652, some came with the Dutch East India Company and settled in Capetown.

1806—Great Britain took possession of the Cape. Religious equality was granted to all. Practically all disabilities against the few Jews living there were removed.

1841—The first Jewish community was organized. In 1849, the first synagogue was established at Capetown.

1880's— Diamond and gold mines were discovered. Increased European immigration brought many Jews who became active in the economic development of the country. In the great exodus from Russia that followed in the next decades, some 40,000 Jews came to South Africa.

1890—The Transvaal Boer Republic was established. Some civic disabilities were imposed against Jews.

1898—Political discontent developed among the Jews. Factions tried to exclude Russian and Rumanian Jews from voting. Chief Rabbi Joseph Herman Hertz (1872–1946) was expelled during the Boer War for his pro-British views.

1930—The government set up a Quota Act, limiting Jewish immigration to South Africa.

1933—When Hitler came to power in Germany, organized anti-Semitism entered South African politics. Greyshirts, subsidized by Germany, were found guilty of circulating the forged *Protocols of the Elders of Zion*. Blackshirts organized street demonstrations that ended with violence. Various defamatory publications were circulated.

1937—The Nationalist Party became imbued with Nazism. The Immigration Act, passed at this time, reduced Jewish immigration to a mere trickle.

1944—Extreme nationalistic groups merged to form a strong united party that imposed racist rule over the whole country.

1961—The Union of South Africa withdrew from the British Commonwealth of Nations and declared itself a Republic. The 110,000 Jews of the Republic enjoy the same rights and are subject to the same disabilities and duties as other citizens.

THE JEWISH COMMUNITY

Early Jewish immigrants engaged in commerce and farming. Following the discovery of diamonds and gold, industrialization began in earnest. Jews were involved in starting the first iron and steel works and the clothing industry. In culture, in politics, and in civic life, Jews have played an important role.

The South African Jewish community is represented by a Jewish Board of Deputies, which acts as its spokesman in dealings with the government and regulates Jewish activities in the whole country. The Jewish children receive Jewish education either in Day Schools or in the afternoon Hebrew school. The Zionist movement is the most active organization and commands the most support from the community. The cities of Capetown, Johannesburg, and Pretoria are the most important centers of Jewish population.

The Jews of Egypt

The history of the Jewish people in Africa could be said to have begun in Egypt, where Jacob, the last of the Patriarchs, settled with his family. His son, Joseph, became Prime Minister to Pharoah in 1525 BCE. After several hundred years of residence, the Israelites were forced into slavery. Moses, the first prophet and lawgiver, led them to Sinai in a great exodus that took place in the year 1492 BCE.

Since that time a number of im-

portant Jewish settlements flourished in the land of the Pharaohs.

586 BCE — When the Temple was
destroyed, Jeremiah the prophet
was forcibly taken to Egypt by
refugee Jews.

331 BCE—The Greeks invaded
Egypt and ended the Egyptian
dynasty. Alexander the Great
established the city of Alexandria, where large numbers of
Jews became residents.

300 BCE—Ptolemy I Soter transferred 100,000 Jews from Palestine
to Egypt. Many of them settled
in Cyrenaica (Libya).

150 BCE—Jason of Cyrene wrote
about the wars of the Maccabees.
About this time, relations between the Greeks and Jews became strained for religious, economic, and political reasons.
Anti-Semitism became an intellectual disease. Much apologetic
literature was written.

First century CE—The rule of Cali-
gula (12–41) was one of senseless
cruelty and despotism. Philo, the
famous Jewish philosopher, headed a delegation who petitioned
the emperor, unsuccessfully, for
protection and redress after a
devastating pogrom.

Living at this time was Apion
(c. 30 BCE–48 CE), an Alexan-
drian grammarian, author, lec-
turer, and traveler, who made
unfounded accusations against
the Jews of Egypt in his writings. As the leader of the Stoic
school of philosophy, he headed
an anti-Jewish delegation before
the Roman Emperor. He was
opposed by Philo, as well as the
historian Josephus who wrote
Against Apion, in which he refuted Apion's slanders.

70 CE—Following the destruction of
the Temple in Jerusalem, many
Jews sought refuge in Egypt.

Cyrenaica became a center of
large Jewish population.

72 CE—The Temple of Onias in the
city of Heliontopolis, where Jews
worshiped, was ordered closed.

30 BCE–641 CE — During Roman
rule, the lives of the Jews were
marred at times by violence, but,
in general, the rule of the Ptolemies was tolerant. Jews were
farmers, artisans, bankers, merchants, and shipowners. In order
to become a government official,
a Jew had to convert, as did a
nephew of Philo who became a
prefect.

Jewish life deteriorated when
the Roman emperors became
Christian, and the church embarked on an active anti-Semitic
campaign. This culminated in
the expulsion of Jews from Alexandria in 415, after bloody riots
instigated by the bishop Cyril.
After that time, the Jewish community was unimportant.

For a brief period after 616,
the Persians occupied Egypt.
They were conquered by the
Arabs in 642. The years that followed were economically trouble-
some for the Jews, but comparatively calm religiously.

642–1517 — The Arab invasion
brought the rule of the Crescent
to Egypt and found Jews concentrated in Cairo. A succession
of Caliphates and dynasties
marked this long period of rule.
Jewish communities became Arab
in character and culture, but remained Jewish in religion.

749—The Abbassides started to
rule. The Caliph Omar imposed
a head tax, a distinctive head
dress, and a large number of
other disabilities upon all Jews,
who kept close ties with the
great academies of learning in
Babylonia.

969–1171—The Fatimids began their rule. Jewish privileges were restored, for the most part, but under the Caliph Hakim, there was fierce persecution. He proclaimed himself the reincarnation of God in 1020.

Records of Jewish life of this time were found in the storeroom of a synagogue in Fustat, near Cairo, by a traveler, Elchanan Adler (1896), who told Solomon Schechter, head of the Jewish Theological Seminary in New York, about them. During the rule of the Fatimids, Fustat was the largest center of Jewish population. This literary find is known as "the Cairo Genizah." The documents reveal conflict between the Palestine and the Babylonian influences in the community and give a detailed description of Jewish life.

They lived in voluntary enclosed areas and spoke a language that was a mixture of Hebrew and Arabic. Rabbinic courts rendered judgments in Arabic. Jews kept slaves and occasionally took two wives. They were well conversant with Arabic literature, wrote poetry, and otherwise lived as exponents of Arabic culture. The occupational pattern became more and more urban with the passage of time.

1517–1881—This was the period of Ottoman Turkish rule. Selim i (1467–1520) was favorably disposed to Spanish refugees.

Under the Turks, there was a resurgence of spiritual life, and close contact with the sages of Safed in Palestine. But the masses still lived in poverty, ignorance, and superstition.

1798—During the conquest by Napoleon, Jews suffered hardships and persecution. At his or-der, synagogues in Alexandria were destroyed, and he exacted heavy contributions from the Jewish community.

1805 — Under Mohammed Ali (1769–1849), Egypt started on the road to modern life. He built schools, sponsored public works, and sent students to study in Europe. He was good to the Jews, championing their cause in the Damascus Affair, restoring many privileges, and opening up economic opportunities that attracted them from Turkey, Syria, and the Balkans.

1881—A British protectorate was established over Egypt, which did not end until recent times. During this time the position of the Jew improved, but as is usual, with better conditions, there was much assimilation and Jewish education became superficial. New synagogues were built, the more affluent Jews were able to move from the old areas, and they came to play a part in public life.

1897—The Zionist movement infused new vigor into Jewish life. Although favorable at first, the government adopted an anti-Zionist policy as part of anti-European reaction which set in as the 20th century began.

1923—Independence was granted to Egypt by Britain, with Fuad i (1868–1936) as the first constitutional monarch. Britain continued to keep troops there and defended the country in World War ii. It did not declare war on the Axis until February, 1945.

1945—The Arab League, composed of seven Arab countries but dominated by Egypt, was organized. One of its avowed purposes, after the State of Israel was created by the United

Nations, was to destroy the new land.

1948—Under Farouk I (1920–1965), Egypt, as part of the Arab League, attacked Israel in an abortive attempt. In retaliation for failure, and using the plight of the Arab refugees from Palestine as a propaganda device, the Arabs in Egypt were aroused to riot against the Jews. There were human casualties, destruction, sequestration of properties of Jews, arbitrary arrests, and detention.

1951—By now, 35,000 Jews had left Egypt, of whom 25,000 settled in Israel. There were anti-Jewish outbreaks, with bombing of synagogues in Alexandria.

1952—A military coup ousted King Farouk in Egypt. Gamal Abdul Nasser took over as President of the country. Rioting in Cairo against Jewish merchants caused considerable destruction of property.

1956—Israel's seizing of the Sinai peninsula resulted in further deterioration of the situation of the Jews in Egypt. Even though Israel withdrew, this did not stop the mass arrests, expropriation, economic boycott, discriminatory taxation, and concentration camps that faced the Jewish population. At least 12,000 fled or were expelled from the country.

1958—Egypt and Syria formed the United Arab Republic as one step in solidifying enemies of Israel.

1961—When Syria seceded, temporarily, from the United Arab Republic, hundreds of Jews had their property sequestered, which meant that they could not leave the country.

1961–70—(See State of Israel)

JEWISH LIFE

The oldest, largest, and best-known Jewish community in Egypt was Alexandria. By the first century CE, there were about a million Jews living in the whole country, with sizable numbers in Cairo, Memphis, Elephantine, and Aswan.

Except for brief periods in early history, the Jews were permitted to worship and live in accordance with their religious beliefs and laws. Each community was autonomous and governed its own internal affairs. The leader, or head, of all the Jews in Egypt was called the NAGID. His power and authority were comparable to those of the Exilarch in Palestine.

The Hellenistic influence left its impress upon the Jews of Egypt. They translated the Hebrew Bible into Greek—the Septuagint. Many Jews had Greek names and large numbers adopted Greek customs. The Hebrew language gave way almost entirely to Greek, at one time.

In addition to the Sephardim and Ashkenazim, there are also Karaites in Egypt, with professional men and religious leaders among them. Each group has its own congregation. The Karaites have their own publications, celebrate the holidays according to the appearance of the full moon, accept only the written and not the oral law.

Over the centuries, Jewish people were segregated in sections similar to the ghettoes of Europe, known as Mellahs, which were usually surrounded by walls and located in the slum section of the cities. It was not unusual for families to live their entire lives in the Mellah.

In 1946, there were about 80,000 Jews in Egypt, but by 1965 fewer than 3,000 remained. They are not considered citizens, have no security, and stay there because they either have no place to go or do not wish to leave what they have.

All the Jews who are left live in either Cairo or Alexandria. They are represented by a council over which the Grand Rabbi presides as the official recognized by the government. Now there is only one rabbi left in Alexandria and one in Cairo whose signature the government accepts. Zionism and contacts with Jews abroad are forbidden.

There is still one Jewish school in Alexandria, which has to accept Moslems. In Cairo there is one Jewish school, one orphanage, and one home for the aged. Most synagogues have closed down, but one in Alexandria and two in Cairo are still functioning. There is no Jewish press.

JEWS TO REMEMBER

PHILO—(20 BCE–c. 40 CE)

He lived in the city of Alexandria and came from a wealthy family. After a trip to Jerusalem, he became completely dedicated to his faith. He was regarded as an outstanding leader of his people and was sent to Rome to defend their rights. He tried to reconcile Jewish and Greek life and could not believe that anti-Semitism was an expression of the cultured Greeks, to whom he felt so close.

He wrote commentaries on the Bible as well as on metaphysics and ethics. In one of his historical works, *Against Apion,* he refuted the false charges leveled against the Jews.

ISAAC BEN SOLOMON ISRAELI—
(c. 860–c. 950)

He is also known as Abu Yakub Ishak ibn Suleiman al-Israili and

as Isacus Judaeus. He wrote a commentary on the Bible, several philosophical works, and several books on medicine, for which he is most famous. He was physician to several Caliphs and conducted a medical school.

SAADIAH GAON—(882–942)

He left Egypt in 928 to become the great Gaon of the academy at Sura. He wrote a Hebrew dictionary called *Agron* and a number of polemics against the Karaites.

MOSES MAIMONIDES—(1135–1204)

This great philosopher came as a refugee from Spain, with his family, in the year 1166, at the age of 13. As personal physician to the Caliph, and as a leader of his people, he was held in high esteem throughout the Jewish world. His reputation and fame, however, were achieved in the field of scholarship.

He was the first to write a scientific commentary of the Talmud, called the *Mishnah Torah,* the purpose of which was to simplify the Biblical and Talmudic laws of Israel. He formulated a system of creeds and beliefs called the *Thirteen Articles of Faith.* His book on Jewish philosophy, *The Guide to the Perplexed,* opened this branch of knowledge and study to the Jewish and non-Jewish world.

SIMON OF CAIRO — (last half of eighth century)

To him is attributed the compendium on the Talmud known as *Halachoth Gedoloth, The Great Law.* Later he made his home in Babylonia.

ISAAC COHEN SHALAL (d. 1525)

He was a prominent Nagid of Egypt and a patron of Jewish learning.

DAVID ABI ZIMRA—(1470–1573)

He was known as RADBAZ, and was a Spanish refugee, who became chief rabbi at Cairo. He wrote a commentary on Maimonides' *Mishnah Torah*.

JEWISH COMMUNITIES

Alexandria	Elephantine
Aswan	Fustat
Cairo	Memphis

The Jews of Morocco

Jews had settled in Morocco, or Mauretania as it was known when Rome conquered it, in 42 BCE. Rome brought Christianity to the country, which was followed by Hellenism in the fourth century. Under the Vandal King Genserich, who conquered Rome and sacked it in 455, the Jews enjoyed equal rights. In the coastal cities, Jewish merchants flourished in the shipping and maritime trades. Inland they earned their living as farmers, vintners, and wine merchants.

Sixth Century

Spanish Jewish refugees from Visigoth persecution brought Western culture, industry, and commerce to Morocco. Christian persecution, however, drove thousands of Jews into the mountains, where they joined Berber tribes who had become converted to Judaism.

Seventh Century

Under Byzantine rule, all synagogues were destroyed. Judaism-professing Berber tribes came to power for a brief period under Kahina, their queen. She united most of the Berber tribes in an un-successful war against the Arabs and was killed in battle. Many tribes were forcibly converted to Islam. Jews were forced to pay heavy taxes and to wear special garb.

Eighth to Thirteenth Centuries

Jews lived in comparative peace, although they were relegated to the MELLAH (salted place or marsh), which became a blighted and poverty-stricken area in time.

In 1032, 6,000 Jews were slaughtered in Fez, and in subsequent persecutions many Jewish women were taken into slavery. In 1062 the liberal Almoravids came to power and conditions improved for the Jews. But in 1147 the Almohades caused a temporary setback in their progress. Old restrictions were renewed and Jews were forced to wear a peculiar costume, not merely the badge. When their dynasty ended (1269), Judaism again came out into the open.

Fifteenth to Nineteenth Centuries

When the expulsions from Spain and Portugal brought many Sephardic Jews to Morocco, much friction resulted between them and the less cultured natives. For many centuries, Jews lived through periods of degradation, discrimination, and occasional fanatical attacks of violence. But, from time to time, there was peace if not prosperity. But in the 19th century conditions became severe. Epidemics took their toll. Education for children, other than religious instruction, was unobtainable. The Jews became protegés of the Sultan, and had no legal rights.

Twentieth Century

With Spanish and, later, French occupation (1912–1955), restrictions were lifted; violence ceased, order was established, and the Jewish status improved. Casablanca became the major center of population, with sizable Jewish communities in Tangier, Fez, Rabat, and Marrakesh. Tetuan, in the Spanish zone, had a considerable Jewish population, where similar conditions prevailed.

> 1940—Anti-Jewish laws of Vichy resulted in demonstrations in the cities, in the ousting of Jews from government positions, and in their forced return to the Mellah. Their rights were not restored until after World War II.

> 1948—When Israel became a nation, emigration started. By 1952, 35,000 had left Morocco.

> 1955—Morocco was granted independence by France. The resultant upheaval caused new outbreaks of anti-Semitic activity, with fatalities and material damage.

> 1956—Jewish emigration to Israel was stopped, temporarily, but as time passed, some passports were issued at various periods.

> 1958—Morocco joined the Arab League and adopted the anti-Jewish program laid down by Nasser, calling for the destruction of the Jewish state.

> 1959—Morocco severed relations with Israel. There are still trickles of emigration, however.

JEWISH LIFE

Most Moroccan Jews resemble the Arabs physically and in social customs, although there are three distinct strains in the total population.

1. The Berber or Mountain Jews
   In 1945 they numbered 30,000. Their education is limited to the Cheder or elementary classes in Hebrew. They are quite pious. About half of them are engaged in handicrafts, with the rest reduced to menial trades or begging.

2. The Sephardic Jews
   They are most numerous and live in the large cities. They, too, are pious, hospitable, and charitable.

3. European Jews
   They came during World War II as refugees and have their own Ashkenazic synagogues. Together with the Sephardic Jews, they are strong Zionists.

Moroccan nationalism and the drive to integrate all minorities has resulted in the Jews now discarding their Arab-Jewish dialect in favor of Arabic and the abandonment of their distinctive non-Moslem garb. Those Jews who are Zionists are suspected of treason by the extreme Arab nationalists, and even the World Jewish Congress was banned by the government. Most Arab-speaking Jews of ancient stock live in Mellahs in extreme poverty under conditions reminiscent of the Middle Ages. In the past, they worked chiefly in fields forbidden to Moslems, like selling liquor or lending money. Some continue to be tailors, carpenters, metalsmiths, peddlers, mattress makers, and importers.

There is a Federation of Jewish communities representing the Jews of Morocco, which is supposed to be only a religious and cultural association, but it also handles political affairs. All Jewish communities have synagogues, but few have rabbis. The Federation also collects money for charity, keeps order in Jewish life, and is responsible for government taxes. The educational system and the Rabbinical Tribunal are headed by a Chief Rabbi.

There is no compulsory education and about one-fourth of the Jewish children receive no instruction of any kind. The schools that do exist are maintained by private charity, by the Alliance Israelite Universelle, or are subsidized by the Jewish community and the government. A seminary was opened in 1947 for the training of Hebrew teachers to staff the Chedarim and the Yeshivoth, and there are two rabbinical seminaries in Tangier. There is one monthly Jewish periodical, written in French.

When Morocco gained its independence in 1955, the Jewish population became more and more insecure, resulting in pressure for emigration. Some 60,000 have gone to Israel with the aid of the Jewish Agency and the Joint Distribution Committee since 1948. In 1961, there were about 160,000 Jews in Morocco, with about 80,000 living in Casablanca. Most of the rural settlements of Jews are being gradually depopulated by emigration. By 1966, there were fewer than 125,000 Jews left in the whole country.

JEWISH PERSONALITIES

HUSHIEL BEN ELCHANAN—
(Tenth–11th Centuries)
Migrated from Italy and headed a Yeshivah in Kairouan. He was a noted Talmudist.

HANANEL BEN HUSHIEL—
(990–c. 1055)
Headed the academy at Kairouan. Wrote commentaries on the Babylonian Talmud and on the Pentateuch.

NISSIM BEN JACOB—(11th Century)
Talmudist and moralist. Headed the academy at Kairouan. Carried on a lengthy correspondence with Hai Gaon of Babylonia. His chief work was *A Key to the Locks of the Talmud,* in which he attempted to explain the methodology of the Talmud.

JEWISH COMMUNITIES

Agadir	Meknes
Casablanca	Rabat
Fez	Safi
Marrakesh	Tangier
	Tetuan

The Jews of Algeria

The Jews in Algeria are a mixture from Africa, Asia, and Europe. Jewish settlements existed in a number of cities in the first century under Roman rule. The history of the country parallels that of Morocco in the early centuries, with some Berber tribes embracing Judaism. Jews suffered disabilities under Christianity and under Byzantine rule, when their synagogues were transformed into churches.

Seventh Century

Sephardic refugees from Visigoth Spain and Portugal became influential in Algerian life and established the patterns of religion and culture that the Jewish community has since followed. When the Arabs conquered Byzantium, their rule was more tolerant.

1130–1269—With the advent of the Almohades, persecution set in and emigration followed. Jews either fled the country, converted to Islam, or submitted to the wearing of distinctive clothes.

1391—Refugees came from Spain and Portugal, bringing with them famous scholars like Isaac ben Sheshet Barfat and Simeon ben Zemach Duran.

1492—More Jews, fleeing from the Inquisition, came from Spain and Portugal.

1518–1830 — Turkish rule. Jews were segregated in Mellahs from the rest of the population and were differentiated by their special dress.

1830—French rule. Some restrictions were removed but Jews were still set apart from others. In an attempt to assimilate, they started to adopt French culture. Poverty, however, continued to be widespread. Mellahs were common in all Jewish areas. About this time European Jews began to settle in large numbers.

1870–1885 — Under French rule Jews were given full citizenship, but French anti-Semitism came at the same time. One of its leaders succeeded in inciting the Moslems against the Jews, with widespread excesses resulting in several cities. The number of Jews in Algeria that received French citizenship was approximately 38,000. This was primarily owing to Adolphe Cremieux, who was the Jewish Minister of Justice in France. During this period there was an influx of European settlers.

1897 — The Dreyfus Affair in France, which attracted world attention, had its repercussions in Algeria. Anti-Jewish excesses became common occurrences.

1917 — Turkey was defeated in World War ɪ and Ottoman power in North Africa was ended. The Moslems, however, still kept the Jews apart from the rest of the population.

1934 — Nazi-inspired anti-Semitic riots in Constantine and other places resulted in hundreds of Jews wounded and scores killed.

1940—The French Vichy government, under German occupation, took anti-Jewish action in Algeria and abrogated the Cremieux laws, with resultant loss of citizenship for Jews. Under German occupation the Jews suffered severely.

1945—The Arab League was organized and a holy war was declared upon the Jews. The high nationalistic feeling of the Moslems became a serious threat to the welfare and security of the Jewish people.

1948—The State of Israel came into being. Thousands of Jews made preparations to leave Algeria.

1954—The Algerian Independence Party was organized and the natives revolted against French rule. Many Jews were held suspect because of their sympathy to France.

1962—France endorsed self-determination for Algeria, but the rightist secret army organization continued to commit atrocities against the natives. Jews were often the innocent victims of these assaults.

1963—Algeria gained its independence from France and became a sovereign state.

JEWISH LIFE

The Jewish community is Sephardic in religion but Arab in culture. The majority of Jews are itinerant peddlers and petty merchants. Some are engaged in more productive work, like painters, carpenters, cigarette makers, jewelers, and the like.

Under French rule, the Jews started to discard some Arab ways and sought to become more Europeanized. Their economic status is bad. Most of them live in overcrowded Mellahs, in great poverty, and with many families living in a single house. The majority subsist on charity dispensed by Jewish social service organizations.

The Alliance Israelite Universelle maintains schools in the larger cities, in cooperation with local Jewish community organizations. There is a federation of all local Jewish councils that convenes biennially and represents all Algerian Jewry. Each of the four large Jewish communities—Oran, Constantine, Algiers, and Bone—has a Chief Rabbi. These are headed by a Grand Rabbi from Algiers.

In 1963 it was estimated that about 130,000 Jews lived in Algeria. All but 4,000 emigrated, most of them to France, when Algeria gained its independence.

JEWISH PERSONALITIES

RABBI ISAAC ben SHESHET BARFAT (1326–1408)
Author of many Responsa and works on Halacha. He was influential among his people and strongly opposed the study of philosophy and Cabala.

SIMEON ben ZEMACH DURAN (1361–1408)
He was called RASHBATZ. He was a Spanish refugee and achieved renown as a codifier, Cabalist, and philosopher. Wrote responsa and diversified works on Jewish studies.

JEWISH COMMUNITIES

Algiers	Guelma
Batna	Mascara
Blida	Mostaganem
Bone	Oran
Colomb-Bechar	Sidi-bel-Abbes
Constantine	Tlemcen
Ghardaia	

The Jews of Tunisia

Tunisian Jews claim that they trace their ancestry to prior to the Babylonian captivity in 586 BCE. True or not, there is archaeological proof that Jewish settlements have existed since the first century CE. Their history follows the pattern of the other North African countries.

Fifth and Sixth Centuries

Jews prospered under the rule of the Vandals, but the Christian church enacted anti-Jewish measures. These were abrogated by Emperor Justinian when in 534 he granted Jews equal rights with the pagans.

Seventh Century

Spanish Jewish refugees, fleeing from the persecution of Visigothic kings, settled in Tunisia. There was a high incidence of intermarriage with pagan Berbers, some of whom adopted Judaism. Jewish life flourished under the Baghdad Caliphate.

1163—A fanatical Almohade Caliph gave the Jews the alternative of conversion or emigration. Many were isolated in ghettos and practically all Jews were forced to wear identifying garments.

1534–1574 — Under Spanish rule the Jews were subjected to various forms of persecution until they reverted to Turkish rule, when they were granted religious autonomy.

1881—With the French occupation the medieval restrictions against the Jews were removed. The new government granted rights and privileges equal to those of the Mohammedans.

1910—Jews permitted to acquire citizenship.

1942—The Nazi army overran Tunisia, rounded up the Jewish youth, and made preparations to destroy the Jewish communities. Before their plans could be carried out they were forced to withdraw from the country.

1948—With the establishment of the State of Israel many Jews prepared to emigrate. After a large scale exodus the government closed the doors to further emigration.

1956—Tunisia gained its independence from France and soon after, a Jewish minister was appointed to the cabinet. President Habib Bourguiba is a moderate, although there are radical elements in the country.

JEWISH LIFE

There are two groups of Jewish people in Tunisia—the Touensa, who are of ancient Jewish stock, and the Grana, who are descended from the Spanish and Portugese settlers. A small number of the former are merchants, traders, and professional men, but most of the people are wretchedly poor.

For some time before the 13th century, Jews were not allowed to live in the city of Tunis, but later obtained permission to live in a ghetto called the HARA, where they remained until 1857.

The Jews on Djerba island live much like their neighbors. They cultivate vineyards and trade in wine. Maimonides lived there in 1163 and reported that the mores of the Jews were similar to those of the Arabs. Most of the 3,500 Jews of Djerba have gone to Israel, leaving about 300 on the island.

In Tunisia the occupation pattern of Jews is like that found in western Europe. However, many still huddle in the ghetto. Culturally the Jews of northern Tunisia are French oriented. In the cities assimilation and intermarriage are increasing.

The Jews of southern Tunisia live on standards below those of the poorest Moslem slum-dwellers. There are no Alliance schools and they are completely removed from the French influence. A Cheder education for boys is the only instruction given.

The outlook for the Jews of Tunisia is not good. The economically depressed conditions of the country, the French-oriented Jews who are identified with foreign colonial power, the self-imposed differences in language, dress and social habits, the antagonism to Israel—all are threats to their future security.

The population estimate for 1959 was 67,000, with 55,000 living in the city of Tunis. Since 1949 over 20,000 Jews have gone to Israel, and about 20,000 to France.

JEWISH COMMUNITIES

Djerba island	Kairouan
Bizerte	Sfax
Gabes	Sousse
Gafsa	Tunis

The Jews of Libya

It is said that before the destruction of the second Temple (70 CE) some 1,000,000 Jews were living in Cyrenaica, which was then a part of Egypt. In 150 BCE, Jason of Cyrene wrote about the history of the Jews of his time. To him is attributed the authorship of the second Book of Maccabees. In 74 BCE Cyrene became a Roman province. About this time bloody riots occurred because of strong differences between the Greeks and the Jews.

115 CE — Revolt against Emperor Trajan. It is reported that in the reprisals that followed nearly all of the Jews of Cyrene were killed or deported.

320 CE—Ptolemy I of Egypt sent Jewish soldiers to upper Libya, where they established permanent Jewish settlements.

Like the other North African countries, Libya came under the successive domination of Carthage, Rome, the Vandals, the Ottoman Empire, and Italy. Not much Jewish history is recorded during the centuries that followed.

1551—Spanish refugees came to Tripoli. Special privileges were granted to the Jews by Sultan Suleiman, the Magnificent.

1911—Italy took over possession of Libya. The position of the Jews remained the same.

1943—15,000 Jews lived in the country. They resided in ghettos called "Al Hara."

1945—After World War II, Libya was placed under British administration. The Jewish population numbered 35,000, owing to large immigration of refugee Jews from Europe.

1948—State of Israel proclaimed. A mass exodus to Israel took place, involving some 30,000 Jews.

1949—The United Nations approved Libya as a sovereign state to become effective in 1952.

1960—Approximately 3,500 Jews remain in Libya.

JEWISH PERSONALITIES

ISAAC BEN SOLOMON ISRAEL (860–950)
He wrote a commentary on Sefer Yetzirah, a work on medieval philosophy.

JEWISH COMMUNITIES

Bengasi	Sabratha
Leptis-Magna	Tobruk
Ola	Tripoli

The Jews of the United States

EARLY HISTORY

The history of the Jews in the United States began in September of 1654 when twenty-three refugees, fleeing from the Portugese Inquisition in Brazil, landed at New Amsterdam, now called New York. This colony was under the rule of the Dutch, who ordered the reluctant Governor Peter Stuyvesant to grant them residence and burgher rights. He consented on condition that the "poor among them shall never become a burden to the community."

Citizenship, however, was withheld from them. Asser Levy petitioned successfully for equal rights for all Jews, including the right to bear arms. However, they suffered the same disabilities as were imposed upon all dissenters of the Dutch Reformed Church, which included Lutherans, Baptists, and Quakers. In 1656 they were permitted to establish a cemetery. In the same year Jews began to settle in Delaware and Connecticut.

1658—A Jewish community sprang up in Newport, R.I. Under the state charter written by Roger Williams it was recorded that no person living in the colony was to be in "any wise molested, punished, disquieted, or called in question for any difference in opinion."

Here in 1763 was built the third synagogue in the United States — "Jeshuath Yisroel" — "Salvation of Israel." It is now known as the TOURO synagogue, named in honor of its first Rabbi, Isaac Touro, and it was declared a national shrine by the United States government in 1947. Although Rhode Island was the first colony to grant religious freedom to all, a 1719 law excluded Jews from voting and holding office.

1664—British rule supplanted the Dutch and most restrictions were removed. It was not until 1686 that the Jews of New York were granted the right to public worship. In 1695 they started a congregation, "Shearith Yisroel"— "The Remnant of Israel," but it was not until 1728 that they were able to build a synagogue, which was located on Mill Street.

1665—Except for Puritan Massachusetts, which withheld religious freedom from Catholics, Quakers and Jews, they were welcome in all the colonies. They went to Delaware in 1656 and to South Carolina in 1665, where the second synagogue to be built was erected in Charleston in 1750, "Beth-Elohim"—"The House of the Lord."

1720—In Pennsylvania, the Quaker William Penn opened his colony to all who believed in the Eternal God. A Sephardic congregation, "Mikveh Yisroel"—"The Collect of Israel," was organized in Philadelphia in 1726.

1733—A fourth congregation was organized in Savannah, Georgia, the year after the first Jews settled there.

1740—Jews were admitted to full citizenship in New York when the words, "upon the true faith of a Christian" were eliminated from the oath for those seeking naturalization. From 1741 to 1748, twenty-four Jews were granted citizenship in New York. By the time of the Revolutionary War, there were 300 Jews in the city.

1750–1775—About 2,500 Jews were settled in the colonies. Some of them were Yiddish-speaking, Ashkenazic Jews from Germany, Poland, and England. The earlier arrivals were Sephardic, of Spanish and Portuguese origin, who were considered the more cultured and dominant group.

Though few in number, the Jews integrated quickly in the mainstream of American life. In the new land of freedom they helped build a "New World." They prized the privilege of private conscience and public worship and they joined the ranks of those who pioneered against all forms of intolerance and bigotry.

When the war for independence came, most of them were on the side of the colonies. A few of the wealthy remained loyal Tories. During the war about 300 Jews served in the regular army. In Charleston, one group of militia men were known as the "Jews' Company."

At financial sacrifice and with

personal devotion, Jews proved themselves to be patriots both on the field of battle and on the home front. As sons of liberty they fought with valor and distinction and they gave financial support when it was needed the most.

1776—The Declaration of Independence was signed.

In it are incorporated the Hebraic ideals emphasizing the dignity of all mankind created equal before God.

1789 — At the inauguration of George Washington as the first president of the United States, Rabbi Gershon Mendez Seixas joined with other religious dignitaries in administering the presidential oath of office.

The Constitution, ratified in 1788 with its Bill of Rights, gave assurance of religious liberty to all. "Congress shall make no law respecting an establishment of religion, or prohibiting the free exercise thereof."

Following the Revolutionary War the United States began to expand westward. Many Jews were among the pioneers and a number of cities were founded and named after them.

Aaronsburg, Pennsylvania—
Aaron Levy
Castroville, Texas—
Henry Castro
Heppner, Oregon—
Henry Heppner
Gilman, Vermont—
Isaac Gilman
Montgomery, Alabama—
Abraham Mordecai

SOME EARLY COLONIAL PERSONALITIES

AARON LOPEZ (1731–1782)

He was a prominent merchant of Newport and helped to develop the seaport and shipping industry. Laid the cornerstone of the Newport synagogue.

MORDECAI SHEFTALL (1735–1795)

Appointed Commissary General for the Continental Army. In the defense of Savannah he was captured by the British and paroled in 1780.

HAYM SALOMON (1740–1785)

He gave large financial support to the Continental Congress in the cause of the revolution. The diary of Robert Morris, Secretary of the Continental Treasury, records that Salomon advanced $658,000 to friends, which was never repaid. He died penniless.

FRANCIS SALVADOR (1747–1776)

He was elected to the Colonial Assembly of South Carolina, the first Jew to hold office in the colonies. He was a revolutionary hero and was killed in the defense of Charleston.

BENJAMIN NONES (1757–1826)

Known as the Jewish Lafayette, he served as staff officer under George Washington. After the war he became active in politics.

HEBREW INFLUENCE ON COLONIAL AMERICA

The Pilgrims in the "New World" were deeply influenced by the Old Testament and the Jewish belief in personal freedom. The first book printed at Harvard College in 1640 was a translation of the Hebrew Psalms. Hebrew was a required course for graduation.

Yale University, founded in 1701, had the Hebrew words "Urim V'Tumim," meaning "Light and Perfection," inscribed on its seal. The Liberty Bell at Philadelphia bore the inscription from the Book of Leviticus, "Proclaim liberty throughout the land, unto all the inhabitants thereof." The motto of the seal of the United States, proposed by Jefferson, Franklin, and Adams, read "Rebellion to tyrants is obedience to God." It depicted Israel crossing the Red Sea. America's first Thanksgiving was patterned after the Hebrew Festival of Succoth. The Puritan fathers used Hebrew names and a number of Mosaic laws were incorporated in the legislatures of the colonies.

1801—David Emanuel of Georgia was the first Jew in the United States to be elected a governor.

1812 — Jews of Spanish origin served in the war of 1812. Some, like Commodore Uriah P. Levy (1792–1862), were noted for distinguished service. Commodore Levy was responsible for the abolition of corporal punishment in the navy.

1824—In Charleston, South Carolina, a dissident group made an unsuccessful attempt to modernize synagogue worship. This was the first endeavor to introduce Reform in the United States.

1843—The B'nai B'rith organization was founded as a welfare, benevolent, and social order.

1849—The California "Gold Rush" brought many Jews to the west, where they engaged in peddling and established small businesses. In 1850 two congregations were established in San Francisco. In 1852, two Jews were elected to the state legislature.

1854—Isaac Mayer Wise, the founder of Reform Judaism in America, established the first Reform congregation in Cincinnati, Ohio. He also started the first

seminary for the training of Reform rabbis, the Hebrew Union College, in 1875, and the Union of American Hebrew Congregations, the parent body for Reform Congregations, in 1873. Reform Judaism developed mostly among the German and Hungarian immigrants.

1864–1868—The Civil War. It is estimated that some 7,500 Jews were involved in the struggle between the North and the South— 6,000 with the Union army and 1,500 with the Confederate forces, out of a total of 200,000 Jews in the entire country. Four Jews held the rank of general. With the exception of a small nucleus of Southern Jews, nearly all the Jews of the United States were opposed to slavery.

1874—The Young Men's Hebrew Association was founded in New York City.

1886—The Statue of Liberty was dedicated on Bedloe's Island in New York Harbor. The American Jewish poetess, Emma Lazarus, wrote the poem "The New Colossus," that is inscribed at the foot of the statue.

1887 — The Jewish Theological Seminary to train conservative rabbis was founded by Rabbi Sabato Morais. In 1902, Dr. Solomon Schechter became its President. The parent body for Conservative synagogues is the United Synagogue of America, established in 1913.

1897—In response to the rapid increase in the number of orthodox congregations, the Rabbi Isaac Elchanan Theological Seminary (Yeshivah College) was formed to train Orthodox rabbis. It has expanded to include a teachers' institute, the first Jewish college of arts and sciences, a graduate school, and the Albert Einstein School of Medicine.

1880–1914—There was a tremendous influx of Jews from central and eastern Europe that gave impetus to the growth of Orthodox Judaism and to Zionism in the United States.

1914–1918—The first World War. Over 250,000 Jews were involved with the armed forces of the country. Ten thousand were commissioned officers. Nearly 3,000 died in service.

1922—Rabbi Stephen S. Wise (1874–1949) founded the Jewish Institute of Religion in New York City to train rabbis and educators. The Hebrew Theological College of Chicago, to train Orthodox rabbis, was started the same year.

1929–1939 — Through the Hitler and the depression years, there was distressing agitation, owing in part to the economic stress and in part to the German-American Bund, which was active from coast to coast.

1939–1945 — The Second World War. About ten per cent (500,000) of the Jewish population served in all branches of the armed forces. Ten thousand died in action. The social and economic discrimination of the prewar years subsided during the war.

1945—The United States became the largest center of Jewish population in the world.

ANTI-SEMITISM

The word "Semitism" has its origin in the descendants of Shem, one of the sons of Noah. Many people are of Semitic stock, including the vast population of the Arab world. Actually, a Semite is a member of the Caucasian branch of the human race, which is characterized by two linguistic stems— the Aryan and the Semitic.

In 1879, Wilhelm Marr of Germany introduced the term "anti-Semitism" as one of derogation against the Jewish people. Any form of hatred, dislike, or disapproval might come within the context of the word. Much of the resentment and ill-will against the Jews stemmed from the deicide charge that held them responsible for the death of Christ, renewed each year at Easter time and with each Jew inheriting the guilt. In earlier history it was also evidenced in the distinction made by Christianity between the Aryan and Semitic stock of man, with the latter implying only Jews and their being relegated to an inferior status.

Traces of anti-Jewish feelings have been evident in the United States from the time of Peter Stuyvesant, governor of New Amsterdam (1647–54). The Jews had to fight for their right to serve in the army, to trade and travel, to establish their own cemetery, and to own property. Many of the original states wrote restrictions into their state constitutions, the last of which was not eliminated until as late as 1868.

During the Civil War there were anti-Semitic outbursts in both the North and the South, with Jews being accused of being responsible for the troubles that prevailed, especially in the South. In some cases newspaper editorials voiced the accusations. General Grant accused the Jews of illegal activities and barred them from doing business with the Tennessee Department. President Lincoln rescinded the order. No rabbi could be a military chaplain until 1862, even though large numbers of Jews served in the armed forces. The acute economic crisis following the war generated a latent vigilante hate movement that focused upon minority groups. One of these was the Ku Klux Klan.

The years following the Civil War were marked with great economic and social change that prepared the country to accept the masses of immigrants who were to come in the next fifty years. As Jews moved into the commercial and manufacturing middle class, anti-Semitism took a different approach. Discrimination was felt in the fields of employment, housing and social relationships. Restrictive covenants kept some neighborhoods free of Jews. Certain industries exercised their prerogative by keeping their establishments white and Protestant. Patterns of exclusion operated in clubs, resorts, and recreational facilities, not publicly owned. All during this time, labor unions experienced their great period of growth, many with the help of Jewish leadership, which caused further antagonism.

During the period preceding World War I, there was little overt, organized hostility, but incidents occurred, periodically, that showed that America was not free of latent anti-Semitisim.

THE KU KLUX KLAN

This was a secret society that flourished in the South after the Civil War. It was organized in 1865 for the purpose of maintaining "white supremacy." After the turn of the century it lost vitality, but in 1915 it was reorganized and in addition to its anti-Negro program it espoused anti-Catholicism and anti-Semitism. It spread throughout a number of southern and northern states and controlled politics in many communities. The membership declined and after World War II an attempt at revival failed as state after state barred them. The movement experienced a resurgence after civil rights legislation was enacted by Congress in 1954, and still emerges, periodically, to do some violence.

RIOTING IN NEW YORK

On July 30, 1902, the funeral of the noted Rabbi Jacob Joseph was held in the lower east side of New York city. As the funeral procession passed a printing plant, workers leaned from the windows, made vulgar and obscene remarks, and threw waste material on the hearse and mourners This was followed by a shower of nuts, bolts, wood blocks and oil-saturated bundles of papers. Some angry Jews retaliated by breaking windows in the factory. The riot squads were summoned and the police fell upon the Jews, brutally beating and abusing them. They were aided by the men in the factory who directed water sprays from fire hoses on the Jews. An investigation concluded that both parties were at fault.

THE LEO FRANK CASE (1884–1915)

Leo Frank was part-owner of a pencil factory in Marietta, Georgia. In 1913, a fourteen-year-old girl was found murdered in the basement of the factory, and before she died she scribbled a note charging an unnamed Negro as her assailant.

On the testimony of a Negro, Jim Conley, who was in the building at the time of the murder, Leo

Frank was arrested and convicted of the crime. Anti-Semitic hysteria became rampant and voices were raised clamoring for his death. A biased jury sentenced Frank to be hanged. Conley was found guilty of being an accessory to the murder and was given a year's sentence in the chain gang.

Governor John H. Slayton sought to avert pre-arranged plans for the lynching of Frank by secretly commuting the sentence to life imprisonment and removing him to safer quarters. For this act he was denounced as "King of the Jews and Traitor."

The chief instigator of the malicious diatribe against Frank and all Jews was Thomas E. Watson, (1856–1922). He was an avowed racist and led repeated attacks against Catholics, Jews, and Negroes. In his personal publication "Watson's Magazine," he wrote in January 1915, "Every student of sociology knows that the black man's lust after white women is not much fiercer than the lust of the licentious Jew for the Gentile."

In August of 1915, Frank was the victim of a prison assault by whites and Negroes. Following an incident in which his throat was cut he was transferred to a prison hospital. A large, armed vigilante group overpowered the warden and guards, abducted Frank, and lynched him on the outskirts of Marietta.

The reaction to this lynching was nationwide. Scathing deunciations in editorials, articles, and sermons were leveled against the perpetrators of this brutal act. Watson defended his actions and continued his bigoted onslaughts against all who opposed him. Using racism in a political campaign he succeeded in winning an election to the United States Senate. At his death he was greatly lauded by his Southern colleagues. He was not only responsible for the lynching of Leo Frank, but successfully poisoned the minds of millions of people against Jews and other minorities.

PROTOCOLS OF THE ELDERS OF ZION (1920s)

The Dearborn Independent, a newspaper owned and published by Henry Ford, turned into an anti-Semitic vehicle, publishing the slanderous "Protocols of the Elders of Zion," a book used in France, Germany, and Russia to associate the Jew with an international conspiracy to dominate the world. Although sued and enjoined by the court to cease publication, Henry Ford never apologized to the Jewish people, nor stopped allowing the dissemination of the forged document through his resources.

FRANKLIN FORGERIES

Benjamin Franklin (1700–1790) was one of the founding fathers of the United States of America. He supported the "freedom of conscience" amendment and was favourably disposed to all minority groups. In 1930 there appeared an extract from a mythical journal supposedly authored by Charles Pinckney, which contained anti-Semitic statements attributed to Franklin. It was exposed as a forgery, but is still used by present-day anti-Semitic propagandists in associating the Jewish people with criminal tendencies.

NUMERUS CLAUSUS

This Latin phrase means "a

closed or limited number," and refers to restricting the number of Jews who desired to attend the higher schools of learning to a limited percentage of the total student body. In effect it is a "quota" system.

In the United States, many schools, especially private institutions, have been known to limit the admission of Jewish students. This is not based on an enunciated national policy. Schools justify their methods of selection by saying that they seek to avoid a concentration of any geographical, national, social, economic, racial, or religious groups in their student body. Except for tax-supported schools, which do not discriminate, each institution claims and defends its right to its own selection practices.

MODERN MANIFESTATIONS

Hiter's Nazism spilled over into the United States as it developed in Germany. The German-American Bund endeavored to spread the Nazi doctrines and practices. Threats were made against Jews individually and accusations made against them as a group. Swastikas were smeared on homes and synagogues. Unrestrained propaganda found sympathetic readers and listeners especially as the economic depression deepened.

Between 1933 and 1949, one hundred and fourteen anti-Semitic organizations were formed. In their wake followed a barrage of hate literature. Father Charles Coughlin used the pulpit of his church in a Detroit suburb, and a magazine, "Social Justice," to fan the flames of prejudice and intolerance against the Jews, until public outrage forced the Church to silence him.

On the march with a program of threats and violence were the Silver Shirts, the Black Shirts, and the Brown Shirts, which last were members of the German-American Bund that spread a Nazi-like doctrine. The Brown Shirts survived the war and under the leadership of George Lincoln Rockwell, who was assassinated by one of his own men, swastikas were again smeared on homes and synagogues, cemeteries desecrated, and bombs thrown. Arms caches and plans of attack were found by civil authorities who investigated these and other hate groups. The silence of the world when millions of Jews were being annihilated in Europe had its counterpart in the silence that greeted the emergence of organized postwar anti-Semitism in the United States.

Patterns of discrimination were considerably modified since the civil rights laws were passed. Progress is noted in the removal of many restrictive covenants, in legislation guaranteeing equal opportunity in employment, and in the abandonment of many restrictions in social clubs. But with the upheaval caused by Negro militants, the Jews were again caught as victims of anti-Semitism. This time the Negroes made them the scapegoats for their frustration. Thus, another injustice was added to the historically recurring cycle.

IMMIGRATION

1815—The first wave of Jewish immigration, until the beginning of the 19th century, is known as Sephardic or Spanish, since most of them were descendants of Jews from Spain and Portugal. They numbered about 3,000 at this time and settled along the Atlantic seaboard.

1815–1880—Following the Napoleonic wars and the collapse of liberal movements in Germany, there came a German-Jewish influx, which can be called the second wave of immigration and which spread throughout the middle west. The Jewish number reached 250,000 in the total United States population of 4,000,000.

New settlements were started at St. Louis (1816), Cincinnati (1817), Chicago (1837), and San Francisco (1849). The Germans' contribution to Jewish life was in the form of organizations to meet their socio-religious needs. The B'nai B'rith, with its subsidiaries, supplied social, cultural, and philanthropic purposes. The Joint Distribution Committee and the American Jewish Committee were outgrowths of interests generated from this group.

1881–1914—The third wave of immigration is known as the East European and included those from Russia, Poland, Austria-Hungary, Rumania, and the Baltic areas. Most of them settled along the eastern coast where, as manual workers, they gravitated to the labor movement. America became the new "Promised Land" for the poor Jews who fled the terror and oppression of the "old country." Jewish population increased to 3,500,000. From 1904 to 1909, over 100,000 Jewish immigrants arrived annually.

They brought with them a rich Yiddish culture, an intense Zionist feeling, and a vigorous Ashkenazic religious life. They considered themselves as living in Galuth—exile. This generation put great emphasis on the education of their children.

1924—A strong anti-foreign senti-ment resulted in the Johnson Act, which set immigration restrictions based on national origins. Jews who were the main victims of oppression were particularly affected, because they lived in countries whose quotas were very low and because the percentage of those originating from such countries was low in the total population in 1890. Their one avenue of rescue was cut off. This also meant that religious and cultural reinforcements from Europe were cut off and would not balance the assimilation tendencies in Jewish life.

1934–1952—During the Nazi holocaust and following World War II, some 300,000 Jews were admitted as refugees and "Displaced Persons."

1952—The McCarran-Walter Immigration and Nationality Act virtually closed the doors to immigration. In 1960 about 6,600 Jews entered the United States.

1965—The national origins basis for immigration remained unchanged until 1965 when a new law was passed. The new criteria did not lift the bars altogether, because it had to be proved that the skills of the applicant were not suppliable by citizens of the country. However, it did provide for reunion of families under certain conditions.

JEWISH POPULATION GROWTH

1818 ...	3,000	1910 ...	2,044,000
1824 ...	6,000	1917 ...	3,389,000
1840 ...	15,000	1927 ...	4,288,000
1848 ...	50,000	1937 ...	4,771,000
1877 ...	200,000	1954 ...	5,250,000
1888 ...	400,000	1957 ...	5,320,000
1897 ...	938,000	1965 ...	5,500,000
1905 ...	1,777,000		

THE JEWISH COMMUNITY

The Jewish people in the United States form the largest concentration of Jews in the world, numbering five-and-one-half million. They possess the fullest measure of religious freedom and security known in their history since the Exile. They are in almost all fields, especially in the clothing industry, in the labor movement, in entertainment, and in merchandising. Jewish names are to be found in farming, building, mining, publishing, chemistry, finance, transportation, and communications. There are relatively few in government, in the lumber or automotive industries, in banking, and many forms of big industries. They have made notable reputations in artistic endeavor, in music, art, and in the English, Hebrew, and Yiddish theater and literature.

The American Jewish community is honeycombed with organizations. The Kehillah, or community council of East European Jewry, was not actually transplanted to the United States, but there were LANDSMANN-SCHAFTEN, or mutual benefit societies, composed of individuals who emigrated from the same areas. The first one was organized by German Jews in New York in 1859, and by the first Polish group in 1870.

The B'nai B'rith was started in 1843; the Free Sons of Israel in 1849, and the B'rith Abraham in 1859. These offered sociability, mutual aid, and health or burial benefits. The B'nai B'rith Order later branched out to include a hospital program, Hillel Foundations on 62 campuses, A.Z.A., and B.B.Y.G. youth programs, a vocational service, and, of late years, projects in Israel.

In the field of education, in addition to the seminaries mentioned in the historical section of this chapter, the parochial Yeshivah or the American-Jewish day school, was started in the middle 1800's. They are still to be found in about 42 communities in 17 states. As public education improved, after-school and Sunday classes for Jewish instruction were started. The Talmud Torah school, unaffiliated with any congregation, developed at the end of the 19th century.

There are two Jewish-founded universities, (1) Yeshivah College in New York City, which was formed in 1915 from the merger of the Etz Chayim Yeshivah (1886), with the Rabbi Isaac Elchanan Theological Seminary (1896) and (2) Brandeis University (1948) at Waltham, Mass., which is nonsectarian and which completed a 50 million dollar building program, recruited a distinguished faculty, and was accredited by Phi Beta Kappa in its 13th year. There is one graduate institution for Jewish higher studies at the Dropsie College for Hebrew and Cognate Learning at Philadelphia, and there are also several centers of advanced Talmudic learning in New York City.

Auxiliary educational institutions developed, such as the Jewish Publication Society of Philadelphia (1888) and the American Jewish Historical Society (1892). There is a Jewish Museum, as well as large collections of Judaica and Hebraica in the various Jewish seminaries. Following World War II, YIVO, the Jewish Scientific Institute, which sponsors research about Jewish life and letters, moved to New York from Europe. In addition, there are teacher-training institutions and a People's University, also in New York City. There are vigorous Anglo-Jewish, Yiddish, and Hebrew publications covering the gamut of all cultural, social, philanthropic, and denominational interests.

The end of World War I saw the emergence of an all-inclusive institution in the community—the community center, which is native to the United States. It evolved from the Young Men's and Young Women's Hebrew Associations and usually houses membership organizations, athletic activities, social functions, a Hebrew School, a summer day camp, adult education, teen-age social and cultural programs, and meeting and dining rooms. By 1960 there were about 350 centers throughout the country, with a membership of over a half-million. These centers are coordinated and serviced by the Jewish Welfare Board, a lay group, which was started originally in 1917 to take care of the needs of Jews in the armed forces, an activity which it still retains.

Because of the legal, social, and vocational problems posed by mass Jewish immigration, several organizations developed. The United Service for New Americans (U.S.N.A.—1945), which itself was a merger of the National Refugee Service and the National Office of Service to the Foreign Born, was joined by the Hebrew Sheltering and Immigrant Aid Society (H.I.A.S.—1909). The latter was formed from a merger between the Hebrew Sheltering House Association (1884) and the Hebrew Immigrant Aid Society (1902). There is also the American ORT, which was founded in Russia (1880) as "the Society for the Encouragement of Handicraft." And there is the National Council of Jewish Women (1893), concerned with immigrants, Jewish welfare problems, and improvement generally.

During World War I, there also developed rescue agencies to meet emergencies in Jewish life due to the war. Reconstruction and rehabilitation were the purposes of the J.D.C.—The Joint Distribution Committee (1914). During the persecutions by Nazi Germany, its tasks multiplied, and to this day it is doing an effective job in transporting to safety, feeding, and sheltering Jews wherever they may be distressed. In 1938, it merged with the United Palestine Appeal, which is the main beneficiary in most cities of organized Jewish Welfare Fund Drives.

Another group of organizations fights persecution, discrimination, and bigotry leveled against anyone, but primarily against the Jews. Included are the American Jewish Committee (1906), which started as a result of the Russian pogroms; the American Jewish Congress (1918), which was interested as a Zionist group in proper representation for the Jewish people at the peace treaty after World War I, but is now active in legal aspects of discrimination; the Anti-Defamation League of the B'nai B'rith (1913), which combats anti-Semitism through education, social action, and agitation for adequate laws; and the Jewish Labor Committee (1934), which speaks for the Jewish labor union's interests.

Pursuant to the promise made to Governor Peter Stuyvesant, Jews have cared for most of their own welfare needs. As time passed, there were so many little philanthropic organizations duplicating efforts that their activities in the larger cities had to be coordinated. In smaller communities, all such welfare usually emanated from the synagogue. In New York City, the Federation of Jewish Charities (1917) was organized to raise over-all funds and establish policy. In time, there came into being a national organization, the Council of Jewish Federations and Welfare Funds. As time passed, governmental relief implemented Jewish help, but specific religious and ritual needs and problems were still handled by Jewish agencies. In a few cases, Jewish facilities were extended to the public, like the National Jewish Hospital in Denver, the Leo N. Levy Memorial Hospital in Hot Springs, the Jewish Braille Institute, and others.

Between 1948 and 1964, American responsibility for the survival of European Jewry, for helping Israel receive the homeless and unwanted Jew everywhere, and for increased community services reached a point where American Jews had provided nearly three-quarters of a billion dollars to meet the needs. Hadassah contributed $125,000,000 in medical care for immigrants into Israel; the Israel Bond Drive netted more than $600,000,000 in long-term loans. The Pioneer Women and ORT supplied large sums for their projects in the new homeland.

Throughout the years of American Jewish history there has been great pressure toward assimilation, starting with the day the immigrant set foot on American soil. The incidence of intermarriage is increasing, especially among the better-educated segments of the Jewish community. More than 80% of college-age youth are in college. Fewer and fewer Jews are public charges. Religious leaders are concerned with the problem of the survival of Judaism, and with what forms are best suited to this survival. Mordecai Kaplan's *Reconstructionist Movement* is the most recent solution offered by Jewish scholars.

The Jewish community became part of the struggle to separate Church and State when it supported the liberals on the Supreme Court in 1963, who said that religious indoctrination belongs in the church and the home, not in the school. In some extreme right-wing sectors this was an excuse for anti-Semitic attacks, which also continues because of their general support of integration. However, unless and until democracy fails to function in these United States, the Jewish population will be as safe as any minority group. So long as there are no periods of economic or political crises, Jews will be allowed to perform their civic functions and accept responsibilities in a free society like anyone else.

The Jews of Canada

While Canada was a French possession, Jews could not settle there in any appreciable numbers, nor could they start any communal organization. As individuals they shared in the commercial development of the colony and participated in the British occupation. The first sizable influx of Jews, who came in the middle of the 18th century, were Spanish-Portuguese. In 1768 they established a congregation, Shearith Israel, in Montreal. A second congregation came into being in Toronto about a century later.

In the 19th century English Jews migrated to Canada and were later followed by refugees from East European persecution. Until the 20th century the total Jewish population was less than 20,000. After the two World Wars they came in large waves, particularly following the advent of Hitler. By 1960, there were about 250,000, with the largest numbers in Montreal, Toronto, and Winnipeg, respectively.

At times the Jews encountered attempts to limit their civil rights. In 1807 a Jew was elected twice to the Quebec Assembly and expelled each time because he could not be sworn in according to his own religion. The Governor dissolved the legislature when it tried to enact a law that would prohibit Jews from holding office. In 1832 Canadian Jews received full equal rights with the passage of a bill known as the "Jews' Magna Charta."

The Jewish communities in Canada have a well-developed cultural, social, and institutional life, with Orthodox Jewry predominating. They are represented in all trades, professions, and industries and are considered on a par with the Jews of the United States.

JEWISH COMMUNITIES

Calgary	Regina
Edmonton	St. Catherine's
Halifax	Saskatoon
Hamilton	Toronto
London	Vancouver
Montreal	Windsor
Ottowa	Winnipeg
Quebec	

The Jews of Latin America

Jewish history in Latin America began with the Expulsions from Spain and Portugal in 1492. With the discovery of the New World by Columbus and with the Spanish and Portuguese conquests, Marrano Jews were among the early colonists. When the Church and the Inquisition came to Latin America, the Marrano Jews became subject to its cruel treatment. What seemed a promising future ended in disillusionment and migration. At the beginning of the 19th century there were very few Jewish communities in South America.

It was not until the 1890's that new immigrants from Turkey, the Middle East, and North Africa came to Argentina. And from East Europe came Jews to settle in Brazil and Uruguay. They were aided by the Jewish Colonization Association (ICA) founded and largely supported by Baron Edmond de Hirsch.

After World War I, when quotas closed the doors of the United States to large-scale immigration, the stream started to flow into the countries of South America and continued through the tragic years of Hitlerism.

Jews never achieved the economic and social position in Latin America that they did in the United States and Canada. Their economic security was also endangered in the 1930's and 40's when Nazi influence became powerful in even the more advanced republics. And since the establishment of the State of Israel, Arab elements throughout Latin America have been responsible for anti-Jewish propaganda and incidents.

The typical Latin-American Jewish community is made up of Sephardim, East European Ashkenazim, and Central European Jews. Language and custom differences divided them, but Zionism and the World Jewish Congress were unifying factors and have helped to counteract anti-Semitism.

Spiritually and culturally, Judaism is on the wane. There is little or no Jewish education except for the very young, and where it is provided, only about one-third of the children take advantage of it. Intermarriage and assimilation have increased sharply. Many synagogues have no rabbinical leadership. The mainstream of Jewish life, where it does exist, follows Orthodox practice in the synagogue and in its culture and literature.

Today, some 620,000 Jews live in the lands of Latin America. The largest communities are in Argentina, Brazil, and Mexico. The smallest, consisting of just a few families, are found in the Caribbean Islands.

MAJOR JEWISH COUNTRIES

Argentina	450,000
Bolivia	4,200
Brazil	130,000
Chile	35,000
Colombia	9,000
Cuba (before Castro)	10,000
Ecuador	3,000
Mexico	30,000
Peru	4,000
Uruguay	40,000
Venezuela	6,000

THE SMALLER COUNTRIES

Aruba	175
British Guiana	30
Barbados	80
Costa Rica	1,200
Curaçao	750
Dominican Republic	600
Dutch Guiana	650
El Salvador	320
Guatemala	1,000
Haiti	200
Honduras	150
Jamaica	1,500
Martinique	100
Nicaragua	200
Panama	2,000
Paraguay	1,500
Puerto Rico	1,450
Trinidad and Tobago	180
Virgin Islands	175
Surinam	410

The Jews of Argentina

Argentina has the largest and most successful Jewish settlement in Latin America. Marrano Jews came from Spain in the 16th century but it was not until 1868 that the first Jewish settlement was founded by Louis H. Brie in Buenos Aires.

The main flux of East European Jews came after the Russian pogroms of the 1880's, when Baron Edmond de Hirsch financed the establishment of a number of colonies under the auspices of the Jewish Colonization Association (ICA). Between 1904 and 1915, 83,000 Jewish immigrants came to Argentina. After World War I, there was a large Sephardic influx from the Mediterranean areas. From 1920 to 1938 immigration averaged from six to seven thousand a year. By 1946 there were 450,000 Jews living in the country.

After World War I, the highly industrialized European countries, especially Germany and Italy, established themselves in Argentina. With them came Fascism, Nazi propaganda, and anti-Semitism. German infiltration in the government was responsible for anti-democratic and anti-American feeling. Although other Latin American countries joined the Pan-American front during World War II, Argentina remained neutral despite her sympathy toward the Axis powers until just before the close of the war, when she joined the Allies for the purpose of having a seat at the peace table.

In 1946, Juan Peron emerged as the dictator after years of Fascist complicity and cooperation. Though seemingly opposed to anti-Semitism, he merely expressed official regret in the face of increased desecrations and outbreaks.

By 1955, resentment against Peron erupted and he fled the country, leaving behind many loyal followers known as Peronistas. The new government sought to bring the country back into the pro-Western democratic community. But unemployment and discontent brought nascent anti-Semitism and outbreaks by youth Fascist groups. The kidnaping of Adolph Eichmann by Israeli agents caused additional terrorism, but in the national elections of 1963 the Peronistas were defeated and a strong democratic leadership emerged.

JEWISH LIFE

About 80% of Argentina's Jews live in Buenos Aires, but small Jewish settlements can be found in more than 500 towns and villages. There are twenty Jewish Colonization Association settlements, some of them having celebrated their 75th anniversary.

Internal Jewish affairs are organized according to Israeli party allegiance, making members of the Mapai party the official spokesmen for the Jewish community. The growth of anti-Semitism, the increasing number of non-practicing Jews, the identification of Jewish university students with leftist political parties, and the general downgrading of religion and Jewish education have become a threat to Jewish community unity and survival.

Jewish education is chiefly on a primary level. Yiddish is fostered through the theater, newspaper, and other cultural enterprises. The Zionist movement is very active, encouraging emigration to Israel. Politically, the Jews are represented by the Delegacion de Asociaciones Israelitas Argentinas (DAIA), composed of delegates from all existing organizations. Local community councils, numbering about 120, are affiliated with a central body called the "Vaad HaKehilloth," which deals with education, culture, religion, and social problems.

The Jewish population in 1964 was about 450,000.

JEWISH COMMUNITIES (500 AND OVER)

Avellaneda	Moisesville
Basavilbaso	Parana
Bernasconi	Resistencia
Buenos Aires	Rivera
Concordia	Rosaria
Cordoba	Santa Fe
Coronel Suarez	San Juan
General Roco	Tucuman
Medanos	

The Jews of Brazil

In the century following the Spanish Inquisition, Marrano Jews left Spain and Portugal for the New World. Many settled in Brazil. Fernando de Noronha, a Brazilian pioneer (1503), is thought to have been a Marrano. When the Inquisition came to Brazil many Jews forsook their religion.

With the Dutch conquest of Brazil in 1631, the Inquisition ceased and many Marranos declared their Jewish faith openly. The Portuguese reconquered the country in 1654, and again many Jews were forced to leave for other havens. Twenty-three of these refugees came to New Amsterdam to establish the first Jewish community in the United States. Two centuries later (1852), with the proclamation of Brazilian independence, Marrano Jews again were able to revert to Judaism.

There were less than 3,000 Jews in Brazil before the 20th century, but the number increased when, in 1924, the United States quota system closed its doors to large-scale Jewish immigration. By World War II, the Jewish population had increased to 110,000, mostly in urban centers.

During the depression, following 1929, Fascist elements were able to gain a foothold and to spread anti-Semitism. This was owing primarily to the decline of Brazil's coffee-based economy. There were about a million-and-a-half Germans and a similar number of Italians among whom Fascist cells proliferated.

In 1934, when Getulio Vargas, the quasi-military dictator, came to power, Nazism went underground. He opposed Zionism, Yiddish newspapers, and the expansion of the Jewish parochial system. His goal was cultural autonomy for the whole country, in which separatism had no place. Following his suicide in 1954, his successor, Joao Cafe Filho, espoused cultural pluralism, dedicated Jewish institutions, and participated in Jewish communal functions.

Succeeding presidents were favorable to the Jews. Juscelino Kubitscheck (1956) refused citizenship to a Latvian Nazi mass-killer. Joao Quadros (1960) ordered the elimination of dictionary definitions derogatory to the Jews.

When Nasser came to power in Egypt, Brazil offered sanctuary to more than 5,000 Egyptian Jews. There are now about 130,000 Jews in Brazil out of a total population of 54,000,000. Most of them are concentrated in the large cities of Rio de Janeiro and Recife.

In the last decade there has been little anti-Semitism manifested in the country. There is a United Zionist organization known as Unificada. Jewish education is supervised by the Federation of Jewish charities. The language of instruction is Portuguese, with some subjects taught in Hebrew or Yiddish.

JEWISH COMMUNITIES

Bahia
Belem
Curitiba
Bello Horizonte
Manaos
Parana
Porto Alegre
Recife
Rio de Janeiro
Salvador
Sao Paulo

The Jews of Chile

Marrano Jews settled chiefly in Santiago during early Spanish rule, but the Inquisition prevented any open observance of Judaism. After gaining independence in 1810, and the granting of religious liberty, Jews began to immigrate, but their population did not exceed 3,000 by 1914. After World War I a Jewish community was formally organized and there are now three synagogues in Santiago and one in Valparaiso. After 1933 there was considerable Jewish immigration, but from 1939 to 1950 it was restricted to 200 to 300 annually. Except for a small number of Hungarian refugees who were permitted to enter in 1957, immigration has practically ceased.

The Jewish community numbers about 30,000, with the largest group, East Europeans, followed in size by the German-speaking group, and then the Sephardim who hail from Greece, Turkey, and Gibraltar. It is administered by the Comite Representativo, which includes 40 affiliated organizations.

As a group, Jews do not play a role in the political life of the country, although there have been a few outstanding citizens. The Zionist federation represents all groups from Herut to Mapam. The prevailing language is Spanish, but Yiddish- and German-speaking groups have their own clubs. There has been little overt anti-Semitism except for that resulting from the agitation of a minority of Arabs during the Israeli-Arab war.

The "Vaad HaChinarch" is responsible for Jewish education. The curriculum is the same as in Spanish-speaking public schools, with additional instruction in Hebrew and Yiddish. Only about 25% of the Jewish children attend these schools.

JEWISH COMMUNITIES

Concepcion
Rancagua
Santiago
Temuco
Valdivia
Valparaiso

The Jews of Colombia

Marranos from Curaçao settled in Barranquilla and Cali early in the 16th century, but were eliminated by the Inquisition. A few Jews came in the middle of the 19th century. It was not until after World War I that they came from Eastern Europe, Palestine, and later from Germany. After 1939 Jewish immigration was forbidden. Now, most of the country's 9,000 Jews are Ashkenazic and live in the three principal cities, Bogota, Barranquilla, and Cali.

Their economic situation is good, with many engaged in industry and trade. All the communities are affiliated with the World Jewish Congress and all the organizations in the various communities are represented on a council or central committee that regulates Jewish life.

The Jews of Cuba

The Inquisition came to Cuba in the 16th century and the Jewish community of Marranos, who had come following the conquest of Spain, were prevented from practicing their Judaism. There is little record of Jewish history until the 19th century, when Rumanian Jews, naturalized in the United States, went to Cuba from Florida.

Jews befriended José Marti, leader for Cuban independence, and helped him fight for the freedom of the country. After World War I, East European and Austrian immigrants came to Cuba, hoping to proceed to the United States, but many stayed as permanent residents. In 1947 Jewish immigration was stopped.

Before the Castro regime, 90% of Cuba's 10,000 Jews lived in Havana. Under the Communist economy they suffered heavily from expropriation and totalitarian rule, which caused large numbers to leave for the United States. It is estimated that about 2,500 remain in the country.

The Jews of Ecuador

A few Ashkenazic families settled in Quito and some Sephardic families in Guayaquil in 1904. Immigration increased during Hitlerism in Europe, when about 3,000 Jews came. Most of them settled in Quito. By 1950 the total Jewish population was 4,000. Their initiative was most evident in the growth of the number of industries. At first they were welcomed, but anti-Semitic propaganda aroused resentment against them. Since 1945

many have left and the economic situation of those who remained is very unsatisfactory. There was no Jewish school in Ecuador until 1954, when two Israeli women started a Kindergarten. The Jewish organizations are dominantly Zionistic.

The Jews of Bolivia

During the Spanish domination (1531–1825) many Marranos came to Bolivia, settling in Potosi as silver miners. The country was then part of Peru and when the Inquisition reached there in 1570, the Jews were persecuted, imprisoned, or burned. Those who survived were assimilated into the Catholic population. The establishment of the republic in 1825 brought religious toleration, and once again Jews settled there.

Immigration began in 1905 but was negligible until the 1920's, when many arrived from Poland, and the 1930's, when many came from Germany. In 1938 the government offered free land to farmers and 200 refugees settled at Villie Sacaba. Between 1933 and 1942, 7,000 Jews immigrated to Bolivia. In 1940 the government issued a decree prohibiting the admission of Jews and even the issuance of transit visas was denied them. The restriction was lifted temporarily in 1947 when the government admitted Jewish war orphans, but since that time there has been little immigration.

There are about 4,200 Jews in Bolivia, most of whom are Ashkenazic and live in Lapas and Cachabamba. Small numbers are found in Oruro, Santa Cruz, Sucre, and Tarija. They are most active in industry and mercantile enterprises, many of which deal with imports.

The Jews of Mexico

The first Jewish settlers were Marranos who came with the conquistadores early in the 16th century from Spain and Portugal. They sought in vain to escape the Inquisition, which was active for two centuries. Jewish practices were forbidden until the beginning of the 19th century, at about which time some German, French, and East European Jews came to Mexico. They were joined by Sephardim from Syria, Turkey, and Greece. By 1910 there were about 10,000 Jews in the country.

After World War I, Jews came from Damascus and Aleppo, and more from European countries. Most of them settled in Mexico City. In 1937 future Jewish immigration was barred completely, but following World War II a few refugees from Hungary were permitted to enter.

By 1959, of the 30,000 Jews in the country, about 2,500 were living outside of Mexico City in 17 provincial towns. Of the total population most are Ashkenazim, many are Sephardim, and there are about 2,000 Indian Jews who claim Spanish-Jewish ancestry. This latter group has its own synagogue in Mexico City.

After World War II, several Fascist parties developed, encouraged by a few leading Catholics and by powerful industrialists who were ready to exploit anti-Semitic unrest in order to discredit the government. In 1956, a vicious anonymous anti-Semitic pamphlet was distributed. Jews were understandably concerned as they watched the subsidized rallies of the Sinarquist Party and the multiplication of anti-Semitic articles and publications sponsored by the Fascist Yel-low Shirts. They were relieved when the workers resisted the development of Fascism, and when the United States made it clear that she would not tolerate either a Fascist or Communist base in Mexico.

The Jewish community enjoys comparative peace of mind in a reasonably healthy community. An outstanding Jewish philanthropist, Elias Surasky, presented school buildings to the government at a cost of more than a million dollars. He also built a lavish Jewish Sports Club for the community, which has no Jewish signs or symbols outside the building, but which is decorated in the hallways by wall paintings of Jewish historical events.

Jews pioneered in the industrial development of the country, especially in the manufacture of textiles, electrical appliances, plastics, metals, and clothing. Many were also engaged in minor commercial activities. Some were tailors, shoemakers, and jewelers. About 10% were in the professions.

The first Jewish community was organized in Mexico City in 1909 by Sephardim from Aleppo, although their synagogue was not built until 1931. The first Ashkenazic group started the "Juventad Israelita" in 1917, and American Jews living in Mexico established a Young Men's Hebrew Association in 1918. As Ashkenazic immigration increased, they also started a congregation, "Nidhei Israel," which numbers over a thousand families.

All Jewish organizations are joined together in a "Comite Central Israelita de Mexico," which is recognized by the government as representing Mexican Jewry. The community maintains Jewish schools that are attended by 85% of all Jewish children. They speak

Spanish, but also learn Hebrew and Yiddish.

JEWISH COMMUNITIES

Guadalajara
Mexico City
Monterey
Tijuana

The Jews of Peru

By the 16th century the Marranos who settled in Peru had achieved a significant position in the trade and commerce of the country. Spain's introduction of the Inquisition in 1569 ended this era. Among the martyrs of the Inquisition was Manuel B'antista Perez, considered the richest man in the country. His wealth was confiscated and only those of his co-religionists who could pay 200,000 ducats to the governor were spared. It was not until 1870 that Alsatian Jews established a community in Peru. Within a half-century they were almost completely assimilated and only a cemetery in Lima remains in mute testimony.

Although there is practically no immigration of Jews, there are manifestations of anti-Semitism in the press and periodic public demonstrations. Only about 30% of the Jews have been granted citizenship. Their economic position, as a whole, is satisfactory, especially in trade and manufacturing. Politically, they are excluded from government positions. Most Jews live in Lima, with a few scattered in smaller cities. The majority are from East Europe, with the rest equally divided between the Sephardim and those who are classified as German-speaking.

JEWISH COMMUNITIES

Arequipa
Ica
Iquitos
Lima
Pinia
Trujillo

The Jews of Uruguay

At the end of the 19th century there were few Jews in Uruguay. By 1925 there were 1,800, most of them coming from East Europe, Turkey, and other oriental countries. Between 1926 and 1943 about 15,000 more came, with an additional few thousand after World War II. Immigration is now restricted.

Uruguay is the most democratic of the Latin American countries with respect to equal rights for the Jews. But a political party with an avowed anti-Semitic platform does exist. The government, however, supports the Zionist cause and is friendly with the state of Israel.

The Jewish population is divided into four groups, each of which has its own synagogue: Ashkenazic, Sephardic, German-speaking, and Hungarian. Most of them live in Montevideo, with large numbers participating in the economic and political life of the country. They are well represented in the field of merchandising, in industry, and as artisans. About one-fourth of the Jewish children attend the schools maintained by the Jewish community. The present population is 40,000. Montevideo, with 36,000, has five synagogues, two Yeshivoth, and six rabbis.

JEWISH COMMUNITIES

Flores
Las Piedras
Mercedes
Montevideo
Minas
Paysandu
Rivera
Rocha
Salto

The Jews of Venezuela

The Jewish community in Venezuela is little over 100 years old, with the first arrivals coming from North Africa in 1850. A few families came from the Caribbean Islands in 1873. By 1935 there were about 1,500 in the country, most of them coming from East Europe and Germany. By the end of World War ii further immigration was barred.

The Jewish community is interested in the State of Israel and in Jewish education. Secularly, they are active in trade, industry, and the professions. Most of them live in Caracas, free of anti-Semitism, although only about 60% of the Jewish population has been granted citizenship. The Jewish population is about 6,000.

JEWISH COMMUNITIES

Caracas
Maracaibo
Maracay
Valencia

9

The Organizational Life of the Jew

The Jewish Community

Within Jewish life there has always been a strong sense of community and a need for some form of central authority, especially when the people were living under foreign and hostile rule. During Bible times, group life centered around the Patriarchs, then the priesthood, Judges, and the Kings. Life in the Diaspora made it necessary to establish authoritative bodies that were recognized by local governments and granted autonomy to control and regulate intra-Jewish affairs.

The structure of the Jewish community today has many semblances to those of the past. Its activities and destiny are interlocked with the problems and needs of world Jewry, but each community is independent, although some local efforts are coordinated under democratically constituted national bodies.

THE COMMUNITY IN BIBLE TIMES

The first known Jewish community centered around the Patriarch Abraham, who was the tribal head of his people. When he traveled from one territory to another, his entire tribe went with him. Scripture tells us that when Jacob journeyed to Egypt to join his son Joseph, a family of seventy souls accompanied him.

During the wanderings of the children of Israel in the wilderness, the institution of the Priesthood, with its divisions and classes, was established. The Tabernacle, with its sacrificial cult, became the center of Jewish life. The responsibilities of the individual to the community became clearly defined and later were mandated in Biblical law. Offerings, tithing, sanctions, and penalties were controlled by the priesthood, but appointed elders were the administrators of the village or community. They were responsible for order and justice in addition to the collection of taxes and the care of the poor.

The unified Patriarch family or "Mishpachah" existed until the time of Moses, when upon the advice of his father-in-law Jethro, he appointed heads, known as ZEKENIM— זקנים —ELDERS or ADMINISTRATORS of the community, over smaller groups into which he divided the people. These leaders ranked according to the number of people under their jurisdiction and were selected for their wisdom and piety. Moses is said to have formed them into a council of seventy members, where they represented their respective groups. (Numbers 11 : 16)

These Elders were not primarily judicial officers, although they came to be called Judges in a later period. Following the death of Joshua, many tribes were ruled by judges who were called MISHPATIM—משפטים. They were military leaders as well as administrators and they assumed all the responsibilities involved in ruling.

With the establishment of the monarchy under Saul and David, the Jewish people experienced greater centralization of communal control. The kings levied taxes, conscripted men for war and labor camps, and enforced the civil laws. Every town had its own community organization, which was responsible to the king. The priesthood, through its Temple organization, regulated the religious life of the people.

As far as is known, this pattern prevailed for centuries until the Exile to Babylonia (586 BCE). After the return to Palestine, the people were guided by a KNESSETH— כנסת —an ASSEMBLY of leaders invested with civil and religious jurisdiction. This body was known as the KNESSETH GADOLAH— כנסת גדולה —THE GREAT ASSEMBLY, and was convened by Ezra the Scribe in 444 BCE. Its size and composition varied from 70 in the days of the Second Temple to 120 in Talmudic times.

THE SANHEDRIN

The word SANHEDRIN— סנהדרין —is the Hebraized form of the Greek word SYNEDRION, which means ASSEMBLY. This council of elders, which functioned as a court and legislature during the Second Commonwealth, resembled both the 70-member Council of Elders appointed by Moses and the Knesseth Gadolah of Ezra's time. Its presiding judge, who was called NASI— נשיא —PRINCE, was the 71st member. Next in authority was the AB BETH DIN— אב בית דין —THE FATHER OF THE HOUSE OF JUDGMENT. The primary functions of the Sanhedrin were to judge all civil and religious cases, determine the new moon, arrange the calendar in leap years, and exercise the right of excommunication. There was a lesser council called SANHEDRIN KETANAH— סנהדרין קטנה —which consisted of 23 members. Its jurisdiction extended to communities outside of Jerusalem and involved only civil and criminal cases.

In Talmudic times, the Sanhedrin became known as ANSHE KNESSETH HA-GADOLAH— אנשי כנסת הגדולה —THE MEN OF THE GREAT ASSEMBLY. This body of scholars carried on the chain of tradition of interpreting the law and making it available to the people. Because of its widely accepted legal decisions it was also known as the BETH DIN HA-GADOLAH— בית דין הגדולה —THE HOUSE OF THE GREAT COURT. Among the specific tasks of the Great Assembly were those of arranging and classifying the Oral Law, instituting prayers and benedictions, and canonizing the Bible.

UNDER GREEK RULE

Jews have lived in semi-autonomous communities ever since the fourth century BCE, when Alexander the Great conquered Palestine. The Egyptian Ptolemies and the Syrian Seleucidan rulers favored limited self-rule for their Jewish subjects. In Alexandria, they were allowed their own legislative and consultative assembly called GERUSIA, and a Jewish administrator or tax-collector, called ALABARCH.

UNDER ROMAN RULE

During Roman rule the Jewish people was permitted to regulate its own religious life, but the political part of the Sanhedrin continued to direct public affairs and administer criminal law under the Roman procurator. The Jewish community Council was known as the MA-AMAD ANSHE HA-IR— מעמד אנשי העיר —LEADERS OF THE PEOPLE OF THE CITY. The members of the council were called PARNASSIM— פרנסים —or ZEKENIM— זקנים, and varied in number from seven to twelve. The officials of the council included a president called RESH MATA— ראש מטה — HEAD OF THE CITY; a court of justice, BETH DIN— בית דין, consisting of at least three members; a SOFER— סופר —COMMUNITY SCRIBE or NOTARY; and appointed representatives for collecting and dispensing charity.

ACADEMIES

Academies were primarily schools of higher learning where rabbinic studies were pursued. They flourished during the Talmudic period in Palestine and Babylonia and exerted a wide influence upon the intellectual and spiritual life of the people. The deliberations of the scholars in the various academies resulted in the accumulation of a vast tradition embodied in an extensive literature. The Palestinian schools that were already in existence became more important after the fall of the Second Temple.

Because of the dual nature of Jewish tradition, embracing learning and law, the academies were referred to as schools of learning and courts of law. Hence such names as YESHIVAH— ישיבה —"House of Session,"

BETH HA-MIDRASH— בית המדרש —"House of Study," SANHEDRIN— סנהדרן "Law Body," and BETH DIN— בית דין —"House of Judgment."

The first academy founded after the fall of the Temple (70 CE) was at Jabneh (Yavneh) by Jochanan ben Zakkai. It succeeded the Sanhedrin as an academy of scholars but it did not have the same legal authority. Other academies were subsequently founded by individual scholars. After the Bar Cochba rebellion in 135 CE, the center of Jewish learning moved north to Galilee, with the central school of authority located at Usha. This was the first of many moves over the centuries during which the Mishnah and the Jerusalem Talmud were codified.

Among the many tasks of the academies were the enactment of new ordinances, fixing the text of the Prayer Book, settling the canonicity of the Bible, rendering decisions in the form of Responsa, and arranging for Kallahs—meetings of scholars and lay officials. Other of the more important academies were located at various times at Tiberias, Pekin, Bet Shearim, Shepharam, Caesarea, Sepphoris, Lydda, Nehardea, Nisibis, Nehar, and Mata Mehasya, but the supremacy of those at Sura and Pumbeditha was recognized by all Jewry.

Although academies continued to exist until the thirteenth century, their real importance ended in the eleventh century. Since then the name has been used for schools of rabbinic studies, but there was no longer the luster lent by the brilliance of the famous scholars attributed to those academies of old.

THE GAONATE

The word GAON— גאון —means "pride" or "excellency," and was accorded to outstanding heads of the two major Babylonian academies at Sura and Pumbeditha. It is derived from the phrase in Psalm 47 : 5— "Gaon Ya-akob"— גאון יעקב —"Pride of Jacob."

The institution of the Gaonate started in 589 and lasted almost 500 years. The Gaonim were recognized as the official authoritative body and spokesmen throughout world Jewry. They sponsored semi-annual Kallahs (Assemblies), which attracted laymen, rabbis and students for the exposition of moot questions on Torah, Talmud, and Diaspora problems. They created a literature known as Responsa, which contained answers and commentaries to questions propounded by Jewish communities. Some of the more outstanding Gaonim were Rav Yehudai Gaon, Rav Saadiah Gaon, Rav Sherira Gaon, and Rav Hai Gaon.

After the eleventh century, the title "Gaon" was used as recognition of the superiority of any outstanding Talmudic scholar, such as Elijah Gaon of Vilna (1720–1797).

DIASPORA— תפוצות —TEFUTZOTH

Diaspora is a Greek word that means "dispersion" and refers to all Jewish people living beyond the borders of Palestine (Israel). Wars have been the major cause of displacing persons and the Jews of Palestine were frequently subjected to exile, which was called "Golah." Not all exiled Jews lived in captivity. Many were free to recreate their Jewish way of life and became permanent residents of their adopted country. The Book of Esther tells us that the Jews who lived in Persia were scattered throughout the provinces. A Jewish colony flourished in Egypt in the fifth century before the common era.

During the Second Commonwealth, many Jews were living in countries neighboring Palestine, particularly in the Greek Isles, the Roman provinces, Egypt, and North Africa. After the fall of the Temple (70 CE), wherever they lived they were labeled as dispersed or Diaspora Jews. Today the world outside the State of Israel is still called the Diaspora.

Diaspora Jews have preserved their culture and adhered to their religion. In the Babylonian countries they developed the Talmud and created many academies of learning. In Spain they produced a "Golden Age" of literature. In Poland they developed the highly organized Vaad, the Community Council. In Eastern Europe they created world-renowned Yeshivoth and noted rabbis. In the United States they have contributed to the moral and spiritual life of the American people.

About ten million Jews live in the Diaspora. The latest populations records show the following :

The United States	5,500,000
Soviet Russia	2,300,000
France	500,000
Argentina	450,000
England	450,000
Canada	250,000
Rumania	130,000
Brazil	130,000
Morocco	125,000
South Africa	110,000

THE COMMUNITY IN THE DIASPORA

After the fall of the Second Temple (70 CE) and the dispersion of the Jews throughout the world, there was no longer any one central authority to regulate all of Jewish life. Each community was allowed to organize independently to provide facilities for worship, to maintain schools, ritual bath houses, a cemetery, and societies for mutual aid. It was convenient for the rulers to have a central authority with which to deal.

The Babylonian Jewish communities were under the jurisdiction of an Exilarch, appointed by the Caliph, assisted by a council consisting of from seven to ten men.

In Portugal the Jews were granted autonomy in civil and criminal matters under a Chief Rabbi ("Rabbi Mor") who was an officer of the Crown. He approved the appointment of rabbis and teachers, supervised the estates of orphans, examined the local community accounts, and collected delinquent taxes. On his staff were a chief Justice ("Ouvidor") who was an expert in Halachah; a Chancellor who was the keeper of the official seal and documents; and a Marshall (Escriteiro) who executed decrees, seizures, and punishments. The internal affairs of the community were regulated by deputies (Procuradores) assisted by selectmen (Tove Ha-ir) or (Homes Boas das Communas), and a notary (Scribe).

In Spain, the Moors allowed self-regulation to the Jewish communities in the form of the ALJAMA, the Arabic word meaning "to gather." The leader was the intermediary between the community and the government. In the 13th century, when Spain became Christian, each bishop ruled the Jews in his diocese, with the aid of elders, rabbis, and religious judges chosen by each "Aljama de los Judios." The head of this council had to be approved by the regional bishop. He had various titles : "Rab de la corte," or Rab Mayor (Court or Chief Rabbi), or "Juez Mayor" (Chief Justice).

The Jews of Moravia in the 16th century had a Chief Rabbi and a Central Council, which continued until 1925 in Czechoslovakia. When the country was under Austrian rule some of the former autonomous rights were curtailed except for the well-organized system of Jewish education.

In France, Germany, and Italy, when there was no publicly recognized central authority, there was still the need for conferences of Rabbis and Jewish lay leaders on common religious and legal problems. Synods were formed in Northern France and the Rhineland, which met periodically to examine and re-affirm the ordinances of previous assemblies. Although early synods were mostly juristic, later ones were concerned with fiscal, defensive, and political matters.

During the Middle Ages in Central Europe, the Jews were considered the personal property of the feudal kings and were governed in their communities by a JUDEN-BISCHOF (Bishop of the Jews) or a JUDEN-MEISTER (Master of the Jews). As the rabbi and tax collector, he had to enforce the king's harsh laws and demands.

Sultan Mohammed, the Conqueror (1451–1481) of Turkey, appointed a "Hacham Bashi" or Chief Rabbi to be the official representative of the Jews before the Turkish government. He sat in the Turkish state council beside the Moslem Mufti and the Greek Orthodox Patriarch. The "Hacham Bashi" apportioned and collected taxes, acted as judge, appointed rabbis, and administered the affairs of the Jewish community. Later, the Jews were allowed to choose their own Chief Rabbi, subject to ratification by the government.

THE KAHAL OR KEHILLAH— קהל–קהלה —COMMUNITY COUNCIL

During part of their history in the Diaspora, the Jewish people was subject to and represented by a central authority vested in a democratically constituted body called the KAHAL—קהל—COMMUNITY COUNCIL. Among East European Jews, where it rose to its most influential form, it was known as the KEHILLAH. It was concerned with all matters affecting the Jew in his relation to the king, the State, and the Church. It was recognized by the government as the agent of the people and spoke for and acted in their behalf. As a self-governing body, it could enforce cooperation by imposing religious sanctions. As an autonomous agency, it had full authority to safeguard and promote the religious, educational, and social life of the people. It lasted in some countries until the 19th century, when it was abolished. But, with variations, it exists in some form in many communities today.

When the Kehillah was at its height, it was responsible for the following :

1. *Taxation*

    Every able-bodied individual had to contribute to the community treasury, not only for its own philanthropic needs, but also for the taxes levied against the entire Jewish community.

2. *Government Representation*

    In economic and political matters, and in dealings with the ruling power, the leaders of the Kehillah were the spokesmen for all the Jews and the bargaining agent when their welfare was involved.

3. *Internal Affairs*

    The council had full legal authority to appoint committees, representatives, and judges to regulate the internal affairs of the community. This included matters of marriage, divorce, and civil suits, the sale and purchase of property, the fixing of standards of weights and measures, the stabilization of prices and wages, the censoring of morals, trying minor criminal cases, and the responsibility for protecting the community. It could impose penalties and decree excommunication.

4. *Religious and Cultural Activities*

The Kehillah was required to establish courts, schools, and synagogues; appoint judges, rabbis, cantors, ritual slaughterers, and overseers of charity; and supervise ritual functions, such as public bath-houses and slaughtering.

5. *Benevolent Institutions*

Every Jewish community undertook the responsibility of caring for the sick and the poor, the widow, the orphan, and the aged. Benevolent societies and fellowships were organized to implement the practice of Tzedakah.

THE KEHILLAH OF THE MIDDLE AGES

The highest form of the KAHAL or KEHILLAH was developed during the 16th to the 18th centuries in Poland. There it was included by various rulers in the Royal Charters that granted complete Jewish autonomy to the communities. While the Kehillah had self-determination, it was wholly dependent upon the government for protection, for which it had to pay special taxes and assessments. Because of its far-reaching functions it became a very powerful institution.

A group of KEHILLOTH were sometimes organized into provincial bodies called MEDINOTH— מדינות. Regional meetings were held to settle litigation between communities, adjudicate appellate cases, and supervise local Kahals. The VAAD HA-MEDINOTH—ועד המדינות—had its own Chief Rabbi, who was recognized as the spokesman for all the Kahals in the province.

THE COUNCIL OF THE FOUR LANDS

In Poland, four Medinoth combined to form the VAAD ARBA ARATZOTH —ועד ארבע ארצות—THE COUNCIL OF THE FOUR LANDS. Represented were the provinces of GREATER POLAND, with its center at Posen; LITTLE POLAND, with its center at Cracow and Lublin; the UKRAINE (PODOLIA-VOLHYNIA), with its center at Astrog and Ludmir; and GALICIA, or RED RUSSIA, with its center at Lemberg. A fifth Vaad, LITHUANIA, participated with the other four at the annual sessions, but withdrew in 1623. The VAAD met twice every year and was attended by SHTADLANIM—שתדלנים —official delegates or representatives. They elected a presiding officer, who was called ROSH HA-KAHAL—ראש הקהלה—THE HEAD OF THE COUNCIL.

These council meetings were also attended by throngs of visitors who came from far and near to hear the decisions of the renowned rabbis and scholars. The gatherings resembled the pilgrimages to Jerusalem in Bible days, with the spirit of festivity prevailing.

In 1746 the VAAD was abolished by the Polish government, and in 1821, when Russia ruled Poland, even the local Kehilloth were disbanded. However, modifications of the basic pattern of communal living and collective management were preserved by those who lived in the ghettos of Poland and Lithuania. As emancipation dawned for the Jews, it brought assimilation and the abandonment of Jewish group living that had been responsible for the continuity and vitality of traditional Judaism.

Community Organizations

Over the centuries the Jewish people has looked to many types of appointed or elected bodies for leadership and direction. Following are some of these community organizations:

BETH AM—בית עם—HOUSE OF THE PEOPLE

A common name designating a place where the people assembled for various purposes.

COMMUNITY COUNCIL

In modern times, Jewish communities in western countries have formed voluntary associations composed of heads of Jewish organizations. The council derives its authority from the constituent organizations and promotes philanthropic, educational, and social functions.

CHEVER IR—חבר עיר—A CITY ASSOCIATION

This was a politico-Jewish community council of early times, representing the Jewish people and responsible to the ruling power.

EDAH—עדה—CONGREGATION

A Biblical name for an assembly or association of people for devotional purposes; also known in Greek times as *synodos, syllogos,* and *synagogue.*

FATTORI

An executive committee of the Jewish community in Italy, responsible to Papal authority for all Jews.

GERUSIA—גרוסא—COUNCIL OF ELDERS

Under Greek rule this Council of Elders functioned in the city of Jerusalem. It was headed by the High Priest and was a self-governing body responsible to the Greek authorities. This Council of Elders became the nucleus for the Sanhedrin.

KAHAL—קהל—or KEHILLAH—קהלה—COMMUNITY or CONGREGATION

A body of elected or appointed men, approved by the government. This group had jurisdiction over religious and most secular affairs in some European countries.

KNESSETH—כנסת—ASSEMBLY PLACE

A place of meeting for general purposes. This was an early name

for the synagogue, which was used not only for prayer and instruction, but also for discussing and settling affairs of the individual
and the group.

MA-AMAD ANSHE HA-IR—מעמד אנשי העיר—LEADERS OF THE PEOPLE

These leaders of the city comprised a governing body of Jews
under Roman rule. It consisted of a president, a court of justice, a
scribe or notary, and appointed representatives for the collection and
distribution of charity.

KNESSETH GADOLAH—כנסת גדולה—THE GREAT ASSEMBLY

This rabbinical body was said to have been founded by Ezra, the
Scribe, after the return from Babylonian exile in 444 BCE. Its concern was primarily with religious matters and Jewish jurisprudence.
In Talmudic times it became known as ANSHE KNESSETH HA-GADOLAH
—אנשי כנסת הגדולה—THE MEN OF THE GREAT ASSEMBLY.

MA-AMADOTH—מעמדות—STANDING COMMITTEES

In Bible times laymen were appointed as committees to be present at the daily sacrifices at the Temple.

MOADEI EL—מועדי אל—MEETING PLACES OF GOD

These meeting places existed in Bible times and were used for
prayers and devotions unaccompanied by sacrifices.

SANHEDRIN—סנהדרין—COUNCIL

This name was applied to the highest Jewish Court and legislative
body during the latter part of the Second Commonwealth. In Talmudic times it was composed of leading rabbis and scholars.

TZIBUR—צבור—CONGREGATION

Members of a house of worship. The term is also used to designate the Jewish community.

ZIKNE HA-IR—זקני העיר—ELDERS OF THE CITY

In early times the heads of the most prominent families constituted an administrative body of the city.

Leaders of the Diaspora

THE NASI OF PALESTINE

At the end of the Second Jewish Commonwealth (70 CE), when the
Jewish community of Palestine was left without any central authority to
regulate its affairs, the office of the NASI—נשיא—which means PRINCE,
came into being. As the titular head of the Jews, he was recognized by
Rome as the spokesman for the Jewish people and in addition to dealing with its military representatives he had to keep order and collect
taxes. He was usually a prominent rabbi or pious layman to whom the
community looked for religious guidance. His jurisdiction extended to all
the communities throughout the country.

The office of Nasi in Palestine was hereditary, insofar as this was possible. After the second century, a descendant of Hillel held the office until the year 425, when it was abolished by Rome. The title, however, continued in current use to designate the lay leader of a Jewish community.

THE NAGID

In Moslem and some Christian countries where Jewish communities flourished, the man whom the government considered the head of the Jewish people was called NAGID— נגיד —LEADER. He directed the religious life of the people and represented them in the Parliament. The title originated in Egypt in the tenth century, from where it spread to Spain. The office lasted until the 16th century in Egypt.

THE ETHNARCH

Jewish communities that existed in Palestine under foreign domination were under the leadership of an appointee of the ruling power. His title was that of ETHNARCH, a Greek word meaning "Ruler of a People." The office was bestowed by the emperors of Rome, first upon Simon the Hasmonean and then upon Herod, who were merely puppet-governors.

THE RESH GALUTA OR EXILARCH

In the ninth century, in Babylonia and Persia, the seat of authority was vested in the office of EXILARCH or RESH GALUTA— ראש גלותא —THE HEAD OF THE EXILES. According to tradition the Exilarch was always a descendant of King David. He was recognized at court, lived in royal state, and was chief tax-collector among the Jews. He appointed judges, regulated commerce, and was the political representative of the Jewish community.

THE GAON

GAON— גאון —means EXCELLENCY and refers, primarily, to the intellectual leader selected by the community to head the leading academies of learning in Babylonia. While the office was technically under the jurisdiction of the Exilarch, the Gaonim were looked upon as the spiritual heads of the community. Their decisions concerning Jewish law were accepted by all the people of the Jewish world.

BISHOP OF THE JEWS

This term was used in Medieval England for a KOHEN or Priest, and in Germany, for the representative of the Jewish people who could be a rabbi or layman. The Latin term EPISCOPUS JUDAEORUM and the Norman-French term L'EVESKE were equivalents for "Bishop of the Jews."

CROWN RABBI

The Crown Rabbi was appointed by the secular authority to represent the Jewish people in their dealings with the state. This was not a sign of recognition or spiritual quality. In Russia, his primary duties were to record births, marriages, and deaths. The PRESBYTER JUDAEORUM in Medieval England was of this type. In Spain he was called RAB DE LA CORTE (Court Rabbi); in Portugal, ARRABI-MOR (Grand Rabbi); and in Sicily, DIENCHELELE (General Judge).

TITLES OF OFFICIALS, FUNCTIONARIES OF STATE, CHURCH, COMMUNITY, AND LEADERS OF THE DIASPORA

Government Officials

Alluf—	אלוף	Military chief
Ebed HaMelech—	עבד המלך	Servant of the King—royal officer
Katzin—	קצין	Commander of the army—ruler—dictator
Mashkeh—	משקה	Cup Bearer to the ruler—butlership
Mazkir—	מזכיר	Recorder—chief counselor—secretary
Melech—	מלך	King—sovereign—ruler
Mishneh—	משנה	Second in command
Mishneh HaMelech—	משנה המלך	Viceroy—Vizier—next to King
Nadib—	נדיב	Nobleman
Nagid—	נגיד	Leader—chief—prince
Nasi—	נשיא	Head of Sanhedrin—prince—chief
Nasich—	נסיך	Prince
Natzib—	נציב	Prefect—commissioner—deputy
Pakid—	פקיד	Overseer—inspector—official
Pechah—	פחה	Governor—prefect
Rosh HaTabachim—	ראש הטבחים	Chief of bodyguard
Sar—	שר	Prince of royal family—commander
Sar HaRatzim—	שר הרצים	Chief of the messengers
Sar HaRechush—	שר הרכוש	Controller of the treasury
Sar al HaTzabah—	שר אל הצבא	General of the army
Saris—	סריס	Chamberlain of the king—palace official—eunuch
Sar M'usim—	שר מעשים	Overseer of forced labor
Shalish—	שליש	Military officer—one of three in command
Sochayn—	סוכן	Minister of the palace
Sofer—	סופר	Secretary of State—recorder—scribe notary—chancellor—interpreter of the Law
Zekenim—	זקנים	Elders—advisers—council members

Priestly Order

Amarcal —	אמרכל —	Auxiliary priest—temple treasurer
Gizbar —	גזבר —	Temple treasurer
Kohen —	כהן —	Priest
Kohen Gadol —	כהן גדול —	High Priest
Kohen Hadyot —	כהן הדיוט —	Low ranking priest
Kohen HaRosh —	כהן הראש —	Head or Chief Priest
Kohen Mishneh —	כהן משנה —	Second in rank to high priest
Levite —	לוי —	Priestly assistant—temple administrator
Memunneh —	ממונה —	Auxiliary priest—deputy
Segan —	סגן —	Prefect—priestly official—governor—ruler

Community Officials

Ab Beth Din —	אב בית דין —	Father of the House of Judgment—Vice-President of the Assembly, or the Sanhedrin
Anshe Ma-amad —	אנשי מעמד —	The Community Council
Beth Din —	בית דין —	House of Judgment—a Court of Justice varying in number of representatives
Chacham —	חכם —	Sage, scholar or teacher—a wise man of the Sanhedrin—title used in Sephardic communities
Chacham Bashi —	חכם באשי —	Title for the Chief Rabbi of Turkey
Chazan Ha-Ir —	חזן העיר —	The Cantor of the city, who was usually appointed by the leaders of the synagogue
Chevrah Kedishah —	חברה קדישא —	Holy Fellowship—burial society
Gabbai —	גבאי —	Second most important community leader—collector—treasurer
Gabbai Cheshbonot —	גבאי חשבנות —	Controllers—treasurers of the community
Gabbai shel Tzedakah —	גבאי של צדקה —	Administrators of charity
Ma-amad —	מעמד —	Presiding officer (Sephardic)—stands—stations—posts—Israelite attendants at Temple sacrifices

Term	Hebrew	Definition
Machalekah Tzedakah	מחלקה צדקה	Distributors of charity
Mahamad	מעמד	Presiding board (Sephardic)
Meshullach	משולח	Messenger—traveling collector for Israeli institutions—collectors of taxes for charity
Mohel	מוהל	Circumciser—religious functionary trained for this ritual
Nasi	נשיא	Prince—chief—head of the Great Assembly or Sanhedrin
Pekidim	פקידים	Presiding head of board (Turkey)
Parnas	פרנס	President of the community or congregation—administrator (German : Barnos)
Parnase HaKnesseth	פרנסי הכנסת	Supporters of the community
Parnassim	פרנסים	Lay leaders of the community
Resh Mata	ריש מתא	Head of council or city (Babylonia)
Sanhedrin	סנהדרין	Body or Council of scholars—men of the Great Assembly
Shammash	שמש	Sexton—caretaker—beadle—assistant to the president of the congregation
Sheliach	שליח	Messenger—agent—representative
Sheliach Beth Din	שליח בית דין	Agent of the court—messenger of the congregation
Sheleechim	שליחים	Collectors
Shivah Tobay Ha-Ir	שבעה טובי העיר	Executive board of seven "good" men of the city
Shomair HaRosh	שומר הראש	Head guardian—leader
Shtadlan	שתדלן	Representative of medieval Jewish community
Shochet	שוחט	Ritual slaughterer
Sofer	סופר	Scribe—notary—recorder—interpreter of the law

Tobay Ha-Ir — טובי העיר — Good men of the city, numbering between seven and twelve

Zekenim — זקנים — Elders—directors of the council—advisors

Functionaries of the Synagogue

Baal — בעל — Leader—master—dignitary

Baal Koray — בעל קורא — Master reader of scripture—one who chants the weekly portion of the Torah

Baal Tefillah — בעל תפלה — Master reader of prayers—cantor—one assigned to read daily, festival, or Holy Day worship services

Baal Tekiah — בעל תקיעה — Blower of the Shofar

Beth Din — בית דין — Court of judgment

Board of Trustees — — Executive board responsible for the administration of the synagogue

Chazan — חזן — Cantor—in Talmudic times he was the Sheliach Tzibur, the Baal Tefillah, and the Chazan HaKnesseth—in modern times, he chants the prayers, sings special renditions of them, trains the choir, reads the Torah and blows the shofar

Chazan HaKnesseth — חזן הכנסת — Director of the services—servant of the synagogue

Chazan Sheni — חזן שני — Assistant cantor

Chazan Ha-Ir — חזן העיר — Cantor of the city

Darshan — דרשן — Expounder—teacher or preacher in the synagogue

Dayan — דין — Judge—trustee—assistant to the president—member of the rabbinical court—assistant to the Chief Rabbi (Sephardic)

Maggid — מגיד — Itinerant preacher

Manhig — מנהיג — Curator—leader—director

Memunnah — ממונה — Deputy—officer

Parnas — פרנס — President of the congregation—guardian

Rabbi — רבי — Teacher—spiritual leader—title given to scholars

Rosh Beth Din — ראש בית דין — Head of the court

Rosh HaKnesseth — ראש הכנסת — President of the congregation

Sandek — סנדק — Godfather at circumcision

Schulklopfer — Synagogue summoner (by knocking on doors of congregants) (German)

Scholnik — סקולניק — Minor official (Polish)

Sheliach Tzibur — שליח ציבור — Messenger of the congregation

Sheleechim — שליחים — Messengers

Shofet — שופט — Judge

Wardens — Officers, trustees, or directors of the congregation (English)

Diaspora Leaders

Abba — אבא — Father—ancestor—master—title of respect (Christian derivative is "Abbot.")

Alabarch — Leader of the Jews in Egypt

Apostoli — Messengers or emissaries (Greek for "Sheleechim")

Archesynagogos — Head of Synagogue (Greek for "Rosth HaKnesseth")

Archipercite — Exilarch—head of session (Greek)

Archon — Presiding judge (Greek)—magistrate of any Jewish community of the Diaspora—responsible for the external management of the congregation

Archpresbyter — Priestly functionary (Greek)—Chief Rabbi in early English history

Barnos — President of the community (German)

Baumeister — Architect—building master (German)

Bishop of the Jews — Christian title for Jewish leaders (Episcopus Judaeorum) in England and Germany

Chacham Bashi חכם באשי — Chief Rabbi (Turkey)

Chaver — Distinguished colleague—fellow

Court Rabbi — Chief Rabbi (Spain)

Crown Rabbi — Chief Rabbi (Russia)

Deodatus Episcopus — Regional head

Ethnarch — Roman title for Jewish leader

Exilarch — Head of Babylonia Jewish community—Head of the Exile—chief collector (Aramaic: Resh Galuta)

Gaon גאון — Head of Babylonian Jewish academies

General Judge — Chief Jewish leader in Sicily

Gerusia — Council of elders—supreme self-governing body in Jerusalem (Greek for "Zekenim")

Grand Rabbi — Title given to Chief Rabbi in France and Portugal

Hochmeister — High official—Austrian title for Chief Rabbi

Judenbishop — Bishop of Jews (Germany)

Judenmeister — Head of the Jews (Austria)

Mahamad מעמד — Presiding board (Sephardic)

Morenu מורנו — Our teachers—rabbis with special learning

Moshiach משיח — Anointed one—messenger—prophet

Moshiach Adonoy משיח אדני — Anointed of the Lord

Pater Synagogue — Father of the synagogue

Patriarch — Title of the founding fathers of Judaism, Abraham, Isaac, and Jacob; also given to leading Palestinian scholars after the first century of the common era

Praefectus Judaeorum — — Head of the Jews

Presbyter — — Christian title for elder—teacher

Rab — רב — Master—teacher—lord—head of a congregation—title of Babylonian expounders of Torah

Rabban — רבן — Our teacher—title given to important personage

Rab Chobail — רב חובל — Captain

Resh Galuta — ראש גלותא — Exilarch

Rishon L'Tzion — ראשון לציון — Chief Rabbi of Israel (Sephardic)

Rosh — ראש — Head—leading official—principal

Rosh Kallah — ראש כלה — Head of the Talmudic academy in Babylonia—leader of the assembly

Rosh HaGolah — ראש הגולה — Leaders of the Exiles—Ethnarch of Babylonia

Rosh HaPerek — ראש הפרק — Head of the session (Egypt and Palestine)—similar to Ethnarch

Roshi — ראשי — Chief—first in rank

Scholnik — — Minor official (Poland)

Tetrarch — — Jewish prince (Roman)

Charity and Welfare Institutions

THE TRADITION OF CHARITY

The essence of Jewish charity may be found in the literal meanings of the words TZEDAKAH—צדקה—which means "Righteousness," and GEMI-LUTH CHASADIM— גמילות חסדים —which means "Acts of Kindness." It is also associated with the word MITZVAH—מצוה—which means a "Commandment," a "Precept," an "Injunction of the Torah." In popular usage a Mitzvah becomes a meritorious deed or a deed of charity. Thus, any form of Tzedakah is a Mitzvah; any act of kindness is carrying out God's commandment; to receive some special honor in the synagogue was a Mitzvah. Colloquially, the term Mitzvah means to live in accordance with the precepts of charity.

It is commanded in the Bible that . . .

> If there be among you a needy man, or of thy brethren in any of thy gates . . . thou shalt not harden thy heart, nor shut thy hand from thy needy brother. . . . For the poor shall never cease out of the land; therefore I command thee saying: 'Thou shalt surely open thy hand unto thy poor and needy brother.'   (Deuteronomy 15 : 8f.)

The obligation of giving charity to those in need is not only a religious responsibility but is one of the oldest and most sacred of Jewish traditions. The rabbis extended the concept to include those who were in need of sympathy and comfort. The practice of charity, therefore, became an act of benevolence as well as relief to the needy; an expression of love of mankind as well as devotion to human welfare. It received its fullest expression in the preachments of the prophets who spoke of God's concern for the poor, the oppressed, and the needy as taking precedence over sacrifices and prayer.

Tzedakah implies alms or things that can be purchased for money, while Gemiluth Chasadim implies personal consideration. The first is given to the poor, while the latter applies to the rich and the poor. There is the inference that the performance of Tzedakah is more incumbent upon the wealthier, whereas Gemiluth Chasidim should be performed by everyone.

In the Jewish tradition poverty is not degrading, for the poor man has a right to share in the blessings of others. In the agricultural economy of Bible times, a system of poor relief was guaranteed to him, especially in three prescribed forms, (1) PEAH—פאה—CORNERS, (2) LEKET—לקט—GLEANINGS, and (3) SHICH-CHAH—שכחה—FORGOTTEN. These are enumerated as follows:

> When you reap the harvest of your land thou shalt not wholly reap the corner (Peah) of your field, neither shalt thou gather the gleaning

(Leket) of thy harvest . . . nor the fallen fruit of thy vine-yard. Thou shalt leave them for the poor and the stranger.   (Leviticus 19 : 9f.)

When thou reapest thy harvest in thy field and hast forgot (Shichchah) a sheaf in thy field, thou shalt not go back to fetch it; it shall be for the stranger, the fatherless, and for the widow.
(Deuteronomy 24 : 19f.)

The Bible term for taxes is MESEEM—מסים. This took the form of tithings and offerings. The poll tax MAS HA-GULGOLETH—מס הגלגלת—was the levy of the half shekel. The shekel was a money weight used in connection with sacred things.

This they shall give . . . every man from twenty years old and upward . . . half a shekel for an offering to the Lord.   (Exodus 30 : 13)

The Mishnah lists tax-gatherers among murderers and robbers, because they contracted with the Romans to deliver certain amounts of money and kept a good share for themselves, using every imaginable method that the people could not avoid.

Another early form of Tzedakah was the tithing for the Levites who were to be supported because they did not receive a share of the inheritance of the land. Later, this tithe was extended so that part of it could be given to the needy. This was called MA-ASER ANI—מעשר עני—A TITHE FOR THE POOR, and was due in the third and sixth years of the Sabbatical period. This type of Tzedakah inferred God's ownership of the soil and its fruits; man's stewardship of the world's goods included making them available to the needy.

And the Levite that is within thy gates; . . . and the stranger, and the fatherless, and the widow which are within thy gates, shall come, and shall eat and be satisfied.   (Deuteronomy 14 : 27f.)

The rabbis considered the amount of charity one was expected to give. A Jew is expected to give between one-tenth and one-fifth of his income to charitable causes. To give less than one-tenth, says the Talmud, was to fall short of one's duty to his fellowmen, but to give more than one-fifth might cause him to lapse from independence to dependence.
(Yoreh Deah 249)

Many guidelines were laid down for individual and community behavior in the exercise of Tzedakah and Gemiluth Chasadim. The rabbis declared that combined action to meet community needs is more practical and productive than individual efforts. But support of public institutions does not exempt one from assisting individuals who appeal for help. Caution in responding to requests is advised, but not to the point of suspecting every applicant for assistance to the degree that harm or ruin to a worthy person or family could result.

The Talmud states that if a person asks for food, no question should be asked or any investigation be made. And Proverbs 3 : 27 tells us "withhold not good from him to whom it is due when it is in the power of thine hand to do it. Say not unto thy neighbor, 'Go, and come again, and tomorrow I will give'; when thou hast it by thee." To do otherwise would be to put the recipient to shame. This consideration for the poor accounts for a special chamber in the Temple where a fund box was kept for the needy. It was the forerunner of the community charity box (Kuppah) of later times. All possible secrecy was maintained in order that no one could see who came for help, nor were the donors known who deposited their charity in the box.

In the daily morning prayer service there is a passage from the Mishnah (Peah 1) that speaks of the meritorious forms of charity.

> These are the things, the fruits of which a man enjoys in this world, while the stock remains for him for the world to come : viz. honouring father and mother, the practice of charity, timely attendance at the house of study morning and evening, hospitality to wayfarers, visiting the sick, dowering the bride, attending the dead to the grave, devotion in prayer, and making peace between man and his fellow; but the study of the Law is equal to them all.

Later, the rabbis selected seven virtues, labeling them as cardinal obligations of charity.

1. Feeding the hungry and giving the thirsty to drink
2. Clothing the naked
3. Visiting the sick
4. Burying the dead and comforting the mourners
5. Redeeming the captive
6. Educating the fatherless and sheltering the homeless
7. Providing poor maidens with dowries

(Moed Katon 27b)

SPECIFIC ACTS OF KINDNESS

From early times it became the responsibility of the community to attend to the care of the needy. Food, clothing, and shelter were their primary concern. In the matter of Gemiluth Chasadim—Acts of Kindness, societies or associations were formed to carry out the directives.

Visiting the Sick—בקור חולים—*Bikkur Cholim*
This was both an individual and community obligation. Volunteers

not only brought cheer and comfort to the suffering and bedridden, but also provided table provisions, medical expenses, and financial aid.

Redeeming the Captive— פדיון שבויים —Pidyon Shevuim

Jewish history recounts many instances of Jews taken into captivity or held as prisoners for ransom. The purpose of this form of charity was to raise money to purchase the freedom of captive Jews.

Clothing the Naked—מלביש ערומים—Malbish Arumim

To provide necessary garments for indigent and distressed people. No one was to suffer shame for lack of apparel.

Attending the Dead—הלוית המת—HaLivayoth HaMaith

A "Holy Fellowship" called CHEVRAH KEDISHA—חברה קדישא— voluntarily undertook the duty of performing the last rites for the the dead. This Mitzvah was also known by the name of CHESED SHEL EMETH—חסד של אמת—"Kindness for the Sake of Truth." The function of this voluntary fellowship is to attend to the dying, to prepare the deceased for burial, and to perform all the functions pertaining to the dead in accordance with Jewish Law and tradition. Any Jew could honor and respect the dead by accompanying the funeral procession to the cemetery.

Comforting the Mourners—נחום אבלים—Nachum Avaylim

Paying a condolence call on the family of the deceased, particularly during the seven days of mourning, and bringing food and necessities when the bereaved were confined to their home is an obligation that is deemed meritorious.

Dowering Poor Maidens—הכנסת כלה—Hachnoseth Kallah

The name literally means "Sheltering the Bride." Its purpose was to provide dowries for poor unmarried girls who had none. Later it was expanded to arrange suitable marriages and to help provide a trousseau and a home.

Sheltering the Homeless—בית יתומים—Beth Yethomim

To educate the fatherless and to provide a home for the orphan became the responsibility of the whole community. This was the forerunner of the modern Orphan Asylum and other child care centers.

Feeding the Hungry—לחם לרעבים—Lechem R'ayvim

This form of Tzedakah is the first of the seven acts of kindness listed in the Talmud. Bread is the "staff of life" and the prophets' interpretation of social justice is that no one should go hungry nor the thirsty lack water.

Acts of Kindness—גמילות חסדים—Gemiluth Chasadim
One of the functions of this society was to alleviate temporary suffering and hardship by loaning monies to those in need without charging interest. Under dire circumstances the loans were not expected to be repaid. This form of charity was the forerunner of the Hebrew Free Loan Societies.

Hospitality to Strangers—הכנסת אורחים—Hachnoseth Orchim
The term literally means "Sheltering the Guests." As a religious society, its main purpose was to welcome indigent strangers and transients and to extend the hospitality of food and lodging during their stay. It was the custom of some families to invite strangers to stay at their homes over the Sabbath week-end. In many communities the synagogue maintained shelters or guest homes. But these practices are fast disappearing as secular agencies minister to transients and there is a paucity of Jewish wayfarers.

Free Matzoth—מעות חטים—Ma'oth Chittim
This term means "Wheat Money." The society collected money to enable people in unfortunate financial circumstances to receive Passover provisions so that the holiday might be celebrated in proper tradition. The theory behind this Mitzvah was that every Jew must have the means to observe and enjoy the Passover festival.

Alms for the Poor—עוזר דלים—Ohzer Dalim
People who were reduced to poverty and were too proud or ashamed to ask for relief were the recipients of aid from this agency.

Good Works—מעשים טובים—Ma-asim Tobim
The Torah doctrine of "Good Deeds" was also supposed to operate in all areas of human relations. Virtuous deeds of note were :

Words of Kindness—דברות חסד—Divroth Chesed
This is the duty of judging one's fellowmen in a favorable light, judging mankind without malice or prejudice, and refraining from speaking ill or passing gossip. It includes raising the intellectual, moral, and social condition by kind words of advice, comfort, and encouragement.

HaBayoth Shalom—הבאת שלום—Bringer of Peace

This involves the effecting of peace and harmony between man and his fellowmen, between members of a family, between parties, and between nations. It is the duty of every individual to prevent strife and dissension and to effect reconciliation wherever possible.

MAIMONIDES' EIGHT DEGREES OF CHARITY

Jewish ethics stress consideration for the feelings of those who are dependent upon charity. Poverty was considered an unfortunate circumstance, shared at one time by a majority of Jews. Since rabbinic tradition declared that the poor should never be put to shame, conscientious attempts were made to enable them to receive help without embarrassing them. This is emphasized in the formulation of degrees of charity by the great scholar, Moses Maimonides, in which he evaluated eight ranks of givers of charity, from the least to the most meritorious :

1. Giving less than is needed and without kindness or grace.
2. Giving inadequately but with good grace.
3. Giving only after a request is made.
4. Giving before a request is made, with donor and recipient knowing each other.
5. Giving without knowing the recipient, but the latter knows the donor.
6. Giving secretly, with the donor knowing the recipient, but the recipient not knowing the donor.
7. Giving so that neither the donor nor the recipient knows each other.
8. Helping the needy to become independent by advancing money or providing opportunities.

THE COLLECTION OF CHARITY

Historically, the money for charitable purposes has come from many and varied sources. Voluntary contributions continue to be the chief one, especially in times of crisis. Individual solicitations, fund-raising campaigns, pledges made during services in synagogues, donations made for happy or sad occasions comprise the main methods used today.

In the past, every member of the Jewish community could be assessed when control was centralized in the Kehillah or when the ghetto was required to raise a certain sum. Every community was required to maintain a public charity fund (KUPPAH) from which the needy received money for clothing, food, and necessities, and transients were provided with lodging. The contributions were assessed weekly by a communal board in proportion to the means and length of residence of the individual. A resident of thirty days in the city was obligated to participate. A three-month resident had to help also with the "Tamchuy"—daily distribution of food (soup kitchen). A six-month resident had to contribute to a clothing fund and a nine-month resident to the burial fund. This system continued to the end of the Middle Ages.

In more modern times, in many cities, there were separate charity boxes (Pushkehs) for specific purposes, such as orphanages, over-seas Yeshivoth, old folks' homes, and so on. In nearly every Jewish home it was customary to find one or more of them, with collectors making periodic visits. Every synagogue had a number of boxes for voluntary contributions from the worshipers. At the cemetery, charity boxes were used by the members of the "Chevrah Kedishah" to solicit contributions from the mourners and visitors. Today, one of the vestiges of these charity boxes is the blue and white Jewish National Fund Box, which raises funds for land purchase and reforestation in Israel. Another echo is found in the KUPPAT CHOLIM— קפת חולים —"Sick Fund," organized in Palestine in 1912 to care for the needs of workers and their families in times of illness. Today, this is better organized and supports a chain of hospitals, ambulances, pharmacies, and sanatoria.

Benevolent Institutions

HEALTH AND WELFARE

Jewish social service was born in the synagogue. When an individual was confronted with any problem of a personal nature that he could not solve, he would seek the counsel and guidance of his rabbi, who would often have to turn to others for assistance. This was especially true in cases of need. In time, this led to the formation of various societies with specific purposes, all motivated by the basic doctrine of Gemiluth Chasadim—Acts of Kindness.

During the Middle Ages in Rome, many such societies were active. In addition to one for visiting the sick, there was one for arranging burials; seven for providing clothes and bedding for children, widows, and prisoners; two supplied poor brides with gifts, clothes, and wedding expenses; one helped people to settle in Palestine; and others maintained lodging for travelers, supported Hebrew schools, and provided holiday and Sabbath needs for the poor and the stranger. The names of the societies were taken from the Bible or Prayer Book, i.e., "Upbringers of Orphans," "Clothers of the Naked," "Crown of the Aged," "Comforters of Mourners," and so forth.

Most of these early tradition-oriented institutions, supported and administered on a personal basis, have given way to modern impersonal social service agencies in whose work the donors do not participate. Laymen sometimes participate, but usually as volunteer aides to the professional workers. Even the CHEVRAH KEDISHA, the holy fellowship concerned with the burial ritual, which operated without a building or a structured organization, is now often staffed with technicians, advisers, and administrators. Despite the changes, the concept of Tzedakah still motivates Jews and the adage that "Charity becomes the Jew" reflects the spirit of compassion, love, and mercy, which is the hallmark of benevolence.

CARE OF THE SICK

Illness of any kind was always considered a calamity, for it not only endangered the well-being of the individual, but it often led to loss of livelihood and financial dependence. It became a community responsibility to provide the indigent sick with a physician, medicine, and family necessities. The health and welfare of a person always has precedence in Jewish law. The Sabbath and Holy Days could be violated in the interest of preserving life. Even the law of fasting on Yom Kippur could be transgressed to permit the sick to eat. The Talmud (Kiddushin 66d) says that "It is forbidden to live in a city in which there is no physician."

THE HEKDESH

The Talmud mentions a PUNDOK— פונדק —or ACHSANYA— אכסניה an inn or a lodging place supported by the community. This was usually built on the high road to provide shelter and food for the sick, for poor transients, and for the homeless.

During the Crusades, in the 11th and 12th centuries, the number of homeless Jews increased greatly, making a community-supported hospice or asylum a necessity. Such an institution was known as the HEKDESH— הקדש —"House Consecrated for the Poor." This was the term used also by the Essenes when they gave their worldly goods to the poor.

The Hekdesh provided free care and medical services for the homeless, aged, infirm, or ill. By the end of the Middle Ages the sick were treated in a separate part of the building, which was referred to as the BETH CHOLIM— בית חולים —HOUSE OF THE SICK. Although the Hekdesh served primarily as an infirmary for transients, it was also open to the local community.

In the ghetto, when the Jewish people had to live under restrictive conditions in highly congested slum areas, the medical facilities of the larger non-Jewish community were usually denied to them. For their self-protection and preservation, they had to set up a system of hygienic and sanitary care, which they based upon the Mosaic laws of purity and cleanliness. However, they, like non-Jews, were afflicted with diseases, and subject to epidemics and plagues that took their toll in great numbers. In addition, there were always traveling mendicants and Jewish refugees who came with their sick and disabled. The problem of their care became a growing burden upon the local Jewish communities. By the middle of the 16th century there was a small Beth Cholim in Berlin that cared for the local citizenry. Other communities set up similar agencies for the care of the sick.

It took centuries for the gradual transformation of the Hekdesh into the hospital in the modern sense. Through the 19th and 20th centuries the growth was so explosive that by 1960, in the United States alone, there were no less than 80 Jewish hospitals and hundreds of organizations for attending the sick.

WORLD-WIDE INSTITUTIONS

Jewish hospitals, built and maintained by Jewish communities, are to be found all over the world. There are three in England. There were thirty in Germany before Hitler, and 112 in Russia before World War i. Until 1940 there was only one in France, founded in 1836. In nearly all instances, the services of these institutions were open to all people, regardless of race or creed.

The first modern organization to establish a health program for the Jewish people was the Society for the Protection of Health of Jews in Russia. The initial letters of its Russian name "Obshchestvo Zdorovje Evteev" (oze) became a symbol of medical aid for Jews. Before Hitlerism and Communism terminated its program, the oze operated some 470 institutions, including hospitals, consultation centers, dispensaries, and dental clinics among Jews of Lithuania, Latvia, Rumania, and parts of Poland.

The Jewish people of Poland created a similar national agency known by the initials "toz." In addition to health care, it promoted a physical culture program for children and adults.

Hadassah, the Women's Zionist Organization of America, has been responsible in large part for medical accomplishments and the development of hospitals and nursing education and services in Israel. This organization provides a nonsectarian preventive and curative program and in cooperation with the Hebrew University has established a medical school and a 500-bed Medical Center, and maintains health stations and clinics throughout the country.

AMERICAN INSTITUTIONS

Jewish health care institutions, on a national basis in the United States, started during the 19th century. The first hospital, supported by Jewish funds but not limited to Jewish patients, was founded in Cincinnati, Ohio, in 1845. The Montefiore Hospital for Chronic Diseases was established in New York City in 1884. Some hospitals under Jewish auspices were sponsored by fraternal organizations, such as the B'nai B'rith, while others received their support from Jewish individuals and organizations. Many are known for effective treatment of, and research centers for, special diseases.

The National Jewish Hospital at Denver

Functioning since 1899, this hospital was the first Jewish institution to offer free treatment and care to tubercular and asthmatic patients on a non-sectarian basis. Its motto is "None May Enter Who Can Pay—None Can Pay Who Enter." The hospital operates a Kosher kitchen for its Jewish patients and maintains a research, educational, and rehabilitation program. It also has departments for research in conjunction with the medical school of the University of Denver in the fields of chest diseases and heart ailments.

Jewish National Home for Asthmatic Children and Children's Asthma Research Institute and Hospital

Located at Denver, Colorado, they maintain a free, non-sectarian medical and research center for children who suffer from chronic asthma and other allergic diseases. When first organized in 1906 it cared for tubercular children and some whose parents were tubercular patients under treatment in Denver.

The American Medical Center at Denver

This institution, organized in 1904, has been known as the "Denver Sanatorium" and the "Jewish Consumptives Relief Society." It is nonsectarian and is recognized by the American Medical Society as a teaching school in tuberculosis as well as a nationwide medical and treatment center for cancer and chest diseases, and for clinical and basic cancer research.

Leo N. Levi Memorial Hospital

Established by B'nai B'rith (1914) at Hot Springs, Arkansas, this institution maintains a free nonsectarian medical center for treatment, research, and medical education in tuberculosis and other chest diseases, cancer and allied diseases, blood diseases, and operable heart ailments.

Ex-Patients Sanatorium for Tuberculosis and Chronic Disease

This institution was organized in 1908 in Denver to provide free treatment and rehabilitation to patients with tuberculosis, asthma, and other chronic diseases.

Deborah Hospital

This hospital, organized in Brown Mills, New Jersey, provides free care for needy patients and corrective surgery in cardiac and pulmonary diseases.

CHILD CARE

Historically, the Jewish family is known for its closeness and its great concern for the well-being of its members. Where families cannot fulfill this function, the Jewish community assumes the responsibility. Sometimes a child is orphaned; divorce may leave the child with only one parent; economic conditions may work hardships on the children. Sickness and poverty often add to the burden of maintaining normal family life. Husbands disappear or desert their families; accidents cause permanent disabilities; children are born crippled or demented. For these and other reasons a family may need help from relatives, friends, institutions, or community agencies.

Traditionally, every Jewish community has accepted the moral mandate to provide religious and secular education of children of the poor, to arrange for the health and welfare of the orphan, to teach him a trade, and to provide dowries and arrange marriages for the fatherless. In modern times, Jewish family services have depersonalized assistance. They now give direct relief as well as provide personal and family counseling, family life education, and psychiatric services directly relating to children.

The field of child-care suffered from over-expansion and duplication in the larger cities, so one of the more recent developments has been to coordinate the efforts by creating clearing bureaus. The first was established in Baltimore in 1919, followed by one in New York City in 1922. Later, there were mergers and consolidations that put all cooperating child-care agencies in one body. The latest such large concentration occurred in New York in 1939.

ORPHAN CARE

In the Jewish tradition, orphans (Yethomim— יתומים) receive special consideration as directed in Deuteronomy 24 : 17, "Thou shalt not pervert the justice due to the stranger, or to the fatherless."

Since orphans are regarded as defenseless, every Jew owed them the duty of preventing infringement on their rights. The prophets considered as unrighteous any injustice against orphans, since all Israel was obligated to "Judge the fatherless and plead for the widow." (Isaiah 1 : 17)

In Talmudic times, orphans were exempt from contributing to public offerings and to the poor fund; they were protected against claims of creditors until they were of legal age; claims upon them did not have to be canceled by the Sabbatical year since they were under the care of the authorities; they could deposit their money for safekeeping in the Temple so it could not be seized by anyone. Orphans without means shared in the tithe that was reserved for the poor and also in the gleanings (Leket) of the field and the forgotten sheaves (Shich-chah). Girls received special consideration when they reached marriageable age, by being provided with trousseaus and dowries. It was considered meritorious that orphans were usually cared for by blood relatives, but it was even more commendable for strangers to assume this responsibility.

With the growth of the Jewish community, the more or less personal attention given to the orphan was transferred to asylums, foster homes, and institutions. In the larger Jewish communities orphanages were established and supported by private and public charities. National organizations like the B'nai B'rith maintained a large orphan home (Bellefaire), organized in 1868 at Cleveland, Ohio, as part of their program for child care. This institution is now a residential treatment center for disturbed children.

Until recent times the orphan home was the only haven for parentless children. There they lived, separated from the community, stigmatized by the unfortunate circumstances that made them wards of the community. Today, the orphan home has been replaced in great part by the foster home in which children are placed and their support provided by Family and Child Care agencies of the Jewish or civic community. In a sense these agencies have become the wards or guardians of the fatherless and the victims of broken homes.

In 1942 there were approximately 100 local children's institutions, cottage-plan systems, orphan asylums, and foster care agencies caring for about 12,000 children, supported by the Jewish communities. But since World War II the size of the orphan problem has slowly diminished because of government aid to dependent mothers and the higher economic standards of living in the families affected. There has been an increase, however, in the number of behavior problems among youth, especially those from broken homes, necessitating increased case work and the establishment of child guidance facilities.

THE CARE OF THE AGED

BETH MOSHAV ZEKENIM— בית מושב זקנים —A HOUSE FOR THE AGED, is one of the benevolent services based on the tradition of honoring parents. In early times the family cared for its own aged, but as society grew more complex, family solidarity tended to disintegrate and the old and feeble members were often left without care and support. The responsibility for their care fell upon the community, possibly as early as the period of the Second Temple, although some rabbis of the Talmudic period placed the beginnings of communal provision back to Bible times. In most cases, the aged were included in those places that sheltered the sick (Bikkur Cholim) and the homeless (Hekdesh). In the Middle Ages nearly every Jewish community had some form of shelter for the aged.

Special homes for only the aged developed in the United States along two lines, the institutional and the noninstitutional types of care. The first type was the Home for Aged and Infirm Hebrews in New York City, opened in 1870. In 1940 there were approximately 66 such institutions, serving 47 cities and caring for about 6,000 men and women. Patients who were financially able contributed to their support.

The largest number of these homes were established between 1910 and 1919. They are to be found in most large cities and usually also serve neighboring communities. Most of them are privately maintained. The minimum ages range from 60 to 70. There has been a rise in the proportion of residents afflicted with chronic ailments and physical handicaps, so there is increased emphasis upon nursing and medical care.

The second type, the noninstitutional care program for the aged, is increasing in scope in recent times. There is a trend in social service agencies toward placing the elderly in boarding homes, or maintaining them in their own quarters when possible. Many receive old-age and other public assistance, and so long as they are healthy, they can live alone.

In most European countries before World War II, the homes for the aged resembled the old Hekdesh. Holland was an exception, with as many as thirteen homes, eight in Amsterdam alone, most of them maintained by the Jewish communities and some by the Boards of Guardians. In England the situation is similar. There are nine homes in London, the oldest having been started as an alms house by the Sephardic community in 1703. The largest home for the Jewish aged in France is in Paris, with others in Bordeaux, Nancy, and Luneville.

Over the years in Palestine there were many homes for those aged Jews who migrated there to study or spend their last days. These were supported by funds collected by solicitors who traveled all over the world. After World War II, with the creation of the State of Israel and the influx of hundreds of aged and infirm European Jews, more modern institutions for their care were developed by both international agencies like the Joint Distribution Committee and the government's Social Service Department. The Jewish tradition of caring for the aged continued.

THE AFFLICTED (The Lame, the Halt, and the Blind)

The Rabbis of the Talmud stated that "the poor, the leper, the blind and the childless are as if dead." (Nedarim 64b) This meant that they were to receive special consideration in all matters pertaining to their welfare, especially in legal cases. The blind were exempt from some of the commandments. They could act as judges but not as witnesses.

While the lame, the halt, and the blind were classed among the unfortunate of society, they were, nevertheless, the charge of the community. Biblical law made provision for their protection : "Thou shalt not put a stumbling block before the blind." (Leviticus 19 : 14) This injunction became the forerunner of social legislation to help and protect the afflicted.

Deaf mutes were classed among the idiots and regarded as irresponsible persons, but they, too, were included in the Mosaic law from being cursed or abused. Children born with mental deficiencies were considered victims of the "Evil Eye," a superstitious belief that the individual was accursed or possessed by some evil spirit.

Special institutions for the afflicted are not maintained by the Jewish communities. Where institutional care is necessary, public welfare agencies make such care available.

ORGANIZATIONS, NATIONAL AND INTERNATIONAL

Community Service—Guidance—Research

The complexity of Jewish social welfare has brought into existence a number of national organizations to act as coordinating agencies and advisory bodies for community welfare funds and institutions. A rough

estimate of the number of local societies, agencies, bureaus, and charitable organizations attending the poor, the sick, and maladjusted throughout the country would be in excess of four thousand. Most communities
have a federation or welfare fund to raise money and to coordinate their
various activities. Local federations, however, rely on national agencies
for guidance and research. The following organizations are some that
offer special services in the fields of social service, education, and philanthropy :

American Jewish Correctional
Chaplains Association, Inc.
(1935)
10 East 73rd Street, N.Y.C.
10021

Program
To rehabilitate Jewish prisoners;
To offer religious and social
services to penal institutions.

Association of Jewish Community
Relations Workers (1950)
31 Union Square, N.Y.C. 10003

Program
To encourage cooperation between Jewish community relations workers and com-
munal workers;
To encourage among Jewish
community relations work-
ers the fullest possible understanding of Jewish life and
values.

B'nai B'rith Vocational Service
Bureau (1938)
1640 Rhode Island Ave., N.W.
Washington, D.C. 20036

Program
To aid in occupational adjustment of Jewish youth and
adults;
To carry out research in problems of occupational adjust-
ments and discrimination.

Council of Jewish Federations and
Welfare Funds (1932)
729 7th Avenue, N.Y.C. 10009
Program
To provide central and regional services in Jewish community campaigns;
To provide information concerning interpretation, budgeting, and social planning.

Jewish Conciliation Board of
America (1930)
225 Broadway, N.Y.C. 10007
A voluntary Social Service
agency.
Program
To adjust and conciliate disputes involving individuals
and organizations.

Jewish Occupational Council
(1939)
156 Fifth Ave. N.Y.C. 10010

Program
To serve as a central service,
research, and coordinating
agency in the field of vocational guidance.

Jewish Peace Fellowship (1941)
43 W. 57th Street, N.Y.C. 10019

Program
To clarify the relationship of
Judaism to Pacifism;
To aid conscientious objectors.

Jewish War Veterans (1896; 1929)
1712 N. Hampshire Ave., N.W.
Washington 9, D.C.
It was organized as the Hebrew Union Veterans organization, but later merged with other groups and adopted its present name in 1929.

Program
To offer patriotic, fraternal, and educational services in behalf of the Jews of the United States;
To uphold and defend the name of the Jew.

National Association of Jewish Center Workers (1918)
55 W. 42nd Street, N.Y.C. 10016

Program
To promote the welfare, training, and professional standards of Jewish Center Workers.

National Community Relations Advisory Council (NCRAC) (1944)
55 West 42nd Street, N.Y.C. 10036
This is a joint planning and policy making agency for a large number of Jewish organizations and community councils.

Program
To formulate policy in the field of community organizations in the United States;
To coordinate the work of national and local agencies engaged in community relations activities.

National Conference of Jewish Communal Services (1899)
31 Union Square W. N.Y.C. 10003

Program
To discuss problems and developments in the various fields of Jewish communal service on a professional basis.

National Council of Jewish Women (1893)
1 West 47th Street, N.Y.C. (10036)
First national Jewish Women's organization in the United States, dedicated to furthering human welfare.

Program
To provide for educational and cultural needs for the Jewish community;
To promote religious education for Jewish children;
To offer programs for social action in the field of legislation;
To work for the mentally and physically handicapped and underprivileged;
To render immigrant aid and service to the foreign born.

National Jewish Welfare Board (1917)
145 E. 32nd St. New York, N.Y. 10016
The central organization for Jewish Centres. YMHA's, and YWHA's throughout the country.

Program
To provide for the religious and welfare need of the Jews in the armed forces and in veterans' hospitals;
To promote physical and cultural well-being of Jews;
To provide chaplains and rabbis to the armed forces and veteran institutions;
To assist disabled veterans and beneficiaries of veterans.

National Jewish Committee on
Scouting (1926)
New Brunswick, N.J. (Boy
Scouts of America)

Program
To stimulate Boy Scout activity among Jewish boys.

IN DEFENSE OF JEWISH RIGHTS

The concept of Tzedakah includes concern for the political and economic status of world Jewry. The Jewish people, throughout its history,
assumed the responsibility of redeeming captives and caring for refugees.
In its time the Kehillah interceded for the welfare and protection of
Jews wherever it was possible or expedient.

The Jewish people of England and France were the leaders in creating
national and international organizations for the protection of the rights
of their co-religionists. In America a number of national organizations
came into being for the same purpose, whether at home or abroad.

From time to time attempts were made to coordinate these agencies
into a unified body to speak for American Jewry, but with little success.
The following organizations comprise a chronological list of self-defense
agencies. Many had auxiliary functions. Some no longer exist.

EUROPEAN ORGANIZATIONS

Board of Deputies of British Jews
(1760)
London, England
This is the first Jewish organization created for the primary purpose of regulating internal Jewish
affairs. Its structure resembled that
of a Kehillah with representatives
from Sephardic and Ashkenazic
synagogues, and secular institutions
totalling 450 members. It is supported by levies paid by the affiliated bodies.

Program
To be the representative
spokesman for British Jewry;
To safeguard the natural rights
that pertain to British citizens;
To help the cause of Jewish
emancipation in other lands;
To alleviate the condition of
the poor and unfortunate;
To combat anti-Semitism

Alliance Israelite Universelle
(1860)
Paris, France
This organization, founded by
Adolph Cremieux as a result of the
Mortara Case, was the first of its
kind to champion the rights of oppressed Jews in France, Eastern
Europe, Asia, and Africa. It was
also the first attempt to unite Jews
of many countries in a joint effort
to counteract anti-Semitism and to
secure citizenship rights and privileges. The work of the Alliance
was political, educational, relief,
and propaganda. Its educational
program included a network of
schools in oriental countries. In
1957, a total of 47,500 children
were in attendance at these
schools. The pioneer agricultural
school in Mikveh Israel (1870) was
founded by the Alliance.

Program
To defend the honor of the

Jewish name wherever it is attacked;

To encourage by every available means the pursuit of useful handicrafts;

To combat, where necessary, the ignorance and vice engendered by oppressors;

To work, by the power of persuasion and moral influence, for the emancipation of Jews who still suffer under the burden of exceptional legislation.

The Alliance rendered effective service to needy Jewry and was recognized as the most influential Jewish organization of the world until World War II. While France was under Hitlerism, the work of the Alliance was temporarily halted.

The Anglo-Jewish Association (1871)
London, England

This association was patterned after the Alliance of France. Although traditionally non-Zionist, it is a principal share holder in the Jewish Colonization Association and supports the Evelina de Rothschild school in Jerusalem. From 1881 to 1944 it cooperated with the Board of Deputies of British Jews in its political activities.

Program

To obtain protection for those who may suffer in consequence of being Jewish;

To advance social, moral, and intellectual welfare of Jews in Eastern Europe and elsewhere.

Israelitische Alliance zu Wien (1873)
Vienna, Austria.

Program

To work for suffering Jews outside of Austria;

To intervene for the protection of Jews;

To combat slander and blood accusation through educational work;

To aid refugees and charitable organizations.

With the liquidation of the Jews under Hitlerism, this organization went out of existence in 1938.

Hilfsverein der Deutsche Juden (1901)
Berlin, Germany

This German Jews' Aid Society was organized to help Jews maintain educational institutions. It assisted thousands of Jews to emigrate when their security was threatened under Nazism.

Program

To provide financial assistance to needy Jews and to support Jewish schools in Eastern Europe;

To aid orphan children of the Ukrainian pogroms.

World Jewish Congress (1936)
15 E. 84 St. N.Y.C. 10028

This international organization was started in Geneva as the successor to the Committee on Jewish Delegations. It is recognized as the central democratic representative of all the Jewish people for the defense of the rights of the Jews everywhere.

Program

To secure and safeguard the rights, status, and interests of Jews and Jewish communities throughout the world;

To represent its affiliated organizations before the United

Nations, the organization of American States, the Council of Europe, governmental, intergovernmental and o t h e r international authorities on matters that are of concern to the Jewish people as a whole;

To promote Jewish cultural activity and to represent Jewish cultural interests before UNESCO;

To organize Jewish communal life in countries of recent settlement;

To prepare and publish surveys on contemporary Jewish problems.

AMERICAN ORGANIZATIONS

American Jewish Committee (1906)
165 E. 56 St. N.Y.C.   10022
The first American Jewish organization created for the defense of Jewish rights at home and abroad. In times of crisis it broadens its activities to include philanthropic and political aid where needed.

Program
To prevent infraction of the civil and religious rights of Jews in any part of the world;

To secure equality of economic, social, and educational opportunity through education and civic action;

To broaden understanding of the basic nature of prejudice through propaganda and to improve techniques for combating it t h r o u g h mass media and educational means;

To promote a philosophy of

Jewish integration by projecting a balanced view with respect to full participation in American life and retention of Jewish identity.

American Jewish Congress (1917)
15 E. 84th St. N.Y.C.   10028
This organization was founded by Rabbi Stephen S. Wise and a group of Zionists for the recognition of Jewish civil, political, and religious rights in central and eastern Europe and in Palestine. Following World War I it sent a delegation to the Paris Peace Conference. It adjourned after that, but was reorganized as a permanent body in 1922. It is active in pressing legal aspects of constitutional guarantees for all minorities. It helped to organize the World Jewish Congress in 1936 and fought vigorously against Nazism.

Program
To protect the rights of Jews in all lands;

To strengthen the bonds between American Jewry and Israel;

To promote the democratic organization of Jewish communal life in the United States;

To foster the affirmation of Jewish religious, cultural, and historic identity;

To contribute to the preservation and extension of the democratic way of life.

Anti-Defamation League   (1913)
315 Lexington Ave. N.Y.C.
10016
This department of the B'nai B'rith is dedicated to helping the persecuted and to defending the name of the Jew.

Program

To combat anti-Semitism and to secure justice for all citizens alike;

To counteract un-American and anti-democratic propaganda;

To promote better group relations;

To disseminate literature concerning Jews and Judaism;

To achieve greater democratic understanding among all Americans through public information, education, and community action.

Jewish Labor Committee (1934)
     25 E. 78 St. N.Y.C.   10021

This was founded by representatives of all branches of the Jewish labor movement in the United States. Before World War II it organized an anti-Nazi boycott and helped rescue 1,500 Jewish labor leaders from Europe. After 1945 it was active in rehabilitating displaced persons. It is strongly Zionistic and supports many projects in Israel.

Program

To combat communist and fascist propaganda and anti-Semitism;

To aid victims of oppression and persecution;

To combat racial and religious intolerance abroad and in the United States in cooperation with organized labor and other groups.

American Committee for Safeguarding Equal Rights of Jews (1938)
N.Y.C.

This organization, also known as the General Jewish Council, was called into being by the B'nai B'rith to represent a united front for combating anti-Semitism and for joint political action in behalf of world Jewry. It included the following big-four defense agencies:

    The American Jewish Committee
    The B'nai B'rith
    The American Jewish Congress
    The Jewish Labor Committee

This attempt to create a single, all-inclusive advisory and coordinating body for the defense of Jewish rights failed because of differences in ideology of the respective member agencies.

Consultative Council of Jewish Organizations (1946) 61 Broadway, N.Y.C. 10006

This body represents the American Jewish Committee, the Anglo-Jewish Association, and the Alliance Israelite Universelle. It is a non-governmental organization with consultative status.

Program

To cooperate, consult, advise, and render assistance to the United Nations and to its Educational, Scientific, and Cultural department (UNESCO), to the International Labor Organization (ILO) and to the Council of Europe on problems relating to human rights and on all matters pertaining to Jews.

Coordinating Board of Jewish Organizations (1947)
     1640 Rhode Island Ave., N.W.
     Washington 6, D.C.

Represents B'nai B'rith, Board of Deputies of British Jews and the South African Jewish Board of Deputies. It is also a non-governmental consultative body.

Program

To represent Jews in the Economic and Social Council of the United Nations;

To protect the status, rights, and interests of Jews as well as related matters bearing upon the human rights of all peoples.

American Jewish League Against Communism (1948)
220 W. 42nd St. N.Y.C. 18

To publicize communist enmity toward Jewry and Judaism, and the American Jews' enmity to communism;

To fight communist infiltration in Jewish life.

JEWISH VETERAN ASSOCIATIONS

Jewish War Veterans of the United States of America (1896) 1712 New Hampshire Ave., N.W. Washington 9, D.C.

This organization was an outgrowth of the Hebrew Union Veterans Organization. In 1923 it became the Jewish War Veterans of the United States of America. It included all veterans of previous wars, thus becoming the oldest veteran organization in this country.

Program

To be of greater service to its country and to one another, and to perpetuate American ideals;

To maintain true allegiance to the United States of America;

To uphold the fair name of the Jew and to fight his battles wherever he is unjustly assailed;

To aid widows and dependents of deceased veterans;

To assist such comrades and their families as may be in need of help;

To gather and preserve the records of patriotic service performed by Jews;

To honor the memory and shield from neglect the graves of heroic dead;

To promote Americanization programs.

National Association of Jewish Chaplains of the Armed Forces (1946) 145 E. 32nd St. N.Y.C. 10016

Program

To promote fellowship among chaplains;

To advance common interest in all chaplains in and out of service.

The Rehabilitation of Jewish Life

Among the sad experiences dotting the pages of Jewish history are those of mass suffering following the heels of war, persecution, pogroms, and enforced migrations. The displacement of Jews in European countries was accompanied by such economic dislocation and insecurity, that organizations came into existence with programs for reconstruction and rehabilitation. Wealthy individuals sought to save human life through planned colonization schemes. Organizations undertook to train people for new modes of livelihood and to adapt them to new environments.

It became the responsibility of national Jewish agencies to provide care for the wandering and homeless Jews. Even before World War II many international organizations were already operating in the field of Jewish economic, social, and educational rehabilitation and were ready to step in where needed.

SOCIETY FOR REHABILITATION AND TRAINING (1880)
Russia (ORT)

This organization is popularly known as the "ORT", the initials for the Russian name "Obstchestvo Resmeslenovo Truda." Its program was at first confined to Russian Jewry but soon spread to other countries of Europe. It became a world organization after World War I, with branches in France, Germany, England, America, and elsewhere. In 1943 the headquarters of the World ORT Union were moved from Berlin to Geneva. The World ORT Union has increased the scope of its work in recent years to 19 countries, including Israel and North America. In America, a number of ORT agencies function under the following names.

American ORT Federation (1924)
222 Park Avenue, N.Y.C. 10003
Women's American ORT (1927)
American Labor ORT (1937)
National ORT League (1937)
Business and Professional ORT (1937)
American and European Friends of ORT (1941)

Program
To reconstruct the lives of the Jews in Eastern Europe in cooperation with national governments;
To extend long-term credits to Jews for the purchase of machines and tools;
To establish and conduct trade schools and to place graduates in permanent positions;
To help in the formation of collective workshops and develop Jewish cooperatives and artisan industries.

JEWISH COLONIZATION ASSOCIATION (1891)
England (ICA)

In the year 1891, a Jewish philanthropist, Baron Maurice de Hirsch of England, founded the Jewish Colonization Association. Aided by liberal contributions from other wealthy Jews, the Association embarked upon a program of enabling Jews to settle in agricultural colonies in Argentina and other countries, including Brazil and Palestine. In 1923, the word Palestine was added to the name (PICA) and in 1927 it became HICEM (in combination with HIAS). Since World War II the work of ICA has been concentrated in the Americas.

Program
To assist and promote the migration of Jews from any part of Europe and Asia;
To establish colonies for agriculture, industry, and commercial purposes;
To maintain agencies and institutions necessary to such settlement work, such as cooperative loan societies, savings banks, and schools.

JEWISH AGRICULTURAL SOCIETY (1900)

386 Park Avenue. N.Y.C. 10016

Founded by joint agreement between the Jewish Colonization Association and the Baron de Hirsch Fund, it helps Jews to settle on farms and aids those already settled.

Program

To encourage farming among Jews in the United States;

To train young men for farm work and to prepare for farm ownership;

To provide information on the most recent scientific developments in agriculture.

OSE—WORLD UNION FOR THE PROTECTION OF THE JEWS (1912) AMERICAN COMMITTEE OF OSE (1939)

8 West 40 St. N.Y.C. 10018

Organized in Russia to combat the high mortality rate among Russian Jews and to alleviate sickness and suffering through preventive measures and hygienic instruction. Until the outbreak of World War II branches of OSE were to be found all over Europe, operating hospitals, dispensaries, summer camps, and clinics.

In Poland, a similar program was started in 1923 and was carried on under the name of TOZ. Its activities were widespread until the advent of Hitlerism. OSE offered the following important services until it went out of existence :

Program

To improve the health of the Jewish people and their medical education;

To popularize hygiene among Jews;

To render moral and physical aid with particular emphasis upon Jewish youth;

To operate a Red Mogen David (Red Cross).

HADASSAH—WOMEN'S ZIONIST ORGANIZATION (1912)

65 E. 52nd St. N.Y.C. 10022

Organized in 1912 by Henrietta Szold for the purpose of conducting health, medical, and social service activities in Israel and of fostering creative Jewish living in America.

Hadassah is the largest Jewish women's organization in the world. Its youth body is known as Junior Hadassah. Also affiliated is the Business and Professional Women of Hadassah.

Program

To help interpret Israel to the American people;

To provide basic Jewish education as a background for intelligent and creative Jewish living in America;

To support a country-wide medical and public health system in Israel, including clinics, hospitals, nurses training, and medical education.

To cooperate in the Youth Aliyah program in Israel in which it pioneered;

To partcipate in the program of the Jewish National Fund;

To support a child welfare and a vocational educational program.

AMERICAN JEWISH JOINT DISTRIBUTION COMMITTEE (1914)

3 East 54th St. N.Y.C. 10022

The Joint Distribution Committee came into existence during the first World War through the merger of three American Relief agencies:

(1) The American Jewish Relief Committee,
(2) The Central Committee for Relief,
(3) The People's Relief Committee.

The original purpose of the JDC was the regulation of welfare disbursements in the war zones of Europe after the war. Subsequently it grew into the largest reconstruction and rehabilitation agency in the world.

The greatest task of the JDC has been to help the victims of Nazism. Wherever they were permitted to operate they were the only agency giving Jews life and hope. Its program today is to administer and distribute funds for relief, rehabilitation, and emigration activities in behalf of Jews overseas, especially victims of mass migrations.

Program
War Relief
Emergency Relief
Reconstruction
Reorganization

UNITED JEWISH APPEAL (1930)

1290 Avenue of the Americas, N.Y.C. 10019

This organization is the national Jewish coordinated fund raising agency for the American Jewish Joint Distribution Committee, the United Israel Appeal, and the New York Association for New Americans. The UJA receives its support from the Welfare Fund Agencies of the local Jewish communities.

VAAD HATZALA REHABILITATION COMMITTEE (1939)

132 Nassau St. N.Y.C. 10038

Program
To aid immigration of rabbis, students, and religious leaders to Israel and the United States;
To send food transports to Israel;
To assist religious academies in Europe and Israel.

JEWISH RESTITUTION SUCCESSOR ORGANIZATION (1947)

3 East 54th St., N.Y.C. 10022

This organization is recognized by the goverment of the United States. It works through the Jewish Agency, the Joint Distribution Committee and some Israeli organizations.

Program
To discover, claim, receive, and assist in the recovery of Jewish heirless or unclaimed property;
To utilize such assets or to provide for their utilization for the relief, rehabilitation, and resettlement of surviving victims of Nazi persecution.

CONFERENCE ON JEWISH MATERIAL CLAIMS AGAINST GERMANY, INC. (1951)

3 East 54th St. N.Y.C. 10022

These funds were secured under an agreement with the German Federal Republic for the relief, rehabilitation, and resettlement of needy victims of Nazi persecution living outside Israel.

Immigration and Refugee Aid

The people of Israel has been characterized as the "Wandering Jew." For the past two thousand years, with few exceptions, the Jew has never been permitted to establish roots in any country of his dwelling. As the Passover Haggadah aptly states it, "champions of God, they marched from one Egypt to another, driven in haste, their property a prey to the rapacious foe, with their bundles on their shoulders, and God in their hearts."

Because hospitality to strangers was one of the primary injunctions imposed upon the Jewish people, the Jew usually found co-religionists to help him wherever he went. Every Jewish community, however bad its own lot might have been, somehow found a place for the refugee. In time, Jewish communities all over the world assumed the obligation of raising funds to help their distressed brethren and to support such traditional institutions as Hachnoseth Orchim (Sheltering Homes), and Pidyon Shebuyim (Redemption of Captives).

Starting in the 1880's, it was natural that American Jewry, once victims of European pogroms and persecution, should take the leadership in offering aid to the newcomer to these shores, as well as to refugees seeking shelter in other parts of the world. This form of Tzedakah is one of Jewry's oldest practices, and many institutions arose to fulfill this function.

The two World Wars created the largest Jewish refugee movements in history. Old agencies were revived. New ones were created or old ones merged to meet the needs of the time. The first communal undertaking was a "Hachnoseth Orchim," the Hebrew Sheltering House Association. In 1909 this was merged with the Hebrew Immigrant Aid Society (HIAS) to become a modern welfare agency, international in scope. It was known as HICEM, in which the HIAS cooperated with ICA (Jewish Colonization Association) and Emigdirect (Emigrations–Direktion), which had been set up in 1921 by the Jewish Emigration Conference in Prague to assist Russian Jews to emigrate.

The League of Nations created a Department for Refugees, but its interest was only juridical. The United Nations extended the program, but the relief aspects were limited. In 1947, the International Refugee Organization was established by the United Nations to deal with Arab refugees from Palestine.

In 1954 HIAS merged with the United Service for New Americans and the overseas migration services of the Joint Distribution Committee to create the United HIAS Service (UHS). This agency provides a world-wide service to help Jews migrate to wherever they feel they can make an economic and social adjustment. So many of those who come to the United States stay in New York City that the program of the New York Association for New Americans is supported nationally through the United Jewish Appeal.

HEBREW IMMIGRANT AID SOCIETY (1909) HIAS
425 Lafayette St. N.Y.C. 10003

This organization, now known as "United HIAS Service, Inc." came into existence through the merger of the Hebrew Sheltering Home, founded in 1880, and the Hebrew Immigrant Aid Society, founded in 1882. Subsequent mergers have made this a world-wide organization.

Program
To provide Jewish migrants with legal documents, transportation, and shelter upon arriving;
Representation and intervention before governmental authorities;
To provide temporary relief needs;
To establish contact with kinsmen and friends;
To secure employment.
Over the years, the following have been absorbed by HIAS :

NATIONAL REFUGEE SERVICE (1939)

This organization was the successor to the National Coordinating Committee (1934). It became part of the United Service for New Americans in 1946.

Program
To aid refugees arriving in the United States;
To give voluntary financial aid, support, and assistance to Jewish or non-Jewish persons;
To act as a national clearing house.

UNITED SERVICE FOR NEW AMERICANS (1946)

This organization was the result of a merger between the National Refugee Service (1939) and the National Office of the Service to the Foreign Born, which was sponsored by the National Council of Jewish Women. In 1954, it became part of HIAS.

Program
Immigration, reception, resettlement, and rehabilitation for Jewish displaced persons and immigrants.

EMIGDIRECT (EMIGRATIONS-DIREKTION) (1921)

This was set up at Prague in 1921 by the Jewish Emigration Conference to aid emigration from Europe, especially Russia.

ICA (JEWISH COLONIZATION ASSOCIATION) (1891)

Philanthropic society founded by Baron Maurice de Hirsch to assist Jews to emigrate from countries of Europe and Asia.

HICEM (1927)

After 1927 the Emigdirect merged with HIAS and ICA to be known as HICEM (initials of the three agencies). When the Emigdirect severed its connection in 1934 to join ORT–OSE, the organization was known as HIAS–ICA. Its purpose was to give information and assistance to Jews emigrating from Europe. With Nazism, the program was extended to find homes for German refugees in other parts of the world. Before the end of World War II, ICA had to withdraw because of lack of funds and in 1945 HIAS alone remained.

During the Nazi period, many committees were formed, the more durable of which were absorbed or merged with other agencies. Some, like the Refugee Economic Corporation and the Dominican Republic Settlement Association ceased their functions.

REFUGEE ECONOMIC CORPORATION (1934)

Program
　　To assist in the economic rehabilitation of refugees and displaced persons;
　　To undertake and assist in the financing and management of enterprises of a banking, credit, industrial, or utility nature;

To find suitable areas of settlement and reconstruct lives of newcomers.

DOMINICAN REPUBLIC SETTLEMENT ASSOCIATION (1939)

Program
　　To settle Jewish and non-Jewish refugees in the Dominican Republic.

BARON DE HIRSCH FUND (1891)

This fund is related to ICA, but it went further in helping Jews fleeing from East Europe.

Program
　　To protect immigrants when they arrived in port;
　　To give them relief and temporary aid;
　　To remove them from urban centers by training and settling them on the land;
　　To impart secondary education in agriculture;
　　To teach mechanical trades;
　　To support the Jewish Agricultural Society (1900) and to promote the Jewish farm movement.

National Religious Bodies

The Jewish religion has been defined as a "Way of Life," and while this connotes definite characteristics, there are many interpretations as to how the Jew should travel along this "way." Orthodoxy insists that the road to God must conform with the principles and traditions revealed to Moses on Sinai. Reform Judaism seeks to interpret God in the pattern of modern life. Within the framework of each may be found divergent and conflicting interpretations. Beyond and between these two dominant groups there are many shadings, from the harmonizing attempts of Conservative Judaism to a humanist concept devoid of the personal idea of God. Following are the more important institutions, organizations, and denominational schools that represent the various branches of Jewish religious life in America :

ORTHODOX

AGUDATH ISRAEL OF AMERICA (1912)

5 Beekman Street, N.Y.C. 10038

This "Union of Israel" is the American branch of the world organization.

Program
To unite Jewry in the Orthodox spirit;
To seek solutions of problems that confront world Jewry in the spirit of true Torah.
Affiliated groups
Pirchei Agudath Israel—Children's division.
Bnos Agudath Israel—Girl's division.
Zeirei Agudath Israel—Youth division.

AGUDATH ISRAEL WORLD ORGANIZATION (1912)

2521 Broadway, N.Y.C. 10025

An international organization of Orthodox Jews, founded at Kattowitz by German, Polish, and Ukrainian Jews. It opposed Zionism and the Mizrachi movement.

Program
To provide research institutes for postwar problems of religious Jewry;
To engage in research and publish studies concerning religious Jewry.

CANTORS ASSEMBLY OF AMERICA (1947)

1109 Fifth Avenue, N.Y.C. 10028

Program
To elevate the general status and standards of the cantorial profession;

To unite all cantors who are traditional Jews;
To conserve and promote the musical traditions of the Jewish people.

HEBREW THEOLOGICAL COLLEGE (1922)

7135 N. Carpenter Rd. Skokie, Ill.

Program
To offer studies in higher Jewish learning along traditional lines;
To train rabbis, teachers, and religious functionaries.

NER ISRAEL RABBINICAL COLLEGE (1933)

4411 Garrison Blvd. Baltimore, Md. 21215

Program
To train rabbis and teachers for the needs of Orthodox Jewry;
To provide complete secular and religious instruction.

RABBINICAL ALLIANCE OF AMERICA (1944)

156 Fifth Avenue, N.Y.C. 10011

Although intended as an alumni association of the Yeshivah Torah VaDaath, it became a representative body of orthodox rabbis. It still supports the Yeshivoth.

Program
To further traditional Judaism and support institutions of higher learning;
To maintain professional competency among its members;
To establish modern orthodox communities in the United States;
To supply all Jewish com-

munities with religious functionaries;
To defend the welfare of Jews the world over.

RABBINICAL COLLEGE OF TELSHE (1941)

28400 Euclid Ave., Cleveland, O.

A college for higher Jewish learning, specializing in rabbinics and Talmudic Study. Conducts preparatory academy, graduate school, and pedagogical institute.

RABBINICAL COUNCIL OF AMERICA (1923)

84 Fifth Ave. N.Y.C. 10011

Organization of ordained orthodox Rabbis in pulpits in North America.

Program
To promote Orthodox Judaism;
To support institutions for the study of Torah.

UNION OF ORTHODOX JEWISH CONGREGATIONS OF AMERICA (1898)

84 Fifth Ave. N.Y.C. 10011

Program
To serve as authoritative central body for the orthodox congregations in the United States and Canada;
Conducts the certification of the U Kashruth service.
Affiliates
National Conference of Synagogue Youth (1954)
Women's Branch (1923).

UNION OF ORTHODOX RABBIS OF THE UNITED STATES AND CANADA (1902) (Agudas Harabonim)

235 E. Broadway, N.Y.C. 10002

Program
To foster traditional Judaism and promote higher Torah learning;
To strengthen authority of orthodox rabbinate;
To disseminate knowledge of traditional Jewish rites and practices among the masses;
To assist in the establishment and maintenance of Yeshivoth in the United States.

UNION OF SEPHARDIC CONGREGATIONS (1929)

8 W. 70th St. N.Y.C. 10023

Program
To promote the religious interests of Sephardic Jews;
To provide leadership for Sephardic congregations;
To distribute Sephardic Prayer Books.

YESHIVA UNIVERSITY (1896) (Yitzchak Elchanan)

186th & Amsterdam, N.Y.C. 10033

Program
A school for undergraduate and graduate work in general and Jewish education; grants rabbinical ordination; maintains a separate High School for boys and girls. Operates the Yeshivah College for men, the Stern College for women, the Albert Einstein Medical School, and a cantorial school. Its Women's organization was founded in 1935.

YESHIVATH TORAH V'DA-ATH AND MESIVTA (1918)

141 S. 3rd St. Brooklyn, N.Y. 11211

Program
Offers Hebrew and secular education from elementary

school through rabbinical ordination;

Maintains a Hebrew Teachers Institute.

Affiliates

Academy of Higher Learning and Research (Beth Midrash Elyon)

CONSERVATIVE

JEWISH THEOLOGICAL SEMINARY OF AMERICA (1856)

3080 Broadway, N.Y.C. 10027

Maintains a theological seminary for the training of teachers and ordination of rabbis.

Affiliates

Teachers Institute Seminary and College of Jewish Studies (1909)

Jewish Museum (1926)

Institute for Religious and Social Studies (1938)

University of Judaism (1947)

Department of Radio and Television (1944)

Maxwell Abbell Research Institute in Rabbinics (1951)

American Jewish History Center (1953)

RABBINICAL ASSEMBLY OF AMERICA (1900)

3080 Broadway, N.Y.C. 10027

Serves as a professional organization for Conservative rabbis.

UNITED SYNAGOGUE OF AMERICA (1913)

3080 Broadway, N.Y.C. 10027

Parent body for conservative congregations and auxiliaries.

Affiliates

National Women's League (1918)

National Federation of Jewish Men's Clubs (1929)

Commission on Jewish Education (1930)

National Academy for Adult Jewish Education (1940)

National Association of Synagogue Administrators (1948)

Educators Assembly (1951)

Youth of United Synagogue (1951)

College Age Organization — ATID (1960)

American Academy for Jewish Research (1920)

REFORM

UNION OF AMERICAN HEBREW CONGREGATIONS (1873)

838 Fifth Avenue, N.Y.C. 10021

Parent organization of Reform congregations in the western hemisphere.

Affiliates

Commission on Jewish Education (1923)

National Federation of Temple Sisterhoods (1913)

National Federation of Temple Brotherhoods (1923)

National Federation of Temple Youth (1938)

Commission on Social Action (1949)

National Association of Temple Administrators (1955)

Commission on Synagogue Administration (1962)

Jewish Chautauqua Society (1893)

HEBREW UNION COLLEGE (1875) —JEWISH INSTITUTE OF RELIGION (1922)

—Merged in 1950

Cincinnati, New York City, Los Angeles, and Jerusalem.

Prepares students for the Rabbinate, Cantorate, and religious school teaching. Assembles, classifies, and preserves Jewish Americana.

Affiliates
Jewish Museum (1913)
American Jewish Archives (1947)
Hebrew Union School of Education and Sacred Music (1947)
Los Angeles College (1954)
American Jewish Periodical Center (1956)
Biblical and Archaeological Institute in Jerusalem

CENTRAL CONFERENCE OF AMERICAN RABBIS (1889)

790 Madison Avenue, N.Y.C. 10021

This Reform Rabbinical Association seeks to conserve and promote the Jewish Religion and learning through its various committees and commissions.

WORLD UNION FOR PROGRESSIVE JUDAISM (1926)

838 Fifth Avenue, N.Y.C. 10021

Promotes and coordinates worldwide efforts on behalf of liberal Judaism.

INDEPENDENT GROUPS

ACADEMY FOR JEWISH RELIGION (1954)

112 East 88 Street, N.Y.C. 10028

A school for the training and ordination of Rabbis for Reform, Conservative and Orthodox groupings.

SOCIETY OF JEWISH SCIENCE (1922)

N.Y.C.

Maintains that Jewish Science is the application of the teachings of Judaism to the practices of life; that religious healing is derived from the God concept in the Hebrew Psalms.

SYNAGOGUE COUNCIL OF AMERICA (1926)

235 Fifth Avenue, N.Y.C. 10016

Provides over-all Jewish religious representation in the United States, acting in the interest of Orthodox, Conservative, and Reform Judaism.

JEWISH RECONSTRUCTIONIST FOUNDATION (1940)

15 West 86th Street, N.Y.C. 10024

This "Society for the Advancement of Judaism" is dedicated to the advancement of Judaism as a religious civilization, to the upbuilding of Israel, and to the reconstruction of Jewish life.

Affiliates
Federation of Reconstructionist Congregations and Fellowships (1954)

AMERICAN COUNCIL FOR JUDAISM (1943)

201 East 57 Street, N.Y.C. 10022

Program
To advance the universal principles of Judaism free of nationalism;
To promote the national, civic, cultural, and social integration of Americans of Jewish faith.

Educational Organizations

The word of God, as embodied in the religion and faith of the Jews, was to be taught "diligently" unto the children of Israel. The synagogue was the first house of learning and in late Bible times, education became compulsory for all boys.

Throughout their history the Jewish people have been called "The People of the Book," not so much because they gave the Bible to the world, but rather because of the extent to which they dedicated themselves to the pursuit of knowledge. The vast literature of the Talmud, Midrash, and kindred writings sprang from the "House of Study" where, at a very early age, the youngster was introduced to Biblical lore.

Today, Jewish education is taught in the Cheder, the Talmud Torah, the Folk School, the Sabbath and Sunday School, and the all-day parochial school, each with its own curriculum, text books, materials, and techniques. Their needs are supplied by a multitude of educational bureaus and commissions, staffed by experts in their respective fields.

In addition to these institutions, a number offer adult courses on Jewish and secular subjects. Following are the more important ones:

AMERICAN ASSOCIATION FOR JEWISH EDUCATION (1939)

101 Fifth Avenue, N.Y.C. 10003

Program

Coordinates, guides, and serves Jewish educators and schools through a community program, publications, and special projects.

ASSOCIATION OF ORTHODOX JEWISH SCIENTISTS (1947)

84 Fifth Avenue, N.Y.C. 10011

Program

To promote the orientation of science within framework of Orthodox tradition;

To relate to the interaction between the Jewish traditional life and scientific developments;

To encourage Orthodox Jewish youth in the study of science and to assist others engaged or interested in scientific pursuits.

B'NAI B'RITH HILLEL FOUNDATION (1923)

1640 Rhode Island, N.W. Washington, D.C. 20036

Program

Provides cultural, religious, and counseling service to Jewish students in colleges and universities.

BRANDEIS INSTITUTE (1941)

1101 Pepper Tree Lane, Brandeis (Santa Susana), Cal. 93064

Maintains summer camp institutes for college students and teen-agers and week-end adult institutes for training for leadership in the American Jewish community.

Program

To instill an appreciation of Jewish cultural and spiritual heritage;

To create a desire for active participation in the American Jewish community.

BRANDEIS UNIVERSITY (1948)
Waltham 54, Mass.

A co-educational, non-sectarian, free-quota school for the study of the arts and sciences, sponsored by the Jewish people of the U.S.

COLLEGE OF JEWISH STUDIES (1924)
72 East 11th St., Chicago, Ill. 60605

Offers Jewish study courses and provides professional training for Hebrew and religious school teachers.

DROPSIE COLLEGE FOR HEBREW AND COGNATE LEARNING (1907)
Broad & York Sts., Philadelphia, Pa. 19132

A non-sectarian school under Jewish auspices; offers post-graduate instruction in higher Jewish and semitic learning.

GRATZ COLLEGE (1893)
10th St. & Tabor Rd., Philadelphia, Pa.

The first Jewish teachers' training school in the U.S.

Program
Prepares teachers for Jewish religious schools;
Provides studies in Judaica and Hebraica;
Maintains a Hebrew high school;
Coordinates Jewish education in the city and provides consultation services to Jewish schools of all leanings.

HEBREW TEACHERS COLLEGE (1921)
43 Hawes St., Brookline, Mass. 02146

Program
To offer higher Jewish learning;
To train Hebrew teachers and community workers;
To promote a constructive knowledge of the Jewish spiritual creations and contributions to the world's culture and progress;
To conduct a four-year parochial high school.

HERZLIAH HEBREW TEACHERS INSTITUTE (1921)
314 W. 91st St., N.Y.C. 10024

Program
To train teachers of Bible, Hebrew language, and Jewish religion for Hebrew elementary, parochial, and high schools;
Conducts schools, institutes, and adult-education courses.

JEWISH CHAUTAUQUA SOCIETY (1893)
838 Fifth Avenue, N.Y.C. 10021

Sponsored by the National Federation of Temple Brotherhoods.

Program
To disseminate authoritative knowledge about Jews and Judaism to educational institutions and Christian Seminar camps and institutes.

JEWISH EDUCATION COMMITTEE (1939)
1776 Broadway, N.Y.C. 10019

Central community service agency for Jewish education in N.Y.

Program
To meet the educational needs of the groups in the com-

munity through cooperation with their official educational agencies.

Affiliates

Council on Jewish Audio-Visual Materials. (1949)

JEWISH INFORMATION SOCIETY OF AMERICA (1959)

72 East 11 St., Chicago, Ill. 60605

Program

To work for a better understanding of the Jewish religion among non-Jews and estranged Jews;

To introduce prospective proselytes to Jewish congregations;

To arrange for their instruction in the Jewish religion.

JEWISH TEACHERS SEMINARY AND PEOPLES UNIVERSITY (1918)

515 Park Avenue, N.Y.C. 10022

This is the only Hebrew-Yiddish seminary in the U.S.

Program

To train men and women in the light of scientific knowledge and historical Jewish ideals for the Jewish teaching profession, research, and community service.

MESIVTA YESHIVAH (RABBI CHAIM BERLIN RABBINICAL ACADEMY) (1905)

1411 Dinsmore Ave., Far Rockaway, N.Y. 11691

Maintains parochial schools, a rabbinical academy, and post-graduate school for advanced Jewish studies.

MIRRER YESHIVA CENTRAL INSTITUTE (1947)

1791–5 Ocean Parkway, Brooklyn, N.Y. 11223

Maintains a high school, rabbinical college, and post-graduate school for Talmudic research; engages in rescue and rehabilitation of scholars overseas.

NATIONAL COUNCIL FOR TORAH EDUCATION (1939)

200 Park Avenue, N.Y.C. 10003

Sponsored by Mizrachi-Hapoel Hamizrachi (Religious Zionists).

Program

To organize and supervise Talmud Torahs;

To prepare and train teachers and to supply educational materials;

Sponsors the National Association for Orthodox Educators and the American Menorah Institute.

NATIONAL COUNCIL FOR JEWISH EDUCATION (1926)

101 Fifth Avenue, N.Y.C. 10003

Program

To further the cause of Jewish education in America;

To raise professional standards and practices and promote welfare of Jewish educational workers;

To improve and strengthen Jewish life.

NATIONAL COUNCIL OF BETH JACOB SCHOOLS (1943)

150 Nassau St., N.Y.C. 10038

Operates Orthodox all-day schools and a summer camp for girls.

NATIONAL COUNCIL OF YOUNG ISRAEL (1912)

3 West 16th Street, N.Y.C. 10011

Program
To educate Orthodox youth in Torah-true Judaism through youth work and study.
Affiliates
Eretz Israel Division (1926)
Employment Bureau (1914)
Armed Forces Bureau (1939)
Institute for Jewish Studies (1947)
Intercollegiate Council (1950)

NATIONAL FEDERATION OF HEBREW TEACHERS AND PRINCIPALS (1944)

120 W. 16th St., N.Y.C. 10011

Program
To organize Hebrew teachers nationally;
To improve professional status and intensify the study of Hebrew language and literature in Jewish schools.

NATIONAL JEWISH INFORMATION SERVICE FOR THE PROPAGATION OF JUDAISM, INC. (1960)

6412½ Olympic Blvd., Los Angeles, Cal. 90048

Program
To convert Gentiles to Judaism and revert Jews to Judaism;
To train Jewish missionaries and offer Jewish instruction through correspondence.

NATIONAL SOCIETY FOR HEBREW DAY SCHOOLS (1944)

(Torah Umesorah)
156 Fifth Ave., N.Y.C. 10010

Program
To establish and service all-day Jewish schools throughout the country;
To conduct teacher training institutes, seminars, and workshops;
To publish and distribute textbooks and materials.
Affiliates
National Association Parent-Teachers Association
National Association of Jewish Day School Administrators
National Council of Yeshiva Principals
National Yeshiva Teachers' Board of License

P'EYLIM-AMERICAN YESHIVA STUDENT UNION (1951)

3 West 16 St., N.Y.C. 10011

Program
To aid and sponsor voluntary pioneer work by American graduate teachers and rabbis in the camps of new villages and towns of Israel.

RABBINICAL ALLIANCE OF AMERICA (1944) (Igud HaRabbanim)

156 Fifth Avenue, N.Y.C. 10010

Program
To further traditional Judaism and support institutions of higher learning;
To establish modern Orthodox communities and supply religious functionaries;
To elevate the position of Orthodox rabbis nationally, and to defend the welfare of Jews the world over.

RESEARCH INSTITUTE OF RELIGIOUS JEWRY (1941)

1133 Broadway, N.Y.C. 10010

Program
To engage in research and publish studies concerning the situation of religious Jews and their world problems.

SHOLOM ALEICHEM FOLK INSTITUTE (1918)
41 Union Square, N.Y.C. 10003

Program
Supports schools of Yiddish learning for the instruction of children in the Yiddish language, literature, and folklore;
To imbue Jews with the significance of Jewish life in America and Israel.

WEST COAST TALMUDICAL SEMINARY (Mesivta Beth Medrosh Elyon) (1953)
11027 Burbank Blvd. N. Hollywood, Cal. 91601

A Yeshiva elementary, high school, and Torah-Talmudic academy; also prepares students for the Rabbinate.

YAVNE HEBREW THEOLOGICAL SEMINARY (1924)
510 Dahill Rd., Brooklyn, N.Y. 11218

A school for higher Jewish learning and the training of rabbis and teachers for American Jewish communities.

Cultural Organizations

It is difficult to separate Jewish cultural institutions from those of Jewish education. They really belong together, since both serve to awaken the Jew to his heritage. Cultural organizations abound. Some have come into existence because of special occasions or observances in Jewish life. Others have been created in response to special needs in the life of the Jew.

ALEXANDER KOHUT MEMORIAL FOUNDATION (1915)
3080 Broadway, N.Y.C. 10027

Program
Publishes works in the field of Talmudic lore, lexicography, and archaeology.

AMERICAN BIBLICAL ENCYCLO-PEDIA SOCIETY (1930)
210 West 91 Street, N.Y.C. 10024

Program
To spread knowledge of the Bible through publication of the Talmudic-Midrashic-Biblical Encyclopedia called Torah Shelemah.

AMERICAN CONFERENCE OF CANTORS (1953)
40 West 68 Street, N.Y.C. 10023

Program
To promote the best of musical tradition;
To introduce new musical concepts of worship through commissions and competitions for contemporary Jewish composers.

THE AMERICAN JEWISH ARCHIVES (1948)
Clifton Ave. Cincinnati 20, Ohio

Program
To serve as a repository for the

important historic records of Jews on the American continent;

Supplies data to individuals and communities on American Jewish history.

AMERICAN JEWISH HISTORICAL SOCIETY (1892)

150 Fifth Avenue, N.Y.C. 10011

Program
Collects and publishes material on the history of the Jews in America.

AMERICAN JEWISH INSTITUTE (1947)

250 West 57 Street, N.Y.C. 10019

Program
Seeks the advancement of Jewish knowledge and culture through the dissemination of data on Jews and Judaism;

Publication of essential literature for speakers and library services.

Affiliate
Jewish Information Bureau (1932)

A clearing house and the publisher of "Index."

CONFERENCE ON JEWISH SOCIAL STUDIES (1935)

1841 Broadway, N.Y.C. 10023

Program
Engages in and supervises scientific studies and factual research with respect to sociological problems involving contemporary Jewish life.

CONGRESS FOR JEWISH CULTURE (1948)

25 East 78 Street, N.Y.C. 10021

Program
To centralize and promote Jewish culture throughout the world;

To unify fund raising for its activities.

Affiliate
World Bureau for Jewish Education. (1948)

Program
To coordinate the work of Yiddish and Hebrew-Yiddish schools in the United States and abroad.

INSTITUTE FOR JEWISH RESEARCH (1925)

1048 Fifth Avenue, N.Y.C. 10028

This organization is known as YIVO, taken from the letters of its Yiddish name, "Yiddisher Visenschaftlicker Organization."

Program
To stimulate, promote, and develop cultural life;

To engage in Jewish Social research.

JEWISH ACADEMY OF ARTS AND SCIENCES (1927)

46 West 83 Street, N.Y.C. 10024

Program
To honor Jews distinguished in the arts and professions;

To encourage Jewish achievement in scholarship and the arts.

JEWISH BOOK COUNCIL OF AMERICA (1940)

145 E. 32 Street, N.Y.C. 10016

Program
To spread knowledge of Jewish books, literature, and authors.

JEWISH BRAILLE INSTITUTE OF AMERICA (1931)

48 East 74 Street, N.Y.C. 10021

Program
To meet the cultural and religious needs of the blind;
To publish books for the blind and maintain a worldwide free Braille lendinglibrary for all people.

JEWISH LITURGICAL MUSIC SOCIETY OF AMERICA (1963)

90-15 68th St. Forest Hills, L.I. 11375

Program
To present, evaluate, promote, and advance Synagogue music.

JEWISH MINISTERS CANTORS ASSOCIATION OF AMERICA (1910)

236 Second Avenue, N.Y.C. 10003

Program
To perpetuate the cantorial profession in its traditional form;
To provide assistance to needy cantors;
Maintains library of cantorial and Hebrew music.

JEWISH MUSEUM (1926)

1109 Fifth Avenue, N.Y.C. 10028

Program
To collect and exhibit Jewish ceremonial objects;
To exchange contemporary art;
To sponsor lectures and related activities.

JEWISH PUBLICATION SOCIETY OF AMERICA (1888)

222 N. 15 Street, Philadelphia, Pa. 19102

Program
To publish and disseminate books of Jewish interest for the purpose of preserving Jewish culture and heritage.

LEAGUE FOR SAFEGUARDING THE FIXITY OF THE SABBATH (1929)

122 W. 76th St. New York City 10023

Program
To promote the observance of the seventh-day Sabbath and to protect such observers.

LOUIS AND ESTHER LAMED FUND, INC. (1939)

19420 Silvercrest, Southfield, Mich.

Program
To bring about cooperation between Yiddish and Hebrew writers and readers;
To foster the development of Jewish culture by providing grants and scholarships.

NATIONAL BAR MITZVAH CLUB (1926)

515 Park Avenue, N.Y.C. 10022

Program
To enhance meaning of the Bar and Bat Mitzvah ceremony;
To develop personal identification with Israel through a three-year program culminating in a summer tour of Israel.

**NATIONAL COMMITTEE FOR
FURTHERANCE OF JEWISH
EDUCATION (1940)**

824 Eastern Parkway, Brooklyn,
N.Y. 11213

Program
   To disseminate the ideals of
   Torah-true education among
   the youth of America.

**NATIONAL JEWISH MUSIC
COUNCIL (1944)**

145 East 32 Street, N.Y.C. 10016

Program
   To promote Jewish music
   activities on a community
   basis.

**OFFICE FOR JEWISH
POPULATION RESEARCH (1949)**

165 East 56th Street, N.Y.C.
10022

Program
   To gather population and
   statistical data on Jews and
   to stimulate national interest in Jewish population research.

**RESEARCH INSTITUTE OF
RELIGIOUS JEWRY (1941)**

1133 Broadway, N.Y.C. 10010

Program
   To engage in research and
   publish studies concerning
   the situation of religious
   Jewry and its problems all
   over the world.

**YIDDISHER KULTUR FARBAND
(1937)**

189 2nd Avenue, N.Y.C. 10003

Program
   To advance Jewish culture,
   and publish and exhibit
   works of contemporary Yiddish writers and artists.

Zionist Pro-Israel Organizations

Zionism, as a national movement, became a reality when in the year
1897 Dr. Theodore Herzl of Vienna founded the World Zionist Congress. Within this Congress were united all Zionists groups throughout
the world, dedicated to the establishment of Palestine as an independent
Jewish homeland. During the centuries of persecution, starting with the
close of the second commonwealth (70 CE), the Jew had dreamed of and
yearned for the restoration and resettlement of the land of the Patriarchs.

As the World Zionist movement grew and became popular, various
ideologies developed resulting in the creation of separate Zionist factions.
All were agreed upon the central idea—the creation of a Jewish national
home, but they differed as to the form Zionism should take. Therefore,
subsequent Zionist congresses were marked by strong differences and conflicts between the Cultural Zionists, Territorialists, Social Democrats,
Labor Zionists, and Religious Zionists. These ideologies have increased
in number and today a multitude of Zionist organizations raise their
voices to appeal to the people for support.

Despite the fact that Israel Statehood was established in 1948, most of these Zionist organizations continue to function, even if only to propagandize. Many of them are fund-raising agencies and carry on their respective programs in Israel and the United States. Following are the more important institutions engaged in pro-Israel activities :

GENERAL

AMERICAN ZIONIST COUNCIL (1939; 1949)
515 Fifth Avenue, N.Y.C. 10022

Program
To serve as a coordinating agency and a public relations arm of all the major American Zionist organizations;
To create a greater appreciation of Jewish culture.

JEWISH AGENCY—AMERICAN SECTION FOR PALESTINE
515 Fifth Avenue, N.Y.C. 10022

Program
Authorized American Agency for the State of Israel;
To work for the development and colonization of Israel;
To absorb Jewish immigrants from Diaspora;
To coordinate Jewish institutions and associations;
To stimulate private investments;
To conduct world-wide Hebrew cultural programs.
Affiliate
Zionist Archives and Library of the Jewish Agency (1939)

JEWISH AGENCY FOR ISRAEL (1949; 1960)
515 Park Avenue, N.Y.C. 10022

Program
To determine the allocation of United Jewish Appeal funds for rescue, rehabilitation, and resettlement programs in Israel.

JEWISH NATIONAL FUND (1910)
42 East 69th Street, N.Y.C. 10027

Its Hebrew name is Keren Kayemeth L'Yisroel—Fund for the Establishment of Israel.
Program
To raise money for the purchase, development, and reclamation of the land of Israel.

KEREN-OR, INC. (Jerusalem Institutions for the Blind) (1958)
1133 Broadway, N.Y.C. 10010
Program
To raise money for the maintenance of the Jewish Institutions for the Blind in Israel.

NATIONAL YOUNG JUDEA (1909)
116 West 14th Street, N.Y.C. 10011

Program
To perpetuate and inculcate American Jewish Youth in the Zionist heritage.

STATE OF ISRAEL BOND ORGANIZATION (1951)
215 Park Avenue, N.Y.C. 10003

Program
To provide large-scale investment funds for the eco-

nomic development of the State of Israel through the sale of the State of Israel bonds.

UNITED CHARITY INSTITUTIONS OF JERUSALEM, INC. (1903)

154 Nassau Street, N.Y.C. 10038

Program
To raise funds for a large number of institutions in Israel.

UNITED JEWISH APPEAL (1927)

515 Park Avenue, N.Y.C. 10022

Program
To raise funds for Israel's immigration and resettlement program;
To be the fund-raising representative of all Zionist parties as well as the Palestine Foundation Fund and the Jewish Agency.

WORLD CONFEDERATION OF GENERAL ZIONISTS (1946)

30 East 42nd Street, N.Y.C. 10017

Program
To promote Zionist education and further Jewish survival in the diaspora;
To encourage private and collective industry and agriculture.

ZEBULUN ISRAEL SEAFARING SOCIETY (1946)

31 Union Square W. N.Y.C. 10003

Program
To encourage seamindedness among Jewish youth;
To assist training schools for seamen in Israel;

To aid disabled sick and old seamen.

ZIONIST ORGANIZATION OF AMERICA (1897) (ZOA)

145 East 32nd Street, N.Y.C. 10016

A propaganda organization for the promotion of Zionism in America.

Program
To safeguard the integrity and independence of Israel as a free and democratic commonwealth by means consistent with the laws of the United States;
To assist in the economic development of Israel;
To strengthen Jewish sentiment and consciousness as a people and promote its cultural creativity.

AMERICAN ZIONIST YOUTH FOUNDATION (1963)

515 Fifth Avenue, N.Y.C. 10022

Program
Coordinates and initiates Zionist youth activities in interpreting Israel to the youth of America;
Sponsors Israel Summer Institutes in America and in Israel.

Affiliates
American Zionist Youth Council (1951)
Student Zionist Organization (1954)

ECONOMIC

AMEIC—AMERICAN ERETZ ISRAEL CORP. (1944)

565 Fifth Avenue, N.Y.C. 67

Program

To further trade between the United States and Israel;

To assist in the economic development of Israel.

AMPAL—AMERICAN PALESTINE TRADING CORP. (1942)

17 East 71st Street, N.Y.C. 10021

Program

To develop trade relations and close ties between the United States and Israel through investment, shipping, and import-exports;

To assist in Israeli development of economic and industrial sources.

PEC—ISRAEL ECONOMIC CORPORATION (1926)

(Formerly Palestine Economic Corp.)

500 Fifth Avenue, N.Y.C. 10036

Program

Fosters economic development of Israel on a business basis through investments.

RASSCO ISRAEL CORPORATION (1950)

535 Madison Avenue, N.Y.C. 10022

Program

To develop investment opportunities in Israel;

To strengthen economic ties between the United States and Israel.

LABOR ZIONISM

HASHOMER HATZAIR (1925)

112 Fourth Avenue, N.Y.C. 10003

The English name for this pro-labor American organization is "The Young Guardians."

Program

To support labor and progressive forces in Israel;

To raise money for the Chalutz movement;

To encourage investment in cooperative industrial enterprises.

Affiliates

Zionist Youth Organization (1925)

Progressive Zionist League (1947)

Americans for Progressive Israel (1950)

LABOR ZIONIST ORGANIZATION OF AMERICA (1905)

200 Park Avenue, N.Y.C. 10003

Program

To aid in building the State of Israel as a cooperative commonwealth;

To promote the philosophy of the Histadruth—the general Federation of Jewish Labor in Israel;

To establish a democratic society throughout the world based on idividual freedom, equality, and social justice;

To strengthen Jewish education and promote the welfare of Jews in all lands.

Affiliates

Poale Tzion—Workers of Zion

Ichud HaBonim—Labor Zionist Youth (1935)

HaShavim—Labor Zionist Aliyah Group

League for Labor Israel (1961)

NATIONAL COMMITTEE FOR LABOR ISRAEL (1923)

33 East 67 Street, N.Y.C. 10021

Program
To raise and provide funds for the Histadruth institutions in Israel;

To assist in the integration of newcomers as productive citizens in Israel;

To promote an understanding of the aims and achievements of Israel labor among Jews and non-Jews in America.

Affiliate
American Trade Union Council for Histadruth.

UNITED LABOR ZIONIST PARTY (1920; 1947)

305 Broadway, N.Y.C. 10007
The Hebrew name for this organization is Achdut HaAvodah-Poale Tzion—The Labor Unity and Labor Zionist Party.

Program
To establish a democratic socialist order in Israel and strengthen Jewish labor movements in the United States.

RELIGIOUS ZIONISM

POALE AGUDATH ISRAEL OF AMERICA, INC. (1948)

147 W. 42nd Street, N.Y.C. 10036

Program
To educate youth to become Orthodox Chalutzim;

To support Kibbutzim, trade schools, and children's homes in Israel.

Affiliates
Ezra-Irgun HaNoar HaChareidi (1953)
To educate and prepare children for life in the Kibbutzim.

Chever HaKibbutzim—League of Religious Settlements (1951)
Women's Division (1948)

RELIGIOUS ZIONISTS OF AMERICA (1911)

200 Park Avenue, N.Y.C. 10003

Most of the Religious Zionist organizations operate under the direction of Mizrachi, a word meaning "Eastern." They seek to rebuild Israel as a Jewish commonwealth in the spirit of traditional Judaism.

B'NAI AKIVA OF NORTH AMERICA (1934)

200 Park Avenue S. N.Y.C. 10003

Program
To interest youth in religious labor Zionism;

Maintains training farms and summer camps.

MIZRACHI-HAPOEL HAMIZRACHI (1909; 1957)

200 Park Avenue S. N.Y.C. 10003
(Religious Workers Party)

Program
To establish and maintain schools and Yeshivoth in Israel;

Supports all-day schools and a maximum program of religious education in the United States.

MIZRACHI HATZAIR (1952)

200 Park Avenue S. N.Y.C. 10003

Program
To inculcate religious Zionism in the youth of America:

To promote Aliyah for Jewish youth to rebuild Israel as a religious society.

MIZRACHI PALESTINE FUND (1928)

200 Park Avenue S. N.Y.C. 10003

Program
To raise funds for the Mizrachi movement.

WOMEN'S ZIONIST ORGANIZATIONS

HADASSAH, WOMEN'S ZIONIST ORGANIZATION OF AMERICA (1912)

65 East 52nd Street, N.Y.C. 10022

Program
To support and conduct health, medical, and social service in Israel;
To support child welfare and vocational-educational projects;
To provide maintenance and education for youth newcomers through Youth Aliyah;
To interpret Israel to American people through education and youth projects;
To foster creative Jewish living in the United States.

Affiliate
Junior Hadassah, Youth Division (1920)

MIZRACHI WOMEN'S ORGANIZATION (1948)

45 East 17th Street, N.Y.C. 10003

Program
To help support and maintain kindergartens, nurseries, girls' homes, and vocational schools in Israel.

PIONEER WOMEN (THE WOMENS LABOR ZIONIST ORGANIZATION OF AMERICA) (1925)

29 East 22 Street, N.Y.C. 10010

Program
To sponsor social welfare, vocational training, and rehabilitation projects in Israel;
To cooperate in a constructive citizenship program;
To promote Jewish education and culture in American life.

WOMEN'S LEAGUE FOR ISRAEL, INC. (1928)

1860 Broadway, N.Y.C. 10023

Program
To provide shelter, vocational training, and social adjustment services to young women newcomers to Israel;
To cooperate in the educational program for young women at the Hebrew University in Jerusalem.

REVISIONIST ZIONISTS

BETAR-BRITH TRUMPELDOR OF AMERICA (1929)

116 Nassau Street, N.Y.C. 10038

Program
To organize Jewish youth and instill in them a love for Israel;
To settle Jewish youth in Israel.

CULTURAL ZIONISM

AMERICAN COMMITTEE FOR BAR-ILAN UNIVERSITY IN ISRAEL, INC. (1952)

641 Lexington Avenue, N.Y.C. 10022

Program
> To support growth and development of the American chartered Bar-Ilan University in Israel;
> To administer American student programs and to arrange exchange professorships in the United States and Israel.

AMERICAN COMMITTEE FOR BOYS TOWN JERUSALEM (1949)

165 W. 46th St., N.Y.C. 10036

Program
> To provide a comprehensive program of academic, vocational, and religious training for Israeli teenagers.

AMERICAN COMMITTEE FOR THE WEIZMANN INSTITUTE OF SCIENCE, INC. (1944)

515 Park Avenue, N.Y.C. 10022

Program
> To support the Weizmann Institute of Science at Rehovoth, Israel.

AMERICAN FRIENDS OF THE HEBREW UNIVERSITY (1931)

11 East 69 St., N.Y.C. 10021

Program
> To foster the growth, development, and maintenance of the Hebrew University of Jerusalem;
> To represent, publicize, and raise money for its support;

To administer American-student programs and arrange exchange professorships in in the United States and Israel.

AMERICAN FRIENDS OF RELIGIOUS FREEDOM IN ISRAEL
(formerly League for Religious Freedom in Israel) (1963)

P.O.B. 2421 Washington, D.C. 20013

Program
> To seek full religious freedom in Israel through separation of church and state;
> To promote public knowledge of religious coercion in Israel and rally American Jewish support to its cause.

AMERICA-ISRAEL CULTURAL FOUNDATION, INC. (Formerly American Fund for Israel Institutions) (1939)

4 East 54th Street, N.Y.C. 10022

Program
> Central fund raising agency for leading educational, cultural, and social welfare agencies;
> Supports projects including the Israel Philharmonic Orchestra, the Habimah theater, the Inbal dancers, Israel Museum, and Academies of Music;
> Sponsors cultural exchange between the United States and Israel.

AMERICAN ISRAEL PUBLIC AFFAIRS COMMITTEE (1954)
(Formerly American Zionist Committee for Public Affairs)

Colorado Bldg., 14th & G. Streets, N.W. Washington, D.C. 20004

Program

To conduct public action bearing upon relations with governmental authorities with a view to maintaining and improving friendship and good will between the United States and Israel.

AMERICAN-ISRAELI LIGHT-HOUSE, INC. (1928)

30 E. 69th Street, N.Y.C. 10022

Program

To provide education and rehabilitation for the blind in Israel.

AMERICAN JEWISH LEAGUE FOR ISRAEL (1957)

11 West 42 Street, N.Y.C. 10036

Program

To unite all those who are committed to the historical ideals of Zionism, independently of class or party.

AMERICAN PHYSICIANS FELLOWSHIP, INC. FOR THE ISRAEL MEDICAL ASSOCIATION (1950)

1622 Beacon St. Brookline, Mass. 02146

Program

To foster and aid medical progress in Israel;

To secure fellowships for selected Israeli physicians;

To aid financially and contribute literature and supplies.

AMERICAN RED MOGEN DAVID FOR ISRAEL (1941)

225 West 57 Street, N.Y.C. 10019

Program

To function as the national membership organization for the counterpart of the Red Cross in Israel;

To purchase medical supplies and ambulances and to maintain blood banks and first-aid stations in Israel.

AMERICAN SOCIETY FOR TECHNION-ISRAEL INSTITUTE OF TECHNOLOGY, INC. (1940)

1000 Fifth Avenue, N.Y.C. 10028

Program

To support the school at Haifa for the promotion of technical and industrial development.

AMERICANS FOR A MUSIC LIBRARY IN ISRAEL (1950)

2451 N. Sacramento Ave., Chicago, Ill. 60647

Program

To promote, encourage, and financially assist musical education in Israel.

DROR HECHALUTZ HATZAIR (1948)

2091 Broadway, N.Y.C. 10023

Program

To foster Zionist programs for youth;

To sponsor work-study seminars and summer camps.

FCH—FEDERATED COUNCIL OF ISRAEL INSTITUTIONS

38 Park Row, N.Y.C. 10038

Program

To secure funds for independent religious, educational, and welfare institutions in Israel, not otherwise maintained.

HAGDUD HAIVRI LEAGUE, INC.
(1929)
(American Veterans of the
Jewish Legion)
426 W. 58 Street, N.Y.C. 10019

Program
To assist Legion veterans in settling in Israel;
To uphold ideals of Jewish Legion, which fought for Palestine liberation.

HISTADRUT IVRITH OF AMERICA
(1916) (Tarbuth)
120 West 16 Street, N.Y.C. 10011

Program
To promote Hebrew language and literature in the U.S. and sponsor Hebrew-speaking camps;
To strengthen the cultural relations between the United States and Israel.

Affiliate
Hebrew Arts Foundation (1939)

THEODOR HERZL FOUNDATION
(1954)
515 Park Avenue, N.Y.C. 10022

Program
To conduct a Zionist adult education program through classes, lectures, and academic conferences;
To issue books and literature on modern Zionism, Israel, and Jewish subjects.

ISRAEL MUSIC FOUNDATION
(1948)
731 Broadway, N.Y.C. 10003

Program
To support the growth of music in Israel and disseminate Israeli music throughout the world.

PALESTINE SYMPHONIC CHOIR
PROJECT (1938)
3143 Central Ave., Indianapolis, Ind. 46205

Program
To settle cantors and Jewish artists in Israel;
To establish a center for festivals of Biblical musical dramas.

SOCIETY OF ISRAEL
PHILATELISTS (1948)
40–67 61 St., Woodside, L.I. 11377

Program
To sponsor chapters and research groups for Israeli philately;
To maintain a philatelic library and support of public and private exhibitions.

UNITED STATES COMMITTEE
FOR SPORTS IN ISRAEL, INC.
(1950)
147 East 42 Street, N.Y.C. 10036

Program
Sponsors U.S. Maccabiah Team and the Orde Wingate Institute for Physical Education;
To promote facilities and training of Israeli personnel.

ANTI-ZIONISM

AMERICAN COUNCIL FOR
JUDAISM, INC. (1943)
201 East 57 Street, N.Y.C. 10022

Program
To advance the universal principles of a Judaism free of nationalism;
To maintain an educational program dedicated to the universal tradition of Judaism.

Fraternal and Benevolent Organizations

Societies for mutual benefit date far back in history. Fraternities or societies for the burial of the dead are mentioned in the Talmud. The 19th century witnessed the rise of the modern fraternal order, with its insurance and endowment features. These societies not only offer pecuniary benefits and cheap insurance, but provide social, educational, and cultural activities. Many of these organizations have been instrumental in shaping the character of American Jewish life.

AMERICAN VETERANS OF ISRAEL (1949)

110–23 63rd Ave., Forest Hills, N.Y. 11375

Program
> To maintain contact among American veterans of Israel's War of Independence and the Aliyah Bet volunteers;
> To foster contacts between America and Israel.

B'NAI B'RITH (1843) (Sons of the Covenant)

1640 Rhode Island Ave., N.W. Washington, D.C. 20036

Program
> To unite Jews through social, cultural, civic, philanthropic, and patriotic activities;
> To promote programs in youth work, community organization, adult Jewish education, aid to Israel, international affairs, service to veterans, and to citizenship and civic projects.

Affiliates
> Anti-Defamation League (1913)
> Hillel Foundations, Inc. (1923)
> National Association of Hillel Directors (1949)
> Vocational Service Bureau (1938)

B'nai B'rith Women
Youth Organization (1924)

B'NAI ZION (1910) (Fraternal Zionist Organization of America)

50 West 57 Street, N.Y.C. 10019

Program
> To promote principles of Americanism, fraternalism, and Zionism;
> To offer life insurance, hospitalization, and other benefits to members;
> To sponsor settlements, youth centers, medical clinics, and the John F. Kennedy evaluation center for the mentally retarded in Israel.

BRITH ABRAHAM (1887)

37 East 7th Street, N.Y.C. 10003

Program
> To provide fraternal benefits to members;
> To support camps for underprivileged children and senior citizens;
> To promote brotherhood, Jewish ideals, Zionist mutual aid, and philanthropic activities.

BRITH SHOLOM (1905)

121 S. Broad St., Philadelphia, Pa. 19107

Program
To promote defense of Jewish rights, civic welfare, and service to the Jewish community.

FARBAND (LABOR ZIONIST ORDER)
575 Sixth Avenue, N.Y.C. 10011

To provide members and families with low-cost fraternal benefits;
To enhance Jewish life, culture, and education;
To support the State of Israel in keeping with the ideals of labor Zionism.

FREE SONS OF ISRAEL (1849)
257 W. 93rd St., N.Y.C. 10025

Program
A benevolent fraternal order based on friendship, love, and truth;
To provide sick and death benefits and to engage in non-sectarian philanthropic activities.

HEBREW VETERANS OF THE WAR WITH SPAIN (1899)
87–71 94 St., Woodhaven, N.Y. 11421

Program
A social and fraternal group to fight bigotry.

INTERNATIONAL JEWISH LABOR BUND (1897; 1947) (World Coordinating Committee of the Bund)
25 East 78 Street, N.Y.C. 10021

Program
To coordinate activities of world bund organizations and represent them in the Socialist International;

To spread the ideas of Jewish Socialism as formulated by the Jewish Labor Bund;
To publish and disseminate literature.

JEWISH PEACE FELLOWSHIP (1941)
Columbia University, Earl Hall, Broadway and 117 Street, N.Y.C. 10027

Program
To support efforts to resolve human conflicts through pacific methods.

JEWISH SOCIALIST VERBAND OF AMERICA (1921)
175 E. Broadway, N.Y.C. 10002

Program
To promote the ideals of social democracy among the Yiddish-speaking working people of America.

PROGRESSIVE ORDER OF THE WEST (1896)
705 Chestnut St., St. Louis, Mo. 63101

Program
To foster benevolence and philanthropy through its fraternal order.

SEPHARDIC JEWISH BROTHERHOOD OF AMERICA (1915)
116 E. 169 St. Bronx, N.Y. 10452

Program
To promote the industrial, social, educational, and religious welfare of its members.

UNITED ORDER TRUE SISTERS, INC. (1846)

150 W. 85 Street, N.Y.C. 10025

Program
To promote cancer treatment and other services through its fraternal and philanthropic activities.

WORKMEN'S CIRCLE (1900)

175 E. Broadway, N.Y.C. 10002

Program
To offer sick benefits and cemetery-funeral provisions;
To foster cultural, social, and educational activities and to support schools for Yiddish instruction.

Affiliates
Division of Jewish Labor Committee (1933)
English-Speaking Division (1927)
Young Circle League (Youth Section) (1927).

WORLD SEPHARDI FEDERATION (1951) (American Branch)

152 W. 42 St., N.Y.C. 10036

Program
To assist Jewish and non-Jewish refugees through relief, resettlement, and rehabilitation programs in Europe, the Middle East, and the United States;
To support institutions in Israel that do not receive support from the United Jewish Appeal or other fund-raising agencies.

Landsmannschaften—Societies

Among early organizations that sprang up in American Jewish life were the Landsmannschaften, composed of immigrants with a common geographical origin. They transplanted many of the institutions of the European Shtetel, built their own synagogues, and continued their social and cultural life in the new setting. Some established mutual aid and free-loan associations. Others aligned themselves with specific causes for the welfare of the Jewish people here and abroad. Since World War II a number of them have disbanded.

AMERICAN ALLIANCE OF POLISH JEWISH SOCIETIES (1908)

1133 Broadway, N.Y.C.

Program
To act in the protection of Jewish interests and rights.

ASSOCIATION OF YUGOSLAV JEWS IN THE U.S. (1940)

247 W. 99 Street, N.Y.C. 10025

Program
To assist Jews of Yugoslav origin, and charitable organizations;
To assist Jewish immigrants in Israel.

UNITED GALICIAN JEWS OF AMERICA, INC. (1904; 1937)

175 Fifth Avenue, N.Y.C. 10010

Program
To represent Galician landsleit all over the world;
To work for the State of Israel.

UNITED HUNGARIAN JEWS OF AMERICA, INC. (1944)
269 W. 76 Street, N.Y.C. 10023

Program
To assist Hungarian Jews in the U.S.;
To maintain rehabilitation center in Ramat Gan, Israel;
To aid needy Jews everywhere.

UNITED RUMANIAN JEWS OF AMERICA, INC. (1909)
31 Union Square W., N.Y.C. 10003

Program
To defend the interests of Jews in Rumania;
To work for their civic and political emancipation and for their economic rehabilitation;
To represent and further the interests of Rumanian Jews in the United States.

Labor Organizations

The Jewish religion, as early as Bible times, laid special emphasis on the equitable treatment and protection of the worker. The Talmud deals at great length with the ethics of labor and mutual obligations of employer and employee.

The ideals of social justice gave voice to the desire of the exploited worker to improve his lot. Under oppressive working conditions in Europe and America, the Jew found himself in the vanguard of trade unionism. In European countries, the Jewish labor movement received its impetus from socialism. The struggle for economic emancipation had political ramifications. Radicalism and revolt offered the best hope to the masses. In America, the struggle for economic emancipation meant freedom from sweat shops, low wages, long hours, seasonal unemployment, unsanitary and hazardous working conditions, and many other evils.

To improve these deplorable conditions and to raise the standard of the working class, attempts were made to organize the workers into unions. The Jewish labor movement struggled with various radical elements, socialistic organizations, strikes, hardships, short-lived gains, and internal dissensions. Owing to devoted efforts on the part of their leaders, over many years, there finally emerged strong Jewish labor organizations that set the pattern, to a large measure, for the American labor movement. Along the way there were developed many radical, intellectual, and socialistic ideologies, some represented by fraternal orders and mutual aid societies. In some respects the entire labor movement might be rightfully called a Jewish movement, since from the days of Mosaic legislation the Jew has always rebelled against the tyranny of economic and political exploitation of man.

EARLY LABOR MOVEMENTS (Di Fareinigte Yiddische Geverkshaften)

The Propaganda Society 1882
Russian Jewish Workers Society 1885
Jewish Workers Society 1885

These organizations, stemming from the European Bund groups, were the forerunners of the Jewish labor movement in America. They sought to propagate the ideals of socialism among the masses and experimented with cooperative movements. Some of the leaders of these societies were Alexander Harkavy, Abraham Cahan, Dr. Abraham Caspe, Bernard Weinstein, M. Zametkin, David Edelstadt, Dr. H. Solotaroff, and N. Aleinikov. In 1888 these organizations gave way to a larger federation of Jewish unions, known as the United Hebrew Trades.

UNITED HEBREW TRADES (1888)

This was the parent institution of the Jewish labor movement in America. From its very inception it has played an important role in the American labor movement. Among its early leaders were Morris Hillquit, M. Zametkin, Louis Miller, R. Lewis, I. Magidow, and Dr. Luibitch.

Program
    To create a network of unions in the Jewish trades;
    To popularize trade unionism among the masses;
    To promote Jewish communal and humanitarian programs;
    To link the Jewish trade movement with the American Labor movement.

UNITED GARMENT WORKERS (1891)

This union of the garment workers was the first attempt in the United States to organize labor on a national scale. Israel Barskey, a crusader among the clothing workers, was one of its founders. Although it started with progressive policies, its subsequent American-born, non-socialist leadership was strongly conservative. Inner dissension resulted in a split in its ranks and in 1914, under Jewish leadership, the Amalgamated Clothing Workers of America was formed.

THE WORKMEN'S CIRCLE (1892)—Reorganised (1900)
175 East Broadway, N.Y.C. 10002

This organization (The Arbeiter Ring) is the oldest and largest benevolent and fraternal Jewish labor society in the nation. It started as a society to unite the workers of the world by a "ring of friendship." The purpose of the Circle is three-fold : (1) Mutual assistance among members in times of need and misfortune, (2) education of members, and (3) organization of co-operative business enterprises. Among its early leaders were Sam Shapiro, B. Feigenbaum, Meyer London, Rose Asch, Dr. B. Hoffman, M. Goldrich, D. Gingold, M. Schwartz, M. Boker, L. Kalman, M. Goldring, L. Cozlin, H. Lasker, and A. Goldesmith.

Program

Provides sick benefits, life insurance, free burial;

Promotes social, cultural, educational, and humanitarian activities;

Operates own sanatorium and medical clinics;

Sponsors and supports daily schools for instruction in Yiddish language, history, and literature.

SOCIAL TRADE AND LABOR ALLIANCE (1895)

This alliance was organized by Daniel DeLeon, a radical labor leader. It was an attempt to win the Jewish worker by injecting a socialist political philosophy into the labor movement.

UNITED HATTERS, CAP, AND MILLINERY WORKERS (1895)
673 Broadway, N.Y.C. 10016

This union is one of the three oldest in America. It was founded in 1873 and reorganized in 1895. In 1901, under the leadership of Max Zaritsky, it became known as the United Cloth Hat and Capmakers Union. In 1934 it changed its name to its present form with the amalgamation of Hatters International and Millinery Workers International.

Unionism in America owes much to the Hatters. To them goes the credit for eliminating prison labor, bringing order out of chaos in its own industry, and driving out racketeering and abuses. Some of the early Jewish leaders of this union were Max Zuckerman, Nathaniel Spector, Abraham Mendelowitz, Alex Rose, Jacob Roberts, Louis Margolin, Max Kaplan, Jack Margolis, Herman Hinder, Lucy Oppenheim, and Max Golden.

INTERNATIONAL LADIES GARMENT WORKERS (1900)
1710 Broadway, N.Y.C. 10019

This union was the first Jewish nationwide labor organization for workers in all branches of ladies' tailoring. Its primary program was to protest and reform the evils of the sweatshops and home labor. It introduced the "Protocol of Peace" concept in labor circles, in which were set up a Committee of Grievances and a Board of Arbitration. Among its early leaders were Herman Robinson, Bernard Braff, Joseph Barondess, Benjamin Schlesinger, and M. Rosenberg.

Program
    To foster education and grant scholarships to able students;
    To maintain a union Health Center and a summer resort called Unity House;
    To participate in national and international drives for communal betterment;
    To contribute to emergent relief projects.

LABOR ZIONIST ORGANIZATION OF AMERICA (1905) (Farband)
575 Sixth Avenue, N.Y.C. 10011

This organization, also known as the Jewish National Workers Alliance of America (Farband), renders fraternal insurance benefits and engages in labor Zionist, educational, and cultural activities. The original name of this organization was the Poale Zion—Workers of Zion. After founding the Jewish National Workers Alliance it embarked on an extensive education program by establishing many secular Jewish folk schools.

Program
    To further the building of the State of Israel as a cooperative commonwealth;
    To promote a universal democratic society;
    To vitalize, strengthen and democratize the structure of Jewish community life in America;
    To enrich the contribution of the individual Jew to the welfare of the United States, to the Jewish people, and to mankind.

AMALGAMATED CLOTHING WORKERS OF AMERICA (1914)
15 Union Square, N.Y.C.

Under the leadership of Sidney Hillman and Joseph Schlossberg, this organization broke away from the United Garment Workers to become one of the great liberal and progressive forces in the American labor movement. To its leadership goes the credit for making collective bargaining a recognized institution in labor circles, establishing the forty-four hour work week, and the popularizing of unemployment insurance.

Program

To maintain sick and health benefits;

To promote the Sidney Hillman Medical Center;

To engage in cooperative and low-cost housing;

To sponsor educational, cultural, and recreational activities;

To support public causes and contribute to relief;

To maintain Amalgamated banks in New York and Chicago.

JEWISH SOCIALIST VERBAND OF AMERICA (1921)
175 E. Broadway, N.Y.C. 10002

The purpose of this organization is to promote and propagandize the ideas of social democracy among the Jewish working people.

JEWISH LABOR COMMITTEE (1933)
25 East 78 Street, N.Y.C. 10021

This organization is composed of representatives from all Jewish labor groups. Its headquarters is known as the "Atran Center for Jewish Culture," and was presented to them by Frank Atran, an industrialist. The terrible plight of the Jews under Nazism brought the Jewish Labor Committee into existence and since then it has dedicated itself to the defense of human rights for everyone everywhere, and to strong support of Israel.

Program

To aid Jewish and non-Jewish labor institutions overseas;

To aid victims of oppression and persecution everywhere;

To combat anti-Semitism and expose racial and religious intolerance in cooperation with other labor groups;

To educate Trade Union members in the ideals of equality and fraternity among all social and religious groups;

To work with all organized labor for civil rights and civic standards.

INTERNATIONAL HANDBAG, LUGGAGE, BELT AND NOVELTY WORKERS (1936)
1733 Broadway, N.Y.C. 10019

This organization paralleled other unions in combining forces to increase their bargaining power. Leaders in this union were Ossip Walinsky, Norman Zukowsky, Norris Fuchs, Philip Lubiner, and Benjamin Feldman.

LABOR ZIONIST ORGANIZATIONS

A number of Zionist organizations have identified themselves with the Jewish labor movement. Some of them have thrown their weight in behalf of American labor. Most of them have given financial and personnel support to the labor movement in Israel. The following Labor Zionist organizations are listed in more detail under the classification of Zionist organizations :

> Poale Tzion (Farband) Labor Zionist Organization of America
> HaPoel HaMizrachi of America—Orthodox Workers
> HaPoel HaTzair—The Young Worker
> Poale Agudath Yisroel—Union of Israel Workers
> HaShomer HaTzair—the Young Guardians
> HaBonim Tzion—Labor Zionist Youth
> League for Religious Labor in Israel
> Achduth HaAvodah Poale Tzion—United Labor Zionist Party
> Histadruth—Socialist Labor Party

SOME JEWISH LABOR LEADERS OF NOTE

Barondess, Joseph (1850–1924)
Labor organizer. Zionist leader. Founder of International Cloak Makers.

Ben Gurion, David (1887–   )
Labor Zionist. One of the founders of the Achdut Ha-Avodah party and Mapai in Israel. General Secretary of the Histadrut.

DeLeon, Daniel (1852–1914)
Radical labor leader. Founder of the I.W.W. Organized Socialist Trade and Labor Alliance.

Dubinsky, David (1892–   )
Organizer of industrial cooperatives. President of ILGWU.

Edelstadt, David (1866–1892)
Poet, propagandist for labor. Contributor to Yiddish literature.

Feigenbaum, Benjamin (1860–1932)
Socialist labor leader. Writer and editor. One of the popularizers of the natural and social sciences.

Gompers, Samuel (1850–1924)
Founder and president of the American Federation of labor.

Hillquit, Morris (1870–1933)
Leader in the organization of the United Hebrew Trades. Labor intellectualist.

Hillman, Sidney (1887–1946)
Organizer of the Amalgamated Clothing Workers of America. First to encourage technological changes and efficiency in industry. Promoted labor banks and housing.

Hoffman, Ben Zion (1874–1954)
Socialist labor writer. Interested in Jewish cultural nationalism.

Hourwich, Dr. Isaac A. (1860–1924)
Labor philosopher and educator. Wrote four-volume work on immigration and labor.

Kaplansky, Solomon (1884–1950)
Engineer and labor Zionist leader. First secretary of The World Poale Tzion Organization.

Katzenelson, Berl (1887–1944)
Labor Zionist. Active organizer of Jewish workers. Writer and editor of labor journals.

Litwak, A. (1874–1932)
His chief interest was in socialist education and culture for the Jewish worker.

London, Meyer (1871–1926)
Socialist labor leader. General council for Workmen's Circle. First socialist elected to Congress (1914).

Pine, Max (1866–1928)
Socialist labor leader and humanitarian. One of the founders of the *Forward*.

Schlesinger, Benjamin (1871–1932)
President of the ILGWU. Manager of the *Forward*. Sought gains for labor through favorable public opinion.

Schlossberg, Joseph (1875–   )
Editor and labor leader. Organizer of Amalgamated Clothing Workers of America.

Schneiderman, Rose (1882–   )
President of Women's Trade Union League. Only woman member of the Labour Advisory Board of the National Recovery Administration, 1933–35; Secretary of the New York State Department of Labor, 1937–44.

Sigman, Morris (1880–1931)
Founder of Independent Cloak Pressers' Union. Strong believer in industrial unionism.

Stokes, Rose Pastor (1879–1933)
Labor agitator, organizer, and writer.

Weinstein, Bernard (1886–1946)
Known as the "Daddy" of Jewish unionism. Organizer of the United Hebrew Trades.

Vladek, Baruch Charney (1886–1938)
Poet and essayist. A founder of the Jewish Labor Committee. Elected to City Council of New York City.

Zaritsky, Max (1885–1959)
Promoter of cooperative commonwealth. Opposed to economic and political exploitation.

Zhitlowsky, Dr. Chaim (1865–1943)
Labor Zionist. Interest in consumers' cooperative movement.

JEWISH LABOR PAPERS

Die Arbeiter Tzeitung (1890)
Die Freie Arbeiter Shtime (1890)
Die Zukunft (1892)
Aben Blatt (1894)
Jewish Daily Forward (1897)

Index

High Priest), 42; JACOB JOSEPH, (Books) 207–8; JO-SEPH, 740; SHABBATAI (SHACH), 754

Halachah (Bible Law), 129, 169, 194, 210, 417, 482, 590, 687 (*See* Codes of Law); Babylonian *Talmud,* 721; and Conservative Judaism, 677; on Dietary Laws, 417; Gaonic literature, 722; L'Moshe M'Sinai, 113; of Mishnah, 169; Orthodox Judaism, 656, 657 (*See also* above and Codes of Law); study of, 687; in *Talmud,* 155, 721; in Tannaitic Midrashim, 169; Targumim, 26

Halachic Writings, 156, 722; basis for Responsa, 230; Midrashim, 169

Halachoth, 114, 157–59; *Gedoloth* of ALFASI (Major Laws), 747, of SIMON of Cairo, 825; Mishnaic, 153

Halavayith Ha-Maith (Funeral Procession), 557, 875

HALBERSTAN, CHAYIM, 233

Ha-LEVI: BENJAMIN ben MEIR, Rabbi, 803; JUDAH, (Book) 196, 204, (Book) 213, 274, 637, 692, 743; NATHAN BENJAMIN (GHAZZATI), 273–74, 694, 812

Half-Holidays (Chol HaMoed), 141; Moed Katan, 138, 140; mourning on, 141; Passover, 338, 367; Succoth, 342, 382, 386

Half-Kaddish (Chatzi), 612

Half-Shekel, 686

Hallel (Prayers of Praise): Chanukah, 388; Rosh Chodesh, 395; service, 383–84, 388, 395, 605–6; Succoth, 384

Hallowed Things (Seder Kodashim) (Order of the Mishnah), 127, 135, 144–46, 689; Eleven Tractates, 144–46; Gemara to, 144

Hallowed Things in *Chagigah* (Mishnaic Tractate), 141

Halt, Care of the, 885

Hamafteach Shel Manule Ha-Talmud, 157

HAMAN, 99, 105, 392, 393, 681

Hamantasch (Purim Pastry), 393

Hamir Dath (Changer of Religion), 499

HAMON, MOSES, of Turkey, 810, 813

HANANEL ben HUSHIEL, Rabbi, 157, 233, 828

HANANIAH (Shadrach), 100, 107

HANNAH, 55; And seven sons, 108, 389

Handles (Stalks) (Mishnaic Tractate). See Uktzin

Hands (Mishnaic Tractate). See Yadayim

Hands, 164
    clean, 490
    laying on of, 313, 590–91
    postures of, during prayer, 360, 363, 600–2
    symbolism of, 602
    washing, 148, 427–28, 599
        upon arising, 148, 427,
        blessing for, 428, 444,
        after burial, 428, 561,
        before and after meals, 427, 444,
        method of, 428,
        Nail water, 428,
        occasions for, 428,
        at Passover Seder, 372,
        Shulchan Aruch on, 428,
        superstition about, 427, 561

Handwriting on the Wall (Book of Daniel), 101

HaPoel HaMizrachi, 713, 914, 927

HaPoel HaTzair, 927

Hara, 831, 832

Haran, 35

HARDOON, SILAS, 633

HARKAVY, ALEXANDER, 923

Harvesting: and the poor, 264; tithe for priests, 137

Hashgacha (Providence), 298

Hashkem (Midrash), 176

Hashomer, 629, 707; Ha-Tzair (Labor Zionists), 714, 913, 927

Mikveh); for purification, 148, 423, 426; witnesses to, 503

Immigrants, Aid to, 652, 896–98

Immigration: into Palestine, 654, 694, 698, 699, 700, 701, 705–8; into the United States, 652–53, 807, 836, 839–40, 845, 846, 847

Immigration and Refugee Aid Organizations, 652, 896–98

Immorality, a Sin, 163

Immortality, 106, 252–58, 278, 281, 298, 547, 549; and the Boethusians, 623; in Conservative Judaism, 549; early views, 255; and the Essenes, 547, 621; Mendelssohn's idea, 215, 781; modern views about, 254, 549–50; Orthodox Judaism (*See* above, Immortality); Pharisees, 254, 547; in philosophical literature, 211–18; in Reconstructionism, 549; in Reform Judaism, 281, 549; and Resurrection, 547; Sadducees, 254, 547; of the soul, 106, 108, 211–18, 252–58, 547; through a son (a Kaddish), 452

Impotence, 454–55; Indications of, 455

Improvement, 165

Impurity, 147, 319, (*See also* Cleanliness, Holiness); ritual cleansing of, 148

Impurity (Niddah) (Mishnaic Tractate), 135, 147, 148, 320, 527

Incantations, 304, 312

Incense Burner (Havdalah), 355

Incest, 286, 453, 527

Incorporeal, 215, 237, 293

Indecency, 122

Independence Day in Israel, 339, 394, 397, 512

India, History of the Jews of, 631–32

Indices, Talmud-centered, 156

Individual: liability for damages, 142; life of, from birth to death, 426–574; responsibility, 74, 99, 110, 118, 262, 296, 598

Infant, Death of, 570

Inferno. *See* Gehinnom

Inheritance, 141

INNOCENT: III, Pope, 734, 738, 767; IV, Pope, 774

Inquisition, 189, 271, 498, 636, 735, 743, 744–47, 829, 832; in Latin America, 847, 848, 849, 850, 851; and Zionism, 695

Insolence, 297

Institute for Jewish Research, 908

Institutions: the afflicted, 885; the aged, 542–43, 879–80, 884–85; American Health, 881–82; benevolent, 878–85; child care, 453, 882–84; health and welfare, 878–85; the homeless, 875, 879–80, 884; names of, during Middle Ages, 878; orphan care, 285, 486, 883–84, 874, 875; of Orthodox Judaism, 485, 656, 657; for the sick, 543–45, 879–80

Instruments. *See* Music

Intercalary Month: 331, 333, 336–37, 392; how determined, 336; in relation to Passover, 336–37

Intermarriage. *See* Marriage

Interment. *See* Burial

International Handbag, Luggage, Belt and Novelty Workers, 926

International Jewish Labor Bund, 920

International Labor Organization, 891

International Ladies Garment Workers, 653, 924–25

Interpreters, Bible, 198–201. *See* Amoraim

Intolerance, 99

Intoxication, 493

Iran. *See* Persia

Iraq (Babylonia): and Israel, 724; Jews of, 720–4

Ireland, 792; discriminatory dress, 792; expulsion and return, 792; Jews of, 792; Synagogue, 792

Irgun, 707, 716

Iron: Curtain, 755, 763; Czar, 757; Guard, 808

Irreverence, 265

ISAAC, 18, 33, 35, 349, 610, 634, 677; AARON, 818; the Blind (ABRAHAM ben ISAAC),

JUNG, LEO, Rabbi, 659

Justice, 290, 297; in Bible, 46, 51, 79, 264, 277, 293, 486–89, 678; Court of (See Beth Din); doctrine of, 51, 678; in ethical literature, 116, 120, 122, 490; of God, 81, 93; Law of, 46, 49, 50, 51, 264, 487; Prophet of, 78, 79; quotations, 488–89; rules of, 142; social, 51, 482, 651; voice of, 72

JUSTINIAN I, Emperor: 732, 745, 820, 830; Code of, 733

JUSTUS of Tiberias, 183

Kaaba Stone, 729

Kabbalat Shabbat, 346

Kabalah (Licensed for Shochet), 418, 595

Kabbalah. See Cabala

Kaddish (Mourner's Prayer), 256, 264, 440, 557, 560, 562–64, 568; daily, 563; Half- (Chatzi), 612; orphan's, 563–64; for a parent, 256, 440, 557, 560; in Reform Judaism, 564; said for whom, 564; a son as, 452; soul redeemed through, 452

Kadesh (Male Temple Prostitute), 618

KADOORIE Family, 633

Kadosh (Holy, Sanctified, Consecrated): derivatives of the word, 265–66; Outer Court, 40, 580

Kahal: 859–61; in Poland, 751–52, 860; abolished in Russia, 757–58, 762, 861

KAHAN, ISRAEL MEIR (CHAFETZ, CHAIM), 210, 755

KAHANA: Rabbi, 175; bar TACHLIFA, 152, 175

KAHANIAH, 635

KTHINA, Queen, 826

KAIDANOVER, AARON SAMUEL, 233

Kalam (Arabic Philosophical Method), 213

KALISCHER, Rabbi ZVI HIRSCH, (Book) 695

KALISHER, ABRAHAM, 754

Kallah. See Bride

Kallah (The Bride) (Smaller Talmudic Tractate), 155; Rabbathi, 442

Kallah (Rabbinical Assemblies), 721; arranged by Academies, 856

KALLEN, HORACE, 218

KALMAN, L., 924

KALONYMOS: family, 233, 777; ben JUDAH, 777; ben KALONYMOS, 736; ISAAC NATHAN ben, (Book) 196, 199

KAMENEV, 762

Kan-Ahora (Evil Eye) (Eyen Ha-Ra), 123, 306, 307, 312, 456, 545. See also Keina Hora

KANT, EMANUEL, 782, 783

KAPLAN: MAX, 924; MORDECAI M., 669

KAPLANSKY, SOLOMON, 928

Kappal. See Yarmulkeh

Kapparot (Sacrifice), 262, 306, 364

Karaites; 225–30, 624–25, 691, 728 in Babylonia, 722
  Bible: authority, 624, fixed reading of text of, 194, 226, interpretation of Commandments, 225–30
  customs and observances, 226
  and dietary laws, 624
  dogma, 226, 624
  in Egypt, 824, 825
  founders of, 228, 624
  GOD, attributes of, 226, 239
  influence on Hebrew, 625
  and intermarriage, 507
  history, 624–25, 627
  and Kashruth, 624
  and the Khazars, 637
  lexicographer, 220
  literature, 227–30
  and Masorah, 225–30, 625
  and the Mezuzah, 624
  Oral Law vs. Rabbinic Interpretation, 624, 647
  principles, 226, 624
  names of, 624
  and Rabbinites, 624, 627, 724, 728
  religion, 227–30
  in Syria, 724

Malach (Messenger or Angel), 316; Chabala (of Destruction), 317; HaB'rith (of the Covenant), 460; HaMashchith (of Destruction), 548; HaMaveth (of Death), 318, 321, 545, 548; HaPanim (of the Presence), 319, 320

MALACHI: 66, 86–87, 376, 488, 509, 681; life of, 87

Malachi, Book of, 24, 25, 86

Malaim (Full Month), 332

Malayalam, 632

Malbish Arumim, 875

Male Child in Judaism, 452

Mameh LaShon (Hebrew as Mother Tongue), 649, 675–76

Mamzer (Illegitimate One), 164, 453–54, 510

Man, 281; body and soul, 252, 546; creation of, 34, 251–52 (See also Creation); free agent, 251; and God (See God and Man); moral duties, 209, 251–52; primordial, 201; relationship with God, 88 (See also God and Man); responsibilities, 118, 251; sin against, 261, 301, 491

MANASSEH, 36, 348; ben ISRAEL, (Book) 196, 789, 816; King of Judah, 61, 64, 67, 71, 108, 677, 680

MANASSES, 107

Manasses, Prayer of, 103, 107

Mandate, British. See Palestine

MANDELKERN, SOLOMON, (Book) 223

Manhig, 869. See also Parnas, 869

Mankind, 487–88

Manna, 37, 347, 583

Manners, Table, 442

MANTINO, JACOB, 735

Mantle of Torah (Me'il), 43, 244

MANUALE, ANGELUS, 735

MANUEL of Portugal, 749

Ma-oth Chittim (Wheat Money), 371, 448, 876

Mapai. See Political Parties of Israel

Mapam. See Political Parties of Israel

Mapath HaShulchan, 159

MAPU, ABRAHAM, 650, 763

MARCELLUS, 686

MARCUS, JACOB R., (Books) 192

MARDUK (BEL) (Babylonian Deity), 720

MARGARET THERESA, 793

MARGARITHA ANTONIUS, 501

MARGOLIN, LOUIS, 924

MARGOLIS: JACK, 924; EPHRAIM Z., 233; MAX, (Book) 192, 225

MARIA THERESA, Empress of Austria, 793, 796, 800

MARR, WILHELM, 780, 786, 836

Marranos (Neo-Christians) (Crypto-Jews), 189, 193, 272, 636–37, 727, 744–47, 814, 817; in England, 789; in France, 767; Kol Nidre, 363; in Latin American Countries, 844, 846, 847, 848, 849, 850, 951; of Portugal, 193, 636, 744; Synagogue, 636; traditions, 630; in Turkey, 810

Marriage (Kiddushin), 290, 294, 508–31

Adultery. See Adultery

age of, 514

annulment of, 539

arranging, 142, 453, 514–15

Badchan (Jester) (Master of Ceremonies), 520

betrothal, 141, 142, 508, 517-18

bigamy, 511

blessings, 521, 522–25

Breaking of glass, 307, 518, 525

bride (Kallah), 155; dowry, 141, 285, 536; fasting, 399, 517; hair, 429, 517; immersion (Mikveh), 426, 517; trousseau, 516

bridegroom, 141, 517

broker, 515–16

celibacy, 284, 509, 526, 621

ceremony (Kiddushin), 155, 263, 306–7

Chalitzah, 141, 513, 540, 548

childlessness, 452

childless widows, 141, 513

children in, 141, 162

Chuppah, 518, 521–22

civil, 771

songs, 94, 520, 605
sterility and impotence, 454–55
superstitions about, 306–7, 520–21, 525
in Sweden, 818
symbols and practices, 518–19
Tallith in, 405, 519
in *Talmud,* 142, 155, 508
throwing rice, 521
Unterfuhrers, 522
vow, 440, 523
walking around groom, 520
wedding ring, 519
wedding rite (Nissu'in), 518, 520
widows, 141, 510–11, 513
Wine, 520
Mars, 310
MARSHALL, LOUIS, 702
MARTI, JOSE, 746, 849
MARTINEZ, FERNANDO, 746
MARTINI, RAYMOND (Marti), 195, 746
Martyrdom, 71, 189, 265, 340; of ELEAZAR and HANNAH, 108; of ISAIAH, 111; of JESUS, 268; of Mar ZUTRA, 726
Martyrs: death of, 186; Fast of the, 340; Ten: 120, 123, 124, 129, 688, Midrash on, 178, 186; MARULLUS, 686
MARX: ALEXANDER, (Book) 192; KARL, 695
MARY, 197
Mas HaGulgoleth (Poll Tax), 873
Masada, 270
Masah (Prophecy), 314
Maschil (Psalm Songs), 88
Masculine Names, 467–69, 470–72
Masechtoth (Treatises in Mishnah), 127; *Ketanoth* (Smaller *Tractates* of *Talmud*), 155
Mashgiach (Overseer), 317, 422, 595
Mashiach. *See* Messiah
Mashkeh (Cup-bearer), 865
Maskilim, 648–50, 761, 785, 798
Masorah (Tradition), 19, 157, 160, 226, 692, 782; Karaites and, 225–30, 625
Masorah of the Six Orders, 160

Masoretes and the Structure of the Bible, 218–19, 226, 227–30; and grammatical forms, 219
Masoreth Ha-Shes Sedarim (Masorah of the Six Orders of the *Mishnah),* 160
Masoretic Bible, 15, 19–20, 27, 31, 67, 219, 226, 681, 728; guides, 155; *Midrash,* 179; and the Samaritans, 27; and the Septuagint, 27
Masquerade, 394
Massacre of the Lepers, 769
Massacres, 693, 697, 750–51, 758–59, 760, 769, 788, 795, 817, 820. *See* Crusades, Black Death
MASTEMA, 323
Master (Baal), 868; of the Covenant, 459; of Narration, 594; of Prayer, 592
MASTER of the GOOD NAME. *See* BAAL SHEM TOB
Masturbation, 528
Matchmaker (Shadchan), 515–16
Materialism, 105
MATTANIAH, 65
MATTATHIAS (High Priest of Modin), 108, 388, 389
Matzah (Unleavened Bread) (Pl., Matzoth), 370–74; Aphikomen, 373, 375; in Blood Libel Accusations, 761, 774, 788; free (Ma-oth Chittim) (Wheat Money), 371, 448, 876; meaning of, 372, 374, 375; prohibited in Russia, 762; three, in Seder, 373, 374
Matzebah (Pillar), 566
Mausoleum, 559
MAUTHNER, FRITZ, (Book) 218
MAXIMILIAN, Emperor, 793
May Laws in Russia, 759, 803
Mazal (Constellation), 309
Mazdaism (Zoroastrianism), 547, 627, 726–27
Mazel Tob, 309, 461, 520
Mazkir (Recorder), 865
Mazzikim (Demon), 311
MAZZINI, 741
Meal: of condolence, 562; at marriage, 520

the River Jordan, 53; of the Cruse of Oil (Chanukah), 387; of ELIJAH (See ELIJAH); of ELISHA, 60; in philosophical literature, 211–18; in places of danger, 163; Rod of Aaron, 327–28; Rod of Moses, 327–28

Miracle Workers, 59, 60, 134, 202–6, 272–74, 644–45; in Scripture, 59, 60

MIRANDOLA, GIOVANNI PICO della, 203

MIRIAM, 37, 47, 329, 338, 605

Mirrer Yeshiva Central Institute, 905

Mirrors and Superstition, 305, 307, 556

MISHAEL (MESHACH), 100, 107

Mishkan. See Tabernacle

°Mishle (Book of Proverbs), 16, 24, 25, 59, 90, 243; Midrash to, 173, 176, 177

Mishloach Manoth (Sending Purim Gifts) (Shalach Monoth), 393, 448

Mishnah (Shas), 111–149, 194, 198, 387, 687–89
arrangement, 124
basic elements, 112
codified, 856
completed by JUDAH HaNASI, 127
Exegesis, Rules of. See Exegesis
expounders (Tannaim). See Expounders, or Tannaim
Father of, 690
and *Gemara,* 154
Halachah. See Halachah
history and development, 113–49, 187
language of, 112
Men of the Great Assembly, 16, 19, 113–27, 244, 609, 854, 862. See also Sanhedrin
names for, 111–12, 127
Orders of, 117, 127, 135–49, 160, 689
period of writing, 112
philology of, 221
preservation of, 113
punishment in, 144

redactors, 114
Responsa based on, 185
scholars of, 128–35, 688
scribes (Soferim), 114
Six Orders of the, 127
Talmud, 154
Torah (Deuteronomy), 49
Torah (Maimonides), 158, 200, 744, 748
Tractates of, 135–49
when written, 113–14
written and oral law, 113

Mishnaioth (Paragraphs of *Mishnah*), 127

Mishneh (Second in Command), 865; HaMelech (Vizier), 865

Mishpachah (Family of Blood Kin), 449, 853

Mishpatim. See Judges

Mission of the Jew, 260, 282

Missionary People, 260, 497

Mithnagdim (Rabbinites), 194, 647–48, 754; Chassidim vs., 208, 645–46, 647, 753; and Karaites, 624, 647, 724, 728

Mitre (Mitznefeth), 43, 44, 603

Mittah (Coffin), 555

Mitzvah (Commandment), 432, 872, 876; Bar (See Bar Mitzvah); Bat (See Bat Mitzvah); going to a funeral, 556–57

Mitzvoth (Righteous Deeds), 127, 256, 515, 544; practice of, 486; Taryag (613), 79, 166, 276, 645; Reduction in Numbers (See Commandments)

Mixed Marriage. See Marriage

Mixed Seating, 658, 668

Mixtures, 139; *Diverse Seeds (Kilayim)* (Mishnaic Tractate), 135, 136–37, 139; Law of, 136, 137, 139, 421–22, 431; prohibited, 136, 137, 139, 421–22, 431

Mizbayach (Altar), 35, 363, 584; Ha-Olah (Brazen Altar), 40, 41, 584

Mizrach (East), 445, 583, 587–88

MIZRACHI, ELIAS, 813

Mizrachi (Religious Zionists), 657, 713; HaPoel Ha-Mizrachi, 713, 914,

Mysticism, 295–96; of Cabala, 201–7, 295, 325, 640–44; in Chassidism, 295; and Divination (*See* Divination); Jewish, 110; of letters and numbers, 201, 640–44; the occult, 312, 640; of words, 201

Mystics, 73, 201–7, 644

Mythology and Folklore, 549–50

Myths: of the Bible, 16, 316–29; in Apocrypha, 102

NAAMAN, 60

NABAL, 57

NABONIDUS, 71

NABOTH, 62

NABOPOLASSAR, 71

Nachash (Serpent Demon), 323

NACHMAN: of Bratislav, (Book) 208; ben JACOB, 151, 166; bar ISAAC, 152

NACHMANI (See ABBAYE NACHMAN ben KAULIL)

NACHMANIDES (MOSES ben NACHMAN) (RAMBAN), 158, (Book) 197, 200, 203, (Book) 205–6, 210, (Book) 215, 231, 234, 692, 744, 746; principles of Judaism, 215

NACHSON ben ZADOK, 722

Nachum (Nahum) Book of, 24, 25, 82–83

NACHUM of Gimzo, 131

Nachum Avaylim, 875

NADAB: Son of AARON, 45; King of Israel, 60, 61, 679

Nadib (Nobleman), 865

NADIR SHAH, 727

NAFTALI, MOSES ben DAVID 229

Nagid (leader), 824, 825, 863, 865

Nahardea (Talmudic Academy), 151–52, 154, 166; closed, 726

NAHAVENDI, BENJAMIN, (Book) 228

NAHUM, 65, 66, 84, 681; on Retribution, 83. *See also* NACHUM

Nails. *See* Finger Nails

Nail Water (Nagel Wasser), 428

Naked, Clothing the, 874, 875

Nakedness, Uncovering, 526

Name, Profanation of (Chillul HaShem), 265

Names

abbreviation, 241, 466

adjective, 465

Anglicized versions, 464

animals, 464, 466

Bible, 22–23, 33, 464

change of, 466, 545

critical illness, 465,545

in Circle, Holy, 464

dates and events, 465

of days, 331

Deity, 464. *See also* God: names)

of demons, 311, 323

divine, 17, 39, 202, 204, 238, 241, 304, 313

of Essenes, 620

of fallen angels, 311, 318, 324

family escutcheon, 324, 466

Feminine

Hebrew, 469–70

Yiddish-Hebrew, 472–73

first, 464

foreign, 465

of God. *See* God

of Israel, 258–60

for Jew, 235–36

for Judaism, 235

Kadosh, derived from, 265–66

Karaites, 624

Kinship, 465

Masculine

Hebrew, 467–69

Yiddish-Hebrew, 470–72

meaning of, 464

of months, 330, 332

multiple, 463

mystical, 313

of Passover, 367

patronymic (Son of), 465–66

physical characteristics, 466

place, 466

places of origin, 466

plants, 464

of Pharisees, 619–20

of practitioners of superstitions, 307

ridiculous, 466

Nazi (Nazism), 649, 652, 707, 755, 772, 779, 786–87, 790, 795, 796, 801, 806, 808, 814, 815, 817, 818, 819, 820, 821, 829, 831, 839, 840, 845, 846, 847, 889, 895

Nazir (Nazirite Vow) (Mishnaic Tractate), 135, 141, 142, 617

Nazirite, 617–18, 634; hair, 429; Law of the, 48, 141, 617; sacrifices, 142; vow, 141, 142, 617

Nebi'im. *See* Prophets

NEBUCHADNEZZAR, 65, 71, 72, 74, 100, 107, 340, 341, 343, 398, 680; dream of, 100; Midrash on captivities under, 178

NECHEMYAH. *See* NEHEMIAH

NECHONY, 114

NECHUNIAH ben HaKANAH, 24, 25, 26, 44, 114, 132, 341, 618, 641

Necromancy, 304, 313, 316

Nedarim (Vows) (Mishnaic Tractate), 135, 141, 142

Nefillath Appayim (Bending the Body), 602

Nega'im (Leprosy) (Mishnaic Tractate), 135, 147

NEHEMIAH, 15, 24, 25, 26, 66, 86, 87, 101, 104, 114, 144, 341, 494, 618, 682; Governor of Palestine, 101; read the Book of the Law, 587

Nehemiah (Nechemyah), 25, 44, 87; Book of, 23, 24, 27, 101

Neighbors, 110, 115, 118, 128, 133, 170, 264, 277, 294; sin against, 162

Ne'ilah Services, 364

Neo-Chassidism, 218

Neo-Christians. *See* Marranos

NERIGLISSAR, 71

Ner Israel Rabbinical College, 899

Ner Mitzvoth (Light of the Commandment) (Index of Talmudic Decisions), 160

NERO, Emperor, 685

Ner Tamid (Eternal Light), 41, 245, 586

Neshamah (Soul), 253, 546. *See also* Soul

Netherlands, 814–16; Jewish communities, 814, 816; Dutch colonies, 814; emancipation, 815; Jewish history in, 814–16; Jews to remember, 815–16; Nazis in, 815

Netherworld, 257, 292, 318, 546

Nethinim (Temple Slaves), 618

NETTER, CARL, 718

Netura (Naturai) Karta in Israel, 275, 718

NEUMAN, ABRAHAM AARON, (Book) 192

NEUMARK, DAVID, (Book) 218

New Amsterdam, 847

New English Bible, 30

New Moon, determining of, 140. *See also* Moon

New Testament: 23, 29, 119, 296, 318; and BEELZEBUB, 318

New Year. *See* Rosh HaShanah

New Year's Day (Rosh HaShanah) (Mishnaic Tractate), 140; kinds of, 140

New Year of the Trees, 344, 395

Nezikin, Seder (Damages) (Order of the Mishnah), 127, 135, 141, 142–44, 155, 689; Gemara of, 143; Ten Tractates, 142–44; Seder Yeshuoth (Salvation), 143

NICANOR, 389

NICHOLAS: I, Czar, 757–58; II, Czar, 760; III, Pope, 269

Niddah (Impurity) (Mishnaic Tractate), 135, 147, 148, 320, 527

Niddah (Impurity of a Menstruous Woman), 526

Night Spirit. *See* Lilith

Ninevah, 71, 80–81, 83, 84, 104, 680, 720

Ninth of Ab, 340, 341, 394, 396–97, 512; Fast of the, 96, 340, 396–97, 398

Nisan (Abib), 332, 333, 338, 357, 366, 398; events of, 338; Tekufoth (vernal equinox), 332, 337

NISI ben NOAH, (Book) 229

NISSIM: Ben David, 271; ben

PESACH. *See* PETER

Pesach. *See* Passover

Pesachim (Passover) (Mishnaic Tractate), 129, 135, 138, 139, 164, 253, 425, 491, 584

Pesara Bible, 32

Peshitta (Syriac Bible), 29

Pesikta (Midrashim), 175

PETACHIAH, of Regensberg, (Book) 190

Petach Tikvah (Colony), 718–19

PETER, (PESACH), 501, 797; the Great, 756, 757; the Hermit, 766

PETHUEL, 77

PETLURA, SIMON, 750; Massacre, 751

PETRUS   ALFONSI   (SEPHARDI, MOSES), 502

P'eylim (American Yeshiva Student Union), 906

PFEFFERKORN, JOHANN JOSEPH, 501, 502, 779, 780

PHANUEL (URIEL), 317

PHARAOH, 36, 37, 368, 408, 677; dream of, 36; HOPHRA, 74; NECHO, 65, 71; RAMESES III, 38

Pharisaic: Judaism, 498; movement, 683

Pharisees (Separatists), 109, 115, 118, 120, 130, 149, 619–20, 644, 682–84; activities, 619–20; admitted to Sanhedrin, 343; belief about death, 257, 298; belief about immortality, 254, 547; differences with Sadducees, 149, 254, 547, 620; history of, 619–20, 622; on Messiah, 257; names, 619–20; and Sabbath candles, 424

Philanthropy, 491; degrees of, 287

Philatelists, Israel Society, 918

PHILIP: II (AUGUSTUS), 766; IV, the Fair, 767; the Tall, 767

PHILIPPSON, LUDWIG, (Book) 215, 784, 786

Philistines, War with, 54, 56, 63, 678

PHILO JUDAEUS, 21, (Book) 183, 215, 216, 218, (Book) 240, 300, 620, 687, 804, 822, 825; state-

ment of principles, 216, 278

Philology,   219–25;   Arabic,   219; Christian scholars of Hebrew, 219; Hebrew, 219; Mishnah, 221

Philosophers, Jewish, 194, 211–18; Arabic, 212, 213; Greek, 213, 214

Philosophic Literature, 211–18; God in, 211–18; immortality, 211–18; soul in, 211–18

Philosophy: Arabic, 212, 213; of Conservative Judaism, 666, 667; of Essenes, 621; literature of, 211–18; mystical, 202–7; of Reform Judaism, 660; and religion, 213, 723

PHINEAS, son of AARON, 52

PHINEHAS, son of ELI, 56

Phrases: about Death, 572–74; derived from the word "Kadosh", 266

Phylacteries (Tefillin) (Lesser Talmudic Treatise), 156

Phylacteries. *See* Tefillin

Physical Characteristics, Names, 466

Physicians and Medicine, 543–44, 879

Pictures and Mourning, 556

Pidyon HaBen (Redemption of First-Born), 48, 145, 439, 453, 473–76, 678; Bible source, 473; blessing for, 439, 475; ceremony, 474, 616; in Orthodox Judaism, 658; observance today, 475–76; rabbinical rules, 476; redemption money, 474, 475, 617; and Reform Judaism, 476

Pidyon Shevuim, 875, 896

Piety, 209, 491, 645

Pilgrimage

Festivals (Shalosh Regalim), 51, 338, 339, 342, 364, 366–86

Bible source, 366

Passover, 51, 338, 366–77

Seudah, 349

Shebuoth, 51, 339, 366, 377–80

Succoth, 51, 342, 366, 380–86

Yizkor on, 364

to shrine, 301

S'michah (Ordination), 485, 590, 687, 693

SMOLENSKIN, PERETZ, 650, 764

SNEJDER, M. B., 225

Sochayn (Minister), 865

Social Justice, 51, 651; taught by Prophets, 482

Social Reform, 82

Social Service, Jewish, 885–88

Socialism, 651–53, 922; in Israel, 717

Socialist Labor Party, 927

Socialist Trade and Labor Alliance, 924

Socialist Verband of America, Jewish, 920, 926

Society: Good, 486; in Proverbs, 91

Society of Israel Philatelists, 918

Society of Jewish Science, 664, 902

Society for Rehabilitation and Train-- ing (ORT), 893

Sociology and Philosophy in Literature, 211–18

Sodom and Gomorrah, 35, 325, 529

Sodomy, 286, 527, 529

SOFER, MOSES SAMUEL, 231, 234

Sofer (Scribe), 589, 595, 855, 865, 867

Soferim (Scribes) (Sofrim), 114, 227, 244, 482, 595

Soferim (Scribes) (Talmudic Tractate), 155

SOKOLOW, NAHUM, 655, 697, 699, 700

Solar Calendar, 331

SOLOMON, King, 43, 57, 58–59, 60, 61, 63, 97, 103, 105, 185, 618, 631, 634, 679, 730, 787; as author, 58, 88, 90, 92, 94–95, 97, 109; children of, 63; death of, 61; legends of, 59, 178, 328–29, 576; Song of Songs, 16, 24, 25, 59, 94–95; Temple of, 58, 328, 576, 583

Solomon, Psalms of (Apocryphal Book), 109

Solomon, Wisdom of (Apocryphal Book), 58, 103

SOLOMON: ben ABRAHAM of Urbina, 219; ben ABRAHAM ibn PARCHON, (Book) 225; ben ADRET, 744; DON, 501; the Exilarch, 625; ibn GABIROL,

(Books) 210, (Book) 216, 742, 768; ben ISAAC (Yitzchaki) (See RASHI); ben JERU-CHAM, (Book) 230; LEVI (*See* PAUL de Burgos) (PAULUS de Santa Maria); ben SAMUEL, (Book) 225; ben SIMON, (Book) 188; ibn VERGA, 189, 813

SOLOTAROFF, H. Dr., 923

SOLOVEICHIK, JOSEPH DOV, 234

Son: of the Commandment(*See* Bar Mitzvah); of David (Messiah), 327; of God, 268, 301, 324; as a Kaddish, 452; of Peace (Shalom Zachor), 461

Son of Sirach (Wisdom of Jesus) (Apocrypha), 21

Soncino Bible, 32

SONCINO Family, 735

Song of Songs (Shir HaShirim) (SOLO-MON), 16, 24, 25, 59, 94–95, 602, 683; canonicity of, 149; Commentary on, 203; Midrashim to, 174; read on Passover, 95; selections from, 95

Song of the Three Holy Children (Apocrypha); 103, 107; passages of, 612

Songs: for Chanukah, 388; for Passover, 376–77; in prayer service, 612; for Sabbath and festivals (Zemiroth), 349, 350, 444; at weddings, 94, 520, 605

SONNENFELS, JOSEPH von, 799

Sons of God (B'nai Elohim), 324, 617

Soothsaying, 304, 315

SOPHER, MOSES, Rabbi, 658

Sorcery, 304, 309, 315, 316

Sotah (The Suspected Woman) (Mishnaic Tractate), 135, 141; Tosefta, 516

Soul, 212, 301, 546; affliction of, 261; body and, 252, 546; Cabala and the, 254, 643; and Chassidism, 258; of a child, 461; concept of, 252; ethical conduct and the, 211–18; fate of the, 255–57; God and the, 213, 301; immortality of, 106, 108, 211, 252–58, 547; Karet (cutting off), 146; Maimonides' Five

the, 54; planting: for the birth
of a child, 457, Tu Beshvat,
343, 394–95; tithes for, 344
Trees, New Year for (Rosh HaShanah
La-Elanoth), 344, 395
Trefah (Unclean), 145, 422; and
Kosher, 414–23
TREITSCHKE, HEINRICH von, 786
Trendel (Dreidel), 391
Trespass Offering, 145, 146, 259, 260
Trespassing (M'ilah) (Mishnaic Trac-
tate), 135, 145, 146
Tribes: division of land among, 52,
678; of Israel, 35, 61, 677; the
Lost Ten, 63, 83, 189–90, 236,
326–27, 328, 627–28, 812;
Twelve Tribes, 43, 110, 677
Trinitarianism, 293, 609
Tripoli, Jews of, 633, 635, 820
TRITO-ISAIAH, 67
TROKI: ISAAC ben ABRAHAM,
(Book) 198, (Book) 230; SOLO-
MON ben AARON, (Book) 230
TROTSKY, LEON, 762
Trousseau, 516
TRUMPELDOR, JOSEPH, 629, 701,
716
Trumpet, Day of Blowing, 357
Trusteeship, 143
Truth, 86, 120, 215, 290, 297, 487,
491
Tsagataish, 637
TSCHLENOW, JEHEIL, 697, 699
Tu Beshvat (Tree Planting) (15th of
Shebat), 343, 394–95
Tunic, 42, 43
Tunisia, 830–31; Christianity in, 830;
communities, Jewish, 831; dis-
tinctive dress, 830; ghettos, 830,
831; history of Jews in, 830;
Islam over, 831; and Israel,
831; Jewish life, 831; Nazis in,
831
Turkemenia, 631
Turkey, 809–13; anti-Semitism, 811;
communities, Jewish, 810, 813;
decline of the Ottoman Empire,
730; discrimination, 810–11;
false Messiahs, 810, 812; history
and life of Jews in, 809–11;
Marranos, 810; noted Jews,

811–13; rulers of, 810; tax, 811
Turkish Rule over Palestine, 693
Turkish-Tataric, 631
Turks in Babylonia, 723
Twenty-Four Books, 23, 24
Two-day Observances: custom (Min-
hag), 335, 381–82, 657; Rosh
Chodesh, 334
TYNDALE, WILLIAM, 30; Bible, 30
Types of Names, 464
Tzadakim, 620
Tzadik (Righteous) (Tzaddikim), 206–
9, 646–47, 753; persecution of,
319
Tzadok (High Priest), 620, 684
Tzedakah (Righteousness) (See also
Charity), 79, 82, 84, 87, 88, 91,
92, 106, 252, 277, 290, 487,
872, 873, 879, 888, 896; boxes,
448, 588, 874, 878; gleaning,
146, 264, 486, 872; tithing for
the poor, 136–37, 297, 873
Tzibur (Congregation), 862
Tzitz (Mitre), 42, 43, 44
Tzitzith (Fringes) (Lesser Treatise of
the Talmud), 156
Tzitzith (Fringes): Bible Source of
Commandment, 402; construction, 403; four corners, 402;
kissing, 403; law of, 48, 402,
678; and MOSES, 402; origin,
402; purpose, 402–3; rules and
regulations, 403; safeguard
against sin, 402; wearing of, by
pious Jews, 404
Tziyun (Monument), 566
Tzum GEDALIA, 342, 398

Uganda, 697, 698
Ukraine, 762
Uktzin (Stalks) (Handles) (Mishnaic
Tractate), 133, 135, 147, 149
Ultimate Deliverer, 327
Unchastity, 301
Unclean Issue (Zabim) (Mishnaic
Tractate), 135, 147, 148
Unclean: bodies, 147, 148; clothing,
147; corpse is, 554–55; food,
148; hands (See Hands, Wash-
ing of); implements, 147;
liquids, 148; Nazirites forbidden

Franco-Prussian, 785; Gibeonites, 52, 53; Greek, 805; Holy, 766; Jericho, 52, 53; between Judah and Israel, 679; of liberation, 704, 709–10; of the Maccabees, 822 (*See* Maccabean Revolt); Medes, 71; Megiddo, 71; Mesopotamia, 54; Midianites, 54; Moabites, 47, 54; Philistines, 54, 56, 63, 678; revolutionary, 833; Rome, 120, 123, 183, 186, 303–96, 684–86; Russo-Turkish, 806, 810; Samaria, 684; Scythian, 71, 84; Serbian-Bulgarian, 803; Sinai Invasion, 710–11, 824; Six Day, 711; Syria, 64, 76, 108, 724–25; Syrian-Greek, 683; World War I, 699, 725, 730, 741, 755, 786, 790, 794, 796, 804, 811, 829, 836, 837, 842, 843, 845, 846, 849, 890; World War II, 695, 696, 707–8, 725, 730, 741, 747, 755, 762, 779, 796, 811, 823, 827, 832, 836, 846, 850, 885

Washing the Corpse, 554–55, 556

Washing the Feet, 427

Washing Hands. *See* Hands, Washing

WASHINGTON, GEORGE, 834

Water: disposing of, 556; drawing of (Libation Ceremony) on Succoth, 120, 140, 385; Holy, 313; and superstition, 305

Waters of life, 329

WATSON, THOMAS E., 838

WAUCHOPE, Commissioner, 707

Way of the World (Talmudic Tractate): *Derech Eretz Rabbah* (Major), 156; *Derech Eretz Zuta* (Minor), 156

Weak, Protect the, 143

Wealth, 128, 165, 303

Wearing the Hat. *See* Head Covering

Wedding Ceremony. *See* Marriage

Wedding Songs, 94, 520, 605

Week, The (Shevuah), 331, 346; prophetical, 332; of Sabbatical Years, 335; of Weeks, 332

Weeks, Feast of. *See* Shebuoth

Weeks, The Three, 340, 398, 512

WEIL, JACOB, 234

WEINSTEIN, BERNARD, 923, 929

WEIZMANN: CHAIM, 655, 698, 702, 706, 712, 715, 790; Institute, 698, 704

Welfare Board, Jewish, 669

Welfare, Social, Organizations, 878–85

Well of Miriam, 329

WELLHAUSEN, JULIUS, 17

Wells (Mikvaoth) (Mishnaic Tractate), 135, 147, 148

WENZEL IV, King of Bohemia, 795

WERTHEIMER: RITTER von, 799; S.A., 174; SAMSON, 781

WESSELY, NAPHTALI HERZ, 782

West Coast Talmudical Seminary, 907

Wheat Money (Ma-oth Chittim), 371, 448, 876

Wheels (Offanim), 320

White Papers, 701–2, 705–7, 716

Wicked, 91, 92, 94, 106

Widows: charity for, 873; childless, 141, 513; grass, 540; marriage of, 510–11, 513; support of, 141

WIERNICK, PETER, (Book) 193

Wife: Agunah, 141, 540–41; apparel provided for, 431; cleanliness of a, 451; conjugal relations, 294, 529–30; consent to divorce, 536; consideration of, 162; and divorce, 449, 536–37; duties of, 450–51; hurting a, 162; -husband obligations, 141, 162, 431, 449–51, 530; initiates divorce, 535–36; the Jewish, 450–51, 516; property rights, 533; in Proverbs, 451; quotations, 531; sexual relations, 529–30; sterility of, 454; tribute to, 92, 451

Wig (Sheitel), 517

Wilderness, 19; wandering in, forty years, 46–47, 49, 678

Will: ethical, 209, 550; freedom of, 125, 211–18, 251, 276, 298; of God, 299, 314, 597

WILLIAM: the Conqueror, 787; Count, of Holland, 814

WILLIAMS, ROGER, 833

Willow (Aravah) (Succoth Symbol), 140, 383; Midrashic interpretations, 384–85

Wills and Testaments, 550